SOCIAL ANTHROPOLOGY
AND OTHER ESSAYS

SOCIAL ANTHROPOLOGY AND OTHER ESSAYS

(Combining *Social Anthropology* and *Essays in Social Anthropology*)

E. E. EVANS-PRITCHARD

THE FREE PRESS, *New York*

Printed in the United States of America

FIRST FREE PRESS PAPERBACK EDITION 1964

Second printing, March 1966

CONTENTS

PREFACE

These six lectures were given on the Third Programme of the B.B.C. in the winter of 1950. Except for a few minor verbal alterations they are printed as they were delivered. I thought it unwise to change, or add to, what was written to be spoken within the limits imposed by the medium of expression and for a particular purpose and audience.

Social anthropology is still little more than a name to most people, and I hoped that broadcast talks on the subject would make its scope and methods better known. I trust that their publication as a book will serve the same purpose. As there are few brief introductory guides to social anthropology I believe that this book may also be of use to students in anthropological departments in British and American universities. I have therefore added a short bibliography.

I have expressed many of the ideas in these lectures before, and sometimes in the same language. I am grateful for permission to use them again to the Delegates of the Clarendon Press and to the Editors of *Man*, *Blackfriars*, and *Africa*.[1]

I thank Mr. K. O. L. Burridge for assistance in the preparation of the lectures and my colleagues at the Institute of Social Anthropology at Oxford and Mr. T. B. Radley of the B.B.C. for critical comments on them.

E. E. E-P.

[1] *Social Anthropology*, an Inaugural Lecture delivered before the University of Oxford on 4 February 1948, the Clarendon Press, 1948; 'Social Anthropology: Past and Present', the Marett Lecture, delivered in Exeter College Hall, Oxford, on 3 June 1950, *Man*, 1950, No. 198; 'Social Anthropology', *Blackfriars*, 1946; 'Applied Anthropology', a lecture given to the Oxford University Anthropological Society on 29 November 1945, *Africa*, 1946.

I

THE SCOPE OF THE SUBJECT

I shall endeavour in these lectures to give you a general account of what social anthropology is. I am aware that even among well-read laymen there is a good deal of haziness about the subject. The words seem to arouse vague associations of either apes and skulls or strange rites of savages and curious superstitions. I do not think that I shall have any difficulty in convincing you that these associations are misplaced.

My treatment of the subject must be guided by this awareness. I must assume that some of you are frankly ignorant of what social anthropology is, and that others believe it to be what it is not. Those who have some acquaintance with the subject will, I hope, forgive me if, therefore, I discuss it broadly and in what may appear to them an elementary way.

In this, my first, lecture I shall tell you what is the general scope of the subject. In my second and third lectures I shall trace its theoretical development. In my fourth lecture I shall discuss that part of its research we call fieldwork. In my fifth lecture I shall illustrate the development of both theory and fieldwork by giving you some examples of modern studies. In my final lecture I shall discuss the relation of social anthropology to practical affairs.

I shall throughout restrict my account as far as possible to social anthropology in England, chiefly in order to avoid difficulties in presentation, for were I to give also an account of the development of the subject in continental countries and in America I should be compelled so to compress the material that what would be gained in comprehensiveness would not compensate for what would be lost in clarity and continuity. This restriction matters less than it would perhaps do in many other fields of learning because social anthropology has to a large extent developed independently in England. I shall, however, mention foreign writers and tendencies where these have markedly affected the thought of English scholars.

Even within these limits it is not easy to give you a clear and simple account of the aims and methods of social anthropology, because there is often lack of agreement about them among social anthropologists themselves. There is, of course, substantial agreement about many matters, but about others there are divergent opinions, and these, as often happens in a small and new subject, tend to become entangled with personalities, for scholars are perhaps more, rather than less, prone than other people to identify themselves with their opinions.

Personal preferences, when it is necessary to express them, are harmless if openly acknowledged. Ambiguities are more dangerous. Social anthropology has a very limited technical vocabulary, so that it has to use everyday language and this, as we all know, is not very precise. Such words as 'society', 'culture', 'custom', 'religion', 'sanction', 'structure', 'function', 'political', and 'democratic' do not always convey the same meaning either to different people or in different contexts. It would be possible for anthropologists to introduce many new words or to give a restricted and technical meaning to words in common use, but apart from the difficulty of getting their colleagues to agree to these usages, were this done on a large scale anthropological writings would soon become a jargon intelligible only to professional scholars. If we have to choose between steering close to the obscurities of everyday speech and the obscurities of specialist jargon I would prefer to risk the lesser perils of everyday speech, for what social anthropology has to teach concerns everybody and not only those who study it professionally.

Social anthropology is a title used in England and to some extent in the United States, to designate a department of the larger subject of anthropology, the study of man from a number of aspects. It concerns itself with human cultures and societies. On the continent a different terminology prevails. There when people speak of anthropology, which to us is the entire study of man, they have in mind only what we in England call physical anthropology, that is to say, the biological study of man. What we call social anthropology would be referred to on the continent as either ethnology or sociology.

Even in England the expression 'social anthropology' has only very recently come into use. The subject has been taught, under the names of anthropology or ethnology, since 1884 at Oxford, since 1900 at Cambridge, and since 1908 in London, but the first university chair which bore the title of *social anthropology* was the honorary professorship held by Sir James Frazer at Liverpool in 1908. The subject has recently received wider recognition and social anthropology is now taught under that name in a number of universities in Great Britain and in the Dominions.

Being a branch of the wider subject of anthropology, it is generally taught in connection with its other branches: physical anthropology, ethnology, prehistoric archaeology, and sometimes general linguistics and human geography. As the last two subjects seldom figure in degree and diploma courses in anthropology in this country I say no more about them; and all I need say about physical anthropology, since it has a very limited overlap with social anthropology at the present time, is that it is a branch of human biology and comprises such interests as heredity, nutrition, sex differences, the comparative anatomy and physiology of races, and the theory of human evolution.

It is with ethnology that we have our closest ties. To understand why this is so it is necessary to know that while social anthropologists consider that their subject embraces all human cultures and societies, including our own, they have, for reasons I will mention later, for the most part given their attention to those of primitive peoples. Ethnologists are dealing with the same peoples, and there is consequently a considerable overlap between the two subjects.

It is important to appreciate, however, that though ethnology and social anthropology make their studies very largely among the same range of peoples they make them with very different purposes. Consequently, though in the past no clear distinction was made between ethnology and social anthropology, they are today regarded as separate disciplines. The task of ethnology is to classify peoples on the basis of their racial and cultural characteristics and then to explain their distribution at the present time, or in past times, by the movement and mixture of peoples and the diffusion of cultures.

The classification of peoples and cultures is an essential preliminary to the comparisons which social anthropologists make between primitive societies, because it is highly convenient, and even necessary, to start by comparing those of the same general cultural type—those which belong to what Bastian long ago called 'geographical provinces'.[1] When, however, ethnologists attempt to reconstruct the history of primitive peoples, for whose past historical records are lacking, they are compelled to rely on inferences from circumstantial

[1] Adolf Bastian, *Controversen in der Ethnologie*, 1893.

evidence to reach their conclusions, which, in the nature of the case, can never be more than probable reconstructions. Sometimes a number of different, and even contrary, hypotheses fit the facts equally well. Ethnology is thus not history in the ordinary sense, for history tells us not that events may have happened, but that they did happen, and not merely that events have taken place, but how and when they happened, and often why they happened. For this reason, and because ethnology can in any case tell us little about the past social life of primitive peoples, its speculations, as distinct from its classifications, have limited significance for social anthropologists.

Prehistoric archaeology is best regarded as a branch of ethnology. It attempts to reconstruct the history of peoples and cultures from human and cultural remains found by excavation in geological deposits. It also relies on circumstantial evidence and, like ethnology, can tell social anthropologists little about the ideas and institutions, in which they would be interested, of the peoples whose bones and artifacts it discovers and classifies. Another branch of anthropology, comparative technology, in the main the comparative technology of primitive peoples, is, as it is usually taught, an adjunct of ethnology and prehistory.

Social anthropology has quite a different task to perform. It studies, as I shall soon demonstrate, social behaviour, generally in institutionalized forms, such as the family, kinship systems, political organization, legal procedures, religious cults, and the like, and the relations between such institutions; and it studies them either in contemporaneous societies or in historical societies for which there is adequate information of the kind to make such studies feasible.

So, whereas some custom of a people, when plotted on a distribution map, is of interest for the ethnologist as evidence of an ethnic movement, of a cultural drift, or of past contact between peoples, it is of interest to the social anthropologist as part of the whole social life of the people at the present time. The mere probability that they may have borrowed it from some other people is not very significant for him since he cannot know for certain that they did borrow it and, even if they did, he does not know when, how, and why they borrowed it. For example, certain peoples in East Africa take the sun for their symbol of God. This to some ethnologists is evidence of Ancient Egyptian influence. The social anthropologist, knowing that it cannot be proved whether this hypothesis is right or wrong, is more concerned to relate the solar symbolism to the whole systems of belief and cult of these peoples. Thus, while the ethnologist and the social anthropologist may make use of the same ethnographic data, they use them for different purposes.

The curricula of university courses in anthropology may be figured by three intersecting circles representing biological studies, historical studies, and sociological studies, the overlapping sections of which are physical anthropology, ethnology (including prehistoric archaeology and comparative technology), and social anthropology. Although these three anthropological disciplines have a common field in primitive man they have, as we have seen, very different aims and methods, and it is through historical circumstances, largely connected with the Darwinian theory of evolution, rather than as a result of a carefully thought out plan, that they are taught together in varying degrees in the universities and are jointly represented in the Royal Anthropological Institute.

Some of my colleagues have indeed expressed themselves dissatisfied with the present arrangement. Some of us would prefer to see social anthropology brought into a closer teaching relationship with psychology or with the so-called social sciences, such as general sociology, economics, and comparative politics, and others of us with other subjects. The question is complex, and this is not the occasion to discuss it. I will only say that the answer given to it much depends on the view taken of the nature of social anthropology, for there is a broad division of opinion between those who regard social anthropology as a natural science and those, like myself, who regard it as one of the humanities. This division is perhaps at its sharpest when relations between anthropology and history are being discussed. I shall leave consideration of this issue till a later lecture, because it is necessary to know something about the early development of the subject to perceive how the division of opinion has come about.

I have briefly, and in an inevitably discursive manner, outlined the position of social anthropology as a university subject. Having cleared the ground to some extent by so doing, I can now devote myself wholly to social anthropology, for that is the topic I am here to discuss and the only one I am competent to discuss. When therefore for convenience I speak in future of anthropology without the qualification 'social' it must be understood that it is to social anthropology that I refer.

I had better deal right away with the questions 'What are primitive societies?' and 'Why do we study them?' before telling you more precisely what we study in them. The word 'primitive' in the sense in which it has become established in anthropological literature does not mean that the societies it qualifies are either earlier in time or inferior to other kinds of societies. As far as we know, primitive societies have just as long a history as our own, and while they are less developed than our society in some respects they are often more developed in others. This being so, the word was perhaps an unfortunate choice, but it has now been too widely accepted as a technical term to be avoided.

It suffices to say at this stage that when anthropologists use it they do so in reference to those societies which are small in scale with regard to numbers, territory, and range of social contacts, and which have by comparison with more advanced societies a simple technology and economy and little specialization of social function. Some anthropologists would add further criteria, particularly the absence of literature, and hence of any systematic art, science, or theology.[1]

We are sometimes criticized for giving so much of our time to the study of these primitive societies. It is suggested that inquiry into problems of our own society might be more useful. This may be so, but for various reasons primitive societies have long held the attention of those interested in the study of social institutions. They attracted the notice of philosophers in the eighteenth century chiefly because they furnished examples of what was supposed to be man living in a state of nature before the institution of civil government. They engaged the attention of anthropologists in the nineteenth century because it was believed that they provided important clues in the search for the origins of institutions. Later anthropologists were interested in them because it was held that they displayed institutions in their simplest forms, and that it is sound method to proceed from examination of the more simple to examination of the more complex, in which what has been learnt from a study of the more simple would be an aid.

This last reason for interest in primitive societies gained in weight as the so-called functional anthropology of today developed, for the more it is regarded as the task of social anthropology to study social institutions as interdependent parts of social systems, the more it is seen to be an advantage to be able to study those societies which are

[1] Robert Redfield, 'The Folk Society', *The American Journal of Sociology*, 1947.

structurally so simple, and culturally so homogeneous, that they can be directly observed as wholes, before attempting to study complex civilized societies where this is not possible. Moreover, it is a matter of experience that it is easier to make observations among peoples with cultures unlike our own, the otherness in their way of life at once engaging attention, and that it is more likely that interpretations will be objective.

Another, and very cogent, reason for studying primitive societies at the present time is that they are rapidly being transformed and must be studied soon or never. These vanishing social systems are unique structural variations, a study of which aids us very considerably in understanding the nature of human society, because in a comparative study of institutions the number of societies studied is less significant than their range of variation. Quite apart from that consideration, the study of primitive societies has intrinsic value. They are interesting in themselves in that they provide descriptions of the way of life, the values, and the beliefs of peoples living without what we have come to regard as the minimum requirements of comfort and civilization.

We therefore feel it an obligation to make a systematic study of as many of these primitive societies as we can while there is still an opportunity to do so. There are a vast number of primitive societies and very few indeed have yet been studied intensively by anthropologists, for such studies take a long time and anthropologists are a very small body.

But though we give chief attention to primitive societies I must make it clear that we do not restrict our attention to them. In America, where social anthropology is better represented in the universities than in the British Empire, a number of important studies of more advanced societies have already been made by American or American-trained anthropologists—in Ireland, in Japan, in China, in India, in Mexico, in Canada, and in the United States itself. I shall give you in a later lecture some account of one of these studies, that by Arensberg and Kimball in Southern Ireland.

For various reasons, among them shortage of personnel and the great number of primitive peoples in our colonial empire, British anthropologists have lagged behind in this matter, but they also are broadening their studies to include peoples who cannot in any sense be described as primitive. During the past few years students of the Institute of Social Anthropology at Oxford have been engaged in studies of rural communities in India, the West Indies, Turkey, and Spain, of the Bedouin Arabs of North Africa, and of English village and urban life.

Also, though not to the same extent in recent years, studies have been made by anthropologists, or from an anthropological point of view, in historic societies, literary sources here taking the place of direct observation. I am thinking of such writings as those of Sir James Frazer on the ancient Hebrews and on certain aspects of Roman culture, of Sir William Ridgeway and Jane Harrison on Hellenic subjects, of Robertson Smith on early Arabian society, and of Hubert on the history of the Celts.

I must emphasize that, theoretically at any rate, social anthropology is the study of all human societies and not merely of primitive societies, even if in practice, and for convenience, at the present time its attention is mostly given to the institutions of the simpler peoples, for it is evident that there can be no separate discipline which restricts itself entirely to these societies. Though an anthropologist may be carrying out research among a primitive people, what he is studying among them are language, law, religion, political institutions, economics, and so forth, and he is therefore concerned with the same general problems as the student of these subjects in the great civilizations of the world. It must be remembered also that in interpreting his observations on primitive societies the anthropologist is always, if only implicitly, comparing them with his own.

Social anthropology can therefore be regarded as a branch of sociological studies, that branch which chiefly devotes itself to primitive societies. When people speak of sociology they generally have in mind studies of particular problems in civilized societies. If we give this sense to the word, then the difference between social anthropology and sociology is a difference of field, but there are also important differences of method between them. The social anthropologist studies primitive societies directly, living among them for months or years, whereas sociological research is usually from documents and largely statistical. The social anthropologist studies societies as wholes. He studies their oecologies, their economics, their legal and political institutions, their family and kinship organizations, their religions, their technologies, their arts, *etc.* as parts of general social systems. The sociologist's work, on the other hand, is usually very specialized, being a study of isolated problems, such as divorce, crime, insanity, labour unrest, and incentives in industry. Sociology is very largely mixed with social philosophy at one end and social planning at the other. It seeks not only to discover how institutions work but to decide how they ought to work and to alter them, while social anthropology has mostly kept apart from such considerations.

However, it is not in this sense that I speak of sociology in these lectures, but in the broader sense in which it is regarded as a general body of theoretical knowledge about human societies. It is the relation of this general body of theory to primitive social life which constitutes the subject of social anthropology. This will be evident when I give you some account of its history because much of our theoretical, or conceptual, knowledge is derived from writings which are in no way, or only indirectly, concerned with primitive societies at all. Therefore I will ask you to keep in mind throughout these lectures two interconnected developments, the growth of sociological theory, of which anthropological theory is only a part, and the growth of knowledge about primitive societies to which sociological theory has been submitted and re-formulated as a specialized body of knowledge relating to them.

I must now give you, in the light of this discussion about the place of social anthropology as a department in a wider field of learning, a clearer idea of the kind of problems social anthropologists investigate. A good way of doing this is to tell you some of the subjects about which post-graduate students of anthropology at Oxford have written theses during the last few years.

I give you the titles of a few which have been awarded degrees recently: 'The position of the chief in the modern political system of Ashanti (West Africa), A study of the influence of contemporary social changes on Ashanti institutions.'; 'The social function of religion in a South Indian community' (the Coorgs); 'The political organization of the Nandi' (East Africa); 'The social structure of Jamaica, with special reference to racial distinctions'; 'The function of bridewealth in selected African societies'; 'A study of the symbolism of political authority in Africa'; 'A comparative study of the forms of slavery'; 'The social organization of the Yao of southern Nyasaland' (Central Africa); 'Systems of land tenure among the Bantu peoples of East Africa'; 'The status of women among the southern Bantu' (South Africa); 'An investigation into the social sanctions of the Naga tribes of the Indo-Burma border'; 'The political system of the Murle' (East Africa); 'The political organization of the Plains Indians' (North America); 'A study of inter-state boundary litigation in

Ashanti' (West Africa); 'Aspects of rank in Melanesia'; 'The social organization of the central and eastern Eskimo'; 'Delict in primitive law' (Indonesia and Africa).

You will, I hope, gain from this sample a general impression of the kind of work social anthropologists do. You will note in the first place that there is nothing very exciting about the subjects of these theses, no seeking after the strange or colourful, no appeal to antiquarian or romantic interests. All are matter-of-fact inquiries into one or other type of social institution.

You will observe also that in so far as the theses discuss particular peoples or series of peoples, they are distributed over all parts of Africa, Southern India, Jamaica, the Indo-Burma frontier, North America, the Polar Regions, islands of the Pacific, and Indonesia. I draw attention to this geographical spread because the vastness of the anthropological field, while offering opportunities for research for the most diverse interests, involves, as I will explain later, certain difficulties in teaching and, to an increasing extent, regional specialization. In the narrowest interpretation of its province it includes the Polynesian and Melanesian peoples of the Pacific, the aboriginals of Australia, the Lapp and Eskimo peoples of the Polar regions, the Mongolian peoples of Siberia, the Negro peoples of Africa, the Indian peoples of the American continent, and the more backward peoples of India, Burma, Malay, and Indonesia—many thousands of different cultures and societies. On a wider interpretation its boundaries include also the more advanced, but still relatively simple, peoples of near and further Asia, north Africa, and parts of Europe—an almost limitless number of cultures and sub-cultures and societies and sub-societies.

You will also note that the sample includes studies of political institutions, religious institutions, class distinctions based on colour, sex, or rank, economic institutions, legal or quasi-legal institutions, and marriage, and also of social adaptation, and of the entire social organization, or structure, of one or other people. Social anthropology thus not only covers societies round the globe but also a number of different studies. Indeed, any adequately staffed department of anthropology tries to cover in its courses of lectures on primitive societies at least the minimum and essential topics of kinship and the family, comparative political institutions, comparative economics, comparative religion, and comparative law, as well as more general courses on the study of institutions, general sociological theory, and the history of social anthropology. It gives also special courses on the societies of selected ethno-geographical regions; and it may provide courses besides on such particular subjects as morals, magic, mythology, primitive science, primitive art, primitive technology, and language, and also on the writings of particular anthropologists and sociologists.

It stands to reason that though an anthropologist may have a general knowledge of all these different ethnographic regions and sociological disciplines, he can be an authority in only one or two of each. Consequently, as in all fields of learning, as knowledge increases there takes place specialization. The anthropologist becomes a specialist in African studies, in Melanesian studies, in American Indian studies, and so forth. He then no longer attempts to master the detail of regions other than those of his choice, except in so far as it is embodied in monographs explicitly devoted to general problems, perhaps religious or legal institutions, in which he is particularly interested. There is already a sufficiently abundant literature on, for example, the American Indians or the African Bantu for a scholar to devote himself exclusively to the one or the other.

The tendency towards specialization becomes yet more marked when the peoples concerned have a literature or belong to a wider culture with a literary tradition. If one has any regard for scholarship one cannot be a student of Arab Bedouin or peasants without a knowledge not only of their spoken language but also of the classical language of their cultural hinterland, or of Indian peasant communities without having some knowledge both of the literature of their language and of Sanskrit, the classical language of their ritual and religious tradition. Also, the anthropologist, besides restricting his researches to certain regions has to devote himself primarily to one or two topics if he is to be master of them and not a jack of all trades. One cannot adequately make a comparative study of primitive legal systems without a good background of general law and jurisprudence, or of primitive art without being well-read in the literature of art.

The circumstances I have related make social anthropology difficult to teach, especially when, as for the most part at Oxford, it is taught at the post-graduate and research level. When a large number of students are working on material in widely separated parts of the world and on a wide variety of problems it is often impossible to give them more than very general supervision. Sir Charles Oman tells us that the same situation confronted those Regius Professors of History at Oxford who tried, unsuccessfully, to conduct classes for post-graduates, for, as he wistfully remarks, 'post-graduate students wander at their own sweet will'.[1] However, the situation is not so difficult in social anthropology as it is in history, for social anthropology is more able to generalize and has a body of general theory which history lacks. There are not only many overt similarities between primitive societies all over the world but they can, at any rate to some extent, be classified by structural analysis into a limited number of types. This gives a unity to the subject. Social anthropologists study a primitive society in the same way

[1] Sir Charles Oman, *On the Writing of History*, 1939, p. 252.

whether it is in Polynesia, Africa, or Lapland; and whatever they are writing about—a kinship system, a religious cult, or a political institution—it is examined in its relation to the total social structure in which it is contained.

Before considering, even in a preliminary manner, what we understand by social structure I will ask you to note a further characteristic of these theses, because it brings out a significant problem in anthropology at the present time and one which I shall discuss again in later lectures. They are all written on sociological themes, that is to say, they deal fundamentally with sets of social relations, relations between members of a society and between social groups. The point I want to make here is that they are studies of societies rather than of cultures. There is an extremely important difference between the two concepts which has led anthropological research and theory in two different directions.

Allow me to give a few simple examples. If you go into an English church you will see that men remove their head-dress but keep their shoes on, but if you enter a mosque in a Muslim land you will observe that men remove their shoes but keep their head-dress on. The same behaviour is customary when entering an English house or a Bedouin tent. These are differences of culture or custom. The purpose and function of the behaviour is the same in both cases, to show respect, but it is expressed differently in the two cultures. Let me give you a more complex example. Nomadic Bedouin Arabs have in some, and basic, respects the same kind of social structure as some of the semi-nomadic Nilotic peoples of East Africa, but culturally the two peoples are different. Bedouin live in tents, Nilotics in huts and windscreens; Bedouin herd camels, Nilotics cattle; Bedouin are Muslims, Nilotics have a different kind of religion; and so forth. A different sort of example, and an even more complex one, would be the distinction we make when we speak of Hellenic or Hindu civilization and Hellenic or Hindu society.

We are here dealing with two different concepts, or two different abstractions from the same reality. Though the definitions which should be given to each and their relation to one another have often been discussed, they have seldom been systematically examined, and there is still much confusion and little unanimity about the matter. Among the older anthropological writers, Morgan, Spencer, and Durkheim conceived the aim of what we now call social anthropology to be the classification and functional analysis of social structures. This point of view has persisted among Durkheim's followers in France. It is also well represented in British anthropology today and in the tradition of formal sociology in Germany.[1] Tylor on the other hand, and others who leant towards ethnology, conceived its aim to be the classification and analysis of cultures, and this has been the dominant viewpoint in American anthropology for a long time, partly, I think, because the fractionized and disintegrated Indian societies on which their research has been concentrated lend themselves more easily to studies of culture than of social structure; partly because the absence of a tradition of intensive fieldwork through the native languages and for long periods of time, such as we have in England, also tends towards studies of custom or culture rather than of social relations; and partly for other reasons.

When a social anthropologist describes a primitive society the distinction between society and culture is obscured by the fact that he describes the reality, the raw behaviour, in which both are contained. He tells you, for example, the precise manner in which a man

[1] Georg Simmel, *Soziologie*, 1908; Leopold von Wiese, *Allgemeine Soziologie*, 1924.

shows respect to his ancestors; but when he comes to interpret the behaviour he has to make abstractions from it in the light of the particular problems he is investigating. If these are problems of social structure he pays attention to the social relationships of the persons concerned in the whole procedure rather than to the details of its cultural expression.

Thus one, or a partial, interpretation of ancestor worship might be to show how it is consistent with family or kinship structure. The cultural, or customary, actions which a man performs when showing respect to his ancestors, the facts, for instance, that he makes a sacrifice and that what he sacrifices is a cow or an ox, require a different kind of interpretation, and this may be partly both psychological and historical.

This methodological distinction is most evident when comparative studies are undertaken, for to attempt both kinds of interpretation at the same time is then almost certain to lead to confusion. In comparative studies what one compares are not things in themselves but certain particular characteristics of them. If one wishes to make a sociological comparison of ancestor cults in a number of different societies, what one compares are sets of structural relations between persons. One necessarily starts, therefore, by abstracting these relations in each society from their particular modes of cultural expression. Otherwise one will not be able to make the comparison. What one is doing is to set apart problems of a certain kind for purposes of research. In doing this, one is not making a distinction between different kinds of thing—society and culture are not entities—but between different kinds of abstraction.

I have spoken earlier of social anthropology's studying the cultures and societies of primitive peoples, because I did not want at that stage to introduce this difficulty. I have stated it, and I shall have to leave the matter there, only asking you to bear in mind that there is still uncertainty and division of opinion about it and that it is a very difficult and complex problem. I shall only say further that the study of problems of culture leads, and I think must lead, to the framing of them in terms of history or psychology, whereas problems of society are framed in terms of sociology. My own view is that while both kinds of problems are equally important, structural studies ought to be made first.

This brings me back to the theses once again. Had you read them you would have noted that they have this in common, that they examine whatever it is they set out to examine—chieftainship, religion, race distinctions, bride-wealth, slavery, land tenure, the status of women, social sanctions, rank, legal procedures, or whatever it may be—not as isolated and self-contained institutions but as parts of social structures and in terms of these structures. What then is a social structure? I shall have to be rather vague and inconclusive in answering this question in my introductory lecture. I shall discuss it again in later lectures, but I may as well say right away that, here again, there is much divergence of opinion on the matter. This is inevitable. Such basic concepts cannot be given precise definition. However, if we are to proceed further, I must give you at any rate a preliminary indication of what is generally implied by the term structure.

It is evident that there must be uniformities and regularities in social life, that a society must have some sort of order, or its members could not live together. It is only because people know the kind of behaviour expected of them, and what kind of behaviour to expect from others, in the various situations of social life, and co-ordinate their activities in submission to rules and under the guidance of values that each and all are able to go about their affairs. They can make predictions, anticipate events, and lead their lives in harmony with their fellows because every society has a form or pattern which allows us to speak of it as a system, or structure, within which, and in accordance with which, its members live their lives. The use of the word structure in this sense implies that there is some kind of consistency between its parts, at any rate up to the point of open contradiction and conflict being avoided, and that it has greater durability than most of the fleeting things of human life. The people who live in any society may be unaware, or only dimly aware, that it has a structure. It is the task of the social anthropologist to reveal it.

A total social structure, that is to say the entire structure of a given society, is composed of a number of subsidiary structures or systems, and we may speak of its kinship system, its economic system, its religious system and its political system.

The social activities within these systems or structures are organized round institutions such as marriage, the family, markets, chieftainship, and so forth; and when we speak of the functions of these institutions we mean the part they play in the maintenance of the structure.

I think that all social anthropologists would accept, more or less, these definitions. It is when we begin to ask what kind of abstraction a social structure is and what precisely is meant by the functioning of an institution that we meet with difficulties and divergence of opinion. The issues will, I think, be better understood after I have given some account of the theoretical development of social anthropology.

II

THEORETICAL BEGINNINGS

In this, my second, lecture and in the following lecture I propose to give you some account of the history of social anthropology. I do not intend to present you with a mere chronological arrangement of anthropologists and their books, but to attempt to trace the development of its general concepts, or theory, using some of these writers and their works as illustrations of this development.[1]

As we have seen, social anthropology is a very new subject in the sense that it has only recently been taught in our universities, and still more recently under that title. In another sense it may be said to have begun with the earliest speculations of mankind, for everywhere and at all times men have propounded theories about the nature of society. In this sense there is no definite point at which social anthropology can be said to have begun. Nevertheless, there is a point beyond which it is hardly profitable to trace back its development. This nascent period of our subject was the eighteenth century. It is a child of the Enlightenment and bears throughout its history and today many of the characteristic features of its ancestry.

In France its lineage runs from Montesquieu (1689–1755). His best known book, *De L'Esprit des Lois* (1748),

[1] General accounts of the history of anthropology can be found in A. C. Haddon, *History of Anthropology*, revised edit., 1934; Paul Radin, *The Method and Theory of Ethnology*, 1933; T. K. Penniman, *A Hundred Years of Anthropology*, 1935; and Robert H. Lowie, *The History of Ethnological Theory*, 1937.

a treatise on political, or perhaps social, philosophy, is best remembered for some rather odd notions Montesquieu had about the influence of climate on the character of peoples and for his remarks on the separation of powers in government. But what is of chief interest to us is that he had the idea of everything in a society and its ambient being functionally related to everything else. One can only understand international, constitutional, criminal, and civil law by considering them in relation to each other and also in relation to the physical environment of a people, their economy, their numbers, their beliefs, their customs and manners, and their temperaments. The object of his book is to examine 'all these interrelations: they form taken together that which one calls the Spirit of the Laws'.[1]

Montesquieu used the word 'laws' in a number of different senses, but in a general sense he meant 'the necessary relations which derive from the nature of things',[2] that is to say, the conditions which make human society possible at all and those conditions which make any particular type of society possible. Time will not allow me to discuss his argument in detail, but it should, I think, be noted that he distinguished between the 'nature' of society and its 'principle', its 'nature' being 'that which makes it to be what it is' and its 'principle' being 'that which makes it function'. 'The one is its particular structure, and the other the human passions which make it work'.[3] He thus distinguished between a social structure and the system of values which operate in it.

From Montesquieu the French lineage of social anthropology runs through such writers as D'Alembert, Condorcet, Turgot, and in general the Encyclopaedists and

[1] *De L'Esprit des Lois*, edited by Gonzague Truc, Editions Garnier Frères, n.d., p. 11.

[2] Ibid., p. 5. [3] Ibid., p. 23.

Physiocrats, to Saint Simon (1760–1825), who was the first to propose clearly a science of society. This descendant of an illustrious family was a very remarkable person. A true child of the Enlightenment, he believed passionately in science and progress and desired above all to establish a positive science of social relations, which were to him analogous to the organic relations of physiology; and he insisted that scientists must analyse facts and not concepts. It is understandable that his disciples were socialists and collectivists, and perhaps also that the movement ended in religious fervour and finally evaporated in a search for the perfect woman who would play the part of a female messiah. Saint Simon's best known disciple, who later quarrelled with him, was Auguste Comte (1798–1857). Comte, a more systematic thinker than Saint Simon, though just as eccentric a person, named the proposed new science of society 'sociology'. The stream of French philosophical rationalism which comes from these writers was later, through the writings of Durkheim and his students and Lévy-Bruhl, who were in the direct line of Saint Simonian tradition, to colour English anthropology strongly.

Our forbears in Great Britain were the Scottish moral philosophers, whose writings were typical of the eighteenth century. The best known names are David Hume (1711–1776) and Adam Smith (1723–1790). Most of them are very little read today. They insisted that societies are natural systems. By this they meant in particular that society derives from human nature and not from a social contract, about which Hobbes and others had written so much. It was in this sense that they talked about natural morality, natural religion, natural jurisprudence, and so forth.

Being regarded as natural systems or organisms, societies must be studied empirically and inductively, and not by the methods of Cartesian rationalism. Thus, the title of Hume's thesis of 1739 was *A Treatise of Human Nature: Being an Attempt to introduce the experimental Method of Reasoning into Moral Subjects*. But they were also highly theoretical thinkers and were chiefly interested in the formulation of what they called general principles and what would today be called sociological laws.[1]

These philosophers had also a firm belief in limitless progress—what they called improvement and perfectibility—and in laws of progress. To discover these laws they made use of what Comte was later to call the comparative method. As they used it, it implied that, human nature being fundamentally everywhere and at all times the same, all peoples travel along the same road, and by uniform stages, in their gradual but continuous advance to perfection; though some more slowly than others.

It is true that there is no certain evidence of the earliest stages of our history but, human nature being constant, it may be assumed that our forefathers must have lived the same kind of life as the Redskins of America and other primitive peoples when they lived in similar conditions and at a similar level of culture. By comparing all known societies and arranging them in order of improvement it is thus possible to reconstruct what the history of our own society, and of all human societies, must have been, even though it cannot be known when or by what events progress took place.

Dugald Stewart called this procedure theoretical, or conjectural, history. It is a kind of philosophy of history which attempts to isolate broad general trends and tendencies and regards particular events as mere incidents. Its method is admirably set forth by Lord Kames: 'We must be satisfied with collecting the facts and circumstances as they may be gathered from the laws of different countries: and if these put together make a regular system of causes and effects, we may rationally

[1] Gladys Bryson, *Man and Society*, 1945, passim.

conclude, that the progress has been the same among all nations, in the capital circumstances at least; for accidents, or the singular nature of a people, or of a government, will always produce some peculiarities.'[1]

Since there are these laws of development and there is a method by which they can be discovered it follows that the science of man these philosophers proposed to establish is a normative science, aiming at the creation of a secularist ethics based on a study of human nature in society.

We have already in the speculations of these eighteenth-century writers all the ingredients of anthropological theory in the following century, and even at the present day: the emphasis on institutions, the assumption that human societies are natural systems, the insistence that the study of them must be empirical and inductive, that its purpose is the discovery and formulation of universal principles or laws, particularly in terms of stages of development revealed by the use of the comparative method of conjectural history, and that its ultimate purpose is the scientific determination of ethics.

It is on account of their attachment to the formulation of general principles and because they dealt with societies and not with individuals that these writers are of particular interest in the history of anthropology. In seeking to establish principles their concern was with institutions, their structural interrelations, their growth, and the human needs they arose to satisfy. Adam Ferguson, for example, in his *An Essay on the History of Civil Society* (1767) and other works writes of such matters as the manner of subsistence, varieties of the human race, the disposition of men to society, the principles of population growth, arts and commercial arrangements, and ranks and social divisions.

The importance of primitive societies for the questions which interested these philosophers is evident, and they

[1] Lord Kames, *Historical Law-Tracts*, vol. i, 1758, p. 37.

occasionally made use of what was known of them, but, outside their own culture and time, Old Testament and classical writings were their main sources. Little was, in any case, as yet known about primitive societies, though the voyages of discovery in the sixteenth century had even in Shakespeare's time led to a general representation of the savage in educated circles, portrayed in the character of Caliban; and writers on politics, law and custom were already beginning to be aware by that time of the great diversity of custom presented by peoples outside Europe. Montaigne (1533–1592), in particular, devoted many pages of his Essays to what we would today call ethnographic material.

In the seventeenth and eighteenth centuries philosophers cited primitive societies in support of their arguments about the nature of rude society in contrast to civil society, that is to say, society before the establishment of government by contract or acceptance of despotism. Locke (1632–1714) especially, refers to these societies in his speculations about religion, government and property. He was familiar with what had been written about the hunting Redskins of New England, and the fact that his knowledge was restricted to only one type of American Indian society much biassed his account.

French writers of the time drew their picture of man in a state of nature from what had been published about the Indians of the St. Lawrence, especially Gabriel Sagard's and Joseph Lafitau's accounts of the Hurons and Iroquois.[1] Rousseau's portrait of natural man was largely drawn from what was known of the Caribs of South America.

[1] Gabriel Sagard, *Le Grand Voyage du Pays des Hurons*, 1632; Joseph François Lafitau, *Moeurs des Sauvages Ameriquains comparées aux Moeurs des Premiers Temps*, 1724. For a general discussion of the influence of ethnographical writings on political philosophy see J. L. Myres, Presidential Address to Section H., *British Association for the Advancement of Science*, Winnipeg, 1909.

I have mentioned the use made of accounts of primitive peoples by some writers of the seventeenth and eighteenth centuries, because we can see in it the beginnings of that interest in the simpler societies as valuable material for theories about the nature and improvement of social institutions which in the middle of the nineteenth century was to develop into what we now call social anthropology.

The writers I have named, both in France and England, were of course in the sense of their time philosophers, and so regarded themselves. In spite of all their talk about empiricism they relied more on introspection and *a priori* reasoning than on observation of actual societies. For the most part—Montesquieu should perhaps be excepted from this stricture—they used facts to illustrate or corroborate theories reached by speculation. It was not till the middle of the nineteenth century that systematic studies of social institutions were made. In the decade between 1861 and 1871 there appeared books which we regard as our early theoretical classics: Maine's *Ancient Law* (1861) and his *Village-Communities in the East and West* (1871), Bachofen's *Das Mutterrecht* (1861), Fustel de Coulanges' *La Cité Antique* (1864), McLennan's *Primitive Marriage* (1865), Tylor's *Researches into the Early History of Mankind* (1865) and his *Primitive Culture* (1871), and Morgan's *Systems of Consanguinity and Affinity of the Human Family* (1871).

Not all these books were concerned primarily with primitive societies. Maine wrote about the early institutions of Rome and, more generally, of the Indo-European peoples, and Bachofen was chiefly interested in the traditions and mythologies of classical antiquity; but those which were least concerned with them dealt with comparable institutions at early periods in the development of historical societies and they dealt with them, as I shall show, in a sociological manner.

It was McLennan and Tylor in this country, and Morgan in America, who first treated primitive societies as a subject which might in itself engage the attention of serious scholars. It was they who first brought together the information about primitive peoples from a wide range of miscellaneous writings and presented it in systematic form, thereby laying the foundations of social anthropology. In their writings the study of primitive societies and speculative theory about the nature of social institutions met.

These authors of the middle of the nineteenth century, like the philosophers before them, were anxious to rid the study of social institutions of mere speculation. They, also, thought that they could do this by being strictly empirical and by rigorous use of the comparative method. We have noted that this method was utilized, under the title of hypothetical or conjectural history, by the moral philosophers. It was given a new and more precise definition by Comte in his *Cours de Philosophie Positive* (1830). As we shall see, it was later to be restated without its historicism by modern anthropology as the functional method.

According to Comte, there is a functional relation between social facts of different kinds, what Saint Simon and he called series of social facts, political, economic, religious, moral, *etc*. Changes in any one of these series provoke corresponding changes in the others. The establishment of these correspondences or interdependencies between one kind of social fact and another is the aim of sociology. It is attained by the logical method of concomitant variations, since in dealing with very complex social phenomena, in which simple variables cannot be isolated, this is the only method which can be pursued.

Using this method, not only the writers to whom I have referred, but also those who came after them, wrote many large volumes purporting to show the laws of the origin and development of social institutions: the development of monogamous marriage from promiscuity, of property from communism, of contract from status, of industry from nomadism, of positive science from theology, of monotheism from animism. Sometimes, especially when treating religion, explanations were sought in terms of psychological origins, what the philosophers had called human nature, as well as in terms of historical origins.

The two favourite topics for discussion were the development of the family and the development of religion. Victorian anthropologists were never tired of writing about these two subjects, and a consideration of some of their conclusions about them will help us to understand the general tone of anthropology at that time, for though they disputed violently among themselves about what could be inferred from the evidence, they were agreed about the aims and methods to be pursued.

Sir Henry Maine (1822–1888), a Scot, a lawyer, and the founder, in England, of comparative jurisprudence, held that the patriarchal family is the original and universal form of social life and that the *patria potestas*, the absolute authority of the patriarch, on which it rests has produced everywhere at a certain stage agnation, the tracing of descent through males exclusively. Another jurist, the Swiss Bachofen, reached a precisely opposite conclusion about the form of the primitive family; and it is curious that he and Maine published their conclusions in the same year. According to Bachofen, there was first everywhere promiscuity, then a matrilineal and matriarchal social system, and only late in the history of man did this system give way to a patrilineal and patriarchal one.

A third lawyer and another Scot, J. F. McLennan (1827–1881), was a great believer in general laws of social development, though he had his own paradigm of stages and ridiculed those of his contemporaries. In his view, early man must be assumed to have been promiscuous, though the evidence shows him first as living everywhere in small matrilineal and totemic stock-groups which practised the blood feud. These hordes were politically independent of one another and each was an exogamous group on account of the custom of female infanticide, which made it necessary for its menfolk to obtain wives from other tribal groups. These early societies eventually developed, by way of polyandry, a patrilineal, in the place of a matrilineal, system of descent, while the family slowly emerged in the form to which we are accustomed. First comes the tribe, then the gens or house, and lastly the family. McLennan's thesis was taken over by yet another Scot, the Old Testament scholar and one of the founders of comparative religion, William Robertson Smith (1846–1894), who applied it to the early records of Arab and Hebrew history.[1]

That versatile man Sir John Lubbock (1834–1913), later Baron Avebury, also traced the development of modern marriage from a state of pristine promiscuity[2]—it was an obsession of writers of the period. The most complicated, and in some respects the most fantastic, product of the comparative method was the construction of the American lawyer L. H. Morgan (1818–1881), who postulated, among other things, no less than fifteen stages of the development of marriage and the family, beginning with promiscuity and ending with monogamous marriage and the family of western civilization. This fanciful scheme of progress has been incorporated, through Engels, into the official Marxist doctrines of communist Russia.

In their reconstructions, these writers made much of the idea of what McLennan called 'symbols' and Tylor called 'survivals'. Social survivals were compared to the rudimentary organs found in some animals and to mute

[1] *Kinship and Marriage in Early Arabia*, 1885.

[2] *The Origin of Civilization*, 1870.

letters in words. They are functionless, or at any rate, if they have a function, it is secondary and different to their original one. Being relics of a preceding age they enable us, these writers thought, to show that a series of social stages which has been worked out by logical criteria is in fact an historical series; and the order of stages being so determined we can attempt to estimate what were the influences which caused development from one stage to the next. For example, Robertson Smith considered, like McLennan before him, that the custom of the levirate is evidence of a preceding state of society in which polyandry was practised. Likewise, Morgan thought that classificatory systems of kinship nomenclature in which a man calls all male kinsmen of his father's generation 'father' and all kinswomen of his mother's generation 'mother', the children of these people 'brother' and 'sister', and their children 'son' and 'daughter', were evidence that sex relations in these societies were at one time more or less promiscuous.

When we turn to the treatment of religion by nineteenth-century anthropologists we find the same aim and method exemplified, though here, as I have mentioned, there is generally a blend of speculations of both an historical and a psychological kind, assumptions about human nature being introduced into the argument. Thus Sir Edward Tylor (1832–1917), who on the whole was more cautious and critical than most of his contemporaries and avoided their stage-making proclivities, tried to show that all religious belief and cult have developed from certain mistaken inferences from observation of such phenomena as dreams, trances, visions, disease, waking and sleeping, and life and death.

Sir James Frazer (1854–1941), whose literary talent first introduced social anthropology to the general reading public, was another great believer in sociological laws. He postulated three stages of development through which all societies pass: magic, religion, and science. According to him, early man was dominated by magic, which, like science, views nature as 'a series of events occurring in an invariable order without the intervention of personal agency.'[1] But though the magician, like the scientist, assumes laws of nature, a knowledge of which he believes enables him to influence it for his own ends, they are in his case not real, but imaginary, laws. In course of time the more intelligent members of society came to see that this was so, and in the resulting state of disillusionment they conceived of spiritual beings with powers superior to man's, who could be induced by propitiation to alter the course of nature to his advantage. This is the stage of religion. Eventually this was also seen to be an illusion and man entered the final, the scientific, stage of his development.

These Victorian anthropologists were men of outstanding ability, wide learning, and obvious integrity. If they over-emphasized resemblances in custom and belief and paid insufficient attention to diversities, they were investigating a real, and not an imaginary, problem when they attempted to account for remarkable similarities in societies widely separated in space and time; and much of permanent value has come out of their researches. Their use of the comparative method allowed them to separate the general from the particular, and so to classify social phenomena.

Thus to Morgan we owe the inception of the comparative study of kinship systems which has since become so important a part of anthropological research. McLennan not only brought together a great mass of evidence to show how common is the rite of marriage by capture in the wedding ceremonies of the simpler societies, but he was also the first to show that exogamy (he invented the

[1] Sir J. G. Frazer, *The Golden Bough. The Magic Art*, 3rd ed., 1922, vol. I, p. 51.

word) and totemism are widespread features of primitive societies and thereby to give us two of our most important concepts; and to him and to Bachofen is due the credit of being the first to draw attention, against the overwhelming bias in favour of patriarchal origins of the family at that time, to the existence of matrilineal societies in all parts of the world, and of recognizing their great sociological importance. Tylor, among many other achievements, showed the universality of animistic beliefs and established the term animism in our vocabulary. Frazer likewise showed the universality of magical beliefs and that their logical structure can be reduced by analysis to two elementary types, homoeopathic magic and contagious magic; and he brought together a great number of examples of divine kingship and of other institutions and customs, and by so doing brought them into relief as widespread social and cultural patterns.

Moreover, their research was much more critical than that of their predecessors. They had, of course, more knowledge from which to generalize, but, in addition to that, they used their knowledge more systematically than the philosophers, of whom Maine complained: 'The inquiries of the jurist are in truth prosecuted much as inquiry into physics and physiology was prosecuted before observation had taken the place of assumption. Theories, plausible and comprehensive, but absolutely unverified, such as the Law of Nature or the Social Compact, enjoy a universal preference over sober research into the primitive history of society and law.'[1]

Philosophical speculations were of little value when unsupported by factual evidence. It was the 'sober research' of Maine and his contemporaries that opened a way to an understanding of social institutions. Their sifting and classification of the material provided an indispensable corpus of ethnographic fact, hitherto lacking, from

[1] *Ancient Law*, 1912 ed., p. 3.

which significant theoretical conclusions could be, and were, drawn and by which they could be tested.

Another virtue found in most of the nineteenth-century writers I have mentioned was that they studied institutions sociologically, in terms of social structure, and not in terms of individual psychology. They avoided arguing deductively, as the philosophers often did, from postulates about human nature, and attempted to explain institutions in terms of other institutions found with them in the same society at the same time or at an earlier period of its history.

Thus when McLennan sought to understand exogamy, he explicitly rejected a biological or psychological determinant of the incest taboo and tried to explain it by reference to the customs of female infanticide and the blood feud and to totemic beliefs. He did not look in human nature for an explanation of the rite of marriage by capture but showed how it can be related to rules of exogamy and how it might be a survival of actual rapine. Likewise he suggested how patriliny might have developed out of matriliny through a combination of the customs of polyandry and patrilocality; and how the worship of animal gods and plant gods and their symbols, and their hierarchical relationship to one another, among the Jews, in India, and in ancient Greece and Rome might have developed out of totemism and a totemic tribal structure.

McLennan rigidly adhered to the thesis that social institutions are functionally interdependent. For instance, he tells us that 'a full explanation of the origin of exogamy requires it to be made out that wherever exogamy prevailed, totemism prevailed; that where totemism prevailed, blood-feuds prevailed; that where blood-feuds prevailed, the religious obligation of vengeance prevailed; that where the religious obligation of vengeance prevailed, female infanticide prevailed; that where female infanticide prevailed, female kinship prevailed. A failure to make good any one of these particulars would be fatal to the entire argument.'[1]

Maine, likewise, was interested in sociological questions—such as the relation of law to religion and morality, the social effects of the codification of law in various historical circumstances, the effect of the development of Rome as a military empire on the legal authority of the father in the family, the relation between the *patria postestas* and agnation, and the movement in progressive societies from law based on status to law based on contract. In his treatment of such problems Maine was forthright in advocating a sociological method of analysis and in condemning what would today be called psychological explanations. 'What mankind did in the primitive state', he argues, 'may not be a hopeless subject of inquiry, but of their motives for doing it it is impossible to know anything. These sketches of the plight of human beings in the first ages of the world are effected by first supposing mankind to be divested of a great part of the circumstances by which they are now surrounded, and then by assuming that, in the condition thus imagined, they would preserve the same sentiments and prejudices by which they are now actuated,—although, in fact, these sentiments may have been created and engendered by those very circumstances of which, by the hypothesis, they are to be stripped.'[2]

In other words, primitive institutions cannot be interpreted in terms of the mentality of the civilized inquirer into them because his mentality is a product of a different set of institutions. To suppose otherwise is to fall into what has been called 'the psychologists' fallacy', so often to be denounced later by Durkheim, Lévy-Bruhl, and other French sociologists.

[1] *Studies in Ancient History* (The Second Series), 1896, p. 28.

[2] *Ancient Law*, 1912 ed., pp. 266–7.

I am not suggesting that the theories of these Victorian anthropologists were sound. For the most part they are not accepted by any anthropologist today, and some of them now appear to be silly not only in the light of our present knowledge but also in the light of the knowledge available at the time they were put forward. Nor am I upholding the method of interpretation. I am merely trying to estimate the significance of these writers for an understanding of the social anthropology of the present day. To appreciate it, and them, we must, I think, bear in mind that the social changes taking place in Europe at the time directed the attention of many thinkers, particularly of philosophers of history, economists, and statisticians, to the role in history of masses, rather than of individuals, and of broad trends, rather than of particular events, and led them to the quest of uniformities and regularities.[1] The study of institutions lent itself easily to this approach, especially when the institutions were those of early man, for which only the outline and direction of development could be surmised, and not the part played in it by individuals or by accidental events, inasmuch as these could not be reconstructed by the comparative method or any other.

But although in some respects these nineteenth-century anthropologists had much the same point of view as those of today, in other respects it differed widely, so widely that it is often difficult for us to read their theoretical constructions without irritation; and at times we feel embarrassed at what seems complacency. In part the difficulty lies in the changes which have taken place in the content of the words used, due, in addition to a general change in outlook, to changes in the meaning of concepts brought about by increase of knowledge; for it must be understood that very little indeed was then

[1] G. P. Gooch, *History and Historians in the Nineteenth Century*, 1949, Chap. XXVIII *et passim*.

known about primitive societies and what were taken for facts were often not facts at all but superficial observations or prejudiced opinion. But even if we make allowance for that, we see now that their use of the comparative method for the purpose of historical reconstructions led them into unjustifiable, and totally unverifiable, conclusions.

These anthropologists of the last century considered that they were writing history, the history of early man, and they were interested in primitive societies not so much in themselves as for the use they could make of them in the hypothetical reconstruction of the earliest history of mankind in general and of their own institutions in particular. Maine's *Ancient Law* has the sub-title *Its Connection with the Early History of Society, and its Relation to Modern Ideas.* The title of Tylor's first book was *Researches into the Early History of Mankind.* Sir John Lubbock's contribution to these studies was called *The Origin of Civilization.* McLennan's essays were brought together in two volumes as *Studies in Ancient History.*

It is not surprising that they wrote what they regarded as history, for all contemporaneous learning was radically historical. The genetic approach, which had borne impressive fruits in philology, was apparent in law, theology, economics, philosophy, and science.[1] There was everywhere a passionate endeavour to discover the origins of everything—the origin of species, the origin of religion, the origin of law, and so on—an endeavour, almost an obsession, to explain always the nearer by the farther.[2]

I mention briefly a few of the major objections to the method pursued in these attempts to explain institutions by seeking to reconstruct their development from supposed origins, for it is important that it should be under-

[1] Lord Acton, *A Lecture on the Study of History*, 1895, pp. 56–8.

[2] Marc Bloch, *Apologie pour L'Histoire ou Métier d'Historien*, 1949, p. 5.

stood why social anthropologists in England have turned away from the kind of interpretations set forth by their predecessors.

We would, I think unanimously, hold today that an institution is not to be understood, far less explained, in terms of its origins, whether these origins are conceived of as beginnings, causes, or merely, in a logical sense, its simplest forms. To understand an institution one is certainly aided by knowing its development and the circumstances of its development, but a knowledge of its history cannot of itself tell us how it functions in social life. To know how it has come to be what it is, and to know how it works, are two different things, a distinction I shall discuss further in my next lecture.

But in the case of these nineteenth-century anthropologists we are not offered critical history, not even as it was understood in the middle of the century, when it was still regarded as a literary art and was in no way the systematic study of sources it has become today. Even then history was at least based on documents and monuments totally lacking for reconstruction of the development of the institutions of early man. In that field historical reconstruction had to be almost entirely conjectural, and it was often little more than plausible guesswork. If one accepts that man is descended from some ape-like creature it may be reasonable to suppose that at one time his sexual relations must have been in some degree promiscuous, and to ask further how it has come about that monogamous marriage has developed from this condition; but the supposition and reconstruction of development are purely speculative. They are not history.

It must be noted also that the comparative method, even when it was used merely to establish correlations, without attempting further to give them a chronological value, had, when applied to social institutions, serious weaknesses which not even the learning and industry of Tylor, or the statistical methods he summoned to his aid, could overcome. The facts submitted to analysis were generally inaccurate or insufficient, and they were also often wrenched from the social contexts which alone gave them meaning. Furthermore, it was found exceedingly difficult, if not impossible, when dealing with complex social phenomena to establish the units to be submitted to analysis by the method of concomitant variations. It is easy to ask how constantly are totemism and clans found together but it is very difficult to define 'totemism' and 'clan' for the purpose of the inquiry. It is even more difficult to give precise definition to such concepts as 'property', 'crime', 'monogamy', 'democracy', 'slavery' and many other terms.

A further difficulty in these investigations, complicated by the spread of institutions and ideas, was to decide what was to be regarded as an instance of the occurrence of a social fact. Does the occurrence of polygamy throughout the Muslim world count as one instance of polygamy or as many? Are parliamentary institutions derived from, and modelled on, the British system in many parts of the world to count as one instance of them or as many?

It will be clear to you from what I have already said that in two important respects nineteenth-century anthropology differed from that of today. It sought to interpret institutions by showing how they might have originated and by what steps they might have developed. We may here leave for further consideration the question of the relevance of historical development for sociological inquiry where the history is known. Most of us would certainly take the view that, since the history of the institutions of primitive peoples is not known, a systematic study of them as they are at the present time must precede any attempt at conjecturing how they may have originated and developed. We would also hold that how they originated and developed is in any case a problem which, however relevant to the problem of how they function in society, is a different problem and one that has to be separately investigated by a different technique.

Another way of expressing this point would be to say that social anthropology and ethnology were regarded by the nineteenth-century anthropologists as a single discipline whereas they are regarded today as distinct.

The second main difference I would like to draw your attention to is only now beginning to emerge clearly in anthropology. In my first lecture I referred to the difference between culture and society. This distinction was scarcely made by the anthropologists of last century. Had they made it, most of them would have regarded culture, and not social relations, as the subject matter of their inquiries; and culture was for them something concrete. They thought of exogamy, totemism, matriliny, ancestor worship, slavery, and so forth as customs—things—and it was an inquiry into these customs, or things, that they regarded themselves as pursuing. Consequently their concepts had always to carry such a heavy load of cultural reality that comparative analysis was bogged down at the outset.

It was not till the end of the century that anthropologists began to classify societies on the basis of their social structures, rather than of their cultures, as a first essential step towards making comparative studies profitable. Social anthropology besides having now separated itself from ethnology has also defined its subject matter as social relations, rather than culture, and has consequently been able to reach a clearer appreciation of its problems and to fashion a method of inquiry into them. Its method is still a comparative method, but it is used for a different purpose and in a different way, and what it compares is different.

Apart from these differences in method one feels also a

moral separation from the anthropologists of last century —or at least I do. Their reconstructions were not only conjectural but evaluatory. Liberals and rationalists, they believed above all in progress, the kind of material, political, social, and philosophical changes which were taking place in Victorian England. Industrialism, democracy, science, and so forth were good in themselves. Consequently the explanations of social institutions they put forward amount, when examined, to little more than hypothetical scales of progress, at one end of which were placed forms of institutions or beliefs as they were in nineteenth-century Europe and America, while at the other end were placed their antitheses. An order of stages was then worked out to show what logically might have been the history of development from one end of the scale to the other. All that remained to be done was to hunt through ethnological literature for examples to illustrate each of these stages. For all their insistence on empiricism in the study of social institutions, the nineteenth-century anthropologists were therefore hardly less dialectical, speculative, and dogmatic than the moral philosophers of the preceding century, even though they felt that they had to support their constructions with a wealth of factual evidence, a need scarcely felt by the moral philosophers.

We are less certain today about the values they accepted. In part, at any rate, the turning away from the construction of stages of development which so occupied them, and the turning towards inductive functional studies of primitive societies, must be attributed to the growth of scepticism whether many of the changes taking place in the nineteenth century can be wholly regarded as improvement; for, whatever the opinion of those who pursue it may be, modern social anthropology is conservative in its theoretical approach. Its interests are more in what makes for integration and equilibrium in society than in plotting scales and stages of progress.

However, I think that the major cause of confusion among nineteenth-century anthropologists was not so much that they believed in progress and sought a method by which they might reconstruct how it had come about, for they were well aware that their schemata were hypotheses which could not be finally or fully verified. It is rather to be looked for in the assumption they had inherited from the Enlightenment that societies are natural systems, or organisms, which have a necessary course of development that can be reduced to general principles or laws. Logical connections were in consequence presented as real and necessary connections and typological classifications as both historical and inevitable courses of development. It will readily be seen how a combination of the notion of scientific law and that of progress leads in anthropology, as in the philosophy of history, to procrustean stages, the presumed inevitability of which gives them a normative quality. Naturally, those who believed that social life could be reduced to scientific laws concluded that similar forms of institutions must have sprung from similar forms and they from similar prototypes. In my next lecture I shall discuss this point further and in relation to the social anthropology of today.

III

LATER THEORETICAL DEVELOPMENTS

In my last lecture I gave you an account of the main characteristics of the writers of the eighteenth and nineteenth centuries who can be regarded in some measure as having studied social institutions in an anthropological way. In both centuries the approach was naturalistic and empirical in intention, if not in practice; generalizing, and above all genetic. Their thought was dominated by the notion of progress, of improvement of manners and customs from rudeness to civility, from savagery to civilization; and the method of investigation they elaborated, the comparative method, was chiefly employed by them for the purpose of reconstructing the hypothetical course of this development. It is in this respect that the anthropology of today is most at variance with that of yesterday.

The reaction against the attempt to explain social institutions by their reconstructed past, to explain what we know something about by what we know next to nothing about, came at the end of last century; and it was particularly directed against those schemes of parallel, seen ideally as unilinear, development which had been so much in favour. Though this genetic anthropology, often, but unfortunately, called evolutionary anthropology, was recast and re-presented in the writings of Steinmetz, Nieboer, Westermarck, Hobhouse,[1] and

[1] S. R. Steinmetz, *Ethnologische Studien zur ersten Entwicklung der Strafe*, 1894; H. J. Nieboer, *Slavery as an Industrial System*, 1900; Edward Westermarck, *The Origin and Development of the Moral Ideas*, 1906; L. T. Hobhouse, *Morals in Evolution*, 1906.

others, it had finally lost its appeal. Some anthropologists, and in varying degrees, now turned for inspiration to psychology, which at the time seemed to provide satisfactory solutions of many of their problems without recourse to hypothetical history. This attempt to construct social anthropology on the foundations of psychology has proved to be, then and since, an attempt to build a house on shifting sands.

There is an undercurrent of psychological assumptions in the stream of anthropological theory in the eighteenth and nineteenth centuries, but though assumptions about human nature were made, and inevitably made, by the writers of the time they did not suggest that customs and institutions could be understood by reference to individual feelings and impulses. Indeed, as we have seen, they often explicitly rejected the suggestion. It must be remembered that there was not at that time anything which could be called experimental psychology, so that when anthropologists even as recent as Tylor and Frazer looked to psychology for aid it was to associationist psychology that they looked; and when this kind of psychology went out of fashion they were left in the outmoded intellectualist interpretations they derived from it.

Other anthropologists were later left in a similar way in the fashion of introspective psychology. I am thinking particularly of writings on such subjects as religion, magic, taboo, and witchcraft—by Marett, Malinowski and others in this country, and by Lowie, Radin, and a number of other anthropologists in America.[1] These writers all, in one way or another, tried to account for social behaviour pertaining to the sacred in terms of feelings or emotional states—of hate, greed, love, fear,

[1] R. R. Marett, *The Threshold of Religion*, 1909; B. Malinowski, 'Magic, Science and Religion', *Science, Religion and Reality*, 1925; R. H. Lowie, *Primitive Religion*, 1925; Paul Radin, *Social Anthropology*, 1932.

awe, amazement, a sense of the mysterious or extraordinary, wonder, projection of will, and so on. The behaviour arises in situations of emotional stress, frustration, or intensity and its function is cathartic, expletive, or stimulating. The development of various modern experimental psychologies showed all such interpretations to be confused, irrelevant, or meaningless. Nevertheless, undeterred by the fate of their predecessors, some anthropologists, especially in America, now attempt to state their findings in that mixture of behaviouristic and psycho-analytical psychologies which is called personality psychology or the psychology of motivations and attitudes.

There are various and particular objections to each of these successive attempts to explain social facts by individual psychology; and there is one common objection to all of them. Psychology and social anthropology study different kinds of phenomena and what the one studies cannot therefore be understood in terms of conclusions reached by the other. Psychology is the study of individual life. Social anthropology is the study of social life. Psychology studies psychical systems. Social anthropology studies social systems. The psychologist and the social anthropologist may observe the same acts of raw behaviour but they study them at different levels of abstraction.

Let me give you a simple example. A man on trial for a crime is found guilty by twelve jurymen and is sentenced by a judge to be punished. The facts of sociological significance are here the existence of a law, the various legal institutions and procedures brought into play by a breach of it, and the action of the political society through its representatives in punishing the criminal. Throughout the process the thoughts and feelings of the accused, the jurymen, and the judge would be found to vary in kind and degree and at different times, just as their ages and the colour of their hair and eyes would be found to vary, but these variations would not be of any concern, or at any rate not of any immediate concern, to the social anthropologist. He is not interested in the actors in the drama as individuals but as persons who play certain roles in the process of justice. On the other hand, to the psychologist, who is studying individuals, the feelings, motives, opinions, and so forth, of the actors are of first importance and the legal procedures and processes of secondary interest. This essential difference between social anthropology and psychology is the *pons asinorum* in the learning of social anthropology. The two disciplines can only be of value —and they can be of great value—to each other if each pursues independently its own research into its own problems and by its own methods.

Apart from the criticisms of the so-called evolutionary theories of nineteenth-century anthropology implied in the ignoring of them by those who sought psychological explanations of customs and beliefs, these theories were attacked from two directions, the diffusionist and the functionalist.

The criticisms of those who became known as diffusionist anthropologists were based on the very obvious fact that culture is often borrowed and does not emerge in similar forms in different societies by spontaneous growth due to certain common social potentialities and common human nature. Where we know the history of an invention, whether in technology, art, thought, or custom, we almost invariably find that it has not been made independently by a number of peoples in different places and at different times but by one people in one place and at a particular moment of their history, and that it has spread, wholly or in part, from this people to other peoples. When we look into the matter further we find that there have been a limited number of centres of important cultural development and diffusion, and also that in the process of borrowing and incorporation into other cultures the diffused traits may undergo all sorts of modifications and changes. Since it can be shown that the inventions for the history of which we have reliable evidence have almost invariably diffused in this manner it is not unreasonable to suppose, when we find similar artifacts, ideas, and customs among primitive peoples in different parts of the world, that these have in the same way spread from a limited number of points of cultural advancement, even though there is no other evidence of their having done so than that contained in their similarity and their geographical distribution; especially if the traits are at all complex and are also found in association.

The bearing of this argument on the genetic theories of the anthropologists of last century, which it did so much to discredit, is obvious. If it could be shown that an institution of some people had through the accidents of history been taken over by them from another people it could then hardly be regarded as a natural and inevitable development of their previous institutions and cited as evidence of some law of growth.

Diffusionist anthropology is still predominant in America. In England it had little lasting influence, partly on account of its uncritical use by Elliot Smith, Perry and Rivers,[1] but also partly because its reconstructions were just as conjectural and unverifiable as the genetic reconstructions it attacked; and the functionalist anthropologists, to whom I now turn, regarded the fight between evolutionists and diffusionists as a family quarrel between ethnologists and none of their affair.

The functionalist objection to both was not only that

[1] G. Elliot Smith, *The Ancient Egyptians*, 1911; W. J. Perry, *The Children of the Sun*, 1923; W. H. R. Rivers, *The History of Melanesian Society*, 1914.

their reconstructions were guesswork, but also that they were trying to explain social life in terms of the past. This is not the procedure of natural scientists, which most writers of this persuasion—and that means most English social anthropologists—consider themselves to be. To understand how an aeroplane or the human body works one studies the first in the light of the laws of mechanics and the second in the light of the laws of physiology. One need not know anything about the history of aeronautics or the theory of biological evolution. Likewise a language can be studied from various angles—grammar, phonetics, semantics, and so forth—without the history of its words having to be known. The history of its words belongs to a different branch of linguistics, philology. In the same way, a history of the legal institutions of the England of today will only show us how they have come to be what they are and not how they function in our social life. To understand how they work requires a study by the experimental methods of the natural sciences. Historical and natural science studies are different kinds of study with different aims, methods, and techniques, and only confusion can result from trying to pursue both together.

In the study of primitive societies it is the task of the historian of primitive peoples, the ethnologist, to discover, if he can, how their institutions have come to be what they are. It is the task of the scientist, the social anthropologist, to discover their functions in the social systems to which they belong. Even with the best sources at his disposal, the historian can only tell us what has been the succession of accidental events by which a society has become what it is. These events could not be deduced from general principles, nor can a study of the events yield them. The nineteenth-century anthropologists were therefore doubly at fault; they were reconstructing history without adequate material for doing so, and they were seeking to establish sociological laws by a method which cannot lead to their establishment. The general acceptance of this position separated social anthropology from ethnology and gave to social anthropology its present autonomy in the wider study of man.

In making these assertions, social anthropologists are maintaining that societies are natural systems of which all the parts are interdependent, each serving in a complex of necessary relations to maintain the whole, and that social life can be reduced to scientific laws which allow prediction. There are here several propositions. The two basic ones, which I shall briefly examine, can be resumed into the statements that societies are systems, and that these systems are natural systems which can be reduced to variables, with the corollary that the history of them is irrelevant to an inquiry into their nature.

That there is some kind of order, consistency and constancy, in social life is obvious. If there were not, none of us would be able to go about our affairs or satisfy our most elementary needs. It will at once also be seen that this order is brought about by the systematization, or institutionalization, of social activities so that certain persons have certain roles in them and so that the activities have certain functions in the general social life. To take an example we have used earlier—in a Court of Criminal Law the judge, the jurymen, the barristers, the clerks, the policemen and the accused, have definite roles, and the action of the Court as a whole has the functions of establishing guilt and punishing crime. The individuals occupying these positions vary from case to case but the form and functions of the institution are constant. It is also obvious that the judge, the barristers, the clerks, and the policemen have professional roles which they can only carry out if there is some economic organization so that they do not, for example, have to grow and prepare their own food but can buy it with the remuneration they receive for the performance of their duties; and also if there is some political organization which maintains law and order, so that they have security in the performance of their duties; and so forth.

All this is so evident that the ideas of social system, social structure, social roles, and the social functions of institutions are found in one form or another in the earliest philosophical reflections on social life. Without going back beyond the names I mentioned in my last lecture, we note that the concepts of structure and function appear in Montaigne's use of the terms *bastiment* and *liaison* in his discussion of law and custom in general, which he compares to 'a structure of different pieces joined together, so connected that it is impossible to disturb one without the whole body feeling it'.[1] The same concept of social system, of which the idea of social function is part, is present throughout Montesquieu's discussion of the nature and principles of different types of society, in which he speaks of the *structure* of a society and the *rapports* between its parts; and we find it, to a greater or lesser degree, in all the eighteenth-century philosophers who wrote about social institutions. In the early nineteenth century it is clearly enunciated by Comte, and though not always explicitly formulated, and though subordinated to the concepts of origin, cause, and stages of development, it is subsumed by all the anthropological writers of that century. Towards the end of it, and increasingly during the present century, greater emphasis was laid on the concept in harmony with a general orientation of thought. Just as earlier the genetic approach was dominant in all fields of learning, so now we find everywhere a functional orientation. There were functional biology, functional psychology, functional law, functional economics, and so forth, as well as functional anthropology.

[1] 'De la Coustume et de ne Changer aisément une Loy Receüe', *Essais*, Nouvelle Revue Française, Bibliothèque de la Pléiade, 1946, p. 132.

The two writers who most specifically directed the attention of social anthropologists towards functional analysis were Herbert Spencer and Emile Durkheim. The philosophical writings of Herbert Spencer (1820–1903) are little read today, but during his life-time they had great influence. He and Comte were alike in their versatility, both attempting to cover the whole of human knowledge and within it to construct a comprehensive science of society and culture, what Spencer called the super-organic.[1] In his view the evolution of human society, though not necessarily of particular societies, is a natural and inevitable continuation of organic evolution. Groups tend always towards increase in size and consequently in organization and therefore in integration, since the greater the structural differentiation the greater is the interdependence of the parts of the social organism. Spencer's use of the biological analogy of organism, dangerous though it has proved to be, did much to further the use of the concepts of structure and function in social anthropology, for he constantly stressed that at every stage in social evolution there is a necessary functional interdependence between the institutions of a society, which must always tend towards a state of equilibrium if it is to persist. He was also a great advocate of sociological laws, both structural and genetic.

The writings of Emile Durkheim (1858–1917) had a greater and more direct influence on social anthropology. Indeed he is a central figure in the history of its development, both on account of his general sociological theories and because he and a band of talented colleagues and pupils applied them with remarkable insight to the study of primitive societies.[2]

[1] *The Study of Sociology*, 1872 onwards; *The Principles of Sociology*, 1882–3.

[2] His best known works are *De la Division du Travail Social: Etude sur L'organisation des Sociétés Supérieures*, 1893; *Les Règles de la Méthode*

Briefly, Durkheim's position was as follows: Social facts cannot be explained in terms of individual psychology, if only because they exist outside and apart from individual minds. A language, for example, is there before an individual is born into the society which speaks it, and it will be there after he is dead. He merely learns to speak it, as his ancestors did, and as his descendants will. It is a social fact, something *sui generis*, which can only be understood in its relation to other facts of the same order, that is to say as part of a social system and in terms of its functions in the maintenance of that system.

Social facts are characterized by their generality, their transmissibility, and their compulsion. All members of a society have, in general, the same habits and customs, language, and morals, and all live in the same common framework of legal, political, and economic institutions. All these things form a more or less stable structure which persists in its essentials over great periods of time, being handed down from generation to generation. The individual merely passes through the structure, as it were. It was not born with him and it does not die with him, for it is not a psychical system but a social system with a collective consciousness quite different in kind from individual consciousness. The totality of social facts which compose the structure are obligatory. The individual who does not abide by them always suffers penalties and disabilities of a legal or moral kind. Usually he has neither the desire nor the opportunity to do other than conform. A child born in France of French parents can only learn French and has no desire to do otherwise.

In emphasizing the singularity of collective life

Sociologique, 1895; *La Suicide; Etude de Sociologie*, 1897; and *Les Formes Elémentaires de la Vie Religieuse: Le Système Totémique en Australie*, 1912. See also many articles and review-articles in *L'Année Sociologique* from 1898 onwards, and those by Hubert, Mauss, and others in the same journal.

Durkheim has been much criticized for holding that there is a collective mind but, although his writing is sometimes rather metaphysical, he certainly never conceived of any such entity. By what he called 'collective representations' he meant what we in England would call a common body of values and beliefs and customs which the individual born into any society learns, accepts, lives by, and passes on. A brilliant study of the ideological content of those collective representations was made by his colleague Lucien Lévy-Bruhl (1857–1939) in a series of books which have had considerable influence in England, though they have been much misunderstood and severely criticized by English anthropologists.[1] Taking for granted that the beliefs, myths, and in general, the ideas, of primitive peoples are a reflection of their social structures and therefore differ from one kind of society to another, he devoted himself to showing how they form systems, the logical principle of which is what he called the law of mystical participation. This was as much a structural analysis as the work of Durkheim, but whereas Durkheim analysed social activities Lévy-Bruhl analysed the ideas associated with them.

Durkheim's importance in the history of the conceptual development of social anthropology in this country might have been no greater than it has been in America had it not been for the influence of his writings on Professor A. R. Radcliffe-Brown and the late Professor B. Malinowski, the two men who have shaped social anthropology into what it is in England today. All of us now teaching the subject in England and in the Dominions are directly or indirectly, for the most part directly, their pupils.

I shall say more about Malinowski (1884–1942) later, especially in my lecture on fieldwork, for if functional

[1] His two best known works are *Les Fonctions Mentales dans les Sociétés Inférieures*, 1912, and *La Mentalité Primitive*, 1922.

anthropology meant more to him than a principle of field techniques it was as a literary device for integrating his observations for descriptive purposes. It was not, properly speaking, a methodological concept, and he never showed himself capable of using it with any clarity when dealing with the abstractions of general theory. Professor Radcliffe-Brown has far more clearly and consistently stated the functional, or organismic, theory of society. He has presented it in a systematic form and with clarity of exposition and lucidity of style.

Professor Radcliffe-Brown tells us that 'the concept of function applied to human societies is based on an analogy between social life and organic life.'[1] Following Durkheim, he defines the function of a social institution as the correspondence between the social institution and the necessary conditions of existence of the social organism; function used in this sense being—I quote Professor Radcliffe-Brown again—'the contribution which a partial activity makes to the total activity of which it is a part. The function of a particular social usage is the contribution it makes to the total social life as the functioning of the total social system.'[2]

Institutions are thus thought of as functioning within a social structure consisting of individual human beings 'connected by a definite set of social relations into an integrated whole'.[3] The continuity of the structure is maintained by the process of social life or, in other words, the social life of a community is the functioning of its structure. So conceived of, a social system has a functional unity. It is not an aggregate but an organism or integrated whole.

Professor Radcliffe-Brown says that when he speaks of social integration he assumes that 'the function of culture

[1] 'On the Concept of Function in Social Science', *American Anthropologist*, 1935, p. 394.

[2] Ibid., p. 397.

[3] Ibid., p. 396.

as a whole is to unite individual human beings into more or less stable social structures, i.e., stable systems of groups determining and regulating the relation of those individuals to one another, and providing such external adaptation to the physical environment, and such internal adaptation between the component individuals or groups, as to make possible an ordered social life. That assumption I believe to be a sort of primary postulate of any objective and scientific study of culture or of human society.'[1]

The elaboration of the concepts of social structure, social system, and social function as defined by Professor Radcliffe-Brown in the last quotation, and as used by social anthropologists today, has been an important aid in the determination of problems of field research. The nineteenth-century anthropologists were content to let laymen collect the facts on which they based their theories, and it did not occur to them that there was any need for them to make studies of primitive peoples themselves. This was because they were dealing atomistically with items of culture, customs, which could be brought together to show either the great similarity or the great diversity of beliefs and practices, or to illustrate stages in human progress. But once it was accepted that a custom is more or less meaningless when taken out of its social context it became apparent both that comprehensive and detailed studies of primitive peoples in every aspect of their social life would have to be undertaken, and that they could only be undertaken by professional social anthropologists who were aware of the theoretical problems in the subject, had in mind the kind of information required for the solution of them, and were alone able to put themselves in the position where it could be acquired.

[1] 'The Present Position of Anthropological Studies', Presidential Address, *British Association for the Advancement of Science*, Section H., 1931, p. 13.

The functionalist insistence on the relatedness of things has thus been partly responsible for, as it has been partly the product of, modern field studies. I shall discuss this aspect of modern social anthropology in my next two lectures.

Functional anthropology, with its emphasis on the concept of social system and hence on the need for systematic studies of the social life of primitive peoples as they are today, thus not only separated, as we have seen, social anthropology from ethnology; it also brought together the theoretical study of institutions and the observational study of primitive social life. We have noted how in the eighteenth century philosophical speculations about the nature and origins of social institutions were occasionally illustrated by reports of explorers about rude societies. We saw then how in the nineteenth century these primitive societies in themselves became the chief object of curiosity of a few scholars interested in the development of culture and institutions, but who relied exclusively on the observations of others, the theoretical thinker and the observer still being divorced. In functional anthropology the two were, as I shall explain more in detail in my next lecture, finally united, and social anthropology in the modern sense of the words came into existence as a distinctive discipline in which theoretical problems of general sociology are investigated by research in primitive societies.

The functional approach had the further effect of changing both the purpose and the use of the comparative method. We saw that the older anthropologists regarded the comparative method as a means of making historical reconstructions in the absence of recorded history, and that the way they used it was to compare examples of particular customs or institutions gathered haphazardly from all over the world. Once the notion of system is accepted as a primary postulate, as Professor

Radcliffe-Brown calls it, the object of research ceases to be ethnological classification and the elaboration of cultural categories and schemes of hypothetical development. It becomes in studies of particular societies the definition of social activities in terms of their functions within their social systems, and in comparative studies a comparison of institutions as parts of social systems or in the relation they have to the whole life of the societies in which they are found. What the modern anthropologist compares are not customs, but systems of relations. This is another matter about which I shall have something further to say in later lectures.

I now come to the second postulate of functional anthropology, that social systems are natural systems which can be reduced to sociological laws, with the corollary that the history of them has no scientific relevance. I must confess that this seems to me to be doctrinaire positivism at its worst. One has a right, I think, to ask those who assert that the aim of social anthropology is to formulate sociological laws similar to the laws formulated by natural scientists to produce formulations which resemble what are called laws in these sciences. Up to the present nothing even remotely resembling what are called laws in the natural sciences has been adduced—only rather naïve deterministic, teleological, and pragmatic assertions. The generalizations which have so far been attempted have, moreover, been so vague and general as to be, even if true, of little use, and they have rather easily tended to become mere tautologies and platitudes on the level of common sense deduction.

Such being the case, I think that we may ask again whether social systems are in fact natural systems at all, whether, for instance, a legal system is really comparable to a physiological system or the planetary system. I cannot see myself that there is any good reason for regarding a social system as a system of the same kind as an organic or inorganic system. It seems to me to be an entirely different kind of system; and I think that the effort to discover natural laws of society is vain and leads only to airy discussions about methods. Anyhow, I am not obliged to prove that there are no such laws; it is for those who say that there are, to tell us what they are.

Those of us who take the view I have expressed about this issue must ask ourselves whether the functionalist claim that the history of an institution is irrelevant to an understanding of it as it is at the present time is acceptable, for the claim rests precisely on a conception of system and law in reference to human affairs which is at variance with our own. A brief consideration of this question will give me the opportunity to outline my own position, for I do not want it to be thought that, in criticizing some of the underlying assumptions of functionalism, I do not regard myself as in other respects a functionalist and follower in the footsteps of my teachers, Professor Malinowski and Professor Radcliffe-Brown, or that I hold that societies are not intelligible and cannot be systematically studied, or that no significant general statements of any kind can be made about them.

In speaking here of history I am not now discussing ethnological hypotheses, whether of a genetic or a diffusionist kind. We may regard that issue as closed. I am discussing the relevance to a study of social institutions of the history of them where this history is known for certain and in detail. This problem was hardly seen by the eighteenth-century moral philosophers and their Victorian successors, because it did not occur to them that the study of institutions could be anything else than a study of their development, the final aim of their labours being a comprehensive natural history of human society.

Sociological laws were consequently conceived of by them as laws of progress. Without the quest for laws—for in that matter American anthropologists are as sceptical as I am—anthropology in the United States is still for the most part historical in its aims. It is for that reason regarded as being more ethnology than social anthropology by functionalist anthropologists in England, who take the view that it is not the task of social anthropologists to investigate the history of the societies they study, and furthermore that a knowledge of their history does not help us to understand the functioning of their institutions. This attitude follows logically enough from the assumption that societies are natural systems which are to be studied by the methods employed, in so far as they are applicable, by such natural scientists as chemists and biologists.

This is an issue which is coming more to the fore today when social anthropologists are beginning to study societies belonging to historical cultures. So long as they were investigating such peoples as Australian aborigines or South Sea Islanders, who have no recorded history, they could ignore history with an easy conscience. Now, however, that they have begun to study peasant communities in India and Europe, Arab nomads, and like communities elsewhere, they can no longer make a virtue of necessity but must choose deliberately to ignore or to take into consideration their social past in making studies of their social present.

Those of us who do not accept the functionalist position in respect of history would hold that, though it is necessary to make separate studies of a society as it is today and of its development in the past and to employ different techniques in each study, and though it may be desirable for these separate studies, at any rate in certain circumstances, to be made by different persons, nevertheless, to know a society's past gives one a deeper understanding of the nature of its social life at the present time; for history is not merely a succession of changes but, as others have said, a growth. The past is contained in the present as the present is in the future. I am not saying that social life can be understood through a knowledge of its past, but that this knowledge gives us a fuller understanding of it than we would have were its past unknown to us. It is also evident that problems of social development can only be studied in terms of history, and furthermore that history alone provides a satisfactory experimental situation in which the hypotheses of functional anthropology can be tested.

Very much more could be said about this question, but you may think that it is a domestic issue which might well be discussed at greater length in a gathering of specialists but is unsuited for detailed argument before a general audience. So, having stated that there is this division of opinion, I will leave the matter there. It is only fair, however, since I have said that I and others, unlike most of our colleagues in this country, regard social anthropology as belonging to the humanities rather than to the natural sciences, that I should tell you what I conceive the method and aim of social anthropology to be.

In my view, it is much more like certain branches of historical scholarship—social history and the history of institutions and of ideas as contrasted with narrative and political history—than it is to any of the natural sciences. The similarity between this kind of historiography and social anthropology has been obscured by the fact that social anthropologists make direct studies of social life whereas historians make indirect studies of it from documentary and other sources; by the fact that social anthropologists study primitive societies which lack recorded history; and by the fact that social anthropologists generally study synchronic problems while historians study diachronic problems. I agree with Professor Kroeber[1] that these are differences of technique, emphasis, and perspective, and not of aim or method, and that essentially the method of both historiography and social anthropology is descriptive integration, even though anthropological synthesis is usually on a higher plane of abstraction than historical synthesis and anthropology more explicitly and deliberately than history aims at comparison and generalization.

As I understand the matter, what the social anthropologist does can be divided into three phases. In the first phase, as ethnographer, he goes to live among a primitive people and learns their way of life. He learns to speak their language, to think in their concepts, and to feel in their values. He then lives the experience over again critically and interpretatively in the conceptual categories and values of his own culture and in terms of the general body of knowledge of his discipline. In other words, he translates from one culture into another.

In the second phase of his work, and still within a single ethnographic study of a particular primitive society, he tries to go beyond this literary and impressionistic stage and to discover the structural order of the society, so that it is intelligible not merely at the level of consciousness and action, as it is to one of its members or to the foreigner who has learnt its mores and participates in its life, but also at the level of sociological analysis.[2] Just as the linguist does not merely learn to understand, speak and translate a native language but seeks to reveal its phonological and grammatical systems, so the social anthropologist is not content merely to

[1] A. L. Kroeber, 'History and Science in Anthropology', *American Anthropologist*, 1935.

[2] Claude Lévi-Strauss, 'Histoire et Ethnologie', *Revue de Métaphysique et de Morale*, 1949.

observe and describe the social life of a primitive people but seeks to reveal its underlying structural order, the patterns which, once established, enable him to see it as a whole, as a set of interrelated abstractions.

Having isolated these structural patterns in one society, the social anthropologist, in the third phase of his work, compares them with patterns in other societies. The study of each new society enlarges his knowledge of the range of basic social structures and enables him better to construct a typology of forms, and to determine their essential features and the reasons for their variations.

Most of my colleagues would, I fancy, disagree with this description of what a social anthropologist does. They would prefer to describe what he does in the language of the methodology of the natural sciences, whereas what I have said implies that social anthropology studies societies as moral, or symbolic, systems and not as natural systems, that it is less interested in process than in design, and that it therefore seeks patterns and not laws, demonstrates consistency and not necessary relations between social activities, and interprets rather than explains. These are conceptual and not merely verbal differences.

You have seen that there are a good number of unresolved methodological and, underlying them, philosophical problems in social anthropology: whether psychological interpretations of social facts should or should not be attempted; whether society and culture should be a single field, or separate fields, of inquiry, and what is the relation between these abstractions; what meaning is to be given to such terms as structure, system, and function; and whether social anthropology is to be regarded as an embryonic natural science or is directing its course to a mirage in pursuit of sociological laws. In all these issues we anthropologists are at sixes and sevens among ourselves, and no amount of argument will resolve the differences of opinion. The only arbitrament we all accept is appeal to the facts—to the judgment of research. In my next lecture I will discuss this side to our subject.

IV

FIELDWORK AND THE EMPIRICAL TRADITION

In my last two lectures I gave you some account of the development of theory in social anthropology. Theory has changed its direction with the increase in knowledge about primitive peoples which it has in each generation been largely responsible for bringing about. It is about this growth of knowledge that I shall speak tonight.

There has always been a popular, though not unhealthy, prejudice against theory as contrasted with experience. However, an established theory is only a generalization from experience which has been again confirmed by it, and a hypothesis is merely an unconfirmed opinion that, judging by what is already known, it is reasonable to assume that further facts will be found by research to be of a certain kind. Without theories and hypotheses anthropological research could not be carried out, for one only finds things, or does not find them, if one is looking for them. Often one finds something other than what one is looking for. The whole history of scholarship, whether in the natural sciences or in the humanities, tells us that the mere collection of what are called facts unguided by theory in observation and selection is of little value.

Nevertheless, one still hears it said of anthropologists that they go to study primitive peoples with a theoretical bias and that this distorts their accounts of savage life, whereas the practical man of affairs, having no such bias, gives an impartial record of the facts as he sees them.

The difference between them is really of another kind. The student makes his observations to answer questions arising out of the generalizations of specialized opinion, and the layman makes his to answer questions arising out of the generalizations of popular opinion. Both have theories, the one systematic and the other popular.

In fact the history of social anthropology may be regarded as the substitution, by slow gradations, of informed opinion about primitive peoples for uninformed opinion, and the stage reached in this process at any time is roughly relative to the amount of organized knowledge available. In the end it is the volume, accuracy, and variety of well authenticated fact which alone counts; and it is the function of theory to stimulate and guide observation in the collection of it. Here, however, I am not so much concerned with popular opinion as with that held by writers about social institutions.

There seems to have been a pendulum swing from extreme to extreme in speculations about primitive man. First he was a little more than an animal who lived in poverty, violence, and fear; then he was a gentle person who lived in plenty, peace, and security. First he was lawless; then he was a slave to law and custom. First he was devoid of any religious feelings or belief; then he was entirely dominated by the sacred and immersed in ritual. First he was an individualist who preyed on the weaker and held what he could; then he was a communist who held lands and goods in common. First he was sexually promiscuous; then he was a model of domestic virtue. First he was lethargic and incorrigibly lazy, then he was alert and industrious. In seeking to change a received opinion it is, I suppose, natural that in the selection and massing of evidence against it an opposite distortion is made.

The dependence of theory on available knowledge in these speculations and the shaping of each by the other may be seen throughout the development of social anthropology. The prevailing opinion about primitive man in the seventeenth and eighteenth centuries, that his life was 'solitary, poore, nasty, brutish, and short', lacked foundation in fact; but it is difficult to see what other conclusion could have been reached from the accounts of contemporary travellers, who for the most part described the primitives they saw in such terms as they have 'nothing that can entitle them to humanity but speech'—this is Sir John Chardin speaking of the Circassians whose country he traversed in 1671[1]—or that they 'differ but little from beasts'—this is Father Stanislaus Arlet speaking about the Indians of Peru in 1698.[2] These early travel accounts, whether they portrayed the savage as brutish or noble, were generally fanciful or mendacious, superficial, and full of inappropriate judgments.

However, it is only fair to say that much depended on the refinement of the traveller and on his temperament and character, and that from the sixteenth century onwards there are not lacking accounts which give sober and factual, if limited, descriptions of native life, such, to mention a few names besides those I have referred to earlier, as the writings of the Englishman Andrew Battel on the natives of the Congo, of the Portuguese Jesuit Father Jerome Lobo on the Abyssinians, of the Dutchman William Bosman on the peoples of the Gold Coast, and of Captain Cook on the natives in the South Seas. They wrote in the spirit of Father Lobo, of whom Dr. Johnson, his translator in *Pinkerton's Voyages*, remarks: 'He appears by his modest and unaffected narration to have described things as he saw them, to have copied

[1] *Pinkerton's Voyages*, vol. IX, 1811, p. 143.

[2] John Lockman, *Travels of the Jesuits*, vol. I, 1743, p. 93.

nature from the life, and to have consulted his senses not his imagination.'[1]

When these early European travellers went beyond description and personal judgments it was generally to establish parallels between the peoples of whom they wrote and the ancients with whom they were familiar from literature, often with the purpose of showing that there must have been some historical influence of the higher cultures on the lower. Father Lafitau thus makes many comparisons between the Huron and Iroquois Redskins and the Jews, the early Christians, the classical Spartans and Cretans, and the ancient Egyptians. In the same manner de la Crequinière, a French traveller to the East Indies in the seventeenth century, sets out to find parallels in India to certain Jewish and classical customs and thus help towards a better understanding of the Scriptures and of the classical writers, for, he says, 'the knowledge of the customs of the Indians, is in no ways useful in itself . . .'[2]

Between the heyday of the moral philosophers and the earliest anthropological writings in a strict sense, between, that is, the middle of the eighteenth century and the middle of the nineteenth century, knowledge of primitive peoples and of the peoples of the Far East was greatly increased. The European colonization of America had been widely expanded, British rule had been established in India, and Australia, New Zealand, and South Africa had been settled by European emigrants. The character of ethnographic description of the peoples of these regions began to change from travellers' tales to detailed studies by missionaries and administrators who not only had better opportunities to observe, but were also men of greater culture than the gentlemen of fortune of earlier times.

[1] *Pinkerton's Voyages*, vol. XV, 1814, p. 1.

[2] *Customs of the East Indians*, 1705, p. viii. (Translated from *Conformité des Coutumes des Indiens Orientaux*, 1704, p. viii.)

Much of accepted opinion about primitive peoples was seen to be wrong or one-sided in the light of this new information, and, as I mentioned in an earlier lecture, the new information was sufficient in bulk and quality for Morgan, McLennan, Tylor, and others to build out of it a self-contained discipline devoting itself primarily to the study of primitive societies. There was at last a sufficient body of knowledge for speculations to be tested and for new hypotheses to be put forward on a solid basis of ethnographic fact.

When it is said that in the end it is the facts which have decided the fate of theories it must be added that it is not the bare facts but a demonstration of their distribution and significance. Allow me to give you an instance. The matrilineal mode of tracing descent had been recorded for a number of primitive societies by ancient and mediaeval historians, for example, Herodotus for the Lycians and Maqrizi for the Beja, and also by modern observers; Lafitau for the North American Redskins, Bowdich for the Ashanti of the Gold Coast, Grey for the Australian Blackfellows, and other travellers for other peoples;[1] but these records were passed over as mere curiosities till Bachofen and McLennan drew attention to their great importance for sociological theory. Had the material been brought together and its importance thereby established before Maine wrote *Ancient Law*, he could hardly have taken the certain line he took in that book and which he was forced to modify in his later writings in the light of this organized evidence.

McLennan is a very instructive example of the relation of a body of knowledge to theories based on it. He was under no illusion about the value of many of his authori-

[1] Joseph François Lafitau, *Moeurs des Sauvages Ameriquains*, 1724; T. H. Bowdich, *Mission from Cape Coast Castle to Ashantee*, 1819; George Grey, *Journals of Two Expeditions of Discovery in North-West and Western Australia*, 1841.

ties, whose accounts he criticized as thin and vitiated by every kind of personal prejudice, but had he been more cautious than he was he could hardly have avoided some of the errors which led him into a succession of false constructions. On the evidence at his disposal he had every reason for being satisfied that matriliny prevailed universally among the Australian aborigines. We now know that this is not the case. It is also not the case, as he thought, that matriliny prevails among the great majority of existing rude races. He also thought that polyandry had the widest possible distribution, whereas in fact its distribution is very limited. He was also wrong in supposing that female infanticide is widely prevalent among primitive peoples.

The most serious error into which McLennan's authorities led him was to suppose that among the most primitive peoples the institutions of marriage and the family are not found or exist only in a very rudimentary form. Had he known, as we now know, that they are found without exception in all primitive societies he could not have reached the conclusions he arrived at, for they depend absolutely on the dogma that neither marriage nor the family exist in early society, a belief not dispelled till quite recently when Westermarck, and after him Malinowski, showed it to be insupportable in fact.[1]

It could be shown with equal facility that most of the theories of other writers of the time were wrong or inadequate on account of the inaccuracy or insufficiency of the observations then recorded. But even where they went most astray these writers at least put forward hypotheses about primitive societies which provided lines of inquiry for those whose vocations and duties necessitated residence, often very lengthy residence, among

[1] Edward A. Westermarck, *The History of Human Marriage*, 1891; B. Malinowski, *The Family among the Australian Aborigines—A Sociological Study*, 1913.

simple peoples; and we get from this time onwards an exchange between scholars at home and a few missionaries and administrators living in backward parts of the world. These missionaries and administrators were anxious both to make contributions to knowledge and to make use of what anthropology could teach them in seeking to understand their wards. They were made aware by their reading of the literature of anthropology that even those peoples lowest in the scale of material culture have complex social systems, moral codes, religion, art, philosophy, and the rudiments of science, which must be respected and, once understood, can be admired.

The influence of anthropological theories of the time is very evident, sometimes for the better, sometimes for the worse, in the accounts they wrote. Not only were they acquainted with theoretical problems being discussed by scholars, but they were often directly in touch with those who propounded them. It became customary for those at home who wanted information to send out lists of questions to those living among primitive peoples. The first of these was that drawn up by Morgan to elicit kinship terminologies, and sent by him to American agents in foreign countries. It was on the basis of their replies that he published in 1871 his famous *Systems of Consanguinity and Affinity of the Human Family*. Later Sir James Frazer drew up a list of questions, *Questions on the Manners, Customs, Religion, Superstitions, etc., of Uncivilized or Semi-Civilized Peoples*,[1] and sent it to people all over the world in order to obtain information which went into one or other volume of *The Golden Bough*. The most comprehensive of these questionnaires was *Notes and Queries in Anthropology*, first published for the Royal Anthropological Institute in 1874 and now in its fifth edition.

Scholars at home sometimes corresponded regularly with those brought into touch with them through their

[1] No date. Probably in the 'eighties.

writings, for example, Morgan with Fison and Howitt in Australia, and Frazer with Spencer in Australia and Roscoe in Africa, In much more recent times administrative officers have taken courses of anthropology in British universities, a development I speak of more fully in my last lecture. Throughout, a most important link between the scholar at home and the administrator or missionary abroad has been the Royal Anthropological Institute which has since 1843, when it was founded as the Ethnological Society of London, provided a common meeting-place for all interested in the study of primitive man.

Many accounts written about primitive peoples by laymen were excellent, and in a few cases their descriptions have hardly been excelled by the best professional fieldworkers. They were written by men with lengthy experience of the peoples, and who spoke their languages. I refer to such books as Callaway's *The Religious System of the Amazulu* (1870), Codrington's *The Melanesians* (1891), the works of Spencer and Gillen on the Aborigines of Australia,[1] Junod's *The Life of a South African Tribe* (1912–13, French edition, 1898), and Smith and Dale's *The Ila-Speaking Peoples of Northern Rhodesia* (1920). Just as the observations of travellers continued to provide valuable information throughout this period when detailed monographs on primitive peoples were being written by missionaries and administrators, so these detailed studies by laymen continued to have great value for anthropology long after professional fieldwork had become customary.

Nevertheless it became apparent that if the study of social anthropology was to advance, anthropologists would have to make their own observations. It is indeed surprising that, with the exception of Morgan's study of

[1] B. Spencer and F. J. Gillen, *The Native Tribes of Central Australia*, 1899; *The Northern Tribes of Central Australia*, 1904; *The Arunta*, 1927.

the Iroquois,[1] not a single anthropologist conducted field studies till the end of the nineteenth century. It is even more remarkable that it does not seem to have occurred to them that a writer on anthropological topics might at least have a look, if only a glimpse, at one or two specimens of what he spent his life writing about. William James tells us that when he asked Sir James Frazer about natives he had known, Frazer exclaimed, 'But Heaven forbid!'[2]

Had a natural scientist been asked a similar question about the objects of his study he would have replied very differently. As we have noted, Maine, McLennan, Bachofen, and Morgan among the earlier anthropological writers were lawyers. Fustel de Coulanges was a classical and mediaeval historian, Spencer was a philosopher, Tylor was a foreign languages clerk, Pitt-Rivers was a soldier, Lubbock was a banker, Robertson Smith was a Presbyterian minister and a biblical scholar, and Frazer was a classical scholar. The men who now came into the subject were for the most part natural scientists. Boas was a physicist and geographer, Haddon a marine zoologist, Rivers a physiologist, Seligman a pathologist, Elliot Smith an anatomist, Balfour a zoologist, Malinowski a physicist, and Radcliffe-Brown, though he had taken the Moral Sciences Tripos at Cambridge, had also been trained in experimental psychology. These men had been taught that in science one tests hypotheses by one's own observations. One does not rely on laymen to do it for one.

Anthropological expeditions began in America with the work of Boas in Baffin Land and British Columbia, and were initiated in England shortly afterwards by Haddon of Cambridge, who led a band of scholars to

[1] *The League of the Iroquois*, 1851.

[2] Ruth Benedict, 'Anthropology and the Humanities', *American Anthropologist*, 1948, p. 587.

conduct research in the Torres Straits region of the Pacific in 1898 and 1899. This expedition marked a turning-point in the history of social anthropology in Great Britain. From this time two important and interconnected developments began to take place: anthropology became more and more a whole-time professional study, and some field experience came to be regarded as an essential part of the training of its students.

This early professional fieldwork had many weaknesses. However well the men who carried it out might have been trained in systematic research in one or other of the natural sciences, the short time they spent among the peoples they studied, their ignorance of their languages, and the casualness and superficiality of their contacts with the natives did not permit deep investigation. It is indeed a measure of the advance of anthropology that these early studies appear today to be quite inadequate. Later studies of primitive societies became increasingly more intensive and illuminating. The most important of these was, I think, that of Professor Radcliffe-Brown, a pupil of Rivers and Haddon. His study of the Andaman Islanders from 1906 to 1908[1] was the first attempt by a social anthropologist to investigate sociological theories in a primitive society and to describe the social life of a people in such a way as to bring out clearly what was significant in it for those theories. In this respect it has perhaps greater importance in the history of social anthropology than the Torres Straits expedition, the members of which were interested in ethnological and psychological problems rather than in sociological ones.

We have noted how theoretical speculation about social institutions was at first only incidentally related to descriptive accounts of primitive peoples, and how later social anthropology may be said to have begun when in

[1] A. R. Brown, *The Andaman Islanders—A Study in Social Anthropology*, 1922.

the nineteenth century these peoples became the chief field of research for some students of institutions. But the research was entirely literary and based on the observations of others. We have now reached the final, and natural, stage of development, in which observations and the evaluation of them are made by the same person and the scholar is brought into direct contact with the subject of his study. Formerly the anthropologist, like the historian, regarded documents as the raw material of his study. Now the raw material was social life itself.

Bronislaw Malinowski, a pupil of Hobhouse, Westermarck, and Seligman, carried field research a step further. If Professor Radcliffe-Brown has always had a wider knowledge of general social anthropology and has proved himself the abler thinker, Malinowski was the more thorough fieldworker. He not only spent a longer period than any anthropologist before him, and I think after him also, in a single study of a primitive people, the Trobriand Islanders of Melanesia between 1914 and 1918, but he was also the first anthropologist to conduct his research through the native language, as he was the first to live throughout his work in the centre of native life. In these favourable circumstances Malinowski came to know the Trobriand Islanders well, and he was describing their social life in a number of bulky, and some shorter, monographs up to the time of his death.[1]

Malinowski began lecturing in London in 1924. Professor Firth, now in Malinowski's chair in London, and I were his first two anthropological pupils in that year, and between 1924 and 1930 most of the other social anthropologists who now hold chairs in Great Britain and the Dominions were taught by him. It can be fairly said that the comprehensive field studies of modern anthropology directly or indirectly derive from

[1] *Argonauts of the Western Pacific*, 1922; *The Sexual Life of Savages*, 1929; *Coral Gardens and their Magic*, 1935.

his teaching, for he insisted that the social life of a primitive people can only be understood if it is studied intensively, and that it is a necessary part of a social anthropologist's training to carry out at least one such intensive study of a primitive society. I shall discuss what this means when I have drawn your attention in a few words to what I think is an important feature of the earlier field studies by professional anthropologists.

These studies were carried out among very small-scale political communities—Australian hordes, Andamanese camps, and Melanesian villages—and this circumstance had the effect that certain aspects of social life, particularly kinship and ritual, were inquired into to the neglect of others, especially of political structure, which was not given the attention it deserved till African societies began to be studied. In Africa autonomous political groups often number many thousands of members, and their internal political organization as well as their interrelations forced the attention of students to specifically political problems. This is a very recent development, for professional research in Africa was not opened till the visit of Professor and Mrs. Seligman to the Anglo-Egyptian Sudan in 1909–1910, and the first intensive study in Africa by a social anthropologist was that carried out by myself among the Azande of the Anglo-Egyptian Sudan, starting in 1927. Since then, most intensive studies of primitive peoples have been made in Africa, and political institutions have received the attention they require, as, for example, in Professor Schapera's account of the Bechuana, Professor Fortes's account of the Tallensi of the Gold Coast, Professor Nadel's account of the Nupe of Nigeria, Dr. Kuper's account of the Swazi, and my own account of the Nuer of the Anglo-Egyptian Sudan.

I will now tell you, so that you may understand better what is meant by intensive fieldwork, what is today required of a person who wishes to become a professional social anthropologist. I speak particularly of our arrangements at Oxford. There a man comes to us with a degree in another subject, and he first spends a year working for the Diploma in Anthropology, a course which gives him a general knowledge of social anthropology, and also, as I explained in my first lecture, some acquaintance with physical anthropology, ethnology, technology, and prehistoric archaeology. He spends a second year, and perhaps longer, in writing a thesis from the literature of social anthropology for the degree of B.Litt. or B.Sc. Then, if his work has been of sufficient merit and if he is lucky, he obtains a grant for field research and prepares himself for it by a careful study of the literature on the peoples of the region in which he is to conduct it, including their languages.

He then usually spends at least two years in a first field study of a primitive society, this period covering two expeditions and a break between them for collating the material collected on the first expedition. Experience has shown that a few months' break, preferably spent in a university department, is essential for sound fieldwork. It will take him at least another five years to publish the results of his research to the standards of modern scholarship, and much longer should he have other calls on his time; so that it can be reckoned that an intensive study of a single primitive society and the publication of its results take about ten years.

A study of a second society is desirable, because otherwise an anthropologist is likely to think for the rest of his life, as Malinowski did, in terms of one particular type of society. This second study usually takes a shorter time because the anthropologist has learnt from his previous experience to conduct research quickly and to write with economy, but it will certainly be several years before his researches are published. To stay this long course of training and research demands great patience.

In this sketch of an anthropologist's training, I have only told you that he must make intensive studies of primitive peoples. I have not yet told you how he makes them. How does one make a study of a primitive people? I will answer this question very briefly and in very general terms, stating only what we regard as the essential rules of good fieldwork and omitting any discussion of special techniques of inquiry. What special techniques we have are in any case very simple and amount to little; and some of them, like questionnaires and censuses, cannot fruitfully be employed unless the people being studied have reached a higher degree of sophistication than is found among simple peoples before their traditional way of life has been much altered by trade, education and administration. There is indeed much to be said for Radin's contention that 'most good investigators are hardly aware of the precise manner in which they gather their data.'[1]

Nevertheless, experience has proved that certain conditions are essential if a good investigation is to be carried out. The anthropologist must spend sufficient time on the study, he must throughout be in close contact with the people among whom he is working, he must communicate with them solely through their own language, and he must study their entire culture and social life. I will examine each of these desiderata for, obvious though they may be, they are the distinguishing marks of British anthropological research which make it, in my opinion, different from and of a higher quality than research conducted elsewhere.

The earlier professional fieldworkers were always in a great hurry. Their quick visits to native peoples sometimes lasted only a few days, and seldom more than a

[1] Paul Radin, *The Method and Theory of Ethnology*, 1933, p. ix.

few weeks. Survey research of this kind can be a useful preliminary to intensive studies and elementary ethnological classifications can be derived from it, but it is of little value for an understanding of social life. The position is very different today when, as I have said, one to three years are devoted to the study of a single people. This permits observations to be made at every season of the year, the social life of the people to be recorded to the last detail, and conclusions to be tested systematically.

However, even given unlimited time for his research, the anthropologist will not produce a good account of the people he is studying unless he can put himself in a position which enables him to establish ties of intimacy with them, and to observe their daily activities from within, and not from without, their community life. He must live as far as possible in their villages and camps, where he is, again as far as possible, physically and morally part of the community. He then not only sees and hears what goes on in the normal everyday life of the people as well as less common events, such as ceremonies and legal cases, but by taking part in those activities in which he can appropriately engage, he learns through action as well as by ear and eye what goes on around him. This is very unlike the situation in which records of native life were compiled by earlier anthropological fieldworkers, and also by missionaries and administrators, who, living out of the native community in mission stations or government posts, had mostly to rely on what a few informants told them. If they visited native villages at all, their visits interrupted and changed the activities they had come to observe.

This is not merely a matter of physical proximity. There is also a psychological side to it. By living among the natives as far as he can like one of themselves the anthropologist puts himself on a level with them. Unlike the administrator and missionary he has no authority and status to maintain, and unlike them he has a neutral position. He is not there to change their way of life but as a humble learner of it; and he has no retainers and intermediaries who obtrude between him and the people, no police, interpreters, or catechists to screen him off from them.

What is perhaps even more important for his work is the fact that he is all alone, cut off from the companionship of men of his own race and culture, and is dependent on the natives around him for company, friendship, and human understanding. An anthropologist has failed unless, when he says goodbye to the natives, there is on both sides the sorrow of parting. It is evident that he can only establish this intimacy if he makes himself in some degree a member of their society and lives, thinks, and feels in their culture since only he, and not they, can make the necessary transference.

It is obvious that if the anthropologist is to carry out his work in the conditions I have described he must learn the native language, and any anthropologist worth his salt will make the learning of it his first task and will altogether, even at the beginning of his study, dispense with interpreters. Some do not pick up strange languages easily, and many primitive languages are almost unbelievably difficult to learn, but the language must be mastered as thoroughly as the capacity of the student and its complexities permit, not only because the anthropologist can then communicate freely with the natives, but for further reasons. To understand a people's thought one has to think in their symbols. Also, in learning the language one learns the culture and the social system which are conceptualized in the language. Every kind of social relationship, every belief, every technological process—in fact everything in the social life of the natives—is expressed in words as well as in action, and when one has fully understood the meaning of all the words of their language in all their situations of reference one has finished one's study of the society. I may add that, as every experienced fieldworker knows, the most difficult task in anthropological fieldwork is to determine the meanings of a few key words, upon an understanding of which the success of the whole investigation depends; and they can only be determined by the anthropologist himself learning to use the words correctly in his converse with the natives. A further reason for learning the native language at the beginning of the investigation is that it places the anthropologist in a position of complete dependence on the natives. He comes to them as pupil, not as master.

Finally, the anthropologist must study the whole of the social life. It is impossible to understand clearly and comprehensively any part of a people's social life except in the full context of their social life as a whole. Though he may not publish every detail he has recorded, you will find in a good anthropologist's notebooks a detailed description of even the most commonplace activities, for example, how a cow is milked or how meat is cooked. Also, though he may decide to write a book on a people's law, on their religion, or on their economics, describing one aspect of their life and neglecting the rest, he does so always against the background of their entire social activities and in terms of their whole social structure.

Such, very briefly and roughly, are the essential conditions of good anthropological fieldwork. We may now ask what are the qualifications required for it. Obviously, in the first place the fieldworker must have had an academic training in social anthropology. He must have a good knowledge both of general theory and of the ethnography of the region in which he is to work.

It is true that any educated, intelligent and sensitive person can get to know a strange people well and write an excellent account of their way of life, and I would say that he often gets to know them better and writes a better book about them than many professional anthropologists do. Many excellent ethnographic accounts were written long before social anthropology was even heard of, for example Dubois's *Hindu Manners, Customs and Ceremonies* (1816) and Lane's *An Account of the Manners and Customs of the Modern Egyptians* (1836) This cannot be denied, but I think that it is also certainly true that, even on the level of translation from one culture into another, without taking structural analysis into account, a man who in addition to his other qualifications has been trained in social anthropology will make a much deeper and fuller study, for one has to learn what to look for and how to observe.

When we come to the stage of structural analysis the layman is lost, because here a knowledge of theory, of problems, of method, and of technical concepts is essential. I can go for a walk and come back and give you an account of the rocks I have seen. It may be an excellent description, but it will not be a geological one. Likewise, a layman can give an account of the social life of a primitive people but, however descriptively excellent, it will not be a sociological account. The difference here is, of course, that in the geologist's study of rocks only scientific knowledge and technical skills and tools are required, whereas in the anthropological study of peoples all sorts of personal and human qualities are involved which the layman may possess and the anthropologist lack. It is possible to put oneself in the position of a man of alien culture, but not of a rock.

Anthropological fieldwork therefore requires in addition to theoretical knowledge and technical training a certain kind of character and temperament. Some men cannot stand the strain of isolation, especially in what are often uncomfortable and unhealthy conditions. Others cannot make the intellectual and emotional transference required. The native society has to be in the anthropologist himself and not merely in his notebooks if he is to understand it, and the capacity to think and feel alternately as a savage and as a European is not easily acquired, if indeed it can be acquired at all.

To succeed in this feat a man must be able to abandon himself without reserve, and he must also have intuitive powers which not all possess. Most people who know what and how to observe can make a merely competent study of a primitive people, but when one has to estimate whether a man will make a study which will be on a deeper level of understanding one looks for more than intellectual ability and technical training, for these qualities will not in themselves make a good anthropologist any more than they will make a good historian. What comes out of a study of a primitive people derives not merely from intellectual impressions of native life but from its impact on the entire personality, on the observer as a total human being. It follows that successful fieldwork may in some degree depend on the suitability of a particular man for the study of a particular people. A man who might fail in the study of one people might succeed in the study of another people. If he is to succeed, his interest and sympathy must be aroused.

If the right kind of temperament is not always found with ability, special training, and love of careful scholarship, it is rarely combined also with the imaginative insight of the artist which is required in interpretation of what is observed, and the literary skill necessary to translate a foreign culture into the language of one's own. The work of the anthropologist is not photographic. He has to decide what is significant in what he observes and by his subsequent relation of his experiences to bring what is significant into relief. For this he must have, in addition to a wide knowledge of anthropology, a feeling for form and pattern, and a touch of genius. I am not suggesting that any of us have all the qualities which make the perfect fieldworker. Some are gifted in one way and some in another, and each uses as best he can what talents he has.

Since in anthropological fieldwork much must depend, as I think we would all admit, on the person who conducts it, it may well be asked whether the same results would have been obtained had another person made a particular investigation. This is a very difficult question. My own answer would be, and I think that the evidence we have on the matter shows it to be a correct one, that the bare record of fact would be much the same, though there would, of course, be some individual differences even at the level of perception.

It is almost impossible for a person who knows what he is looking for, and how to look for it, to be mistaken about the facts if he spends two years among a small and culturally homogeneous people doing nothing else but studying their way of life. He gets to know so well what will be said and done in any situation—the social life becomes so familiar to him—that there ceases to be much point in his making any further observations or in asking any further questions, Also, whatever kind of person he may be, the anthropologist is working within a body of theoretical knowledge which largely determines his interests and his lines of inquiry. He is also working within the limits imposed by the culture of the people he is studying. If they are pastoral nomads he must study pastoral nomadism. If they are obsessed by witchcraft, he must study witchcraft. He has no choice but to follow the cultural grain.

But while I think that different social anthropologists who studied the same people would record much the same facts in their notebooks, I believe that they would write different kinds of books. Within the limits imposed by their discipline and the culture under investigation anthropologists are guided in choice of themes, in selection and arrangement of facts to illustrate them, and in judgment of what is and what is not significant, by their different interests, reflecting differences of personality, of education, of social status, of political views, of religious convictions, and so forth.

One can only interpret what one sees in terms of one's own experience and of what one is, and anthropologists, while they have a body of knowledge in common, differ in other respects as widely as other people in their backgrounds of experience and in themselves. The personality of an anthropologist cannot be eliminated from his work any more than the personality of an historian can be eliminated from his. Fundamentally, in his account of a primitive people the anthropologist is not only describing their social life as accurately as he can but is expressing himself also. In this sense his account must express moral judgment, especially where it touches matters on which he feels strongly; and what comes out of a study will to this extent at least depend on what the individual brings to it. Those who know anthropologists and their writings as well as I do, would, I think, accept this conclusion. If allowances are made for the personality of the writer, and if we consider that in the entire range of anthropological studies the effects of these personal differences tend to correct each other, I do not think that we need worry unduly over this problem in so far as the reliability of anthropological findings is in question.

There is a broader aspect to the question. However much anthropologists may differ among themselves they are all children of the same culture and society. In the main they all have, apart from their common specialist knowledge and training, the same cultural categories and values which direct their attention to selected characteristics of the societies being studied. Religion, law, economics, politics, and so forth, are abstract categories of our culture into which observations on the life of primitive peoples are patterned. Certain kinds of fact are noticed, and they are seen in a certain kind of way, by people of our culture. To some extent at any rate, people who belong to different cultures would notice different facts and perceive them in a different way. In so far as this is true, the facts recorded in our notebooks are not social facts but ethnographic facts, selection and interpretation having taken place at the level of observation. I cannot now discuss, but only state, this general question of perception and evaluation.

I must say in conclusion that, as you will have noted, I have been discussing anthropological field research and the qualities and qualifications required for it in the light of the opinion I expressed in my last lecture that social anthropology is best regarded as an art and not as a natural science. Those among my colleagues who hold the opposite opinion might have discussed the questions with which I have been concerned in this lecture in a rather different way.

V

MODERN ANTHROPOLOGICAL STUDIES

I endeavoured in my second and third lectures to give you some account of the theoretical development of social anthropology, which has meant more or less in practice the development of theories about primitive societies or what in the last century would have been called the institutions of early man, and in the century before, rude society. In my last lecture I briefly reviewed the growth of our knowledge about these primitive societies, and I explained how descriptive accounts of them had improved, both in quality and in quantity, from the casual observations of explorers, through the detailed records of missionaries and administrators, to the intensive studies of modern professional research. The theories have been shaped and reshaped by this steady growth in knowledge and they have on their side, in each reformulation, directed observation into deeper layers and into new fields of the social life of primitive peoples and thereby led to further increase in knowledge.

The great development in research has produced a new orientation in the aims and methods of social anthropology. I will give you in this lecture a brief account of some of the tendencies it has given rise to, and I will then discuss a few anthropological monographs, in which fieldworkers have recorded and arranged their observations, as examples of the kind of inquiry in which social anthropologists now engage. We have seen how they make their observations. We will now examine how they organize them and the use to which they put them.

The essential point to remember is that the anthropologist is working within a body of theoretical knowledge and that he makes his observations to solve problems which derive from it. This emphasis on problems is, of course, a feature of any field of scholarship. Lord Acton told his history students to study problems and not periods. Collingwood told his archaeological students to study problems and not sites. We tell our anthropological students to study problems and not peoples.

The earlier fieldwork monographs were for the most part descriptive accounts of one or other people without much attempt at systematic analysis, though pseudo-historical speculations were sometimes taken for such. Each study consisted of a succession of chapters treating seriatim and in detail a different aspect of social life: environment, racial characteristics, demography, vital statistics, technology, economy, social organization, *rites de passage*, law, religion, magic, mythology, folklore, pastimes, etc. Modern fieldwork monographs are generally intended to give more than merely a description of the social life of a people with interpretations of the more popular kind which any description of one culture in terms of another necessarily entails. They aim at an analytical and integrative description which will bring out those features of the social life which are significant for an understanding of its structure and for general theory.

This followed necessarily as soon as the student of theory began to conduct his own field research. It means that the facts, that is, the observations recorded in the anthropologist's notebooks, are not set forth in his publications as a description of what a primitive people do and say, but to show that what they do and say, apart from its intrinsic interest, illuminates some problem of one or other aspect of culture or institutional life. In other words, in deciding what he is to put into his book and what to leave out of it, he is guided by the relevance of the material for a particular theme designed to bring out significant features of some system of social activities.

I had better say here that in this writing-up side of his work the social anthropologist faces a serious difficulty. We have noted that he makes a study of the entire life of a people. Is it his duty to publish a full record of all his observations on every aspect of their life? The historian is not faced here with the same difficulty. He can select from the material at his disposal what is relevant to his theme and neglect the rest. What he leaves out of his books is not lost. The anthropologist, and to a large extent the archaeologist also, are in a very different position, for what they do not record may be, and often is, lost for ever. The anthropologist is not only the collator and interpreter of sources. He is the creator of them.

It has therefore often been held that it is the duty of a fieldworker not only to record, but also to publish, everything he has observed, whether it has any interest for him or not, on the ground that the first task of anthropology at this time is to assemble as large a body of facts as possible while there are still primitive societies to be studied. The anthropologist is recorder, not arbiter. For him to decide that one fact is important and another fact unimportant is to prejudge the interests of future generations. This is a difficulty which we try to meet in various ways. The prevailing practice tends to be for the fieldworker to publish monographs on one or other aspect of the life of a primitive people which seems to him to have particular importance, using for the purpose only such facts as are relevant to his selected themes and are sufficient to illustrate them. The rest are published in learned journals or are recorded in mimeographed or microfilm form.

The enormous mass of information which can be collected during a two years' study of a primitive people makes, even if this solution is adopted, for a change, already very noticeable, in anthropological method. We have seen that in the past anthropologists were devotees of the comparative method. Whether the aim was to reconstruct history or to reach general descriptive formulas the procedure was the same. A great number of books were read and the information bearing on the subject of inquiry was extracted from them and pieced together to make a new book. Without entering again into a consideration of the value of this kind of literary comparative study, it is a matter of plain experience that it is a formidable task which cannot be undertaken by a man who is under the obligation to publish the results of the two or three field studies he has made, since this will take him the rest of his life to complete if he has heavy teaching and administrative duties as well. As almost all social anthropologists do fieldwork today the situation is a general one.

It is evident that in these circumstances social anthropology would soon disintegrate into an endless succession of disconnected studies if there were not a common method of research to take the place of the older use of the comparative method. This is supplied today, as a result of social anthropology having become a field, or observational, study by what would in the natural sciences be called the experimental method. What I mean by this will be clear to you if I take an example.

An anthropologist has made a study of religious cults in some primitive society and has reached certain conclusions about their role in social life. If he formulates these clearly and in terms which allow them to be broken down into problems of research it is then possible for the same, or another, anthropologist to make in a second society observations which will show whether these conclusions have wider validity. He will probably find that some of them hold, that some of them do not hold, and that some hold with modifications. Starting from the point reached by the first study, the second is likely to drive the investigation deeper and to add some new formulations to the confirmed conclusions of the first. We now have a hypothesis about the religious cults of primitive peoples derived from a study of them in two societies. A third study is now made, and then a fourth and a fifth. The process can be continued indefinitely. If the studies are systematic and each is used to test the conclusions reached up to that point and to advance new hypotheses which permit verification, each will reach, as knowledge increases and new problems emerge, a deeper level of investigation which in its turn will lead to a clearer definition of concepts. Every new study, if it is of any value, not only tells us about a certain institution in the particular primitive society studied, but sheds light on significant features of that institution in other societies, including those in which the importance of these features may not have been realized by earlier investigators. Field research of today is in this sense experimental. It is also, in a rather different sense, comparative; but it is very unlike what used to be called the comparative method, which has largely been abandoned, partly for the reason I have given and partly because it seldom provides answers to the questions asked.

A further change of direction follows from what I have been saying. Not only the method but to some extent the aim of research has changed. It stands to reason that field research is incompatible with those schemes of social development favoured by nineteenth-century anthropologists. One cannot observe events which have long passed and of which no memory has been preserved. In a field study of a primitive people there is no means one can use to prove or disprove the hypothesis that they were once matrilineal or lived in a state of sexual promiscuity.

Apart from this, the scope of inquiry is inevitably narrowed into small problems within the limits of which inquiry is possible and may lead to fruitful conclusions. Ambitious efforts at world-wide synthesis give way to humbler and less spectacular inquiries. Whereas the nineteenth-century anthropologist sought to answer such questions as 'What is the sociological significance of religion?', no anthropologist, or at any rate no sensible anthropologist, would ask such a question today. Rather he seeks to determine, for instance, the part played by the ancestor cult in a social system of the type we call a segmentary lineage system among certain African peoples. Instead of attempting to paint on a grand canvas the development of the notion of responsibility, or the development of the state, in the whole human race, the anthropologist of today concentrates on such small problems as can be investigated by direct inquiry and observation, such as the function of the feud, or the position of chieftainship of a certain kind, in societies where the social activities centred around these institutions can be seen and studied. Instead of discussing whether primitive societies are communistic or individualistic the anthropologist of today makes a detailed study of the complex of rights, some corporate and some personal, centred in property, maybe in land or in cattle, in a particular society to discover how these rights are related to one another and to the social systems in which they figure, kinship systems, political systems, systems of cult, and so forth.

The viewpoint in social anthropology today may be summed up by saying that we now think we can learn more about the nature of human society by really detailed intensive and observational studies, conducted in a series of a few selected societies with the aim of solving limited problems, than by attempting generalizations on a wider scale from literature. As a result we are just beginning to know a little bit about the social life of primitive peoples.

The emphasis placed by modern social anthropology on intensive fieldwork studies in which limited problems are tackled has had a further consequence to which I would like to draw your attention before giving you some examples of modern studies. I have remarked in earlier lectures that the nineteenth-century anthropologists were cultural realists. They were interested in customs, and customs were to them independent entities. They were things one society had and another society did not have. Even so sociologically minded a writer as McLennan regarded exogamy, totemism, matriliny, and so forth as items of custom, which, added up, made cultures. Consequently a people either had rules of exogamy or they did not have them; they were either totemistic or they were not; they were either patrilineal or matrilineal.

This kind of cultural taxonomy is slowly being discarded by English social anthropologists. Much could be said on this subject, but it must suffice to say that the modern anthropologist tends to think more in terms of society than of culture—of social systems and values and their interrelations. He asks not so much whether people have rules of exogamy but, for example, what is the significance of these rules for the study of their intercommunity relations. He is not content to know that people have totemic beliefs but seeks to discover how these beliefs may reflect values of descent and the solidarity of groups based on descent. He does not consider that to know that people trace descent through women, and not through men, is significant knowledge in itself. He investigates rather, again for example, how their matrilineal mode of tracing descent affects the brother-sister relationship or the mother's brother-sister's son relationship. Some of these modern studies, as you will see shortly, are more abstract and structural than others—there is a good deal of divergence of opinion about methods of analysis—but they all tend to be, compared with earlier studies, sociological and functional. I now give you some illustrations.

I start with the summary of one of Malinowski's books because he was the first professional anthropologist to do intensive fieldwork through the native language. Although he collected a vast amount of material about the Trobriand Islanders and published several volumes on them before his death, he gave only a partial account of this people, and we are still in the dark about some of their most important activities, particularly about their political organization and their kinship system. The book I am going to discuss, *Argonauts of the Western Pacific* (1922), though long-winded and written in a journalistic style, may be regarded none the less, and not only because of its priority but on its merits, as a classic of descriptive ethnography.

The book is about one set of activities of the Trobriand Islanders which they call *kula*. They and the inhabitants of some neighbouring islands form a kind of league for the exchange of certain objects, long necklaces of red shell and bracelets of white shell. In the system of exchange the necklaces pass through communities one way round the circuit of islands, and the bracelets pass the opposite way round. These objects have no practical value but only a ritual and prestige value, the prestige consisting in the renown a man gets by receiving, possessing, and then passing on particularly esteemed objects. Those men who take part in these exchanges have partners in the islands they visit. The exchanges take place with formality and decorum, and there must be no haggling; though when the ritual exchanges are completed ordinary commercial transactions, bargaining for food or articles of practical use, takes place. The *kula* proper, however, is the system of ritual exchange within which the necklaces and bracelets go round the island communities in everlasting circuit.

To carry out these exchanges the chiefs of villages and groups of nearby villages organize large trading expeditions. This means the preparation of canoes, nautical knowledge, knowledge of magical spells to aid against the chances of the adventure, and knowledge of tradition and myth to guide the Argonauts in their voyages and negotiations. Therefore Malinowski felt that he had to give in the compass of a single book an account of all these, and many other, matters. He had to give us detailed accounts of magic and myth, to describe the scenery for us, to tell us how the natives cultivate their gardens, what is the social position of their women, how they construct and sail their canoes, and so on—even what went on inside himself as well, for he was there too. He paints a picture of the living reality of Trobriand society which brings to the mind the novels of Emile Zola.

We see very clearly in this his first, and I think his best, book on the Trobriand Islanders his conception of what constitutes a social system and a functional analysis of it. To him a social system is a succession of activities or events, and not a set of abstractions. To go on an expedition, Trobriand Islanders make canoes. In making canoes, they utter magical spells. These spells have stories, or myths, accounting for their origin. They also belong to someone by inheritance from his maternal uncle. In the making of a canoe and in planning the expedition there is organization of labour and direction by the chiefs. The chiefs have authority largely because they are richer than commoners. They are richer because they have bigger gardens. They have bigger gardens because they have several wives. To Malinowski all these different activities form a system because each is dependent on all the others and the function of each is the part it plays in the total set of activities which have a direct or indirect bearing on the exchange of the ritual objects of the *kula*.

It is true that in a sense they do form a system of activities, and this mode of impressionistic presentation of social life is very effective, but, properly speaking, the theme is no more than a descriptive synthesis of events. It is not a theoretical integration, though theoretical problems are discussed in interludes in the course of the story. There is consequently no real standard of relevance, since everything has a time and space relationship in cultural reality to everything else, and from whatever point one starts one spreads oneself over the same ground. A description of social life in terms of various aspects of it on this level of events leads inevitably to endless repetitions and to so-called theoretical conclusions which are no more than redescriptions in more abstract language, since discrete correlations can hardly be perceived if one does not depart from concrete reality. Malinowski might have started from chieftainship and described the *kula* in relation to that institution, or he might have written his book on magic and described the *kula* and chieftainship in relation to that.

It is because he seldom made abstractions that Malinowski failed to see clearly what is perhaps the most significant feature of the *kula*, the bringing together, through the acceptance of common ritual values, of politically autonomous communities. Also, comparison between the social life of a people so described and the social life of other peoples similarly portrayed is limited to assessment of cultural similarities and divergences and cannot be of a structural kind, for which abstraction is required. Nevertheless, some excellent and important ethnographic studies of a number of primitive peoples made on what is still very largely the level of cultural realism by students of Malinowski have enriched the literature of our subject: for example, Professor Firth's *We, the Tikopia* (1936), Miss Hunter's *Reaction to Conquest* (1936), Professor Schapera's *A Handbook of Tswana Law and Custom* (1938), and Dr. Richards's *Land, Labour and Diet in Northern Rhodesia* (1939).

Abstraction can mean several different things. It can mean treating only a part of social life for particular and limited problems of investigation, taking the rest into consideration only in so far as it is relevant to these problems, or it can mean structural analysis through the integration of abstractions from social life. As an example of the first procedure I will discuss Dr. Mead's *Coming of Age in Samoa* (1929). This is a discursive, or perhaps I should say chatty and feminine, book with a leaning towards the picturesque, what I call the rustling-of-the-wind-in-the-palm-trees kind of anthropological writing, for which Malinowski set the fashion.

The aim of the book is to show that the difficulties of adolescence, particularly those of adolescent girls, which are so common and troublesome a feature of American life, do not occur in Samoa and may therefore be regarded as a product of a particular type of social environment, as due to the restraints of civilization and not to nature. Dr. Mead therefore sets out to show us in what way Samoan conditions of adolescence are different from those of American adolescence. With this end in view she tells us everything she observed about the social setting of the Samoan girl, how, in a broad sense, she is educated, what her childhood is like, and about her place in the life of the household, village, and wider community, and her variety of sexual relations with young men. The description is always with particular reference to the problem of the investigation, the moulding of the personality of the growing girl by social conditions and the reactions of this personality to the physiological changes of puberty.

The conclusion of the study is that there are no differences between American girls and Samoan girls in the process of adolescence itself. The differences lie in the response to it. In Samoa there is no stress or crisis but an orderly development of interests and activities. 'The girls' minds', Dr. Mead tells us, 'were perplexed by no conflicts, troubled by no philosophical queries, beset by no remote ambitions. To live as a girl with many lovers as long as possible and then to marry in one's own village, near one's own relatives and to have many children, these were uniform and satisfying ambitions.'[1]

The American girl at the same time of her life suffers from strains and stresses because her social environment is different. What are the significant differences? Dr. Mead is of the opinion that the most important are to be found in the absence in Samoa of deep personal feelings and of conflicting values. The Samoan girls do not care very deeply about anyone or anything, and in particular they do not set high hopes on any one relationship. This is partly due to the fact that they are not brought up in a narrow family circle but in a wider circle of kin, so that both authority and affection are spread over a large number of persons. Even more important is the homogeneous culture of the Samoans. They all have the same standards of behaviour. There is only one set of religious beliefs and there is only one code of morals. Consequently in these matters Samoan adolescents do not have to make choices, inevitably affecting their relationships with those around them, and they therefore avoid the conflicts which follow from having to choose between different sets of values and the maladjustments and neuroses which result from the conflicts. The American adolescent, on the contrary, is confronted in her social environment with

[1] P. 157.

so many various and conflicting values that she has to make a choice, and choice is the forerunner of conflict.

The book I have just discussed differs from most modern field monographs in that no analysis of Samoan social structure is presented, even in outline, so that it is difficult to see the facts related in any sort of perspective. Nevertheless, it is a good example of the single-problem kind of study, and it is written by a highly intelligent woman.

I am now going to give you the argument in two books of my own. I must apologize for doing so, but it is easier to present an analysis within a culture that is familiar to one than in an unfamiliar culture. These two books illustrate the use of abstraction of a rather different kind. The first is a study of a system of ideas and the second a study of a system of political groups.

My first book, *Witchcraft, Oracles and Magic among the Azande* (1937), is about a Central African people. It is an attempt to make intelligible a number of beliefs, all of which are foreign to the mentality of a modern Englishman, by showing how they form a comprehensible system of thought, and how this system of thought is related to social activities, social structure, and the life of the individual.

Among the Azande any misfortune can be, and generally is, attributed to witchcraft, which the Azande consider to be an internal organic condition, though its action is believed to be psychic. The witch despatches what they call the soul, or spirit, of his witchcraft to cause damage to others. The sufferer consults oracles, of which the Azande have a number of different kinds, or a diviner, to discover who is injuring him. This may be quite a complicated and lengthy procedure. When the culprit is revealed he is requested to withdraw his malign influence.

If in a case of sickness he does not do so and the invalid

dies, the kinsmen of the dead man could in the past take the affair to their prince's jurisdiction and exact vengeance or compensation, or they could make, as they invariably do in the circumstances today, lethal magic to destroy the witch. In addition to this lethal magic the Azande have a vast body of magical knowledge and techniques, some requiring membership of special magical associations, which are largely used to protect their persons and activities from witchcraft.

Witchcraft, oracles, and magic thus form a complex system of beliefs and rites which makes sense only when they are seen as interdependent parts of a whole. This system has a logical structure. Granted certain postulates, inferences and action based on them are sound. Witchcraft causes death. Therefore a death is evidence of witchcraft, and the oracles confirm that witchcraft caused it. Magic is made to avenge the death. A neighbour dies soon afterwards and the oracles determine that he died a victim to the magic of vengeance. Each bit of belief fits in with every other bit in a general mosaic of mystical thought. If in such a closed system of thought a belief is contradicted by a particular experience this merely shows that the experience was mistaken, or inadequate, or the contradiction is accounted for by secondary elaborations of belief which provide satisfactory explanations of the apparent inconsistency. Even scepticism supports the beliefs about which it is exercised. Criticism of a particular diviner, for example, or distrust of a particular oracle or form of magic, merely enhances faith in others and the system as a whole.

An analysis of a great number of situations in which discussions about witchcraft arose and of comments on the notion by Azande on many occasions showed further that it provides them with a philosophy of events which is intellectually satisfying. At first sight it looks absurd to hold that if termites have gnawed away the supports of a granary and it falls on a man sitting in the shade beneath and kills him, this is an act of witchcraft; but the Azande do not suppose, any more than we would, that the collapse of the granary is not the immediate cause of death. What they say is that it would not have collapsed at a particular moment when a particular man was sitting under it unless the man had been bewitched. Why should it not have fallen at a different moment or when a different man was sitting under it? It is easy to account for the collapse of the granary. That was due to termites and the weight of millet in it. It is also easy to account for the man being under it. He was there for shade in the heat of the day. But why did these two chains of events coincide at a certain point in space and time? We say that the coincidence was chance. The Azande explain it by witchcraft. Witchcraft and the granary operating together killed the man.

The notion of witchcraft gives the Azande not only a natural philosophy but also a moral philosophy, in which is contained also a theory of psychology. Even if a man is a witch, his witchcraft does not harm people unless there is an act of will. There has to be a motive and this is always to be found in the evil passions of men, in hatred, greed, envy, jealousy, and resentment. Misfortunes spring from witchcraft, and witchcraft is directed by evil intentions. Azande do not blame a man for being a witch. He cannot help that. It is the evil in him which makes him harm others that they denounce. I may add that Azande are well aware of what psychologists call projection, that when a man says that another hates him and is bewitching him it is often the first who is the hater and the witch; and that they also realize the significant part played by dreams, or what is now called the subconscious, in the evil passions of men. It is also necessary to point out that the dogma that it is evil which, through witchcraft, causes misfortune cannot be pleaded as an excuse for actions which are due to vice or ignorance. Witchcraft only causes undeserved misfortunes. A man who commits adultery or is disloyal to his king or who fails in some enterprise, such as pot-making, through lack of skill is responsible for the penalties or failures his actions incur.

Since a witch only injures a man when he is ill-disposed towards him, a sufferer from sickness or other misfortune places the names of his enemies before the oracles, and consequently it is an enemy whom the oracles, declare to be the man bewitching him. Accusations of witchcraft consequently only arise between persons whose social relations with one another permit states of enmity to form. Their incidence is determined by the social structure. For example, the relations between children and adults are not such that enmity is likely to arise between them, so that children are not accused of bewitching adults. For a similar reason nobles are not accused of bewitching commoners, though in this case there is the further reason that no commoner would dare to accuse a noble of witchcraft. Likewise, since in Zande society women do not have social relations with men other than their kin and their husbands—and they would not injure their kin—they are only accused of bewitching their female neighbours or their husbands, and not other men.

The oracles have an order of importance. Some are less certain in their revelations than others and action cannot be taken on their statements till these are confirmed by the highest authority, the poison oracle. The poison oracle in its turn is regarded as having more or less significance according to the social status of its owner. A case may therefore go from one poison oracle to another, as in our country a case may go from one court to another, till a final verdict is given by a king's oracle, beyond which there is no appeal. The legal machinery which operates in cases of witchcraft is thus ultimately in the hands of a king and his representatives, which makes the social action the belief entails one of the main supports of royal authority. The operation of witchcraft beliefs in the social life are also closely connected with the kinship system, particularly through the custom of vengeance, but I have already said enough to show how what at first sight seems no more than an absurd superstition is discovered by anthropological investigation to be the integrative principle of a system of thought and morals and to have an important role in the social structure.

My second book, *The Nuer. A Description of the Modes of Livelihood and Political Institutions of a Nilotic People* (1940), is about a very different kind of people and society and deals with very different kinds of problems. The Nuer are semi-nomadic cattle herdsmen living in marsh and savannah country in the southern Anglo-Egyptian Sudan. They form a congeries of tribes and, since they have no chiefs and no legal institutions, the task which seemed to be of first importance was to discover the principle of their tribal, or political, integration. It was evident that the Nuer, having a very simple material culture, are highly dependent on their environment and it became clear from an examination of their oecology that the pursuit of a pastoral life in difficult conditions made a fairly wide political order necessary if they were to maintain their way of life. This political order is provided by the tribal structure. A study of the different local communities within a Nuer tribe revealed the fact that each is identified politically with a lineage, though most of its members do not belong to this lineage, and that all these lineages are branches of a single clan. Each of the territorial divisions of a tribe is thus co-ordinated with a corresponding branch of this dominant clan so that relations between the parts of a tribe, both their separateness and their unity, are conceptualized and expressed within a framework of values of descent.

Leaving on one side a number of other matters investigated against this general structural background, I will discuss very briefly the Nuer concepts of time as an example of the kind of problem we investigate and the kind of structural analysis we make.

I can only outline the argument, which shows in part how the conceptualization of natural changes as points of reference in time-reckoning is determined by the rhythm of social activities and in part how the points are reflections of structural relations between social groups. The daily tasks of the kraal are the points of reference for each day, and for longer periods than a day the points are the phases of other recurrent activities, such as weeding or the seasonal movements of men and their herds. The passage of time is the succession of activities and their relations to one another. All sorts of interesting conclusions follow. Time has not the same value at one season of the year that it has at another. Also, since the Nuer have, properly speaking, no abstract system of time-reckoning they do not think of time, as we do, as something actual, which passes, can be wasted, can be saved, and so forth; and they do not have to co-ordinate their activities with an abstract passage of time, because their points of reference are the activities themselves. Thus, in a certain month one makes the first fishing dams and forms the first cattle camps, and since one is doing these things it must be that month or thereabouts. One does not make fishing dams because it is November; it is November because one makes fishing dams.

The larger periods of time are almost entirely structural. The events they relate are different for different groups of people so that each group has its own system of time-reckoning in addition to a common system which refers to events of outstanding significance to them all. Also, male Nuer are stratified by age into divisions or sets, a new age-set starting about every ten years. I will not enter into the details of this arrangement but merely say that the time that events happened is often denoted by reference to these divisions. Hence intervals between events are not reckoned in time concepts, as we understand them, but in terms of structural distance, of the social difference between groups of persons. Nuer also reckon history in terms of their genealogies of descent. Now it can be shown that the depth to which descent is traced in any particular situation corresponds to the size of the group of kin concerned, so that here time is a reflection of units of social structure. Events have a position in structure but no exact position in historical time as we understand it. In general it may be said that among the Nuer time is a conceptualization of the social structure and the points of reference in the system of reckoning are projections into the past of actual relations between groups of persons. It co-ordinates relationships rather than events.

Many steps in so short an exposition must be obscure to you. This does not matter, because I am not trying to prove the soundness of the argument but to show you the method of analysis pursued. You will have seen that here again what the method amounts to is to make some part of the social life intelligible by showing how it is integrated with other parts. This can only be done by making abstractions and interrelating them logically.

I mentioned in my first lecture that social anthropology, although it has generally in the past restricted its attention to primitive societies, has not entirely done so, and is not considered by us to be a study of primitive societies but of all human societies. To show you that we also study civilized societies I will take as my final example of anthropological field monographs a book on the peasantry of Southern Ireland, Professor Arensberg's *The Irish Countryman* (1937). It is an excellent example of structural analysis in which the author sets forth simply and concisely the main conclusions reached by an investigation made in County Clare by himself and Professor Kimball.

Southern Ireland is a country of small farms, the greater part of the farming families supporting themselves on from fifteen to thirty acres, living off the land and selling their surplus products for such necessities as flour and tea. The farmers run their farms on the labour of their families, though they receive some help from kinsmen, the network of kinship ties uniting the members of a village and of neighbouring villages having a fundamental role in the organization of Irish country life. The author discusses these and many other topics. I will briefly recount what he says about two of them, marriage and the relations between countryman and townsman.

We are told that 'Marriage is a turning point round which rural life hinges. It is a structural centre.'[1] The smallest farmers have the largest families, and marriage takes place for both sexes at a later age than in any other country for which records are kept. Owing to the small size of the farms a family can usually marry off only one son and one daughter. When the son who is to get the farm marries, his bride brings him a dowry, usually between about £250 and £350—it must be roughly equivalent to the value of the farm, and is therefore a measure of the family's social status. Part of it goes to the husband and his parents, who after the marriage retire from management of the farm, and part is used to help the other sons who, since the farms are not divided

[1] p. 93.

among the children, must either migrate to the towns to earn their living in trade, a profession, or the church, or emigrate. By this means it is possible to maintain family continuity on a farm, blood and land being closely associated, but only at the expense of the other, generally younger, sons. The author shows in this way how marriage, inheritance, social controls, and migration and emigration all form part of the social system of small farms.

The family system of the farm has its counterpart in the local market towns and this, as you will see, accounts for the dying out of the town families. The younger sons of the farmers go to the towns as apprentices and their daughters as wives. A trader lives on country custom, and this is given only to kinsmen. Consequently a shop-keeper or publican marries his son who is to take over from him his shop or pub to a country girl, who will bring with her not only her dowry but also the custom of her part of the countryside. Town and country, the distributive unit and the productive unit, are thus bound together not only economically but through ties of kinship. But urban life affects the outlook of the men, who, bit by bit, can no longer meet the countryman halfway. They lose rural ways and interests, and this is even more so with those born in the towns, the second generation migrants. So the shopkeeper's and publican's families move into professions or into larger towns. They become part of a social milieu in which the countryside has no part, and new blood fills their places in the market town and succeeds by virtue of its country connections, bringing with it new bonds of kinship. We see thus how the economic system, through the exchange of farm products for articles of trade, and the kinship system, through intermarriage between town and country, are bound up together in the general social system of the Irish countryside.

One of the ways in which the connection between townsmen and their country cousins is maintained and expressed is by debt. The countryman is always in debt to his shopkeeper kinsman, and this chronic debt is part of their social relationship. Indeed, when a countryman is angry with a shopkeeper he pays his debt to withdraw his custom and sever their relationship. The debt, like the dowry, is a measure of status, being a sign of one's ability and willingness to support that network of social obligations which gives oneself and one's family a place in social life. The debt passes down the generations from father to son. It is the bond between the family and kin of the farmer and the family and kin of the shopkeeper by which they express in each other confidence and social obligation. Debt is thus shown in a new light, as one of the mechanisms by which a social system is maintained. It cannot be understood merely in economic or legal terms but only in relation to kinship and other features of the total social structure; and moral judgment about it has to be made in the light of this broader understanding.

These few examples—all I have time to give—will, I trust, have shown you the type and diversity of problems with which social anthropologists are today concerned. Once again, you will note that they are not inquiries into the strange or romantic but into matter-of-fact problems of sociology, problems which, moreover, as I shall have occasion to emphasize in my next, and final, lecture, are of general importance, and not important merely within their particular ethnic and geographical setting. It is of significance for us in our own society to learn that the Trobriand Islanders expend their greatest energies in pursuit of honour and not of profit; that if the Samoans lack a diversity of ends, and the greater variety of personality these ends engender, they have personal security and the happiness that goes with it; that though modern science rejects the assumptions on which the Zande system of beliefs is based the system has a philosophic and moral validity; that to understand Nuer concepts of time we have first to understand their social structure; and that in Southern Ireland debt serves to uphold harmonious relations between countryman and townsman. These and many other fruitful, if tentative, conclusions have obviously significance for the understanding not only of the particular societies in the study of which they were reached but for the understanding of any society, including our own.

VI

APPLIED ANTHROPOLOGY

In my earlier lectures I tried to give you a general idea of what social anthropology is in terms of university teaching, of its development as a special department of knowledge, and of the manner and problems of its research. In this final lecture I shall discuss the question most anthropologists must have been asked from time to time. What is the purpose of studying social anthropology?

This question can be variously interpreted and answered. It might be interpreted as an inquiry about the motives that make a man take up social anthropology as a profession. Each anthropologist would probably here give different answers from those of his colleagues. For many of us, including myself, the answer would be either 'I don't quite know' or, in the words of an American colleague, 'I guess I just like going places.'

However, the question generally has the different sense of: What is the use of knowledge about primitive societies? An answer to the question in this form has to be divided into a discussion about its use for the primitive peoples themselves and for those who are responsible for their welfare, and a discussion about its value to the men who study it—to ourselves.

Since social anthropologists mostly study primitive societies, the information they collect and the conclusions they come to obviously have some bearing on problems of the administration and education of primitive peoples. It will at once be acknowledged that if it is the policy of a colonial government to administer a people through their chiefs it is useful to know who are the chiefs and what are their functions and authority and privileges and obligations. Also, if it is intended to administer a people according to their own laws and customs one has first to discover what these are. It is evident also that if it is intended to change a people's economy, for example to alter their system of land tenure, to encourage them to grow export crops, or to institute markets and a money economy, it is of some advantage to be able to estimate, at any rate roughly, what social effects these changes are likely to bring about. If, for example, the system of land tenure is changed there may be repercussions on the people's family and kinship life and on their religion, because family and kinship ties and religious beliefs and cults may be closely bound up with their traditional system of tenure. It is evident also that if a missionary wishes to convert a native people to Christianity some knowledge of their own religious beliefs and practices is required. Otherwise apostolic teaching is impossible, because it has to be through the native language, that is, through the religious concepts of the natives.

The value of social anthropology to administration has been generally recognized from the beginning of the century and both the Colonial Office and colonial governments have shown an increasing interest in anthropological teaching and research. For a good number of years past colonial cadets, before taking up their appointments, have received, among other courses of instruction, instruction in social anthropology at Oxford and Cambridge, and more recently in London. Since the last war colonial officials have been brought home for refresher courses at these three universities and some of them choose social anthropology for special study as an optional subject. In addition, administrative officers have often taken the Anthropological Tripos at Cambridge and occasionally the Diploma or a postgraduate degree in Anthropology at Oxford, and a great many have kept in touch with anthropological developments through membership of the Royal Anthropological Institute.

Colonial governments recognized that while a general and elementary knowledge of anthropology is of value to their officers it is not in itself sufficient to enable them to carry out research, even if they had, as they have not, time and opportunity to conduct it; but the governments have occasionally seconded officers in their service, who have received some further training in anthropology and have shown an aptitude for research, to make studies of peoples in their territories. Some important studies have been made in this way, the most remarkable being the research embodied in the series of volumes by Rattray on the Ashanti of the Gold Coast. Valuable work of the same kind was also done by Dr. Meek in Nigeria and by F. E. Williams and E. W. Pearson Chinnery in New Guinea. It must be said, however, that even at their best the writings of these administrator-anthropologists seldom satisfy the professional scholar. It may perhaps be assumed that they are also not entirely satisfactory from the administrative point of view, because, except in Tanganyika Territory, this mode of conducting research has, I believe, been abandoned by colonial governments.

The government of the Anglo-Egyptian Sudan has always preferred, I think wisely, to finance expeditions by professional anthropologists to carry out special pieces of research or to employ them on short-term contracts for the same purpose, and with intervals research has been going on in that country, successively by Professor and Mrs. Seligman, myself, Dr. Nadel, and Mr. Lienhardt from 1909 to the present time. This method has the advantage that while the anthropologist is gaining experience which will later enable him to take a university post the government is getting its inquiries made by a fully trained man acquainted with the most recent developments in the subject.

Since the last war the Colonial Office has shown greater interest in social anthropology. It has organized and financed anthropological research in a good number of the colonial territories. This means of getting research done has not been, in my assessment of the results, entirely successful. I strongly support the opinion of those who hold that research is best carried out through university departments, which are then made responsible for the selection and training of the student, for supervision of his research, and for the writing-up and publication of its results. The present policy of the Colonial Office is to organize research through local research institutes. One of these, the Rhodes-Livingstone Institute in Northern Rhodesia, has been operating since 1938, and three new institutes for social research have recently been founded, one at Makerere in Uganda, a second at Ibadan in Nigeria, and a third at Kingston in Jamaica. I think myself that this will not prove to be a substitute for the organization of research through university departments, though local institutes can have a useful function as local centres from which research by students of the universities can be carried out—a role like that of the British Institutes at Rome, Athens, and Ankara.

This has been appreciated elsewhere. An extremely important development for anthropologists has been the creation of Treasury Studentships for research into the languages and cultures of the Far East, the Near East, Eastern Europe, and Africa. Experience during the last war showed that there was a lamentable ignorance about these parts of the world, and a Royal Commission under the chairmanship of the Earl of Scarbrough concluded that this state of affairs could only finally be changed by the building up of a tradition of scholarship in the languages and cultures with which it was concerned.

The admirable plan they proposed included the strengthening of university departments and the creation of new university departments, the provision of studentships for research from the universities by men who would eventually take up teaching posts in them, and the foundation of institutes as local research centres in the parts of the world where these researches would be carried out. In this way it is ensured not only that research is conducted but also that a tradition of scholarship is built up and maintained.

These Treasury Studentships have enabled social anthropologists to carry out in various regions research which might otherwise have been beyond their means; for anthropological research in distant parts is very expensive, and the various endowments which generously help us—such as the Emslie Horniman Anthropological Scholarship Fund, the Goldsmiths Company's Postgraduate Travelling Scholarships, the Leverhulme Grants Committee, and the Viking Fund—cannot cover more than a very small portion of the research urgently required.

Missionary bodies in this country have not shown that they consider some acquaintance with anthropology a useful adjunct to the training of those who are to serve in the missions among primitive peoples. This is partly due to the poverty of the missions, which cannot afford to send their volunteers to the universities where anthropology is taught. It is also partly due, I think, to the suspicion with which anthropology has been regarded in missionary circles. The suspicion has not perhaps been unfounded, for anthropology has always been mixed up with free-thought and has been considered, not unjustly, as anti-religious in tone, and even in aim. Also, missionaries feel, naturally enough, that, as Gabriel Sagard says in his introduction to his book on the Hurons (1632), 'The perfection of men does not consist in seeing much, nor in knowing much, but in carrying out the will and good pleasure of God.' Nevertheless, many individual missionaries have taken a deep interest in anthropology and have realized its value for their own work. Their attitude is well expressed by Pasteur Junod of the Swiss Romande Mission, the author of one of the finest anthropological monographs yet written. He tells us that his aim in collecting the information embodied in this book was partly scientific and partly to help administrative officers and missionaries and to enlighten South African opinion about the natives: 'To work for Science is noble; but to help our fellow men is nobler still.'[1] Another missionary, Dr. Edwin Smith, part-author of an excellent account of the Ba-ila people of Northern Rhodesia, has recently been President of the Royal Anthropological Institute.

In the past it has been chiefly administrators and missionaries who have found that some knowledge of anthropology has helped them to carry out their duties more agreeably and effectively. In the changed situation of today technical experts have become increasingly important in our colonial empire—the doctor, the agricultural officer, the forestry officer, the veterinary officer, the engineer, and so on, and also the trader and representatives of mining and other business interests. At present most of them are expected to carry out their various jobs among peoples about whose way of life and ideas they often know next to nothing.

You will ask how a knowledge of anthropology helps Europeans in their dealings with native peoples. Many anthropologists have for a long time spoken about applied anthropology much as one speaks about applied medicine or engineering. Those who have spoken thus have regarded social anthropology as a natural science which aims at the establishment of laws of social life; and once theoretical generalizations can be established

[1] *The Life of a South African Tribe*, 1913, p. 10.

an applied science becomes feasible. We have seen that this normative element in anthropology is, like the concepts of natural law and progress from which it derives, part of its philosophical heritage. As I have earlier said, the eighteenth-century moral philosophers, the nineteenth-century ethnologists, and the majority of the social anthropologists of today have, implicitly or explicitly, taken the natural sciences for their model and assumed that the purpose of anthropology is by prediction and planning to control social change. This assumption is summed up in the phrase 'social engineering'.

It is not surprising therefore that from its earliest years theoretical social anthropology has often been strongly tinged with socialism, especially in France, where both Saint Simon and Comte tried to start positivist religions. It is, I think, clearly the driving impulse behind the work of Durkheim and his colleagues. Their general point of view is well expressed by one of them, Lévy-Bruhl, in an excellent short exposition, *La Morale et la Science des Moeurs* (1903). According to him ethical systems have no effect on conduct whatsoever. They cannot have, because they are merely rationalizations of custom, what is done being right. If a people, for example, kill all twins at birth the practice is moral for that people. Morals are simply rules which actually determine conduct in any society and they therefore vary with variations in the social structure. The moral is what is normal to a given social type at a given phase of development. The task of reason is therefore to mould behaviour by a practical art of ethics derived from a scientific study of social life. This is much the standpoint of almost all writers about social institutions at that period. It was only to have been expected that it should have been shared by many social anthropologists.

Such anthropologists have constantly stressed the

application of their findings to affairs, the emphasis in England being on colonial problems, and in America on political and industrial problems. Its more cautious advocates have, it is true, held that there can only be applied social anthropology when the science of man is much more advanced than it is today; but we find even so cautious and eminent an authority as Professor Radcliffe-Brown writing: 'With the more rapid advance of the pure science itself, and with the co-operation of colonial administrations, we might even look forward to a time when the government and education of native peoples in various parts of the world would make some approach to being an art based on the application of discovered laws of anthropological science.'[1] Less cautious and more popular writers on anthropology, especially in America, have made far-reaching claims for the immediate application of anthropological knowledge in social planning.

If this, what may be called the natural science, view is accepted, it is quite logical to hold further that, since sociological laws are applicable to any society, their main use is rather in the planning of our own society than in controlling the development of primitive societies, which may be regarded as the guinea-pigs of sociological research. After all, it is not only in Africa that there are problems of government, of ownership, of labour migration, of divorce, and so forth. What we discover, for example, about the breakdown of family life among the peoples of our colonial territories can, if a general formula can be derived from the knowledge, be applied to the breakdown of family life in England and America. 'The debt we owe the society that supports us', an American anthropologist, Professor Herskovits, tells

[1] A. R. Radcliffe-Brown, 'Applied Anthropology', *Report of Australian and New Zealand Association for the Advancement of Science*, Section F., 1930, p. 3.

us, 'must be made in terms of long-time payments, in our fundamental contributions towards an understanding of the nature and processes of culture and, through this, to the solution of some of our own basic problems.'[1] What we learn from the yellow and black, as Kipling said in a very different context, will help us a lot with the white.

I have, I hope, made it abundantly and repeatedly clear in these lectures that I do not believe that there can ever be a science of society which resembles the natural sciences. It is not, however, necessary to enter into that question all over again, for I do not think that there is any anthropologist anywhere who would seriously maintain that up to the present time any sociological laws have been discovered; and if there are no laws known, they cannot be applied.

This does not mean that social anthropology cannot be, even in a narrow and technical sense, applied in any way. It only means that it cannot be an applied science like medicine or engineering. Nevertheless, it is a systematic body of knowledge about primitive societies and, like all knowledge of the kind, it can be used to some extent and in a common-sense way in the running of affairs. In the administration and education of backward peoples decisions have to be made, and those responsible for making them are more likely to make wise decisions if they know what the facts are. They are also more likely to avoid serious blunders. Two wars were fought against the Ashanti of the Gold Coast before it was discovered that the Golden Stool of this people, the surrender of which the government had demanded, was believed by the Ashanti to contain the soul of their whole people and could in no circumstances be given up. That anthropological knowledge has been, or can be, of this kind of

[1] Melville J. Herskovits, 'Applied Anthropology and the American Anthropologist', *Science*, 6 March 1936, p. 7.

assistance to administration is evident and has often been stressed by both anthropologists and administrators. It is well summed up in the words written by Professor W. H. Flower in 1884: 'It is absolutely necessary for the statesman who would govern successfully, not to look upon human nature in the abstract and endeavour to apply universal rules, but to consider the special moral, intellectual and social capabilities, wants, and aspirations of each particular race with which he has to deal.'[1]

Obvious though the observation may be, it is I think worth emphasizing that these 'special moral, intellectual and social capabilities, wants, and aspirations' have to be discovered, and also that experience has proved that anthropologists are able to discover them more accurately and quickly than other people. They know what to look for and how to look for it. Time will not allow me to give you more than one example to illustrate how specialist research has been of value to administrations and missions. Among many African peoples one of the ways in which marriage is brought about is by the bridegroom's family and kin handing over cattle to the bride's family and kin. It was for a long time thought that this bridewealth was a purchase and that girls were being sold for cattle. The transaction was therefore condemned by missionaries and forbidden by governments. When it was shown by anthropological research that the transfer of cattle is no more the purchase of a wife than the payment of dowry in western Europe is purchase of a husband, and that the condemnation and abolition of it not only weakened the bonds of marriage and family ties, but also tended to bring about the very degradation of women which they were intended to prevent, a different view began to be taken of it. This is the kind of matter on which laymen might look to anthropology for guidance;

[1] W. H. Flower, The President's Address, *Journal of the Anthropological Institute*, 1884, p. 493.

for the nature and functions of bridewealth can only be discovered by anthropological research.

Besides being in a better position than other people to discover what the facts are, anthropologists are sometimes more likely to estimate correctly the effects of administrative action, because their training accustoms them to look for repercussions where laymen might not look. They may therefore be fairly asked to assist colonial governments, not only by telling them what the facts are, so that policy can be implemented in the light of them, but also by telling them what the effects of any policy are likely to be. It is not an anthropologist's task, however, to suggest what policy should be adopted. Anthropologists may, by their discovery of the facts, influence the means employed in attaining ends of policy and the outlook of those responsible for shaping it, but the knowledge about primitive societies they collect and publish cannot determine what policy is to be pursued.

Policy is determined by overriding considerations. It does not require an anthropologist to tell us that doubtless the people of Bikini Island would be happier if their home had not been turned into a testing ground for atomic bombs. It would also be in vain were anthropologists to explain to governments, as indeed they have done, that if head-hunting among communities in islands of the Pacific is prohibited the peoples concerned may deteriorate and die out. The governments would reply that head-hunting must be stopped regardless of consequences because it is repugnant to natural justice, equity and good government. This is, I think, a good example because it illustrates that ends are determined by values which are axiomatic and do not derive from factual knowledge of circumstances. If those who control policy believe in material prosperity, literacy, democratic institutions, or whatever it may be, they feel that they have to give them to the peoples of their colonial empire.

Whether they are doing right or wrong is a question for moral philosophy, not for social anthropology.

To avoid compromising scholarship anthropologists should eschew questions of policy; and I feel that I should say further that even as fact-finders there is in their dependence for support on governments an element of danger for anthropology and a possibility of conflict between the views of anthropologists and those of governments about what constitutes anthropological research. An anthropologist may be particularly interested, let us say, in some problems of primitive religion and therefore wish to devote a great deal of his attention to them, whereas—governments not generally being interested in such matters—the administration may want chief attention given to problems of labour migration. Or a government may want research done solely into a people's system of land tenure, whereas the anthropologist takes the view that you cannot understand their system of land tenure without a study of their entire social life. Naturally enough, the anthropologist is interested in problems of anthropology, whether these have any practical significance or not. Equally naturally, a colonial government is interested in practical problems, whether they have any theoretical significance or not. Difficulties have arisen on this account. I think myself that the only ultimate solution is for colonial governments to have anthropological posts on their establishments, as they have posts for educationalists, geologists, botanists, parasitologists, and other experts. Some anthropologists will then choose an academic career and others a career in the service of administrations.

I have myself done a considerable amount of research for the government of the Anglo-Egyptian Sudan. As the view of this government about social anthropology corresponds, if I have understood it rightly, with my own, a statement of it will enable me to give you my own opinion about the value of social anthropology to administration. The Sudan Government has, as I have mentioned earlier, for a long time and very generously supported anthropological research. In doing so it has allowed anthropologists to study pretty well where, what, and how they liked. They have chosen the man and let him choose the plan. I think that they have been wise enough to do this because they have never been under the illusion that anything the anthropologist discovered was likely to have any great practical importance. They felt rather that a government ought to some extent to encourage scholarship, and they believed—and this is the point I want to stress—that a knowledge of the languages, cultures, and social life of the peoples of the Sudan has an immense value for administrative officials and others, quite apart from whether it solves any immediate practical problems or not.

One can, I think, look at the matter in this way. If a man were to take a diplomatic or business appointment in France, life would be much more agreeable for him, not to speak of the French, and he would make a much better diplomat or business man, were he to learn the French language and to know a good deal about French social life and the working of their institutions. It is the same with a man living among a primitive people. If he knows what they are saying and what they are doing, and their ideas and values, he will not only have a much deeper understanding of the people but will also probably administer them more justly and effectively.

A seventeenth-century traveller, de la Crequinière, whom I have quoted in an earlier lecture, expresses this point of view succinctly. After giving advice to travellers, based on his experience of the East Indians, to keep an inquiring mind but to remain steadfast in their own religion, to tolerate and try to understand strange customs and to behave well in foreign lands, to avoid falling in love, which is distracting, to avoid gambling and confidence tricksters, and to study history, languages and geography, he concludes: 'He who knows how to travel as he should, will reap great advantages: he will improve his mind by his remarks, govern his heart by his reflections, and refine his carriage by conversing with honourable persons of many countries; and after this, he will be much better qualified to live genteelly, for he will know how to accommodate himself to the customs of different people, and so in all probability to the different humours of those he is obliged to visit: by this means he will never do anything to others, which he knows to be contrary to their inclination; which is almost the only point wherein consists what we now call, the Art of Living.'[1]

I do not believe that anthropological knowledge can be applied to any extent in the arts of administration and education among primitive peoples in any other than in this very general cultural sense—in the influence it has in shaping the attitude of the European towards native peoples. The understanding of a people's way of life generally arouses sympathy for them, and sometimes deep devotion to their service and interests. The native, as well as the European, is then benefited.

I will briefly mention one further particular use social anthropology may have for the peoples whose life is investigated and described. We would ourselves have been richer, and deeply grateful, had some Roman anthropologist bequeathed to us an exact and detailed description of the social life of our Celtic and Anglo-Saxon ancestors. One day native peoples all over the world may be glad to have just such a record of the life of their forbears written by impartial students whose

[1] *Customs of the East Indians*, 1705, p. 159. (Translated from *Conformité des Coutumes des Indiens Orientaux*, 1704, pp. 251–2.)

ambition is to give as full and as true an account as they can.

Social anthropology may occasionally resolve problems of administration. It makes for a sympathetic understanding of other peoples. It also provides valuable material for the historian of the future. But I do not myself attach as much importance to any service it is or may be in these respects as to the general attitudes, or habits of mind, it forms in us by what it teaches us about the nature of social life. It accustoms us to viewing any social activity in any society in the context of the whole social life of which it is part; and also, to see always the particular in the light of the more general.

The social anthropologist aims at revealing the structural forms or patterns which lie behind the complexity and apparent confusion of actualities in the society he is studying; and he does this by seeking to make abstractions from social behaviour and to relate these to one another in such a way that the social life can be perceived as a set of interconnected parts, as a whole. This can, of course, only be done by analysis; but the analysis is made, not as an end—to resolve social life into isolated elements—but as a means—to bring out its essential unity by the subsequent integration of the abstractions reached by analysis. This is why I have stressed that for me social anthropology, whatever else it may be, is an art.

The social anthropologist aims also at showing, by comparing one society with another, the common features of institutions as well as their particularities in each society. He seeks to show how some characteristics of an institution or set of ideas are peculiar to a given society, how others are common to all societies of a certain type, and how yet others are found in all human societies—are universals. The characteristics he looks for are of a functional order, so that he is here again, but on a higher level of abstraction, looking for a dynamic order in social life, patterns which are common to all societies of the same general type and patterns which are universal. Whether he is attempting to reach conclusions about one society or about many or all societies, his procedure is the same: to reach, by analysis, abstractions from complex social actualities, and then to relate these abstractions to one another in such a way that total social relations can be presented as a design, and so perceived by the mind in perspective and as an interconnected whole, with their significant features brought into relief. He is to be judged by whether he succeeds in doing this, and not by whether what he writes is immediately useful.

It is in the light of this conception of the aims of social anthropology that I would ask you to consider its significance for us as persons and its value as a small part of the knowledge of our culture. Since I have this conception of its aims, you will understand why I have emphasized in these lectures that a study of primitive societies is worth pursuing for its own sake, whether or not it can be put to any practical or scientific purpose. I am sure that none of you would hold that a knowledge of ancient Athens, of medieval France, or of renaissance Italy is valueless merely because it does not help us very much in a practical way to solve problems of our own society at the present time, or because it does not aid us in formulating sociological laws. I need not therefore try to convince you that knowledge which cannot be put to any immediate practical purpose, or cannot be reduced to scientific formulae, may yet have great importance both for individuals in their own lives and for our whole society.

Some of you may be thinking, however, and one sometimes hears it said, that it is all very well reading about ancient Athens, medieval France, and renaissance Italy, but who wants to read about a lot of savages? Those who ask this question call us barbarologists. I find this view hard to understand, and it has certainly not been that taken by inquiring minds ever since knowledge of stranger peoples, and in particular of primitive peoples, began to filter into the thought of western Europe. I have remarked in earlier lectures how from the sixteenth century onwards educated men were interested in the reports of travellers about savage peoples, in the remarkable similarities of thought and behaviour no less than in the wide divergences of culture they revealed; and how philosophers were particularly engaged by those reports which described primitive institutions. I fancy that they were more interested in the institutions of the Caribs and the Iroquois than in those of medieval England.

Their curiosity is easy to understand, for primitive peoples must have an interest for anyone who reflects at all on the nature of man and society. Here are men without revealed religion, without a written language, without any developed scientific knowledge, often entirely naked and having only the crudest tools and habitations—men in the raw, as it were—who yet live, and for the most part live happily, in communities of their kind. We cannot imagine ourselves living, far less living contentedly, in such conditions, and we wonder—and I think we *should* wonder—what it is which enables them to live together in harmony, and to face courageously the hazards of life with so little to aid them in their battle against nature and fate. The mere fact that savages have no motor cars, do not read newspapers, do not buy and sell, and so on, far from making them less, makes them more, interesting; for here man confronts destiny in all its harshness and pain without the cushioning of civilization, its anodynes and consolations. No wonder the philosophers thought that such men must live in constant fear and misery.

That they do not do so is because they live in a moral

order which gives them security and values which make life bearable. For closer inspection shows that beneath this superficial simplicity of life there lie complex social structures and rich cultures. We are so used to thinking of culture and social institutions in terms of material civilization and size, that we miss them altogether among primitive peoples unless we search for them. We then discover that all primitive peoples have a religious faith, expressed in dogmas and rites; that they have marriage, brought about by ceremonial and other observances, and family life centred in a home; that they have a kinship system, often a very complicated system and wider than anything of the kind in our own society; that they have clubs and associations for special purposes; that they have rules, often elaborate rules, of etiquette and manners; that they have regulations, often enforced by courts, constituting codes of civil and criminal law; that their languages are often extremely complex, phonetically and grammatically, and have vast vocabularies; that they have a vernacular literature of poetry, rich in symbolism, and of chronicles, myths, folk tales, and proverbs; that they have plastic arts; that they have systems of husbandry which require considerable knowledge of seasons and soils and of plant and animal life; that they are expert fishers and hunters and adventurers by sea and land; and that they have great stores of knowledge—of magic, of witchcraft, and of oracles and divination—to which we are strangers.

It is surely a prejudice and a fashion to hold that these cultures and societies are not as much worth knowing about as others, that an educated man should know about ancient Egypt, Greece, and Rome but need know nothing about Maoris, Eskimoes, or Bantu. This is surely the same mentality as that which centred in post-renaissance and post-reformation time for so long turned its back on the Middle Ages, and centred in space in the Mediterranean and northern Europe treated the history, literature, art, and philosophy of India as of no account. This ethnocentric attitude has to be abandoned if we are to appreciate the rich variety of human culture and social life. The sculptures of West Africa must not be evaluated by the canons of Greek sculpture. The languages of Melanesia must not be treated as failures to conform to the rules of Latin grammar. Magical beliefs and practices are not in the least understood by measuring them by the rules of western science. The hordes of the Australian aborigines are not to be judged against Birmingham and Manchester. Each people has confronted in its own way the problems that arise when men live together and try to preserve their values and hand them down to their children, and its solutions are as worthy of our attention as those of any other people. A primitive society may be small, but is a beetle or a butterfly less interesting than an ox?

This brings me to a more general aspect of social anthropology, what it teaches us, not about primitive societies as such, but about the nature of human society in general. What we learn about one society can tell us something about another and therefore about all societies, whether historical or of our own time.

Let me take some limited and historical examples. Much has been written about the pre-Islamic Bedouin of Arabia, but there are many questions about their social structure which are difficult to answer from the historical evidences. One way of shedding light on these problems is to study the social structure of the Bedouin Arabs of today, who in most respects lead the same kind of life as those of ancient times. Much has been written about the feud in early periods of English history, but here again we are greatly helped towards solving many problems concerning it by a study of how feuds work in barbarous societies of the present day. It is difficult for us now to understand witch trials which took place in, let us say, seventeenth-century England. We can learn a lot about them by a study of witchcraft in central African societies, where people still believe in witches and hold them responsible for damage to their neighbours. One has, of course, to act with great caution in seeking from a study of social phenomena in one society interpretative guidance in the study of similar phenomena in another society; but in fact, however much in some respects the phenomena may differ, in other and basic respects they are alike.

What I am saying is fairly obvious. In every society, however simple, we find some kind of family life, recognition of ties of kinship, an economy, a political system, social status, religious cult, ways of settling disputes and of punishing crime, organized recreation, and so forth, together with a material culture, and a body of knowledge of nature, of techniques, and of tradition. If we want to understand the common features of any kind of institution in human societies in general, and also to understand the different forms it takes and the different roles it plays in different societies, we are clearly aided by a study of the simpler societies as well as of the more complex. What we discover in the study of a primitive society about the nature of one of its institutions makes this institution more intelligible to us in any society, including our own. If we are attempting to understand Islam, for instance, or Christianity or Hinduism, it is a great help towards our understanding of it if we know that certain features of it are universals, features of all religions, including those of the most primitive peoples; that others are features of certain types of religion, and yet others are distinctive of that religion alone.

Fundamentally, I would put the case for social anthropology in this way. It enables us, from one angle, to see mankind as a whole. When we get accustomed to the anthropological way of looking at human cultures and societies we move easily from the particular to the general and back again. If we talk of the family, we do not mean just the family of western Europe of today, but a universal institution, of which the family of western Europe is only one special form with many distinctive peculiarities. When we think of religion we do not think only of Christianity but of the vast number of cults which are practised, and have been practised, throughout the world. Only by understanding other cultures and societies does one see one's own in perspective, and come to understand it better against a background of the totality of human experience and endeavour. If I may revert to my last lecture—Dr. Margaret Mead gained some understanding in Samoa of American problems of adolescence; Malinowski shed light on problems of incentives in British industry by his study of Trobriand exchange of ritual objects, and I think that I gained some understanding of communist Russia by studying witchcraft among the Azande. To sum it all up, I believe that social anthropology helps us to understand better, and in whatever place or time we meet him, that wondrous creature man.

SELECT BIBLIOGRAPHY

GENERAL

Bryson, Gladys, *Man and Society*, Princeton, 1945.
Firth, Raymond, *Human Types*, London, 1938.
Forde, C. D., *Habitat, Economy and Society*, London, 1934.
Haddon, A. C., *History of Anthropology*, London, 1934.
Hodgen, M. T., *The Doctrine of Survivals*, London, 1936.
Kroeber, A. L., *Anthropology*, New York, 1923 (new edit. 1948).
Lowie, R. H., *The History of Ethnological Theory*, London, 1937.
Notes and Queries in Anthropology, London, 1874 (6th edit. to appear in 1951).
Penniman, T. K., *A Hundred Years of Anthropology*, London, 1935.
Radin, Paul, *The Method and Theory of Ethnology*, New York and London, 1933.

THEORETICAL WORKS

Eighteenth Century

Dunbar, James, *Essays on the History of Mankind in Rude and Cultivated Ages*, London, 1780.
Ferguson, Adam, *An Essay on the History of Civil Society*, Edinburgh, 1767.
Hume, David, *A Treatise of Human Nature*, London, 1739–40.
Kames, Lord, *Historical Law-Tracts*, Edinburgh, 1758.
Monboddo, Lord, *Of the Origin and Progress of Language*, Edinburgh, 1773–92.
Montesquieu, Baron de, *De L'Esprit des Lois*, Geneva, 1748. (English trans., *The Spirit of the Laws*, by T. Nugent, New York, 1949).
Saint Simon, Comte de, *Oeuvres de Saint Simon et d'Enfantin*, Paris, 1865.

Nineteenth Century

Bachofen, J. J., *Das Mutterrecht*, Stuttgart, 1861.
Bastian, Adolf, *Der Mensch in der Geschichte*. Leipzig, 1860.
Comte, Auguste, *Cours de Philosophie Positive*, Paris, 1830 onwards.
Coulanges, Fustel de, *La Cité Antique*, Paris, 1864 (English trans., *The Ancient City*, by William Small, Boston and New York, 1882.)
Durkheim, Emile, *De la Division du Travail Social*, Paris, 1893 (English trans., *The Division of Labour in Society*, by George Simpson, New

York, 1933.); *Les Règles de la Méthode Sociologique*, Paris, 1895 (English trans., *The Rules of Sociological Method*, by Sarah A. Solway and John H. Mueller., Glencoe (Illinois), 1938.

Frazer, Sir James, *The Golden Bough*, London, 1890.

Hubert, H., and Mauss, M., 'Essai sur la Nature et la Fonction du Sacrifice', *L'Année Sociologique*, T. 11, Paris, 1897–98.

Maine, Sir Henry, *Ancient Law*, London, 1861; *Village-Communities in the East and West*, London, 1871.

McLennan, J. F., *Primitive Marriage*, London, 1865; *Studies in Ancient History*, London, 1886 and 1896.

Morgan, Lewis H., *Systems of Consanguinity and Affinity of the Human Family*, Washington, 1871.; *Ancient Society*, London, 1877.

Smith, W. Robertson, *Kinship and Marriage in Early Arabia*, London, 1885; *Lectures on the Religion of the Semites*, London, 1889.

Spencer, Herbert, *The Study of Sociology*, London, 1872 onwards; *The Principles of Sociology*, New York, 1882–83.

Steinmetz, S. R., *Ethnologische Studien zur ersten Entwicklung der Strafe*, Leiden and Leipsig, 1894.

Tylor, Sir Edward, *Researches into the Early History of Mankind*, London, 1865.; *Primitive Culture*, London, 1871.

Westermarck, Edward, *The History of Human Marriage*, London, 1891.

Twentieth Century

Benedict, Ruth, *Patterns of Culture*, Boston and New York, 1934.

Cassirer, Ernst, *An Essay on Man*, New Haven, 1944.

Collingwood, R. G., *The Idea of History*, Oxford, 1946.

Durkheim, Emile, *Les Formes Elémentaires de la Vie Religieuse*, Paris, 1912 (Engl. trans., *The Elementary Forms of the Religious Life*, by J. W. Swain, London, 1915.)

Ginsberg, M., *Reason and Unreason in Society*, London, 1947.

Grönbech, V., *The Culture of the Teutons*, 2 vols., Copenhagen and London, 1931. (Trans. from the Danish ed. of 1909–12.)

Hobhouse, L. T., *Morals in Evolution*, London, 1906.

Hubert, H. and Mauss, M., 'Esquisse d'une Théorie générale de la Magie', *L'Année Sociologique*, T.VII, Paris, 1902–3.

Lévy-Bruhl, L., *Les Fonctions Mentales dans les Sociétés Inférieures*, Paris, 1912 (English trans., *How Natives Think*, by Lilian A. Clare London, 1926); *La Mentalité Primitive*, Paris, 1922 (English trans. *Primitive Mentality*, by Lilian A. Clare, London, 1923.)

Lévi-Strauss, C., *Les Structures Elémentaires de la Parenté*, Paris, 1949.

Lowie, R. H., *Primitive Society*, London, 1920.

MacIver, R. M., *Society*, London, 1937.

Malinowski, B., *Magic, Science, and Religion and other Essays*, Glencoe (Illinois), 1948.

Marett, R. R., *The Threshold of Religion*, London, 1909.

Mauss, M., 'Essai sur le Don', *L'Année Sociologique*, N. S. 1, Paris, 1923–4.

Nieboer, H. J., *Slavery as an Industrial System*, The Hague, 1900.

Radcliffe-Brown, A. R., *The Social Organization of Australian Tribes* (*Oceania Monographs*, No. I,) Melbourne, 1931; *Structure and Function in Primitive Society—Essays and Addresses*, London, *In the press*.

Rivers, W. H. R., *Kinship and Social Organization*, London, 1914; *Social Organization*, London, 1926.

Simmel, Georg, *Soziologie*, Leipzig, 1908.

Tawney, R. H., *Religion and the Rise of Capitalism*, London, 1926.

Teggart, F. J., *Theory of History*, New Haven, 1925.

Van Gennep, A., *Les Rites de Passage*, Paris, 1909.

Vinogradoff, Sir Paul, *English Society in the Eleventh Century*, Oxford, 1908; *Outlines of Historical Jurisprudence*, Oxford, 1920.

Weber, Max, *Wirtschaft und Gesellschaft*, 1921–23. (English trans., *The Theory of Social and Economic Organization*, by A. R. Henderson and Talcott Parsons, London, 1947.)

Wiese, Leopold von, *Allgemeine Soziologie*, Munich and Leipzig, 1924.

FIELDWORK MONOGRAPHS

Arensberg, Conrad M., and Kimball, Solon T., *Family and Community in Ireland*, Cambridge, Mass., 1940.

Brown, A. R., *The Andaman Islanders*, Cambridge, 1922.

Drake, St. Clair and Cayton, Horace R., *Black Metropolis*, New York, 1945.

Evans-Pritchard, E. E., *Witchcraft, Oracles and Magic among the Azande*, Oxford, 1937; *The Nuer*, Oxford, 1940.

Firth, Raymond, *We, the Tikopia*, London, 1936.

Fortes, M., *The Dynamics of Clanship among the Tallensi*, Oxford, 1945; *The Web of Kinship among the Tallensi*, Oxford, 1949.

Fortes, M. and Evans-Pritchard, E. E., (editors), *African Political Systems*, Oxford, 1940.

Fortune, R. F., *Sorcerers of Dobu*, London, 1932.

Hunter, Monica, *Reaction to Conquest*, London, 1936.

Junod, H. A., *The Life of a South African Tribe*, 2 vols., Neuchatel and London, 1912–13.

Kuper, Hilda, *An African Aristocracy: Rank among the Swazi*, Oxford, 1947.

Lafitau, Joseph François, *Moeurs des Sauvages Ameriquains*, Paris, 1724.

Malinowski, B., *Argonauts of the Western Pacific, London*, 1922; *Crime and Custom in Savage Society*, London, 1926; *Coral Gardens and their Magic*, London, 1935.

Mead, Margaret, *Coming of Age in Samoa*, London, 1929; *Growing up in New Guinea*, London, 1931.

Nadel, S. F., *A Black Byzantium*, Oxford, 1942.

Peristiany, J. G., *The Social Institutions of the Kipsigis*, 1939.

Rattray, R. S., *Ashanti Law and Constitution*, Oxford, 1929.

Redfield, Robert, *The Folk Culture of Yucatan*, 1941.

Rivers, W. H. R., *The Todas*, London, 1906,

Schapera, I., *A Handbook of Tswana Law and Custom*, Oxford, 1938; *Married Life in an African Tribe*, Oxford, 1940.

Seligman, C. G. and B. Z., *The Veddas*, Cambridge, 1911.

Smith, E. W., and Dale, A. M., *The Ila-Speaking Peoples of Northern Rhodesia*, London, 1920.

Spencer, Sir Baldwin and Gillen, F. J., *The Arunta*, 2 vols., London, 1927.

PREFACE

TO THE OTHER ESSAYS

These lectures and essays might be no more than a heterogeneous miscellany were it not that (apart from the fact that, unlike a symposium, they were written by the same person) they are illustrative of the different levels at which anthropologists find that they have to think and write, those of general theory and method, of literary analysis, and of field research. At each level the experience gained on the others is brought to bear on whatever problems are under consideration. These levels correspond to the way we at Oxford organize the training of students who intend to become professional anthropologists. They are first given a general grounding in theory, for which descriptive ethnography provides the examples. They then apply their knowledge of theory in a systematic study of literary sources presented as a thesis. The final stage is intensive field research, the results of which are presented in a second thesis. The anthropologist has thus at one end of his study to be concerned with broad general principles and at the other with the minutiae of some particular people's behaviour and thought. This operation on different levels makes social anthropology a more complicated study than, for example, history, which is usually on the single level of documentary analysis, for, though it has plenty of methods and techniques, it cannot be said to have a comparable body of explicit theoretical knowledge or anything similar to the observations and participation of our field research. The lectures and essays brought together in this volume are also illustrative of developmental trends in social anthropology, of changes in interest and emphasis, over a period of some thirty years, as our knowledge has increased and some of our theoretical propositions have had to be reformulated accordingly.

The essays fall into three parts, corresponding to the three levels I have mentioned. The first consists of three lectures treating of anthropology and anthropologists in a very general way; the second consists of a lecture and an essay based, the lecture entirely and the essay mostly, on other people's observations; and the third consists of four papers primarily embodying my own observations, with regard to different topics, made during some twenty months research into the way of life of a Central African people between the years 1926 and 1930.

Although some of the points made in the Marett Lecture have been repeated in the lecture delivered at Manchester I have decided to include it in this volume because it stated a point of view very different from, and even contrary to, that of most of my colleagues at the time it was written and had, I venture to think, a catalytic action then required. The lecture delivered at Manchester discusses the relations between social anthropology and history in greater detail. The Aquinas Lecture is an attempt to place sociological and anthropological theories of religion in a general setting of the thought and institutions of their time. Theories purporting to explain the religious beliefs and practices of primitive peoples cannot adequately be appreciated without reference to the social milieu in which they were propounded. The Frazer Lecture gives a sociological interpretation of what Sir James Frazer called divine kingship, the Shilluk people of the Southern Sudan being the *locus classicus* for that subject. The article on Zande kings and princes brings together the impressions made on early European travellers by the rulers of a famous Central African people (called Niam-Niam in much of the literature). Of the four articles based on my own field research among the Azande the first treats of the notions that people have about conception and pregnancy, a subject little studied in detail by anthropologists and one about which much more requires to be known if we are to assess rightly the significance of statements that some peoples in Australia and Melanesia are ignorant of the father's rôle in begetting children. The essay on blood-brotherhood aims at determining the nature of the effective rite, widespread in Africa and found elsewhere, by which a new relationship is established. The essay on Zande theology, or rather on the lack of it, attempts, besides setting forth the evidence, to present a model of how such evidence should be interpreted. Though I stand by the facts recorded in these early essays on conception, blood-brotherhood, and theology and the conclusions reached by analysis of them I would, were I to re-write them today, express myself differently. It stands to reason that points made thirty years ago might be made with less emphasis today. The final essay, on *sanza* or what we now call double-talk, is intended, whilst illustrating the tortuous complexity of a particular primitive language, to direct attention to a subject which offers scope for much original research.

I have left the lectures and essays, much though I would have liked to have recast parts of some of them, almost entirely as they were first written, only here and there substituting for the sake of clarity or consistency one word for another. Such additions as I have inserted in 'Zande Kings and Princes' are marked by square brackets.

I make grateful acknowledgement for permission to republish these lectures and essays to the Editor of *Man* (the Marett Lecture), the Editor of *Blackfriars* (the Aquinas Lecture), the Manchester University Press ('Anthropology and History'), the Syndics of the Cambridge University Press (the Frazer Lecture), the Editor of *Anthropological Quarterly* ('Zande Kings and Princes'), the Editor of *Sociologus* ('Heredity and Gestation as Azande see them'), the Editor of *Africa* ('Zande Blood-Brotherhood'), the Editor of *Sudan Notes and Records* ('Zande Theology'), and the Editor of the *Bulletin of the School of Oriental and African Studies* ('*Sanza*, a Characteristic Feature of Zande Language and Thought').

1

SOCIAL ANTHROPOLOGY: PAST AND PRESENT

The Marett Lecture, 1950

Mr. Rector, Fellows and Scholars, I have been greatly honoured by your invitation to deliver this lecture in commemoration of Rector Marett, a great teacher of social anthropology and my friend and counsellor for over twenty years. I am touched also, Mr. Rector, at delivering it in this familiar hall.[1]

I have chosen to discuss a few very broad questions—questions of method. The considerable advances made in social anthropology during the last thirty years and the creation of new departments in several universities would seem to require some reflection on what the subject is, and which direction it is taking, or ought to take, for anthropology has now ceased to be an amateur pursuit and has become a profession. There is a division of opinion on these matters among anthropologists themselves, broadly between those who regard the subject as a natural science and those who, like myself, regard it as one of the humanities, and this division, which reflects quite different sentiments and values, is apparent whenever there arises a discussion about the methods and aims of the discipline. It is perhaps at its sharpest when the relations between anthropology and history are being discussed, and since consideration of this difficult question brings out the issues most clearly, I shall devote a large part of my lecture to it. To perceive how these issues have come about it is necessary to cast our eyes back over the period of the genesis and early development of the subject.

Eighteenth-Century Origins

A subject of scholarship can hardly be said to have autonomy before it is taught in the universities. In that sense social anthropology is a very new subject. In another sense it may be said to

[1] Delivered in Exeter College Hall, Oxford, 3 June 1950.

have begun with the earliest speculations of mankind, for everywhere and at all times men have propounded theories about the nature of human society. In this sense there is no definite point at which social anthropology can be said to have begun. Nevertheless, there is a point beyond which it is hardly profitable to trace back its development. This nascent period of our subject was the middle and late eighteenth century. It is a child of the Enlightenment and bears throughout its history and today many of the characteristic features of its ancestry.

In France its lineage runs from Montesquieu and such writers as D'Alembert, Condorcet, Turgot, and in general the Encyclopædists, to Saint-Simon, who was the first to propose clearly a science of society, and to his one-time disciple Comte, who named the science sociology. This stream of French philosophical rationalism was later, through the writings of Durkheim and his students and Lévy-Bruhl, who were in the direct line of Saint-Simonian tradition, to colour English anthropology strongly.

Our forebears were the Scottish moral philosophers, whose writings were typical of the eighteenth century: David Hume, Adam Smith, Thomas Reid, Frances Hutcheson, Dugald Stewart, Adam Ferguson, Lord Kames and Lord Monboddo. These writers took their inspiration from Bacon, Newton and Locke, though they were also much influenced by Descartes. They insisted that the study of societies, which they regarded as natural systems or organisms, must be empirical, and that by the use of the inductive method it would be possible to explain them in terms of general principles or laws in the same way as physical phenomena had been explained by the physicists. It must also be normative. Natural law is derived from a study of human nature, which is in all societies and at all times the same. These writers also believed in limitless progress and in laws of progress. Man, being everywhere alike, must advance along certain lines through set stages of development, and these stages can be hypothetically reconstructed by what Dugald Stewart called conjectural history, and what later became known as the comparative method. Here we have all the ingredients of anthropological theory in the nineteenth century and even at the present day.

The writers I have mentioned, both in France and England, were of course in the sense of their time philosophers and so regarded themselves. In spite of all their talk about empiricism they relied more on introspection and *a priori* reasoning than on observation of actual societies. For the most part they used facts to illustrate or corroborate theories reached by speculation. It was not till the middle of the nineteenth century that systematic studies of social institutions were conducted with some attempt at scientific rigour. In the decade between 1861 and 1871 there appeared books which we regard as our early classics: Maine's *Ancient Law* (1861), Bachofen's *Das Mutterrecht* (1861), Fustel de Coulanges' *La Cité antique* (1864), McLennan's *Primitive Marriage* (1865), Tylor's *Researches into the Early History of Mankind* (1865), and Morgan's *The Systems of Consanguinity* (1871). Not all these books were concerned primarily with primitive societies, though those that were least concerned with them, like *Ancient Law*, were dealing with comparable institutions at early periods in the development of historical societies. It was McLennan and Tylor in this country, and Morgan in America, who first treated primitive societies as a subject which might in itself engage the attention of serious scholars.

Nineteenth-Century Anthropology

The authors of this decade, like those of the generation before them, were anxious to rid the study of social institutions of mere speculation. They, also, thought that they could do this by being strictly empirical and by rigorous use of the comparative historical method. Using this method they, and those who followed them, wrote many large volumes purporting to show the origin and development of social institutions: the development of monogamous marriage from promiscuity, of property from communism, of contract from status, of industry from nomadism, of positive science from theology, of monotheism from animism. Sometimes, especially when treating religion, explanations were sought in terms of psychological origins as well as in terms of historical origins.

These Victorian anthropologists were men of outstanding ability, wide learning and obvious integrity. If they over-emphasized resemblances in custom and belief and paid insufficient attention to diversities, they were investigating a real and not an imaginary problem when they attempted to account for remarkable similarities in societies widely separated in space and time; and much of permanent value has come out of their researches. Nevertheless, it is difficult to read their theoretical constructions today without irritation, and at times we feel embarrassed at what seems complacency. We see now that though their use of the comparative method allowed them to separate the general from the particular, and so to classify social phenomena, the explanations of these phenomena which they put forward amounted to little more than hypothetical scales of progress, at one end of which were placed forms of institutions or beliefs as they were in nineteenth-century Europe and America, while at the other end were placed their antitheses. An order of stages was then worked out to show what logically might have been the history of development from one end of the scale to the other. All that remained to be done was to hunt through ethnological literature for examples to illustrate each of these stages. It is evident that such reconstructions not only imply moral judgements but must always be conjectural; and that in any case an institution is not to be understood, far less explained, in terms of its origins, whether these are conceived of as beginnings, causes or merely, in a logical sense, its simplest forms. For all their insistence on empiricism in the study of social institutions the nineteenth-century anthropologists were hardly less dialectical, speculative and dogmatic than the moral philosophers of the preceding century, though they at least felt that they had to support their constructions with a wealth of factual evidence, a need scarcely felt by the moral philosophers, so that a very great amount of original literary research was undertaken and vast repositories of ethnological detail were stocked and systematically arranged, as, to mention the largest of these storehouses, in *The Golden Bough*.

It is not surprising that the anthropologists of the last century wrote what they regarded as history, for all contemporaneous learning was radically historical, and at a time when history in England was still a literary art. The genetic approach, which had borne impressive fruits in philology, was, as Lord Acton has emphasized, apparent in law, economics, science, theology and philosophy. There was everywhere a passionate endeavour to discover the origins of everything—the origin of species, the origin of religion, the origin of law and so on—an endeavour always to explain the nearer by the farther which, in reference to history proper, Marc Bloch calls '*la hantise des origines*'.

In any case, I do not think that the real cause of confusion was, as is generally supposed, that the nineteenth-century anthropologists believed in progress and sought a method by which they might reconstruct how it had come about, for they were well aware that their schemata were hypotheses which could not be finally or fully verified. The cause of confusion in most of their writings is rather to be looked for in the assumption they had inherited from the Enlightenment that societies are natural systems or organisms which have a necessary course of development that can be reduced to general principles or laws. Logical consistencies were in consequence presented as real and necessary connexions and typological classifications as both historical and inevitable courses of development. It will readily be seen how a combination of the notion of scientific law and that of progress leads in anthropology, as in the philosophy of history, to procrustean stages, the presumed inevitability of which gives them a normative character.

The Twentieth Century

The reaction against the attempt to explain social institutions in terms of parallel, seen ideally as unilinear, development came at the end of the century; and though this so-called evolutionary anthropology was recast and re-presented in the writings of Westermarck and Hobhouse it had finally lost its appeal. It had in any case ceased to stimulate research, because once the stages of human development had been marked out further investigation on these lines offered nothing more exciting than attachment of labels written by dead hands. Some anthropologists, and in varying degrees, now turned for inspiration to psychology, which at the time seemed to provide satisfactory solutions of many of their problems without recourse to hypothetical history. This has proved to be, then and since, an attempt to build a house on shifting sands. If I say no more in this lecture about the relation between psychology and anthropology it is not because I do not consider it important, but because it would require more time than I can spare, and also more knowledge of psychology than I possess, to treat adequately.

Apart from the criticism of evolutionary theory implied in the ignoring of it by those, including Rector Marett, who sought psychological explanations of customs and beliefs, it was attacked from two directions, the diffusionist and the functionalist. Diffusionist criticism was based on the very obvious fact that culture is often borrowed and does not emerge by spontaneous growth due to certain common social potentialities and common human nature. To suppose otherwise and to discuss social change without reference to events is to lapse into Cartesian scholasticism. This approach had, unfortunately, little lasting influence in England, partly, no doubt, on account of its uncritical use by Elliot Smith, Perry and Rivers. The other form of attack, the functionalist, has been far more influential, as it has been far more radical. It condemned equally evolutionary anthropology and diffusionist anthropology, not merely on the grounds that their historical reconstructions were unverifiable, but also, and simply, because both were historical approaches, for in the view of writers of this persuasion the history of a society is irrelevant to a study of it as a natural system.

The same kind of development was taking place at the same time in other fields of learning. There were functional biology, functional psychology, functional law, functional economics and so forth. The point of view was the more readily accepted by many social anthropologists because anthropologists generally study societies the history of which cannot be known. Their ready acceptance was also partly due to the influence from across the Channel of the philosophical rationalism of Durkheim and his school. This influence has had, on the whole, not only a profound but a beneficial effect on English anthropology. It injected a tradition which was concerned with broad general questions into the more piecemeal empirical English tradition, exemplified by the way in which theoretical writers like Tylor and Frazer used their material and by both the many firsthand accounts of primitive peoples written by travellers, missionaries and administrators and the early social surveys in this country. On the other hand, if students are not firmly anchored by a heavy weight of ethnographic fact, they are easily led by it into airy discussions about words, into arid classifications, and into either pretentiousness or total scepticism.

The Functional Theory

The functional or organismic theory of society which reigns in social anthropology in England today is not new. We have seen that it was held in their several ways by the early and mid-Victorian anthropologists and by the moral philosophers before them, and it has, of course, a very much longer pedigree in political philosophy. In its modern and more mechanistic form it was set forth at great length by Durkheim and, with special reference to social evolution, by Herbert Spencer. In yet more recent times it has been most clearly and consistently stated by Professor Radcliffe-Brown. Human societies are natural systems in which all the parts are interdependent, each serving in a complex of necessary relations to maintain the whole. The aim of social anthropology is to reduce all social life to laws or general statements about the nature of society which allow prediction. What is new in this restatement of the theory is the insistence that a society can be understood satisfactorily without reference to its past. Almost without exception the eighteenth-century moral philosophers presented their conception of social systems and sociological laws in the form of history in the grand style—a natural history of human societies; and, as we have seen, the enduring passion of their Victorian successors was seeking for origins from which every institution has developed through the working of laws of progress. The modern version of a naturalistic study of society, even if lip-service is sometimes paid to the possibility of a scientific study of social change, claims that for an understanding of the functioning of a society there is no need for the student of it to know anything about its history, any more than there is need for a physiologist to know the history of an organism to understand it. Both are natural systems and can be described in terms of natural law without recourse to history.

The functional orientation, by its insistence on the interrelatedness of things, has been largely responsible for the comprehensive and detailed professional field studies of modern anthropology, such as were entirely unknown to the anthropologists of the nineteenth century, who were content to let laymen collect the facts on which they based their theories. It is also largely due to it that the anthropologist of today sees more clearly than his predecessors that an understanding of human behaviour can only be reached by viewing it in its full social setting. All social anthropologists now accept that the entire activities of primitive societies must be systematically studied in the field, and all have the same holistic approach when they come to set down and interpret their observations.

But a theory may have heuristic value without being sound, and there are many objections to the functional theory. It is no more than an assumption that human societies are systems of the kind they are alleged to be. Indeed in the case of Malinowski the functional theory, in spite of the wide claims he made for it, was little more than a literary device. The theory assumes, moreover, that in the given circumstances no part of social life can be other than what it is and that every custom has social value, thus adding to a naïve determinism a crude teleology and pragmatism. It is easy to define the aim of social anthropology to be the establishment of sociological laws, but nothing even remotely resembling a law of the natural sciences has yet been adduced. What general statements have been made are for the most part speculative, and are in any case too general to be of value. Often they are little more than guesses on a common-sense or *post factum* level, and they sometimes degenerate into mere tautologies or even platitudes. Also, it is difficult to reconcile the assertion that a society has come to be what it is by a succession of unique events with the claim that what it is can be comprehensively stated in terms of natural law. In its extreme form functional determinism leads to absolute relativism and makes nonsense not only of the theory itself but of all thought.

If for these and other reasons I cannot accept, without many qualifications, the functional theory dominant in English anthropology today, I do not assert, as you will see, that societies are unintelligible or that they are not in some sense systems. What I am objecting to is what appears to me to be still the same doctrinaire philosophy of the Enlightenment and of the stage-making anthropologists of the nineteenth century, with only the concept of evolution substituted for that of progress. Its constructions are still posited dialectically and imposed on the facts. I attribute this to anthropologists always having tried to model themselves on the natural sciences instead of on the historical sciences, and it is to this important issue that I now turn. I must apologize to historians if, in considering it, what I say may seem obvious to them. My observations would be hotly disputed by most of my anthropological colleagues in England.

Anthropology and History

In discussing the relations between history and social anthropology it is necessary, if the discussion is to be profitable, to perceive that several quite different questions are being asked. The first is whether a knowledge of how a particular social system has come to be what it is helps one to understand its present constitution. We must here distinguish between history in two different senses, though in a literate society it is not so easy to maintain the distinction as when speaking of non-literate societies. In the first sense history is part of the conscious tradition of a people and is operative in their social life. It is the collective representation of events as distinct from events themselves. This is what the social anthropologist calls myth. The functionalist anthropologists regard history in this sense, usually a mixture of fact and fancy, as highly relevant to a study of the culture of which it forms part.

On the other hand they have totally rejected the reconstruction from circumstantial evidences of the history of primitive peoples for whose past documents and monuments are totally, or almost totally, lacking. A case can be made out for this rejection, though not in my opinion so strong a case as is usually supposed, for all history is of necessity a reconstruction, the degree of probability attending a particular reconstruction depending on the evidence available. The fact that nineteenth-century anthropologists were uncritical in their reconstructions ought not to lead to the conclusion that all effort expended in this direction is waste of time.

But with the bath water of presumptive history the functionalists have also thrown out the baby of valid history. They say, Malinowski the most vociferously, that even when the history of a society is recorded it is irrelevant to a functional study of it. I find this point of view unacceptable. The claim that one can understand the functioning of institutions at a certain point of time without knowing how they have come to be what they are, or what they were later to become, as well as a person who, in addition to having studied their constitution at that point of time, has also studied their past and future is to me an absurdity. Moreover, so it seems to me, neglect of the history of institutions prevents the functionalist anthropologist not only from studying diachronic problems but also from testing the very functional constructions to which he attaches most importance, for it is precisely history which provides him with an experimental situation.

The problem here raised is becoming a pressing one because anthropologists are now studying communities which, if still fairly simple in structure, are enclosed in, and form part of, great historical societies, such as Irish and Indian rural communities, Bedouin Arab tribes, or ethnic minorities in America and other parts of the world. They can no longer ignore history, making a virtue out of necessity, but must explicitly reject it or admit its relevance. As anthropologists turn their attention more to complex civilized communities the issue will become more acute, and the direction of theoretical development in the subject will largely depend on its outcome.

A second question is of a different kind. We ask now, not whether in studying a particular society its history forms an integral part of the study, but whether in making comparative sociological studies, for example of political or religious institutions, we ought to include in them societies as presented to us by historians. In spite of their claim that social anthropology aims at being a natural history of human societies, that is, of all human societies, functionalist anthropologists, at any rate in England, have, in their general distaste for historical method, almost completely ignored historical writings. They have thereby denied themselves access in their comparative studies to the valuable material provided by historical societies structurally comparable to many of the contemporaneous barbarous societies which they regard as being within their province.

A third, and to me the most important question, is a methodological one: whether social anthropology, for all its present disregard of history, is not itself a kind of historiography. To answer this question we have first to observe what the anthropologist does. He goes to live for some months or years among a primitive people. He lives among them as intimately as he can, and he learns to speak their language, to think in their concepts and to feel in their values. He then lives the experiences over again critically and interpretatively in the conceptual categories and values of his own culture and in terms of the general body of knowledge of his discipline. In other words, he translates from one culture into another.

At this level social anthropology remains a literary and impressionistic art. But even in a single ethnographic study the anthropologist seeks to do more than understand the thought and values of a primitive people and translate them into his own culture. He seeks also to discover the structural order of the society, the patterns which, once established, enable him to see it as a whole, as a set of interrelated abstractions. Then the society is not only culturally intelligible, as it is, at the level of consciousness and action, for one of its members or for the foreigner who has learnt its mores and participates in its life, but also becomes sociologically intelligible.

The historian, or at any rate the social historian, and perhaps the economic historian in particular, will, I think, know what I mean by sociologically intelligible. After all, English society in the eleventh century was understood by Vinogradoff in quite a different way from the way it would have been understood by a Norman or Anglo-Saxon or by a foreigner who had learnt the native languages and was living the life of the natives. Similarly, the social anthropologist discovers in a native society what no native can explain to him and what no layman, however conversant with the culture, can perceive—its basic structure. This structure cannot be seen. It is a set of abstractions, each of which, though derived, it is true, from analysis of observed behaviour, is fundamentally an imaginative construct of the anthropologist himself. By relating these abstractions to one another logically so that they present a pattern he can see the society in its essentials and as a single whole.

What I am trying to say can perhaps be best illustrated by the example of language. A native understands his own language and it can be learnt by a stranger. But certainly neither the native himself nor the stranger can tell you what are its phonological and grammatical systems. These can only be discovered by a trained linguist. By analysis he can reduce the complexity of a language to certain abstractions and show how these abstractions can be interrelated in a logical system or pattern. This is what the social anthropologist also tries to do. He tries to disclose the structural patterns of a society. Having isolated these patterns in one society he compares them with patterns in other societies. The study of each new society enlarges his knowledge of the range of basic social structures and enables him better to construct a typology of forms, and to determine their essential features and the reasons for their variations.

I have tried to show that the work of the social anthropologist is in three main phases or, otherwise expressed, at three levels of abstraction. First he seeks to understand the significant overt features of a culture and to translate them into terms of his own culture. This is precisely what the historian does. There is no fundamental difference here in aim or method between the two disciplines, and both are equally selective in their use of material. The similarity between them has been obscured by the fact that the social anthropologist makes a direct study of social life while the historian makes an indirect study of it through documents and other surviving evidences. This is a technical, not a methodological, difference. The historicity of anthropology has also been obscured by its pre-occupation with primitive societies which lack recorded history. But this again is not a methodological difference. I agree with Professor Kroeber that the fundamental characteristic of the historical method is not chronological relation of events but descriptive integration of them; and this characteristic historiography shares with social anthropology. What social anthropologists have in fact chiefly been doing is to write cross-sections of history, integrative descriptive accounts of primitive peoples at a moment of time which are in other respects like the accounts written by historians about peoples over a period of time, for the historian does not just record sequences of events but seeks to establish connexions between them. Nor does the anthropologist's determination to view every institution as a functioning part of a whole society make a methodological difference. Any good modern historian aims—if I may be allowed to judge the matter—at the same kind of synthesis.

In my view, therefore, the fact that the anthropologist's problems are generally synchronic while the historian's problems are generally diachronic is a difference of emphasis in the rather peculiar conditions prevailing and not a real divergence of interest. When the historian fixes his attention exclusively on a particular culture at a particular and limited period of history he writes what we would call an ethnographic monograph (Burckhardt's *Culture of the Renaissance* is a striking example). When, on the other hand, a social anthropologist writes about a society developing in time he writes a history book, different, it is true, from the ordinary narrative and political history but in all essentials the same as social history. In the absence of another, I must cite my own book *The Sanusi of Cyrenaica* as an example.

In the second phase of his work the social anthropologist goes a step farther and seeks by analysis to disclose the latent underlying form of a society or culture. In doing so, he goes farther than the more timorous and conservative historians, but many historians do the same. I am not thinking of philosophers of history like Vico, Hegel, Marx, Spengler and Toynbee, nor of those who can be exclusively particularized as social historians or writers of the *Kulturgeschichte* school like Max Weber, Tawney, and Sombart or Adam Smith, Savigny and Buckle, but of historians in the stricter and more orthodox sense like Fustel de Coulanges, Vinogradoff,

Pirenne, Maitland, or Professor Powicke. It is perhaps worth noting that those historical writings which we anthropologists regard as examples of sociological method generally deal with early periods of history, where the societies described are more like primitive societies than the complex societies of later periods of history, and where the historical documents are not too vast to be grasped and assimilated by a single mind; so that the total culture can be studied as a whole and contained in a single mind, as primitive cultures can be studied and contained. When we read the works of these historians we feel that we and they are studying the same things in the same way and are reaching out for the same kind of understanding of them.

In the third phase of his work the anthropologist compares the social structures his analysis has revealed in a wide range of societies. When a historian attempts a similar study in his own field he is dubbed a philosopher, but it is not, I think, true to say, as it is often said, that history is a study of the particular and social anthropology of the general. In some historical writers comparison and classification are quite explicit; always they are implicit, for history cannot be written except against a standard of some kind, by comparison with the culture of a different time or people, if only with the writer's own.

I conclude therefore, following Professor Kroeber, that while there are, of course, many differences between social anthropology and historiography they are differences of technique, of emphasis and of perspective, and not differences of method and aim. I believe also that a clearer understanding that this is so will lead to a closer connexion between historical and anthropological studies than is at present provided by their meeting points in ethnology and prehistoric archæology, and that this will be greatly to the benefit of both disciplines. Historians can supply social anthropologists with invaluable material, sifted and vouched for by critical techniques of testing and interpretation. Social anthropologists can provide the historian of the future with some of his best records, based on careful and detailed observations, and they can shed on history, by their discovery of latent structural forms, the light of universals. The value of each discipline to the other will, I believe, be recognized when anthropologists begin to devote themselves more to historical scholarship and show how knowledge of anthropology often illuminates historical problems.

Social Anthropology as one of the Humanities

The thesis I have put before you, that social anthropology is a kind of historiography, and therefore ultimately of philosophy or art, implies that it studies societies as moral systems and not as natural systems, that it is interested in design rather than in process, and that it therefore seeks patterns and not scientific laws, and interprets rather than explains. These are conceptual, and not merely verbal, differences. The concepts of natural system and natural law, modelled on the constructs of the natural sciences, have dominated anthropology from its beginnings, and as we look back over the course of its growth I think we can see that they have been responsible for a false scholasticism which has led to one rigid and ambitious formulation after another. Regarded as a special kind of historiography, that is as one of the humanities, social anthropology is released from these essentially philosophical dogmas and given the opportunity, though it may seem paradoxical to say so, to be really empirical and, in the true sense of the word, scientific. This, I presume, is what Maitland had in mind when he said that 'by and by anthropology will have the choice between being history and being nothing'.

I have found, both in England and America, that students are often perturbed at these implications. There is no need for them to be, for it does not follow from regarding social anthropology as a special kind of historiography rather than as a special kind of natural science that its researches and theory are any the less systematic. When therefore I am asked how I think that social anthropology should proceed in the future I reply that it must proceed along much the same lines as do social history or the history of institutions, as distinct from purely narrative and political history. For example, the social historian seeking to understand feudal institutions would first study them in one country of Europe and get to know all he can about them there. He would then study them in other European societies to discover which features were common to European civilization at that time and which were local variations, and he would try to see each particular form as a variation of a general pattern and to account for the variations. He would not seek for laws but for significant patterns.

What more do we do, can we do or should we want to do in

social anthropology than this? We study witchcraft or a kinship system in a particular primitive society. If we want to know more about these social phenomena we can study them in a second society, and then in a third society, and so on, each study reaching, as our knowledge increases and new problems emerge, a deeper level of investigation and teaching us the essential characteristics of the thing we are inquiring into, so that particular studies are given a new meaning and perspective. This will always happen if one necessary condition is observed: that the conclusions of each study are clearly formulated in such a way that they not only test the conclusions reached by earlier studies but advance new hypotheses which can be broken down into fieldwork problems.

However, the uneasiness I have noted is not, I think, on this score, because it must be evident to any student who has given thought to the matter that those who have most strongly urged that social anthropology should model itself on the natural sciences have done neither better research than those who take the opposite view nor a different kind of research. It is rather due to the feeling that any discipline that does not aim at formulating laws and hence predicting and planning is not worth the labour of a lifetime. This normative element in anthropology is, as we have seen, like the concepts of natural law and progress from which it derives, part of its philosophical heritage. In recent times the natural-science approach has constantly stressed the application of its findings to affairs, the emphasis in England being on colonial problems and in America on political and industrial problems. Its more cautious advocates have held that there can only be applied anthropology when the science is much more advanced than it is today, but the less cautious have made far-reaching claims for the immediate application of anthropological knowledge in social planning; though, whether more or less cautious, both have justified anthropology by appeal to utility. Needless to say, I do not share their enthusiasm and regard the attitude that gives rise to it as naïve. A full discussion of it would take too long, but I cannot resist the observation that, as the history of anthropology shows, positivism leads very easily to a misguided ethics, anæmic scientific humanism or—Saint-Simon and Comte are cases in point—*ersatz* religion.

I conclude by summarizing very briefly the argument I have tried to develop in this lecture and by stating what I believe is likely to be the direction taken by social anthropology in the future.

Social anthropologists, dominated consciously or unconsciously, from the beginnings of their subject, by positivist philosophy, have aimed, explicitly or implicitly, and for the most part still aim—for this is what it comes to—at proving that man is an automaton and at discovering the sociological laws in terms of which his actions, ideas and beliefs can be explained and in the light of which they can be planned and controlled. This approach implies that human societies are natural systems which can be reduced to variables. Anthropologists have therefore taken one or other of the natural sciences as their model and have turned their backs on history, which sees men in a different way and eschews, in the light of experience, rigid formulations of any kind.

There is, however, an older tradition than that of the Enlightenment with a different approach to the study of human societies, in which they are seen as systems only because social life must have a pattern of some kind, inasmuch as man, being a reasonable creature, has to live in a world in which his relations with those around him are ordered and intelligible. Naturally I think that those who see things in this way have a clearer understanding of social reality than the others, but whether this is so or not they are increasing in number, and this is likely to continue because the vast majority of students of anthropology today have been trained in one or other of the humanities and not, as was the case thirty years ago, in one or other of the natural sciences. This being so, I expect that in the future there will be a turning towards humanistic disciplines, especially towards history, and particularly towards social history or the history of institutions, of cultures and of ideas. In this change of orientation social anthropology will retain its individuality because it has its own special problems, techniques and traditions. Though it is likely to continue for some time to devote its attention chiefly to primitive societies, I believe that during this second half of the century it will give far more attention than in the past to more complex cultures and especially to the civilizations of the Far and Near East and become, in a very general sense, the counterpart to Oriental Studies, in so far as these are conceived of as primarily linguistic and literary—that is to say, it will take as its province the cultures and societies, past as well as present, of the non-European peoples of the world.

2

RELIGION AND THE ANTHROPOLOGISTS

The Aquinas Lecture, 1959

When I was considering what subject to treat in the Aquinas Lecture,[1] which you had so kindly invited me to deliver, in the state of near-despair one reaches on such occasions I went to an Oxford bookshop where a selection of volumes may be bought for sixpence each and bought one at random in the hope that I might derive some guidance from it. *The True History of Joshua Davidson* (1872) was an at-one-time popular work of fiction by a socialist republican, Eliza Lynn Linton, though it was published anonymously. It is a story of Jesus returning to earth in mid-nineteenth-century England and of how he acted in the situation then confronting him. At the end of the book the authoress says that 'if sociology is a scientific truth, then Jesus of Nazareth preached and practised not only in vain, but against unchangeable Law'. This gave me an idea for my address for, though she was speaking of the doctrines of Political Economy current at that time and as she understood them, it appeared to me that it might be of interest to you were I to discuss the attitude of sociologists, and social anthropologists in particular, towards religious faith and practice. It has been for the most part bleakly hostile.

It is scarcely possible to discuss social science in this country without some reference to its French background. We may regard it, if only for convenience, as beginning with Montesquieu in his great book *L'Esprit des Lois* (1748). In it he set out to discover the laws of social life, the necessary conditions of its existence in its various forms, but he did not, in my opinion, think of these laws in a deterministic or mechanical sense. He frequently discusses

[1] The Aquinas Lecture, delivered on March 7, 1959, at Hawkesyard Priory.

religion, almost always in a naturalistic way, examining people's beliefs simply as social phenomena and endeavouring to determine only what is their social function; and as far as his personal convictions are concerned he is probably to be regarded as a Deist, although in outward matters he remained a loyal son of the Church, in spite of his satirical writings about some of its features, writings which were placed on the Index. From him the line of development of sociological thought in France runs through Turgot and the Physiocrats to the unfortunate Condorcet. Condorcet held that social phenomena are just as natural as those of the inorganic and organic sciences and therefore could be, and should be, studied by the same methods and with the same ends in view as such sciences as physics and biology. There are inexorable laws of social life and social development, and these could be discovered and formulated as a kind of social mathematics, in the light of which a new social world could be constructed. Religion would have no place in it, and certainly there would be no priests, charlatans necessary, no doubt, in early phases of development, but charlatans just the same and also the greatest obstacle in the path of further human progress.

However, the second founder of social science was not Condorcet. It was unquestionably Henri de Saint-Simon, though, because he wrote no comprehensive treatise and for other reasons, that title has gone to Comte. Saint-Simon, whose followers may be regarded as the precursors of totalitarian philosophy, heralds of the Fascist, Nazi, and Communist forms of society, was a greater believer in social laws, in progress, in social planning and the regeneration of mankind; and it is hardly necessary to add that he was an anticlerical and a Deist (of a rather eccentric kind), for almost everybody was at that time who had any pretensions to being a philosopher. Indeed, as Mill remarks in his essay on Bentham, in the more advanced nations of the continent in the second half of the eighteenth century there was scarcely one educated person left who retained any allegiance to the old opinions and institutions. Nevertheless, Saint-Simon realized the necessity of religion in some form or other—'the character of organic epochs is essentially religious'—and he envisaged a secular religion of humanity—man is 'God himself in the finite order'—an idea his followers put into effect—church, dogmas, rituals, pope, and all—with slightly ludicrous results. Even though Saint-Simon wished to reduce Christianity to a system of ethics, the development of his religiosity, set forth in his *Nouveau Christianisme*, published just before his death in 1825 by his followers, alienated his sympathizers among the English intellectuals, including J. S. Mill and Thomas Carlyle, who translated the book; and he became regarded as a crank. It also alienated the British workers, on whom the socialist propaganda of the strangely garbed Saint- Simonian missionaries had at first made some impression, for the combination of religiosity with authoritarianism produced, in the words of one of their educated spokesmen, an impression of 'Gothic barbarity and imposture'. So the Saint-Simonian movement in England, as in France, died out, leaving, however, a heresy which had more lasting influence, the Comtian heresy.

Comte quarrelled with his master, this more or less lunatic genius ('*nullum magnum ingenium sine mixtura dementiae fuit*'): and the pupil, though not so original a thinker, achieved more fame and exercised a wider influence. Indeed, his strange, paranoiac, figure dominated the social thought of the nineteenth century as Montesquieu had dominated that of the eighteenth century. Some of the most used words in his six volumes of the *Cours de Philosophie Positive* are 'necessary', 'indispensable', and 'inevitable'. There are rigid, inexorable laws of social life, determining the necessary conditions of existence of any society at any point of time and also the evolution of every society through the same phases—the theological, the metaphysical, and the positivist or scientific. Such a philosophy of history was clearly incompatible with traditional Christianity or, indeed, with most systems of religious thought. Nevertheless, Comte, like the Saint-Simonians, was a great admirer of the Catholic Church: Protestantism, Deism, and Metaphysical Humanism he could not abide, no expressions of contempt being too severe for them. But if the Church, with its admirable organization, was the mother of civilization and the promoter of personal freedom, all things, alas, have their day. It had to pass as all things have to pass in the course of historical development by the laws of evolution. Catholico-feudal institutions were even then in the final stage of demolition by metaphysical propaganda, which, critical, negative and transitory though it was, and however much one despised it, belonged to an inevitable phase of history; and when the work of destruction was finally accomplished there would emerge the new altruistic, pacific, industrial and scientific age. But later Comte, like Saint-Simon before him, realized that there has to be a religion of some sort and set about founding a new one, a secularist church with himself as high priest, 'an incongruous mixture of bad science with eviscerated papistry' as Huxley acidly called it. Or, to quote one of his countrymen, Georges Sorel, one might as well worship the *Bibliothèque Nationale.* In this country the Comtist cult, supported by George Eliot, George Henry Lewes, and Frederick Harrison among others, has survived into the present day, the Reader in Social Anthropology at Oxford till 1935, Dr. Marett, having been at one time some sort of Comtist; and a Comtist, or Secularist, church still functions in London and, I believe, in one or two other towns; and is not its hagiographical genealogy framed as a curiosity on the walls of Blackfriars' library in Oxford!

At the end of last century and into the first two decades of the present century there was writing, also in France, a man whom we may regard as the third founder of the science which has grown into what we now call social anthropology, Emile Durkheim. He also claimed to be a sociological determinist, who in his earliest essay expresses indignation at Montesquieu's laxity in this respect; though he did not always live up to his claims and the laws he sought were functional rather than historical or evolutionary. Religion had, therefore, to be explained in terms of social function. It is not, as the English anthropologists of his time supposed, an illusion: illusions do not survive centuries and they do not constitute the matrix in which have been formed law, the sciences and the arts. It has an objective basis, the society itself; men worship in the gods symbols of their own collectivities. If it follows from this that there can be no transcendent personal God, it also follows that religion must find a place in every society, for it is a product of the action of social life itself. So we find, at the end of his *Les formes élémentaires de la vie religieuse* (1912), Durkheim, like Saint-Simon and Comte before him, envisaging a secular religion reminiscent of the rationalist religions of the French Revolution, and since, he says, there can be no religion without a church, a secularist church dedicated to the noblest aspirations of mankind.

It has always seemed odd to me how these three men combined a deterministic philosophy, a belief in the regeneration of the human race as an inevitable evolutionary process, with an almost fanatical reforming zeal and at times a vituperative indignation towards all who differed from them. Doubtless, like the Marxists, they felt that, though the process was inevitable, it could be hastened by those who were wise enough to discern its direction and honest enough to declare it. It is also curious that they should have combined evolutionary determinism with a Utopian philosophy. It would seem that the evolutionary laws were to cease to operate when conditions of which they approved should have come about; and in this also they resemble Marxist theoreticians. The objective forces that in the past have governed history at that point pass under man's control and then man makes his own history; in Engels' famous aphorism, 'It is the ascent of man from the kingdom of necessity to the kingdom of freedom.'

What was happening in Great Britain in the period from Comte to Durkheim? Saint-Simonism and Comtism here met with other powerful trends of opinion in intellectual, and then in more popular circles, the principal one being utilitarian doctrines from Adam Smith and Bentham to Mill the younger, those doctrines Mrs. Linton opposed in her novel to the teachings of Jesus. The Utilitarians were unsparing of religion in any shape or form, especially the morbid Bentham, for whom all priests were simple impostors. Another powerful trend was the theory of evolutionary development, first associated with the names Buffon, Lamarck and Erasmus Darwin; and here we may particularly mention Herbert Spencer, not only because he became a leading exponent of evolutionism but also because he may be regarded as the nineteenth-century founder of social science in England, the English Comte, though he would have intensely disliked being so designated. Man, he ceaselessly proclaimed, is subject to invariable laws of development, though these immutable laws are highly complex and most difficult to define. As for religion, it is both untrue and useless; and a basis for morals is much better sought in a scientific study of social life. God, if there is one, is unknowable, and also otiose; but religion is perhaps best explained as the projection of subordination to rulers into propitiation of their doubles after death.

Spencer's dislike of every kind of ecclesiasticism, dogma and ceremony was shared by the social historian Buckle, whose *History of Civilization in England* (1851), little read today, made a great impression on his contemporaries. It is true God exists, but neither he nor human will plays any part in history, which is a record of a sequence of causes and effects of which man is a helpless spectator.

But if Spencer clearly formulated the theory of gradual modification of species or structure, through use or disuse of functions, against the prevailing theory of special creation, and if he extended his evolutionary ideas to include the social or super-organic, it was Darwin and Wallace who in 1858 and following years added the two biological features which caused so great a stir and scandal, the notion of natural selection through the survival of the fittest, an idea which seems to have come to both of them after reading Malthus' *Essay on Population*, and that of the place of man among the primates in the evolutionary process. Both were a further blow to accepted, and it must be added complacent, religious opinion, which reacted violently, uncritically, and even unfairly, suggesting that those who thought like Darwin were not only infidels but were infidels because they wanted to be free from moral restraints. This might not have happened had Darwin at the outset been supported by his fellow scientists, but this was far from being the case. As is well known, Darwin's theories had an enormous influence on sociological thought, as seen, for example, in Bagehot's *Physics and Politics*. As is also well known, Darwin slowly lost his faith, and with it all taste for the arts, during his forty years as a neurotic invalid. As for Wallace, he threw himself into a variety of movements, some sensible, others not—spiritualism, socialism, phrenology, anti-vaccination, anti-colonialism and pacifism.

Another influence which was beginning to make itself felt in the first half of the nineteenth century was biblical criticism, making its first impact on the lay intellectual world in Strauss' *Leben Jesu* (1835), translanted into English by George Eliot, and the writings of Christian Baur; and it gathered momentum as the century advanced, making a further impact in Renan's *Vie de Jésus* (1863) and causing much tribulation among the faithful. Many apparent absurdities in the Scriptures had, of course, been ridiculed by the eighteenth-century Deists—Voltaire, Diderot and others—but now for the first time the Bible was subjected to total, minute, and often devastating literary criticism which was too scholarly to be lightly dismissed as simple prejudice.

In the eyes of orthodox Bible Christians this was bad enough, but worse was to come. Following the success of comparative philology, comparative mythology and comparative religion (a science of religion) began to turn the pagan gods and goddesses, and by implication those of the higher religions as well, into sun and moon and stars and to treat all religious beliefs and rites as phenomena of the same order and, again by implication, of the same validity. This pointed to a relativism in which Christianity was not the one true faith but just one religion among others, all equally false. The famous Max Müller, it is true, trod warily—the Bishop of Gloucester had already condemned attempts 'to put into competition the sacred books of India and the Holy Scriptures'. Not so some of the others, who represent an intellectual movement culminating in Sir James Frazer.

It was in such a climate of Comtism, utilitarianism, Biblical criticism, and the beginnings of comparative religion that social anthropology, as we now understand it, came into being. It was a product, as were ultimately all the others, of eighteenth-century rationalist philosophy, and more particularly of the stream of thought from Hobbes and Locke, through Hume and the Scottish moral philosophers, sceptics and Deists. Its founders were such men as McLennan, Lubbock, Tylor, and, later, Frazer, all great believers in laws of social evolution and in the necessary interdependence of institutions, and all, if one may judge from their writings and from what information one otherwise has about them, agnostics and hostile to religion. Consequently, when they discussed it they tried to explain it away by some theory of psychological or sociological causation, explanations which now seem to us remarkable for their triviality but which were widely accepted at the time. Spiritual Being for Tylor was an illusion, a sort of hallucination brought about by the reflection of immature minds on such phenomena as death, dreams and trance. Religion was also an illusion to Frazer. All are familiar with *The Golden Bough* (1890), in which he sets forth his paradigm of phases of thought through which all peoples pass—magic, religion, and finally science; and you will recollect how in his preface to that book he compares Christian beliefs to venerable walls mantled over with ivy and mosses (venerable but about to be demolished by the battery of the comparative method) and how at the end of it he stands on the shores of Lake Nemi, where once the sacred pagan kings held sway, and listens to the church bells of Rome ringing the Angelus (one religion goes and another comes, and seen from the point of view of rationalism and science they are all much alike, all children of fancy). The purpose of *The Golden Bough* was to discredit revealed religion by showing how one or other of its essential features, e.g. the resurrection of a man-god, are analogous to what we find in pagan religions. The same purpose is only too evident in the writings of Salomon Reinach, a French small-model Frazer—the Mass is a survival of a savage totemic feast, Christ was a mock-king in an annual burlesque, and so forth.

All the leading sociologists and anthropologists contemporaneous with, or since, Frazer were agnostics and positivists—Westermarck, Hobhouse, Haddon, Rivers, Seligman, Radcliffe-Brown and Malinowski; and if they discussed religion they treated it as superstition for which some scientific explanation was required and could be supplied. Almost all the leading anthropologists of my own generation would, I believe, hold that religious faith is total illusion, a curious phenomenon soon to become extinct and to be explained in such terms as 'compensation' and 'projection' or by some sociologistic interpretation on the lines of maintenance of social solidarity. It has been, and is, the same in America. Morgan, the founder of social anthropology in that country, refused to have anything to do with religion and he particularly abhorred ritualistic religion (he was quite shocked by what he saw going on in St. Barnabas' church when he visited Oxford. Needless to say, he detested the Roman Church). Among the last generation of distinguished American anthropologists there was not one, as far as I know, who gave assent to any creed, unless agnosticism be accounted one, or who regarded all religious belief as other than illusion; and I do not know of a single person among the prominent sociologists and anthropologists of America at the present time who adheres to any faith. Religion is superstition to be explained by anthropologists, not something an anthropologist, or indeed any rational person, could himself believe in.

I do not discuss the situation in other countries, for the influences which have chiefly shaped social anthropology in England have either been a native product or have come from France and America. It may, however, be remarked that such sociological writings in other countries as have left their mark on our thinking have been mainly anti-religious in tone. For Marx, as everyone knows, religion was a futile ideological superstructure maintained by, and for, class privilege. Religion, Engels tells us, was one of the means employed by the bourgeoisie to keep the 'lower orders' in their place—'*Die Religion muss dem Volk erhalten werden*' ('religion must be kept alive for the people')—but, he adds, 'no religious tenets will ever suffice to prop up a tottering society'. For Freud it was comparable to obsessional neurosis, the product of wish-fulfilment and the father-complex: does he not call his book on religion *The Future of an Illusion* (1928)? And for Jung, it has little more than a therapeutic value, if I understand him rightly. The best-known Italian sociologist, Vilfredo Pareto, never ceases in his *Trattato di Sociologia generale* (1916) sneering at all and every theological dogma; and though the German sociologist Max Weber cannot be described as being hostile to religion his personal position was negative, or, as he puts it, he was neither anti-religious nor irreligious but 'religiously absolutely unmusical'.

In general, therefore, it may be said that sociologists and anthropologists have been either indifferent or, more often, hostile to religion, though in different ways, for the Catholic agnosticism, if it may be so called, of men like Saint-Simon and Comte was in many ways a different brand of agnosticism from that of men who had a Protestant background like Spencer and Tylor or the Jewish agnosticism of Durkheim and Lévy-Bruhl.

There were, of course, a few who retained their faith, and in the battle some of these earnest souls got shot by their own side to the benefit of their adversaries. I do not see how the Abbé Loisy could have been other than excommunicated, but I think Renan was harshly treated and that it was being over-cautious to have made difficulties for the great Semitic scholar, the Dominican Père Lagrange. It is an old and wise maxim of the Church: *in necessariis unitas, in dubiis libertas, in omnibus caritas.* Protestant scholars were even more vulnerable, for their churches were more committed to defend the Book on which the Reformation was based. Sir Charles Lyell, who regarded himself as a Theist, was denounced because his *Principles of Geology* (1830) seemed to discredit the Pentateuchal accounts of the Creation and the Deluge. What an outcry was raised in the Anglican communion when the courageous Cornishman Bishop Colenso of Natal announced that he was not prepared to accept and did not think that any clergyman should be asked to accept, and furthermore that he was not prepared to teach the Zulus of Natal what appeared to him to be impossible, and therefore incredible, happenings recorded in the books of the Old Testament, especially in Deuteronomy; a challenge for which he was excommunicated by the Bishop of Cape Town in 1863. The founder in this country of comparative philology, comparative mythology, and comparative religion, Max Müller, was also a casualty, though a minor one. He was a staunch Protestant ('the Protestants are better Christians than the Romans') and a devout one, but one of the reasons he was not elected to the Chair of Sanskrit at Oxford in 1860 was that it was said his teaching was subversive of the Christian faith—'unsettling'. Furthermore, he was a German. Then, to give a final example, in the Presbyterian communion, Robertson Smith, one of the most notable biblical scholars and anthropologists of the nineteenth century, was charged before his synod with heresy, his chief offence having been to have written what today would appear to most people a moderate and sensible article on the Bible in the *Encyclopaedia Britannica* in which he made certain critical remarks about the dating, order, and composition of the books of the Old Testament, and although he was not convicted of heresy he was deprived of his Chair of Hebrew at Aberdeen in 1881 for causing a scandal.

On the whole, it may be said that the criticisms levelled at the teaching of the Churches from all sides were most damaging. The Catholics suffered least and the Anglicans most. The Catholic Church counted for too little in England at this time, and being familiar with different modes, or levels, of interpretation of the Bible, it was less committed to a fundamentalist position. Furthermore, an attack on Papistical superstition, however commendable in itself, entailed the dubious company of Anglican divines, the 'state-appointed teachers of rectitude', as Spencer called them, members of a Church which was, in Huxley's words, 'pretty much a preparatory school for Papistry'. It is no mere chance that some of the most influential critics came from dissenting or extreme evangelical homes—Spencer, Darwin, Huxley, Tylor, and the economist Harriet Martineau, are examples—and we may believe that their animosity to revealed religion was not inspired solely by love of truth but was also a reaction to the dreariness of their religious upbringing, and also that their hatred of ecclesiasticism and sacerdotalism was a protest against Tory interests and pride of class as well as against the State Church to which privilege was allied. The non-conformist conscience was more sensitive to social conditions than the Church conscience. It was the 'dissenting vermin that crawl about in dirty alleys' who most felt the needs of the poor. It was the little preachers of the chapels, not the squarsons, who sympathized with the Felix Holts. It must be remembered too that these men were excluded from the universities till 1871, a further grievance to be set against the Church. (In spite of Oxford being the home of reaction, Herbert Spencer was mortified to find that his books were text-books there, whereas that undenominational home of enlightenment, University College, London, would not even have them in its library.) The 'Establishment', as we have now learnt to call them, the few cultured, well-connected, influential and rich who really understand affairs and can control them with urbanity from behind the scenes (I am not certain who they now are, though it appears that the Warden of my college is an *ex officio* member) deplored these Non-conformists, if perhaps not as much as those whom that anecdotal writer Mr. Montagu Williams, Q.C., calls 'men of Eastern origin' or 'very polished gentlemen as far as grease went'.

The melancholic Huxley proved to be the most formidable foe of the State Church. The tactics of this agnostic—he invented the word—for whom, as for Spencer, Tylor and Darwin, all religion began with and is rooted in ghost-worship and all creeds childish, were to challenge some, taken literally, scientifically unacceptable Bible story, such as the Noachian Flood story, and then, having routed his opponents on his own chosen field, to point out that if this story was not historically true there was no reason why one should accept any other Old Testament stories, the authority for all being alike, and, if this were so, then what happens to Christian theology, which must stand or fall with the historical trustworthiness of the Jewish scriptures? This does not follow, but some defenders of the Book played into his hands—Gladstone in particular—by accepting that it did.

It is difficult not to sympathize with the Huxleys rather than with the Wilberforces (the 'Soapy Sams'). It was monstrous that men of science should be attacked, even vilified, for expressing opinions on matters within their own province by men ignorant of these matters. Moreover, there was some truth in Huxley's contention that all Protestantism had ever achieved was to have replaced the infallibility of the Church by the infallibility of the Bible, and some justice in his complaint that those who proclaimed the right of private judgement wished to deny it to him. Moreover, the Bible had become a fetish and the quoting of scriptural texts a nuisance. Dickens is scarcely making a caricature of Jonas Chuzzlewit when he makes him complain of his father's temerariousness in living to over seventy: 'Where's his religion, I should like to know, when he goes flying in the face of the Bible like that!' Also, the

State Church had long been in a deplorable condition, as Methodism bears witness, and it had furthermore become identified with the class interests of the land-owners—Dr. Arnold regarded it as the private preserve of the Tory aristocracy—and of the industrialists, so that anyone in revolt against the Mr. Bounderbys of the time and the appalling conditions of the poor found himself almost inevitably against the endowed and established Church which only too often, when not silent, found some sanctimonious excuse for exploitation (pauperism was due to idleness, improvidence and vice) or was satisfied with moral exhortations and the chill recompense of the hereafter; so it is not surprising that behind the earnestness of the critics they could not entirely conceal their pleasure at her exegetical discomfitures. Anyway, as Huxley very sensibly used to point out, it was no use blaming the scientists, social or otherwise, for deterioration of the Faith. The harm, if such it was, which so many religious people claimed was being done by their inquiries and comments had been done long ago by the Christians themselves and by sceptical philosophers. Why blame the geologists, the anthropologists, and the biblical scholars when the dykes had been breached centuries before?

Nor should we withdraw our sympathy merely because most of the critics were crashing bores, smug and full of intellectual conceit. What could today seem more dreary than the Mills, Spencer, Buckle, Galton, John Morley and the rest of them? But their opponents, the long-winded Gladstones, were equally tedious. Indeed, I must confess that I find the whole period when these controversies were at their height exceedingly tedious: its interminable wars against the weak—Zulus, Ashanti, Benin, Afghans, Burmese, Egyptians, Sudanese and Boers—H. M. Stanley, Lord Randolph Churchill in South Africa, the Prince at Baden Baden . . . and for good measure, though of an earlier vintage, Dr. Arnold at Rugby.

The critics are rather to be blamed, if at all, for allowing indignation, not unmixed with malice, to cloud their scientific judgement. A biologist does not attack some form of animal life, nor does an astronomer denounce the planetary system. Why therefore should those who held, and hold, that religion is just one social institution among others and that all institutions are just as much natural systems, or parts of them, as organisms and celestial bodies, feel called upon to undermine it? This point was well made by Benjamin Kidd in his at one time well-known book *Social Evolution* (1894). If, he said, social scientists were to inquire unemotionally into the social function of a phenomenon so universal and so persistent they would discover that the vitality of societies, even their existence, is bound up with religion, and that it is precisely through religious systems that social evolution, or progress, has been brought about, for it is the most significant of evolutionary forces, the chief agent in natural selection. History shows us that the socially most efficient peoples were, and are, the most religious, and we may therefore draw the conclusion that 'through the operation of the law of natural selection the race must grow ever more and more religious'. This was the pragmatist position taken up, much later, by the social anthropologist Dr. R. R. Marett: 'Religion is all along vital to man as a striving and progressive being.' It was a commonplace of the period. We find it in Sorel, Croce, and many, many others. If what they said is true, it was absurd to describe the higher forms of religion, as Grant Allen did, as so much 'grotesque fungoid growth'.

The point made by Kidd was obvious, and even that dour rationalist hypochondriac Herbert Spencer had to admit at the end of his life that a religious system of some sort is a constituent of every society which has made any progress in civilization and may be a necessary one; and we have already noted the efforts of the Saint-Simonians and Comtists to found secular religions, attempts Kidd considered to be futile because all religions are ultra-rational and based upon beliefs in the supernatural. So were the rationalists' batteries turned on themselves.

Nevertheless, the pragmatic defence of religion could also be an embarrassment, for, though it might seem to be effective as a counter-attack, it was also an avowal of the irrelevancy of the truth or otherwise of theology; and no one is going to accept a religious faith merely because a sociologist says it is socially useful. An even greater embarrassment were the desperate efforts to save the ship by jettisoning its entire cargo. Overboard went prophecies, miracles, dogma, theology, ritual, tradition, clericalism, and the supernatural, everything which Matthew Arnold regarded as unnecessary accretions of folkloristic elements and their derivatives, the products of men's imagination, of their mythopoeic tendencies, of their fascination with thaumaturgic arts—in a word the *aberglaube* of Christianity. Out of what was left Christianity was to be recast. This substitute religion was to be based upon a code of conduct suitable for Victorian gentlemen, a basis suffused with emotion and solid enough to support the slender abstraction, 'the Eternal Power, not ourselves, which makes for righteousness'. The sanction behind right conduct would simply be that it makes for happiness. When a man does right he feels good. Whatever else this reconstruction may have amounted to, it was not the Christian religion of the past, whether Catholic or Protestant, and it was unlikely to appeal to what were sometimes called 'the lapsed masses'.

However, though some social scientists, like Kidd, had second thoughts about religion, in general the battle of the Bible continued as a desultory engagement into the present century, and if it could not be said that either side won a complete victory, it could be said that there appeared to be very little left of the Bible. Bits and pieces of the Old Testament were strewn everywhere, Deuteronomy having been more or less demolished. Nor had the Gospels escaped the barrage, nor even the Acts and the Epistles. Those who sought to retire behind allegorical interpretations, what Huxley called the flight to allegory to escape absurdity, often added to the confusion.

So, many who had been brought up on strict Bible Christianity were thrown into disarray, and the period ends with cries of dismay or of despairing hope: 'Vague half-believers of our casual creeds', 'ignorant armies clash by night', 'I falter where I firmly trod', and so forth.

Looking back, we may sometimes wonder what all the fuss was about. No one today is troubled by Jonah and the whale or Lot's wife or the Gadarene swine, about which Gladstone and Huxley had so memorable a debate; no one cares how many mother-goddesses are brought to light or how many sacred kings are killed; and it incommodes no one that there are many resemblances between Christian rituals and primitive rituals. This is partly because the Churches have ceased to defend positions which it was neither required nor expedient to defend and indeed have learnt to thank the scientists for having rid them of encumbrances: 'Such a release of religion from the bonds of imperfect science is all to the good,' says Whitehead with much good sense. But it is also because the successors to these scientists are more or less indifferent, feeling that as religion no longer dominates thought as it used to do, even in the popular fiction of the time, there is little motive for attacking it. The earlier generation argued unceasingly about religious matters because they cared strongly about them, and although they argued about such topics as Lot's wife and the Gadarene swine, which do not appear to us today to have the importance they attached to them, they realized that more fundamental issues were at stake. Even those who were hostile to Christianity could not escape the religious climate of the time. To be hostile is at least a kind of tribute. But by the end of the century the climate had changed. The Canadian naturalist and Darwin's faithful admirer, Romanes (who endowed a famous lecture at Oxford), was regarded as slightly odd when, after having written under a nom-de-plume an attack on religion in 1876, he rather apologetically said that he had come to see 'that faith is intellectually justifiable', adding, however, and humbly, 'I as yet have not that real inward assurance'. It was no longer thought remarkable that a scientist should say that he was an agnostic, but rather that he should say that he was not, as Lord Kelvin occasioned surprise by doing in 1900; and the scientist was in this matter not peculiar but representative of the intellectual society of the time, for it was no longer thought to be daring in such circles to be an agnostic. Indeed, as Engels, with his attractive, if heavy, irony, remarks, writing round about 1880, the introduction and spread of salad oil in England had been accompanied by the spread of continental scepticism, till agnosticism, if not yet considered quite 'the thing' was at least more respectable than the more extreme forms of Dissent (he had much contempt for the scientific man who, instead of calling himself plainly a materialist, 'translates his ignorance into Greek and calls it agnosticism'). People increasingly ceased to know even what they were indifferent about, and even to declare oneself an agnostic seemed to be a rather pointless commitment. One might almost have said with Dickens' Mr. Tigg, 'I don't even believe that I don't believe, curse me if I do!'

Once it became accepted that the controversies of the past for the most part lacked both significance and substance, and once also a climate of indifference prevailed, it is understandable that a spirit of mutual tolerance should bring to an end disputations between the religious and the natural scientists. But this was only possible because fundamentally there never were any real grounds for dispute between what natural science teaches about the nature of the physical world and what the Churches teach about faith and morals. After all, there cannot be a stronger assertion of natural law than belief in miracles. But this is not the case between the claims of social scientists, or very many of them, and those of the Churches. Here then there is still conflict, and there is bound to be, for, as Mrs. Linton's character saw, sociological determinism and the teachings of Jesus are irreconcilable.

I have tried to give you a sketch of the historical development leading up to the present-day situation to show how social anthropology has been the product of minds which, with very few exceptions, regarded all religion as outmoded superstition, suited no doubt to a pre-scientific age and historically justified, like classes in the eyes of the Marxists, for a given period, but now useless, even without ethical value, and worse than useless because it stood in the way of a rational regeneration of mankind and social progress. It was taken for granted that the theological interpretation of phenomena had been ousted from one department of nature after another and that scientific investigations had only to be extended into social life for its exclusion from the world of reality to be complete. All that would be left to theology then would be some vague metaphysical conceptions. This was the theme of Tyndall's Presidential Address to the British Association for the Advancement of Science at Belfast in 1874; and Huxley stated the matter succinctly in 1892: 'As natural knowledge has widened, supernatural knowledge has shrunk and has grown vague and questionable; and the historical evolution of humanity is being more and more accompanied by a co-ordinate elimination of the supernatural from the occupation of men's thoughts.'

I have attempted no more than to present a fragment of a chapter of the history of certain ideas. Such as I have described it has been the attitude of anthropologists towards religion. I do not discuss it beyond saying that I believe we shall not hear much more of sociological laws as they have been conceived of by so many writers of the past, and indeed of the not so distant past, and that that will be much to the benefit of anthropology; though if the anthropologists of my own generation take the same view they have yet to say so. Moreover, and of course, if the past claims of sociology and anthropology cannot in this respect, as I think, be sustained this would prove nothing with regard to any religion except that it is not contradicted by the conclusions of these particular branches of knowledge. It would merely answer the question posed by Joshua Davidson's biographer. Nor would it mean that the believers among anthropologists would be more or fewer than they have been and are, for the study of anthropology probably affects faith little either one way or the other.

I have only to add that the position today in Great Britain is much what it has been in the past, save in one particular. The majority of anthropologists are indifferent, if not hostile, to religion —atheists, agnostics, or just nothing—and a minority are Christians. The particular is that of the Christians a considerable proportion are Catholics. In fact the situation is more or less that on the one side are the indifferents and on the other side the Catholics with, as far as I am aware, little in between. Here again, I believe there is nothing in the nature of anthropology which has brought about this situation, for it would seem to be a general tendency in the intellectual life of our times—a realization, as Comte long ago most clearly saw, that Protestantism shades into Deism and Deism into agnosticism, and that the choice is between all or nothing, a choice which allows of no compromise between a Church which has stood its ground and made no concessions, and no religion at all.

3

ANTHROPOLOGY AND HISTORY[1]

1961

In 1950 I delivered the Marett Lecture at Oxford.[2] In it I said that I regarded social anthropology as being closer to certain kinds of history than to the natural sciences. I will not say that there was a storm of protest, but I had certainly, as the criticisms levelled at me showed, run into a bad patch of anti-historical prejudice. The influence in this country of Malinowski and Radcliffe-Brown, both extremely hostile to history, was still dominant; but elsewhere too there had been hostility, or at least indifference, to historical method. Durkheim, though perhaps not anti-historical, had been ahistorical, at any rate in the sense that his developmental studies were in the field of evolutionary typology rather than of history proper. His attitude to history was ambiguous and cannot, I think, be accepted.[3] In spite of appearances, on the whole anthropology in the United States, as Kroeber has said, had been fundamentally 'anti-historical in tendency';[4] and even the *Kulturkreislehre* school in Germany and Austria, though historical in form, took its concepts in large measure, as Kluckhohn has observed,[5] not from history but from the natural sciences, for example, its basic concepts of *Schichten* (layers or strata).

It is easy to understand how this turning away from history came about. The precursors and founders of our science had

[1] A Lecture delivered in the University of Manchester with the support of the Simon Fund for the Social Sciences.

[2] Evans-Pritchard, E. E., 'Social Anthropology: Past and Present', *Man*, 1950, No. 198.

[3] Durkheim, E., *L'Année Sociologique*, vol. 1, 1898, 'Preface'; vol. 2, 1899, 'Preface'.

[4] Kroeber, A. L., 'History and Science in Anthropology', *American Anthropologist*, 1935, p. 558.

[5] Kluckhohn, C., 'Some Reflections on the Method and Theory of the Kulturkreislehre', *American Anthropologist*, 1936, pp. 166–7.

attempted, mistaking irreversibility for inevitability, to formulate laws of historical development by which all human societies pass through a determined succession of stages. Even those who did not do this (*e.g.*, Adam Ferguson, John Millar, Sir Henry Maine, Robertson Smith) sought to explain any institution in terms of its origins, or at any rate of its antecedents, which is the characteristic feature of historicist methodology. The so-called functionalist critics of these (also so-called) evolutionary theories had no difficulty in exposing their inadequacies, but a somewhat similar way of handling ethnological facts is scarcely concealed in their own procedures. The search for diachronic laws was for a time to be abandoned in a search for synchronic laws; but it is precisely, as I think Comte saw, the diachronic laws which must first be established for they alone can validate the synchronic laws. Alexander Spoehr has neatly expressed the point: 'the very meaning of functional dependence is that change in one variable results in change in a dependent variable'.[1] On both sides confusion was due, I believe, to failure to understand the difference between natural and normative laws, a failure for which Montesquieu must take some of the blame. Further confusion was added by the fact that while the functionalists were getting their sights on the evolutionary writers the (once again so-called) diffusionists were already sniping at them, holding that social and cultural developments are brought about by contacts of peoples and borrowing of ideas, techniques, and institutions rather than through the operation of evolutionary laws, which are a fatuous abstraction. But the diffusionists were often as uncritical and dogmatic as those whose views they attacked, and sometimes they attempted to formulate universal laws not fundamentally different from those of their opponents. As the diffusionists claimed that they used historical methods of research their inattention to rules of evidence caused a further revulsion from history.

The functionalist critics of both evolutionists and diffusionists should have challenged them, not for writing history, but for writing bad history. As it was, they dropped the history and kept the pursuit of laws, which was often precisely what made the history bad. Moreover, they were ignorant of historical research and seem to have thought that the spurious history they were

[1] Spoehr, A., 'Observations on the Study of Kinship', *American Anthropologist,* 1950, p. 11.

attacking was typical of history as a whole, and so rejected historical explanations of any kind. They justified this by a methodological distinction between generalizing sciences (thus classing social anthropology with the natural sciences) and particularizing sciences like history. This would be legitimate were history merely a record of a succession of unique events and social anthropology a set of general propositions; but in practice social anthropologists today generalize little more than historians do. They do not deduce facts from laws or explain them as instances of laws, and if they see the general in the particular, so does the historian.

Here we must distinguish between types of history, if only roughly and for the purpose of exposition. I wish to make it clear that I am not speaking of those historians who are content to write narrative histories, *histoire-historisante*, battle-history, a history of great events, mostly political. Nor am I speaking of the philosophers of history from Vico and Bossuet to Hegel and Dilthey and the Spenglers and Toynbees of today, those writers of whom Professor Aron speaks so sadly.[1] I am speaking of the *historiens-sociologues*, those who are primarily interested in social institutions, in mass movements and great cultural changes, and who seek regularities, tendencies, types, and typical sequences; and always within a restricted historical and cultural context. Perhaps I should give now a few examples of those I have in mind. Others will be mentioned later, but shall we start with the names of Maitland, Vinogradoff, Pirenne, Bloch, Lucien Febvre and Glotz? Such historians speak as gaily as we of organisms, patterns, complexes, networks of relations, intelligible wholes, *Zusammenhang*, *ensembles*, principles of coherence, *un tout*, etc. History is not a succession of events, it is the links between them. And like us, sociological historians have their models and ideal types to help them to represent the nature of the real. Marx and Weber are examples, and if it be objected that they are philosophers of history we might, following Marrou,[2] cite Fustel de Coulanges. *Civitas*, feudality, class, capitalism, revolution, are all general abstractions implying an ideal type.

Indeed I do not see how there can be an abstraction which is not a generalization as well. No events are unique. The battle of Hastings was only fought once, but it belongs to the class 'battle', and it is only when it is so considered that it is intelligible, and

[1] Aron, R., *Introduction à la Philosophie de l'Histoire*, 1948, p. 285.

[2] Marrou, H-I., *De la Connaissance Historique*, 1954, p. 161.

hence explicable, for, for the historian, intelligibility is explanation; and this, I suppose, is why Cassirer calls historical knowledge a branch of semantics or hermeneutics.[1] Another version of the generalizing versus particularizing sciences theme is the statement sometimes made that social anthropology is much more comparative than history and that this is as it should be, since it is the object of a natural science to pick out similarities and of history to pick out differences. The truth of the matter is this: both sociological historians and social anthropologists are fully aware that any event has the characters of uniqueness and of generality, and that in an interpretation of it both have to be given consideration. If the specificity of a fact is lost, the generalization about it becomes so general as to be valueless (this is what has happened to several of our categories, for example, 'tabu', 'totemism', and more recently 'lineage'; the general statements about phenomena of a certain type, or supposed type, have become so general as to have lost all significance). On the other hand, events lose much, even all, of their meaning if they are not seen as having some degree of regularity and constancy, as belonging to a certain type of event, all instances of which have many features in common. King John's struggle with his barons is meaningful only when the relations of the barons to Henry I, Stephen, Henry II, and Richard are also known; and also when the relations between the kings and barons in other countries with feudal institutions are known; in other words, where the struggle is seen as a phenomenon typical of, or common to, societies of a certain kind. The specificity of King John and Robert FitzWalter as individuals loses much of its importance when they are viewed in their rôles as representatives of a characteristic set of social relations. Of course, things would have been in some respects different if someone else had been in John's place, but they would have been in other, and more fundamental, respects the same. An historical fact thus shorn of its unique features escapes also temporality. It is no longer a passing incident, a sort of accident, but is, as it were, taken out of the flux of time and achieves conceptual stability as a sociological proposition. When we speak of 'Gresham's law' we have transcended the uniqueness of Henry VIII's debasement of the currency and Sir Thomas Gresham's high-handed and unscrupulous activities in the Low Countries.

*

[1] Cassirer, E., *An Essay on Man*, 1944, p. 195.

I now turn to the consequences for social anthropology of its breach with history. I will enumerate some of them briefly.

1. Anthropologists have tended to be uncritical in the use of documentary sources. It does not seem to have occurred to Frazer in citing source after source in *The Golden Bough* to have indicated on what grounds he accepts their authority. In his *Elementary Forms of the Religious Life* Durkheim subjects other theorists of religion to remorseless criticism, but not the writers about the Australian Aboriginals on which he bases his own. So elementary a precaution applies also to our own field monographs, which we take far too much on trust. I am sure that few of us would satisfy all the requirements of those stern, if somewhat unimaginative, arbiters of historical method, Langlois and Seignobos.[1] It is sometimes forgotten that the social anthropologist relies on direct observation only in his rôle of ethnographer and that when he starts to make comparative studies he has to rely on documents, just as the historian does. The relevance of the techniques of historical criticism has, it is only fair to add, been recognized by some of the more historically-minded ethnologists, German writers in particular, but many anthropologists seem to be oblivious of them.

2. Anthropologists have seldom made very serious efforts to reconstruct from historical records and verbal tradition the past of the people they have studied. It was held that this was an 'antiquarian' interest and that it was irrelevant to a functional study of institutions to know how they have changed. It must however now be obvious that in the case of most primitive societies, if the anthropologist is desirous of understanding the nature of their indigenous institutions, he can only do so with the aid of documents and of verbal recollections. Even so early an observer as Roscoe (in the 1880's) had to present us with a reconstruction from verbal accounts of the functioning of the court and administration of the Baganda kings.[2] I am aware that in recent years anthropologists have paid more attention to the histories of primitive peoples, but they have seldom gone beyond what is sometimes called sketching in the historical background. We have not yet learnt, I venture to say, how to treat historical material sociologically. (I would add a plea that as far as possible verbal traditions be recorded in the form of texts, which permit the sources to speak for themselves and in

[1] Langlois, Ch. V. and Seignobos, Ch., *Introduction aux Études Historiques*, 1898, *passim*.

[2] Roscoe, J., *The Baganda*, 1911.

their own idiom and without selection and interpretation by the ethnographer, as well as bearing witness that he really understands a language and its structure.)

3. Owing to lack of such reconstructions the impression is given that prior to European domination primitive peoples were more or less static, and while this may be true for some, it is certainly untrue for others; among the many examples Africa can furnish, I mention the Zulu, the Basuto, the Barotse, the Azande, and the Mangbetu. In some parts of the world, as in some parts of Africa, in North America, and in the Arctic regions there are documentary evidences which enable us at least to indicate what sort of developments have taken place over several centuries. Without knowing them we view a society in false perspective, two-dimensionally; and I agree with Boas when he says that to have an intelligent understanding of a complex phenomenon 'we have to know not only what it is, but also how it came into being'.[1] I am speaking of ethnographical history. Ethnological research raises somewhat different questions. All that need be said here under that heading is that while such research is legitimate it can be valuable only if exercised, as Sapir has warned us,[2] with the greatest caution and the most rigorous adherence to rules of evidence. I give for examples the conclusion that there were Indonesian contacts with Madagascar (Tylor's demonstration) and that some of the more important African food-plants came from America after its discovery by Europeans.

4. A people's traditional history is important for the further reason that it forms part of the thought of living men and hence part of the social life which the anthropologist can directly observe. We have to distinguish the effects of an event, the battle of Waterloo for instance, from the part played in the life of a people by the memory of the event, its representation in oral or written tradition, between *Geschichte* and *Historie*, *storia* and *storiografia*. It is in the second sense of history, I suppose, that Croce says that all history is contemporary history,[3] but he does not put the matter so well as Collingwood,[4] who saw the history of the past incapsulated in a context of present thought, and though thus belonging

[1] Boas, F., 'History and Science in Anthropology: a Reply', *American Anthropologist,* 1936, p. 137.

[2] Sapir, E., *Time Perspective in Aboriginal American Culture, a Study in Method,* 1916, *passim.*

[3] Cassirer, E., *ibid.*, p. 178.

[4] Collingwood, R. G., *An Autobiography,* 1939, p. 114.

to the present it is separated from it. Anthropologists of today and yesterday, owing to lack of interest in history, have not in this matter asked themselves some important questions. Why among some peoples are historical traditions rich and among others poor? Almost seventy years ago Codrington[1] noted that 'A point of difference between the Polynesian and Melanesian sections of the Pacific peoples is the conspicuous presence in the former, and the no less conspicuous absence in the latter, of native history and tradition'; but he gives no reason for this. Again, Dr. Southall has recently remarked[2] that knowledge and interest in past events among the Alur is much greater than among neighbouring peoples to the west of the Nile and Lake Albert, but he likewise does not suggest why this should be so. Another question concerns the content of tradition. What sort of events are remembered and to what social attachments and rights do they relate (*e.g.*, the rights of a family or clan to lands or the rights of a line of descent to office)? Malinowski[3] has paid some attention to this matter, but not systematically, and to 'myth' rather than to history. Then, what mnemonics are employed as points of reference in tradition—features of landscape (history is often attached to places rather than to peoples, as de Calonne[4] has pointed out, or, as Frederica de Laguna[5] has remarked, speaking of the Tlingit of Alaska, peoples conceptualize their geography in history); features of the social structure (genealogies, age-sets, royal successions); and artifacts (heirlooms)? Then again, to what extent do environmental conditions affect tradition and a people's sense of time? Travellers in Central Africa have remarked how all material evidences of an invasion, a migration, an occupation, pass away, in the absence of stone structures, in a few years with the gnawing of termites and the growth of vegetation, and with the evidences perhaps also memory of the events. The student of historical traditions thus has a triple rôle to play: recorder, historian, and sociologist. He records a people's traditions, he assesses their historical validity and gives them a time notation (the record at this stage looks like a monkish chronicle with a commentatorial critique), and finally he makes a sociological interpretation of them.

[1] Codrington, R. H., *The Melanesians*, 1891, p. 47.
[2] Southall, A. W., *Alur Society*, 1953, p. 5.
[3] Malinowski, B., *Myth in Primitive Psychology*, 1926, *passim*.
[4] Calonne-Beaufaict, *A.* de, *Azande*, 1921, pp. 8–9.
[5] Laguna, F. de, *The Story of a Tlingit Community*, 1960, pp. 16 *seq.*

5. It is a measure of the lack of interest anthropologists have shown in the past of the simpler societies that they have made little attempt—Malinowski[1] was an exception—to make a clear differentiation between history, myth, legend, anecdote, and folklore. Let us consider for a few moments how myth is treated. If the anthropologist does not use the blanket-word 'tradition' beneath which to include all stories about the past he tends to use 'history' to refer to what seems to him to be more or less probable, and 'myth' to refer to what seems to him to be improbable or impossible. But myth and history are in important respects different in character, not just in the degree to which they can be substantiated by appeal to evidence or to the laws of natural science. Hence a story may be true yet mythical in character, and a story may be false and yet historical in character. I cannot more than touch on so large a question and must be content to state baldly some distinctive characteristics of myth. It is not concerned so much with a succession of events as with the moral significance of situations, and is hence often allegorical or symbolical in form. It is not incapsulated, as history is, but is a re-enactment fusing present and past. It tends to be timeless, placed in thought beyond, or above, historical time; and where it is firmly placed in historical time, it is also, nevertheless, timeless in that it could have happened at any time, the archetypal not being bound to time or space. Then the very improbabilities, even absurdities, in many myths are not to be taken, as in an historical record, literally and hence as naïvety and credulity, but are of the essence of myth which, just because the events lie outside human experience, demands an act of will and of imagination. Then, myth differs from history in that it is regarded differently by the people to whose culture both belong. They do not regard historical happenings and mythical happenings as happenings of the same order. No Greek, except on the stage, ever saw Cloud-gathering Zeus, Keen-eyed Athene, or Hermes the Speedy-comer.

6. I now turn to a rather different set of consequences of anthropologists ignoring history. We deal with social facts, and a vast quantity of such facts are in the corpora and registers of historians and in their general and special histories, and if any generalizations are to be made which are to hold good for all, or most, phenomena of the same kind the data of history must be used,

[1] Malinowski, B., *ibid.*, *passim*.

even if only selectively and to test conclusions reached by studies of primitive societies. Moreover, the history of periods in which there are many close analogies to what the anthropologist studies in contemporaneous primitive societies can furnish us with terms and concepts which, used with discretion, can be of great value to us. I am thinking of such periods as those of the Merovingians and Carolingians; but I have in mind also sociological historians of any period. I cite a few names (mostly of persons with whose writings I was familiar in my student days) other than those I have already mentioned: Guizot, Gierke, Kovalevsky, Savigny, Petit-Dutaillis, Alfred Zimmern, Ganshof, Fichtenau, or such historians of modern times as Max Weber and Tawney on capitalism and Calvinism, Wright on Elizabethan bourgeois culture, and the Hammonds on village, town, and skilled labourers. However, the histories nearest to our own writings are those of early periods, partly for the reason I have given and partly also, I suppose, because, in the paucity of detailed information about events and personalities, their authors have to treat of institutions and social structures, much as we do; though it will not have escaped you that a good number of the names I have mentioned are those of lawyers—men accustomed to relating particular cases to general principles—(as, indeed, were those of some of the men we regard as the founders of social anthropology: Maine, Bachofen, McLennan, Morgan, etc.). Many historians have been as much sociologists as historians, for example, Grönbech, the historian of the Teutons, Pederson, the historian of the Hebrews, and Henri Hubert, the historian of the Celts. History and sociology fuse in the writings of economic historians (*e.g.*, Rostovtzeff and Simiand), historians of ideas (*e.g.*, Troeltsch and Nygren), historians of art (*e.g.*, Hauser), the school, mostly French, of the historical geographers (Vidal de la Blache has the place of honour), and, perhaps one should add, some historians of languages and military historians.

7. Furthermore, in turning our backs on history we have turned them on the builders of our science who, up to as late as Hobhouse and Westermarck, had as their primary aim to discover the principles or developmental trends in social evolution, an aim which can only be attained if the facts of history are used. Some contemporaneous anthropologists do indeed speak of 'social change', but this expression can mean no more than 'history', and it is evident that the experimental situation of history is much deeper and more

varied than anything anthropologists can observe of primitive societies changing in contact with European civilization.

8. Now, I would say that the tendency in the past, and even today, to overestimate what are called functional ethnographic studies of primitive societies at the expense of developmental studies, and even to ignore historical facts altogether, has prevented us from testing the validity of some of the basic assumptions on which our studies have for long rested, that for example, there is an entity which can be labelled 'society' and that such an entity has something called a 'structure', which can be further described as a set of functionally interdependent institutions or sets of social relations. These are analogies from biological science and, if they have had their uses, they have also proved to be highly dangerous. On them has been based the argument that just as we can understand the anatomy and physiology of a horse without requiring to know anything about its descent from its five-toed ancestor, so we can understand the structure of a society and the functioning of its institutions without knowing anything about its history. But a society, however defined, in no way resembles a horse, and, mercifully, horses remain horses—or at least they have done so in historic times—and do not turn into elephants or pigs, whereas a society may change from one type to another, sometimes with great suddenness and violence. Do we then speak of a society at different points of time or do we speak of two different societies? Except in a few very remote parts of the world, there are no primitive societies which have not already undergone vast changes. New social systems have come into being, and it is precisely in relation to such historical changes that such terms as 'society', 'structure', and 'function' have to be defined. Indeed, I would say that a term like 'structure' can only be meaningful when used as an historical expression to denote a set of relations known to have endured over a considerable period of time. Some have tried to wriggle out of the difficulties involved in the study of primitive societies in process of rapid transformation by extending the organic analysis and saying that they are then in a pathological condition, but though there may be a means of discovering what is normal to societies of a certain type in the sense of what is general in, or common to, them, one cannot speak of 'normal' in the sense of the physiological analogy, because what is normal in a certain type of society may be abnormal in the type of society into which it is developing, and

vice versa. I do not think that Durkheim succeeded in giving a satisfactory definition of social pathology.

Moreover, I think it must be accepted that far from the history of a society or of an institution being irrelevant to a functional study of it, we only fully understand it when we can view it not only in the present but also retrospectively, for, as we all know from our personal experience of events, there is a sense in which it is true that we can know more about the past than about the present. We know what its potentialities were and what were its enduring qualities. De Tocqueville knew much better than anyone who took part in the French Revolution what, sociologically speaking, was happening at the time, and he even had a greater knowledge of the plain facts. Indeed, it has often been pointed out that vast social changes have taken place without even the clearest contemporary minds being conscious of what was happening, and —here now is the point I wish to establish—the nature of the institutions involved in the process of change could not adequately have been understood till placed in the crucible of history. Professor Lévi-Strauss,[1] though from a rather different viewpoint, has made much the same observation, that those who ignore history condemn themselves to not knowing the present, because historical development alone permits us to weigh and to evaluate in their respective relations the elements of the present. The point which I think we both wish to make is neatly summarized by Professor Louis Dumont[2] in the phrase: 'history is the movement by which a society reveals itself as what it is'.

9. Lastly, and I only touch on this point, historiography in itself provides an important field of sociological study, a sociology of historiography, in which the historians themselves and their books are the phenomena under investigation. What historians once wrote about the Reformation or the Hanoverian Succession or the American Revolution is not what they now write, and this is not just because more is now known about these events. It is also because the climate of opinion has changed with vast political and other social changes. This, therefore, is a study of historical knowledge as part of the content of social thought of a changing present; and such a study would be a section of the sociology of knowledge.

[1] Lévi-Strauss, C., *Anthropologie Structurale*, 1958, p. 17.

[2] Dumont, L., 'For a Sociology of India', *Contributions to Indian Sociology*, no. 1, 1957, p. 21.

I might add that a sociology of social anthropology could be included in it, for what anthropologists inquire into, observe, and record, and the inferences they draw from their observations, also change from generation to generation.

*

I have mentioned some consequences of ignorance of history. I am not suggesting, however, that the historians are not losing as much, or even more, than we are by the collapse of the bridge between the two disciplines. I am quite convinced that they are; and I might add that if few of us read some history few of them appear to read any social anthropology, though more, I think, in France than in England, for such names as Granet, Bloch and Dumézil at once come to mind. This is a pity, for we have advantages not possessed by them; and I would say furthermore that these advantages should enable us, were we to enter the conventional fields of history, to shed light on some of its problems. The chief of these advantages is our own field experience and the field experience of our colleagues. There is a big difference between reading about feudal institutions in capitularies and annals and living in the midst of something similar for a couple of years or more, between shall we say, reading about Louis IX in scanty texts and talking to him and observing his actions daily over many months. Paradoxically, the reason, or certainly one of the reasons, why British social anthropologists have not conducted historical research has been precisely this emphasis on field research, or perhaps we should rather say an over-emphasis on field research for its own sake and a too exclusive interest in primitive peoples simply because they are primitive. This has had the result that many of us spend the rest of our lives writing up our field notes and also that we have therefore not usually had time or opportunity to acquire, in addition to our own skills and linguistic qualifications, those required for historical research. (To carry out research in Africa I have myself had to learn a number of languages—one Semitic, one Hamitic, two Nilotic, and one Sudanic—and to acquire a lesser knowledge of other African tongues.) Such anthropo-historical studies as have been made in the past were made, not by anthropologists who became scholars in one or other department of history, but by classical scholars like Frazer, Ridgeway, and Jane

Harrison, and Semitic scholars like Robertson Smith and Cook who acquired a knowledge of the anthropology of their day and applied it in their studies. One of the few genuinely historical books written by an anthropologist *de carrière* is my own book *The Sanusi of Cyrenaica.*

An anthropological training, including fieldwork, would be especially valuable in the investigation of earlier periods of history in which institutions and modes of thought resemble in many respects those of the simpler peoples we study. For such periods the historian struggles to determine a people's mentality from a few texts, and anthropologists cannot help wondering whether the conclusions he draws from them truly represent their thought. Their wonder turns to astonishment when they find that the thought of the ancient Greeks and Hebrews is presented by excellent historians as far more uncritical, naïve, yes, even childish, than that of savages on a much lower technological and cultural level. And though we may know something about what the poets of Charlemagne's court wrote, can we know equally what they thought or even what their writings meant; and how, I must ask, can an Oxford don work himself into the mind of a serf of Louis the Pious? I hope, though not very optimistically, to see the day when a course of social anthropology, including some field research, regarded not so much as an end in itself as a means, will be regarded as a valuable part of an historian's training.

*

What then, since the historian can be equally a sociologist, and the sociologist an historian, are the main differences between history and social anthropology, the question being asked in the sense of differences between social anthropology as it is understood by most of us in England today and history as it is understood by the more sociologically minded historians? They are not of aim or method, for fundamentally both are trying to do the same thing, to translate one set of ideas into terms of another, their own, so that they may become intelligible, and they employ similar means to that end. The fact that an anthropologist studies people at first-hand and the historian in documents is a technical, not a methodological difference. Nor does the fact that anthropological studies can as a rule be of a people only over a short period of time constitute a vital difference. Some historians also cover only a few years (Namier, for example). It is true that the historical past of the historian, till we get near the borderline with archaeology, is much better documented, but this merely means that the volume of facts is greater and that events and personalities are in consequence more sharply delineated. That on the whole we study small societies and the historians as a rule study larger ones is not an important divergence, and in point of fact some primitive and barbarous societies are as large as those studied by classical and mediaeval historians. Nor is it of methodological significance that, owing to our main interest being in primitive societies, what we write about is often ignored by historians. For example, we write books on magic and witchcraft because they are prominent in many primitive societies, but histories of both in western civilization can be, and indeed have been, written.

Now, magic and witchcraft may appear to be somewhat recondite subjects, so I must press the point by noting that in the main historians write about political events and, even when sociologically orientated, political institutions, while we are just as much interested in domestic and community relations, which are as important, whether in a primitive society or in our own, though they have largely been neglected by historians. Is there any history of marriage and the family or of kinship in England? Furthermore—and here we come to an important difference between the two disciplines, at any rate as they are at present constituted—such historical writings as there are on such topics as magic and the family tend to miss many of the problems familiar to us on account of our special training and field experience; and in my opinion this is also the case with many other topics which historians more commonly discuss, for example, the nature of early law, kingship, the institution of the feud, etc. The questions we have learnt to ask ourselves and our informants, arising from our personal contact with social reality, questions forced on us, as it were, by the pressure of recurrent situations, are not asked and the answers are therefore not given. Nor in any case do the documents yield the abundant material we possess on such topics as I have mentioned, partly because the societies we study are so rich in it, and partly because we can observe behaviour directly and ask questions which elicit replies, whereas the historian can only observe behaviour in documents, and when he questions them they are often dumb.

So whilst it may be difficult to make a clear theoretical distinction between history and social anthropology it would be true to say that in practice we tend to approach our data from a rather different angle and consequently to write about them in a rather different manner. In such a study as, for instance, the place of the Crown in English public life today, or indeed at any particular time, we would not consider it necessary, as most historians would, to trace the history of the kingship in detail and perhaps over centuries, because we would be more interested in a particular set of interconnected social relations at a particular point of time, whether the present present or the past present, rather than in its development, which would for us have only a limited relevance. It would always have some, if only because the place of the crown at any period of history is better understood when compared with its place at other periods. The use we require to make of historical data depends on its significance for whatever problem we may be investigating. We can study some sociological problems of language without recourse to philology; but when Meillet wished to have a sociological explanation of the circumstances in which words change their meaning he naturally had to study such changes in the histories of languages.[1]

What I have said about the Crown leads me to make a further observation to illustrate a difference of orientation, due largely to the emphasis we place on fieldwork as part of our training. Historians write history, as it were, forwards and we would tend to write it backwards. The historian of the British Parliament—Pollard, for example—begins with the Witenagemot, or thereabouts, and then traces its development to the present day. In doing this he might not feel the need to go near Westminster, and he might even feel that it would be a disadvantage to do so. In the light of knowledge gained about the past he might then interpret the present, or rather he might think that this is what he is doing. We, on the other hand, would be inclined to proceed in the reverse direction, to make a study of parliament today—its procedures, its parties, its pressure groups, its organization in the constituencies. the professional, class, and religious distribution of its members, etc., and then in the light of what we have learnt about the present to interpret phases of its development in the past.

[1] Meillet, A., 'Comment les Mots changent de Sens', *L'Année Sociologique*, vol. IX, 1906.

But this difference is largely illusory, because, as a matter of fact, the historian interprets the past in terms of his own experience of the present, and I do not see how it could be otherwise. The facts he studies would be meaningless if he were not able to draw some analogy between them and those of the present. Hence one may say that only the historian who understands the present can understand the past. I am not speaking of some sort of empathy, which I distrust, but of an understanding of the categories of peoples of other times through the experience of his own norms, ideas, and values. We may go further and say that if there were not a broad overlap between our present culture and all cultures, and also a basic psychology which is common to all peoples, neither the historians of peoples of distant times and places nor the anthropologists living among primitive peoples would be able to understand them at all. They would even lack the categories in which to describe their observations, for example, law, religion, economics, etc., categories which, it is true, have sometimes to be stretched to serve their purpose. So, if we overtly have a preoccupation with the present and take the past to some extent for granted, the historian in his preoccupation with the past very much takes the present for granted. Hence a sort of paradox: if the present has to be evaluated retrospectively, when it has become the past, the past has to be evaluated in the light of the present.

It could further be urged that though anthropologist and historian might study the same facts they would in any case study them for different ends and use them differently, that the anthropologist searches the past of a society only to discover whether what he is inquiring into in the present has been a constant feature over a long period of time, to make sure that some correlation he thinks he can establish is in fact an interdependency, to determine whether some social movement is repetitive, and so forth, and not to explain the present by antecedents and origins. This is a complex problem. It confronted Ferdinand de Saussure[1] in his discussion of the difference between synchronic language and diachronic language (more or less between grammar and phonetics), and I think it was from him that the terms synchronic and diachronic were introduced into British anthropology. I shall only say further that I believe an interpretation on functionalist lines (of the present in terms of the present) and on historical lines (of the present in terms

[1] Saussure, F. de, *Cours de Linguistique Générale*, 1949, pp. 127 *seq.*

of the past) must somehow be combined and that we have not yet learnt to combine them satisfactorily. One can understand only up to a point, I would hold, social conditions in England today in terms of the present set of social relations. One requires also to view them as a culmination of manifold historical changes, such as those two great wars have brought about. Moreover, this contrast between what the anthropologist does and what the historian does is only valid when the anthropologist restricts himself to the study of a society at a particular point of time—a present present or a past present. I do not see how it can be valid when he studies social development over a long period. Very little, however, has yet been attempted on these lines. It must be said also that in recent decades even less has been attempted in the way of comparative developmental studies aiming at reaching general statements true of all, or most, societies; and one may be justifiably sceptical about whether they can be reached or, if they can, they will not prove to be so general as to be of little value.

*

So, I may as well oblige my critics by confessing that I can see no vital difference between sociological history and what some anthropologists like to call social dynamics or diachronic sociology or the study of social change or processual (*sic!*) analysis. Indeed, in a broad sense, I would say that social anthropology and history are both branches of social science, or social studies, and that consequently there is an overlap of relevance between them and each can learn much from the other. The failure of some to see this I attribute to the following causes. (1) Snobbery, a desire to keep up with the Joneses, the natural scientists. When will people get it into their heads that the conscientious historian, and also the conscientious anthropologist, is no less systematic, exacting, and critical in his research than a chemist or biologist, that it is not in method that social science differs from physical science but in the nature of the phenomena they study? That this has not been clearly understood derives, as Professor Popper[1] rightly says, from an unfortunate equation of determinism and scientific method. (2) If, in contrast to the vast amount of general historical research done, there have been few sociological historians, there have been, in recent decades, far fewer historical anthropologists, and since there

[1] Popper, K. R., *The Open Society and Its Enemies*, vol. 2, 1945, p. 306.

are few social anthropological developmental studies (genuinely historical as distinct from evolutionary speculation) it is difficult to perceive wherein lies, or rather would lie, the differences and similarities of treatment; and consequently it has been by no means easy for me to present a very coherent comparison between the two subjects, or for others to appreciate their affinities. It is understandable that we have made few such studies because our research has been for the most part among peoples who either lack historical records or for whom they are scanty, but it must also be said that even when the opportunity has abundantly offered itself anthropologists have declined to take it. I think that when they do, it may be difficult to distinguish between at least certain kinds of history and certain kinds of social anthropology. I believe further that it will be necessary for them to do so. (3) There is at present not only a divergence of interests with regard to problems and subjects but an almost total detachment of terrain. The vast majority of European historians still spend their lives in adding to mountains of fact about the past of one or other European people. Anthropologists find this material too remote, both territorially and also in most cases with regard to topics, from what they are themselves doing, and they do not think it would profit them much were they to read about Magna Carta, the Becket controversy, Charles the Bold, the Conciliar movement, the growth of Venice, or the *Kulturkampf*. The reverse is also true. An historian of seventeenth-century France or eighteenth-century England does not, naturally, feel inclined to read books on the Hottentots or the Masai.

This situation can be, and I believe will be, changed, and for several reasons, some of which I enumerate. (1) In recent years there has been a growing interest among anthropologists in the history of the simpler peoples they have studied, either from the point of view of history as a record of events which have brought about social changes or from the point of view of history as a representation of these events in the thought of the present day, or from both points of view. I cannot attempt to give full evidence of this growth of interest so I will only cite two writers as examples of it, Professor Barnes[1] and Dr. Cunnison.[2] (2) Anthropologists are

[1] Barnes, J. A., 'History in a Changing Society', *Rhodes-Livingstone Journal*, no. 11, 1951.

[2] Cunnison, I., 'History on the Luapula', *Rhodes-Livingstone Papers*, no. 21, 1951.

more interested than they used to be in societies and cultures which are far from simple and undeveloped—in the Near and Far East for example. Then history cannot be ignored. Professor Dumont[1] is quite right to insist on the interdependence of the social anthropology of India and Indology. (3) The pursuit of laws by use of the comparative method, which led inevitably in developmental studies to the formulation of invariable stages of development and consequently gave the historical approach a bad name, has now, at least in practice, been abandoned. So we can return to the historical interests of the founders of our science without the embarrassments such a return would have entailed thirty years ago; and even the comparative method need cause no blushes if used with caution and within narrow limits, both in scale and formulation. (4) As I have earlier said, anthropologists have a contribution to make to history, and I believe that in the future some will conduct research in the more conventional fields of history. (5) It is probable that historians will increasingly change the direction of their interests. It is understandable that in the past they should have restricted their activities to European history, but it is no longer so in the world in which we live today. When, instead of adding to our knowledge of Charles the Bold and the Conciliar movement, they show more initiative and write histories of non-European peoples and cultures they will better appreciate how relevant to their studies is our own research. In case this should seem to do historians an injustice, I must ask how many scholars there are in England who could write a history of India or some part of it (and I do not mean a history of British rule in India), or of China (not just the Boxer wars), or of the South American Republics, or of the peoples of Africa or some part of Africa (again, I do not mean a history of British conquest and administration)? You could count them on the fingers of both hands, if most of them had been amputated.

*

Maitland[2] has said that anthropology must choose between being history and being nothing. In the sense I have outlined, and in which also I believe he wrote, I accept the dictum, though only if it can also be reversed—history must choose between being social anthropology or being nothing—and I think Maitland might have

[1] Dumont, L., *ibid.*, p. 7. [2] Maitland, F. W., *Selected Essays*, 1936, p. 249.

accepted the stipulation. He says in the same essay, 'The Body Politic', it is somewhat ironical to note, speaking of the lesson taught by Comte about the interdependence of social phenomena, 'It seems to me that the people who have learnt that lesson are not the sociologists but the historians.'[1] I agree, therefore, with Professor Lévi-Strauss,[2] if not in his demarcation of the respective spheres of history and social anthropology, at any rate in his conclusion that the difference between them is one of orientation, not of aim, and that the two disciplines are *indissociables*.

[1] Maitland, F. W., *ibid.*, p. 247.

[2] Lévi-Strauss, C., *ibid.*, p. 31.

4

THE DIVINE KINGSHIP OF THE SHILLUK OF THE NILOTIC SUDAN

The Frazer Lecture, 1948

Introduction

The central theme of *The Golden Bough* was the divine kingship, and it has seemed to me appropriate that a lecture established in its author's honour and now dedicated to his memory should be on that subject. I propose, therefore, to examine one of the examples of divine kingship cited by Sir James Frazer, that of the Shilluk of the Anglo-Egyptian Sudan, and to discuss it as a problem of social structure.

It was recorded as early as 1905 that it was a Shilluk custom to kill their kings[1] and much information about the Shilluk kingship in general has since been collected. Professor and Mrs. Seligman studied the institution in 1909–10 and it was they who brought it to the notice of Sir James Frazer and into the main stream of ethnological theory. Apart from the writings of the Seligmans and a number of articles by other hands there are two monographs on the Shilluk, *The Shilluk People* by Professor Diedrich Westermann, who conducted linguistic research among the Shilluk in 1910, and Father Wilhelm Hofmayr's *Die Schilluk*, largely based on the observations of Father Banholzer and other of his fellow Catholic missionaries, which date from the beginning of the century. Father Hofmayr himself worked among the Shilluk from 1906 to 1916. There has, indeed, long been a considerable body of knowledge about the Shilluk and I would not have considered it profitable to discuss the Shilluk kingship afresh were it not that new light has

[1] Banholzer, P. and Giffen, J. K., *The Anglo-Egyptian Sudan* (edited by Count Gleichen, 1905), ch. VIII, p. 199.

recently been shed on their social structure, and more particularly on the place of the kingship in it, by officers of the Sudan Political Service. It is significant that two of them studied anthropology before joining the Sudan Service, Mr. P. P. Howell at Cambridge, from where he had carried out some research among the Shilluk before joining the Service, and Mr. W. P. G. Thomson at Oxford. It is from this literature, and especially from the more recent accounts, that I have drawn the material for my lecture, for though the Shilluk live in a part of the world with which I am very familiar, my contact with them has been slight.

The Shilluk are the most northern of the Nilotic peoples and have been for centuries in contact with the Arab population of the northern Sudan. Their country was first subjected to intermittent taxation and raiding by the Turks about 1820 and was finally conquered by them in 1867 and became part of the Ottoman Empire. When the Turkish Administration succumbed to the Sudanese Mahdi the Shilluk were involved in a struggle against this new ruler and afterwards against his Khalifa. Lord Kitchener arrived in Shillukland at the end of 1898 and since that time the people have been under Anglo-Egyptian administration. I mention these political events because they have strongly influenced the Shilluk kingship for close on a century, during which the kings have been executed, exiled, deposed, and nominated, by foreign governments. The funerary rites of a dead king and the procedures of election and investiture of a new king were probably not performed in the full traditional manner during this period.

Social Structure

The hamlets of the Shilluk, who number about 110,000 souls, are almost continuous, like beads on a string, along the west bank of the Nile from near Lake No to about lat. 12 N. with a number of settlements on the east bank and along the lower reaches of the Sobat. Their country is treeless savannah, but unlike their cousins the Nuer and Dinka, they are predominantly agricultural and sedentary, for their long river frontage gives them adequate water and grazing in the dry season for the comparatively few cattle (about 25,000) they possess.[1] The brief account I give of their

[1] I am indebted to Mr. John Donald of the Sudan Political Service for the most recent figures of human and bovine population.

social structure is mostly derived from articles in *Sudan Notes and Records* by Mr. Pumphery and Mr. Howell.[1]

The hamlets (*myer*, sing. *pac*), built from 100 yards to a mile or so apart on high ground parallel to the river, vary in size from one to fifty homesteads; a homestead (*gol*), the residence of a family (*gol*), consisting usually of two huts encircled by a fence. Each hamlet is occupied by members of an extended family, or small lineage, with their wives, and the homesteads of this group are arranged in a rough horseshoe shape around a common cattle-byre, which shelters the animals in the rains and is used as a club at all seasons, and a common kraal. The headman of a hamlet (*jal dwong pac*) who is also the head of a lineage in the settlement of which it forms part represents the hamlet on the council of the settlement and receives in consequence a robe of honour from the king or from the chief of the settlement. If his hamlet is only a subsidiary seat of a lineage in the settlement he is regarded merely as its senior member.

The settlement to which I have just referred is called *podh*, a word which has a number of meanings but generally designates a group of hamlets, occupied by different lineages, which, though there may be much competition between them, unite for defence, for the ritual of age-sets (an institution otherwise of little political importance), and in intersettlement and national affairs, and have a common chief. There are about a hundred of these settlements in Shillukland, each having a population of from less than 100 to more than 600 adult males. They are structurally distinct groups of a political kind though the distance that divides a settlement from adjacent settlements may be no greater than that which separates a hamlet from its nearest neighbours in the same settlement.

In every settlement there is a dominant lineage, the *dyil*, the owners of the soil, with whom the various stranger and immigrant accretions (*wedh*) identify themselves politically and with whom they form a separate social community with its own corporate life. This lineage is generally dominant in numbers as well as in virtue of the prestige derived from its traditional association with the settlement site. The chief of the settlement is chosen from it and by its members, though the stranger lineages have some say in the election, which must be confirmed by the king (*reth*) of the Shilluk.

[1] M. E. C. Pumphrey, 'The Shilluk Tribe', *S.N. and R.* (1941); P. P. Howell, 'The Shilluk Settlement', *ibid.* (1941).

Even when a stranger lineage, sometimes a branch of the royal clan (*kwareth*), becomes more numerous in a settlement than its dominant lineage and dispossesses its members of the chieftainship they still retain some prestige as owners of the soil. Unity in a settlement and the authority of its chief are said to depend on its integration around a powerful dominant lineage. I must, therefore, say something here about Shilluk lineages.

There has been, and still is, some obscurity about Shilluk descent groups. There are said to be in Shillukland about one hundred groups designated by the word *kwa* (descendants) followed by the name of the ancestor of the group. These are often described in the literature as exogamous clans but many of them might perhaps be better spoken of as lineages. They have a typical lineage structure with its characteristic branching off in response to the formation of new territorial units. Colonies of the same lineage are found in several settlements, so that in any settlement several different descent groups are represented, one of them, as I have already explained, being always dominant in it and identified with the settlement politically. Although the dispersed lineages of a clan do not intermarry, and sometimes acknowledge their common descent in other ways, a man generally thinks in terms of his localized lineage, reference being usually to the ancestor who founded the lineage in his settlement. It is interesting to note a further common feature of lineage systems: the descendants of a man who has settled with his wife's people trace their descent through the wife to the lineage in whose home they live. This practice is, as among the other Nilotic peoples, one of the ways in which stranger lineages are grafted into the genealogical structure of the dominant lineage in a settlement. However, until we know more than we do at present about the distribution of lineages, about their genealogical structure, and about the part they play in inter-settlement relations it will not be possible to estimate fully their political significance.

All the Shilluk settlements compose a common polity, the kingdom of Shillukland. They are segments of an organization. It seems that in pre-Turkish times there was a tendency for contiguous settlements to combine for war against other settlements or under the leadership of an outstanding personality, but such combinations were not permanent, or even consistent enough for us to speak of them as political groups. The Turkish Administration tried to give greater consistency to them so that they could be used as administrative units, and the Anglo-Egyptian Government has done the same and calls them divisions and appoints a chief for each. Previously they appear to have been little more than districts or localities, and the only chiefs between the king and the chiefs of settlements were those of Ger, northern Shillukland, and Luak, southern Shillukland, whose functions had, as we shall see, a ritual rather than an administrative character, and those of Muomo and Tonga, the settlements which are the northern and southern marches of Shillukland, whose functions were also partly ritual. In Shilluk speech Muomo and Tonga correspond exactly, Professor Westermann tells us, to the expression of the ancient Hebrews: from Dan unto Bersheba.[1] Northern Shillukland and southern Shillukland are the arches of the politico-religious kingdom of the Shilluk of which the kingship is the keystone. That segmentation has taken this particular form is doubtless due to the peculiar ribbon-distribution of the Shilluk settlements.

The whole Shilluk people recognize a single head and we can therefore speak of the Shilluk nation and of their king, and it is with his place in the national polity that this lecture is particularly concerned. According to Shilluk tradition the present king is the thirty-first of his line. All the kings are believed to be descended from Nyikang, the leader of the Shilluk in their heroic age, who led them into their present homeland, conquering it from its inhabitants and dividing it among the lineages of his followers; and Nyikang, or, as we would say, the spirit of Nyikang, is believed to be in every king and to have passed from king to king down the line of his successors. Nyikang is thus a mythological personification of the timeless kingship which itself symbolizes the national structure, a changeless moral order.

The rule of succession is that only a son of a king can be invested with the kingship. As many sons of kings have never succeeded to the throne, there are today numerous and widely diffused branches of the royal clan whose members are ineligible for royal office and lack authority, unless they are also chiefs of settlements, although they are treated with deference by commoners in virtue of their descent. Indeed, the royal clan is easily the largest single clan in the whole country, being said to comprise perhaps a fifteenth of the nation. In some areas its members are more numerous than com-

[1] Diedrich Westermann, *The Shilluk People. Their Language and Folklore* (1912), p. xx.

moners and have supplanted commoner lineages in the chieftainship of settlements. This process, which continues today, has been going on for a long time, for it is said that Abudok, the eighth ruler (and only queen) of the Shilluk, prophesied that one day the royal clan would eat up the rest of the Shilluk.[1] It results from the custom of sending pregnant wives of a king from the royal capital to bear their children in other, generally their natal, settlements. Their daughters are not allowed to marry and therefore do not start lines of descent which would count as sisters' sons to the royal house. Their sons are brought up by settlement chiefs, often their mothers' brothers, and not in the capital. When a prince (*nyireth*) marries he builds a separate hamlet near that of the settlement chief who has reared him and there his descendants live. Some lineages of the royal clan, the *ororo*, have been formally deprived of their noble status and can now intermarry with their parent clan. They are said to be descendants of Ocolo, the fifth king, who were degraded by his successor, but Father Hofmayr's and Father Crazzolara's accounts[2] would suggest that some of them may be descended from nobles degraded by other kings, and further research will probably confirm this. They are few in number but they hold the important chieftainship of Tonga settlement and they play a leading part in the royal funerary and investiture rites. A king always has some of their daughters among his wives and it is said to be their duty to smother him in certain circumstances.

The emergence of what may be called aristocratic status has been accompanied by the formation of numerous groups of persons of the category of *bang reth*, royal clients. They are descendants of retainers of past kings—captured enemies, certain homicides, persons who have become possessed by the spirit of Nyikang, and poor men who have attached themselves to the court—and have been given the fictional collectivity of exogamous lineages. They are said to be rather more numerous than the royal clan. During a king's lifetime his special band of retainers used, until the practice was discouraged by the Government, to live near the capital in a hamlet of their own, but when their master was buried in his natal settlement some of them moved there with his elderly widows, and their

[1] Westermann, *op. cit.*, p. 149.

[2] Wilhelm Hofmayr, *Die Schilluk* (1925), pp. 66, 83 and 261–2; P. J. P. Crazzolara, 'Beiträge zur Kenntnis der Religion und Zauberei bei den Schilluk', *Anthropos* (1932), p. 185.

descendants remained there to tend his shrine. Also, when a prince was 'planted out', as the Shilluk say, in a settlement, his father sent some of his retainers to live there and these became *bang nyireth*, a prince's clients. They served the prince during his lifetime, and after his death their descendants continued to live near the prince's descendants as a fictitious lineage. Consequently, where there is a branch of the royal clan in a settlement there is usually a lineage of clients in the same settlement. The clients are merged in the general category of commoners, *colo*, of which word 'Shilluk' is an Arabic corruption, though it is said of them that they have a slightly lower social status than members of other commoner clans because they have no traditional rights in the settlements in which they live.

The development of the Shilluk kingship has thus produced, though not in a very pronounced or rigid form, a social hierarchy of royal house, nobility (other members of the royal clan), and commoners (including persons of client origin).

The Kingship

If we are to understand the place of the kingship in Shilluk society we must, I think, beware of attempts to define it in terms of judicial and administrative functions and view it rather as a ritual office and in a wider political context. In 1903 Father Tappi wrote that the authority of the king is 'absolute'.[1] Professor and Mrs. Seligman have described the king as 'absolute head—temporal and spiritual—of a state whose territory is divided into a number of provinces, each administered by a chief directly responsible to the sovereign and acting as his proxy',[2] and Professor Westermann has also written of the power of the king as 'absolute'.[3] Father Hofmayr says that 'Mit dem Regierungsantritt ist der König Herr des Landes, das er nach Belieben vergeben kann, und Herr sogar des Eigentums seiner Untertanen'.[4] These statements would seem to require some modification. As Mr. Pumphrey has pointed out, it is unlikely that the so-called 'provinces' were in fact more than districts or that they were in any sense administrative departments

[1] P. C. Tappi, 'Notes Ethnologiques sur les Chillouks', *Bull. Soc. Khediv. de Géog.* (1903), p. 122.

[2] *Pagan Tribes of the Nilotic Sudan* (1932), p. 39.

[3] *Op. cit.*, p. xlvii.

[4] *Op. cit.*, pp. 150–1.

before they were made into something of the kind by foreign governments.[1] Moreover, though doubtless the king exercised considerable influence in the country and may have confirmed settlement chiefs in office, he did not nominate them. They were heads of settlements in virtue of their position as heads of lineages dominant in those settlements and although they had certain duties to the king it is, I think, wrong to describe them as being in any sense administrative officials. To use such terms as 'state', 'government', and 'administration' in speaking of the Shilluk political system would appear to me, in the light of what is now known of it, to be a mistake.

It is true that the more recent authorities imply rather than explicitly state what in their opinion is the position of the king. Mr. Howell and Mr. Thomson speak of 'the theoretical omnipotence' of the king and of a 'theoretically omnipotent monarchy'.[2] Mr. Pumphrey says that in the old days 'justice was probably rough and large-scale fighting more prevalent than litigation'.[3] Indeed, feuds appear to have been rampant in the past, and it is not very clear how they were composed. We are told that major disputes were sometimes brought before the king, but he can hardly be said to have tried such cases. If he intervened at all it was to support partially one side to a quarrel. We are told that when a settlement waged 'unjustifiable' war on another or refused persistently to listen to the king he might raise a 'royal levy' from the adjacent settlements and with this force and his own retainers raid the recalcitrants, seizing their cattle and burning their homesteads. He kept some of the cattle for himself and the rest were taken by those who supported his action. The raiding force would generally be strong enough to discourage resistance.[4] Compensation for injury seems, therefore, to have been obtained by self-help, sometimes backed by royal intervention. Without confirmation I am not inclined to accept Father Hofmayr's statement that compensation for homicide was paid to the king alone.[5] A different picture of the king's part in the settlement of disputes is painted by Mr. Oyler of the American Mission, who witnessed the settlement of a feud, which had been going on in a district for more than three years, by

[1] *Op. cit.*, pp. 18–19.

[2] Howell, *op. cit.*, p. 57; P. P. Howell and W. P. G. Thomson, 'The Death of a Reth of the Shilluk and the Installation of his Successor', *S.N. and R.* (1946), p. 8.

[3] *Op. cit.*, p. 19.

[4] *Ibid.*, p. 12.

[5] *Op. cit.*, p. 162.

the joint intervention of the king and the Government. From his account it is evident that the king could not have imposed a settlement had the disputants not been ready to accept one, that the part played in it by the king was that of peacemaker and not of judge, and that his participation can better be described as sacerdotal than as governmental.[1] The king of the Shilluk reigns but does not govern.

The king's sacerdotal rôle in the settlement of feuds gives us a clue to what is confirmed by a great weight of further evidence: his sacral position in Shilluk society. Our authorities, indeed, speak of the king as the 'Hoherpriester des Landes',[2] of 'the royal and priestly line' and of its 'priestly function',[3] and of the king as 'the high priest of the tribal religion'.[4] Both his functions and his status are primarily of a ritual order. He makes sacrifices on important occasions, especially for rain and for victory in war, and it is his duty to provide cattle for the sacred herds of Nyikang at Nyilual and Wau and a canoe for Nyikang's shrine at Nyibodho. Nyikang, the culture hero of the Shilluk, their first king, and the creator of their nation, is immanent in him and this makes him the double pivot of Shilluk society, the political head of the nation and the centre of the national cult. The kingship is the common symbol of the Shilluk people and, Nyikang being immortal, an abiding institution which binds past and present and future generations.

The correspondence of political structure with religious cult can be seen at every point of the structure. The territorial segments of the nation and their association with lineages is, as we have noted, validated by the myth of Nyikang's parcelling out of his conquests among the clans, the strands of which are, moreover, caught up into a single mythological point, Nyikang. Some trace their descent from his companions, some from his collateral relatives, others from the original inhabitants of the country conquered by him, and yet others from men who played some part in his saga. The lineage heads who are the chiefs of settlements have ritual duties to the kingship: in particular, ceremonial services at the king's investiture, the building of huts at Fashoda, which is both the royal capital and the cult centre of Nyikang, and the upkeep of Nyikang's other shrines and those of past kings. These shrines are widely distributed

[1] 'The Shilluk Peace Ceremony', *S.N. and R.* (1920), pp. 296–9.
[2] Hofmayr, *op. cit.*, p. 152.
[3] Banholzer and Giffen, *op. cit.*, p. 197. [4] Pumphrey, *op. cit.*, p. 19.

throughout the country so that every section of it participates in the cult of Nyikang, who is, it must be borne in mind, not only the semi-divine hero of Shilluk mythology but also the king at every period of their history. Indeed, the shrines of Nyikang, what Professor Seligman calls his cenotaphs, are indistinguishable from the tomb-shrines of dead kings and they have the same ceremonial functions in the life of the people: in the rain-making ceremonies, at harvest-time, and in times of sickness and pestilence.[1] The religion and cosmogony of the Shilluk are bound up with the political system through the identification of Nyikang with the king. The kingship stands at the centre of Shilluk moral values.

We can only understand the place of the kingship in Shilluk society when we realize that it is not the individual at any time reigning who is king, but Nyikang who is the medium between man and God (*Juok*) and is believed in some way to participate in God as he does in the king. 'Nyikang is the *reth*, but the *reth* is not Nyikang.'[2] The participation of Nyikang in the king raises the kingship to a plane above all sectional interests, whether local or of descent. All the Shilluk share in the kingship, however their loyalties may pull them apart in other matters, because in Nyikang are centred all those interests which are common to all the people: success in war against foreigners and the fertility and health of men, cattle, crops, and of those wild beasts which are of service to man. Professor Westermann tells us that 'everything they value most in their national and private life, has its origin in him'.[3] Mr. Howell and Mr. Thomson tell us that when a king dies the Shilluk say '*piny bugon*', 'there is no land'[4]—the centre of the Shilluks' world has fallen out. It is restored by the investiture of a new king, for though kings may perish the kingship, that is Nyikang, endures. Mr. Oyler tells us: 'They say that if Nikawng should die, the whole Shilluk race would perish.'[5]

Because of the mystical values associated with the kingship and centred in the person of the king he must keep himself in a state of

[1] Prof. C. G. Seligman, 'The Cult of Nyakang and the Divine Kings of the Shilluk', *Report of the Wellcome Tropical Research Laboratories* (1911), pp. 221 and 225.

[2] Howell and Thomson, *op. cit.*, p. 8.

[3] *Op. cit.*, p. xliii.

[4] Howell and Thomson, *op. cit.*, p. 18.

[5] Rev. D. S. Oyler, 'Nikawng and the Shilluk Migration', *S.N. and R.* (1918), p. 115.

ritual purity, by performing certain actions and observing certain prescriptions, and in a state of physical perfection. Our authorities say that the Shilluk believe that should the king become physically weak the whole people might suffer, and, further, that if a king becomes sick or senile he should be killed to avoid some grave national misfortune, such as defeat in war, epidemic, or famine. The king must be killed to save the kingship and with it the whole Shilluk people.

This would seem to be the reasoning behind Shilluk statements that the king may be strangled, or suffocated, or walled up in a hut and left to die there, if he fails to satisfy his wives or shows signs of illness or senility. In view of the great importance Sir James Frazer and others have attached to these statements I must confess that I consider them of interest more as an indication of the mystical nature of the kingship than as evidence that the kings were, in fact, ever killed in the ways mentioned or for the reasons given. It is true that Professor and Mrs. Seligman state categorically that 'there is not the least doubt that kings of the Shilluk were killed with due ceremony when they began to show signs of old age or ill health',[1] but I have failed to find convincing evidence that any Shilluk king was put to death in either circumstance, although some of the kings must have qualified long before they died for execution on the grounds alleged; and I am persuaded that the story of kings being walled up in a hut is a confusion arising from the usual walling up of the remains of a dead king, the bones being buried after decomposition of the flesh. In the absence of other than traditional evidence of royal executions in Shilluk history and in view of the contradictory accounts cited I conclude that the ceremonial putting to death of kings is probably a fiction. It possibly arises from the dual personality of the king, who is both himself and Nyikang, both an individual and an institution, which accounts also for the linguistic convention that a king does not die but disappears just as Nyikang is said not to have died but to have disappeared, in his case in a storm. I will return to this question of regicide after I have reviewed the procedures of election and investiture of kings to show what light they shed on the nature of the kingship.

[1] *Report of the Wellcome Tropical Research Laboratories*, p. 221; also *Pagan Tribes of the Nilotic Sudan*, pp. 90–2. Howell and Thomson say (*op. cit.*, p. 19) that ceremonial strangulation is traditional for all members of the royal clan.

Royal Election and Investiture

The phases of the investiture of a new king were excellently described by Mr. P. Munro[1] of the Sudan Political Service, who was an eye-witness of the investiture of King Fafiti Yor, the twenty-ninth king, in 1918. However, the recent accounts by Mr. Howell and Mr. Thomson, who were able to make detailed observations on what happened on the death of King Fafiti Yor in 1943 and on the election and investiture of his successor, King Anei, in 1944 and again (Mr. Thomson) on the death of King Anei and on the election and investiture of King Dak Fadiet in 1945, are descriptively fuller and analytically more illuminating and are therefore followed in the present summary.

On the death of a king his corpse is walled for some months in a hut and his bones are then buried in his natal hamlet, and not in the royal capital. The remains are disposed of, and the mortuary ceremonies conducted, by royal clients, *ororo*, and members of the royal clan (the head of which is not the ruling king but the chief of Fadiang settlement). It is more a clan, than a national affair. The election of the new king, which takes place a few days after his predecessor's death, is, on the contrary, an affair of the whole Shilluk people, who participate in the election through the chiefs of the north and the south, to whom I have already referred.

These persons reflect in their rôles in the election and in the ceremonies of investiture the structural dichotomy of Shillukland. We have seen that the Shilluk kingdom has a double configuration, political in its territorial setting, in its division into north and south and marches and settlements, and ritual in its religious setting, its arrangement in relation to the cult of Nyikang. In the ritual configuration the dichotomy is represented by the ceremonial division of the country into Gol Dhiang the northern division, and Gol Nyikang, the southern division, which correspond structurally to the political division of the kingdom into Ger, the northern half, and Luak, the southern half, though geographically they are not exactly coterminous. The chiefs of the ceremonial divisions in this ritual representation of the Shilluk polity are also the political chiefs of Golbany and Kwom, the two settlements which are to the north and south adjacent to the capital and cult-centre, Fashoda,

[1] P. Munro, 'Installation of the Ret of the Chol (King of the Shilluks)', *S.N. and R.* (1918).

which is almost where the halves meet and is the focal point in the ceremonies of investiture.

I wish to emphasize that the procedure of election ensures that the prince selected to be king must have the backing of the whole country. Mr. Thomson tells us that 'the choice rests entirely with the chiefs of Gol Dhiang and Gol Nyikang'[1] and cannot take place unless they agree, and it is clear that agreement does not depend on the personal feelings of the two men but that they are spokesmen for the halves of the country they represent. The other members of what Mr. Howell and Mr. Thomson call the 'electoral college' and which they say 'is a very conscious survival of the traditional structure of the Shilluk tribe'[2] have 'only to listen to the decision'[3] of these two men. The other members are the two influential chiefs of the northern and southern marches, Muomo and Tonga, nine chiefs of settlements who are descended from the original chiefs among whom Nyikang divided Shillukland when he conquered and settled his followers in it, and three important chiefs of branches of the royal clan which have become dominant in powerful settlements in the country. Thus the backing, if only passive, of all parts of the kingdom is necessary before a prince can be invested with the kingship. The participation of the halves of Shillukland in the making of a king is further emphasized in the intense opposition between them expressed in the drama of the investiture, which at the same time enacts the conquest and settlement of the country by Nyikang and his followers.

Without the collective participation of the halves of the country the investiture of a king, which takes place about a year after his election, cannot be held. The ceremonies would seem to have precisely this function, for the kingship represents the whole country and a king can only be made by rites in which the whole country takes part. Hence also in the investiture all sections of the population are represented. The royal clan, its dispossessed branch, the commoner clans, especially those whose ancestors were among the original followers of Nyikang, and the client clans, all have essential rôles in the drama. Different settlements in different districts of Shillukland and different clans are responsible for performing various parts of the ceremonial and for providing the various objects

[1] W. P. G. Thomson, 'Further Notes on the Death of a Reth of the Shilluk, 1945' (manuscript).

[2] *Op. cit.*, p. 29.

[3] Thomson, *op. cit.*

required in its enactment: silver and cloth from the Arabs of the north (presumably obtained by raiding in the old days), ostrich feathers for the effigies of Nyikang and his son, skins of the rare Mrs. Gray antelope from Fanyikang island for the ceremonial robes of the king and the other more important participants in the ceremony, sacred spears, royal drums, fibre of the dom palm for ceremonial robes, cowrie shells, new huts, beasts for sacrifice, and so forth.

I will recount briefly the chief phases by which the kingship envelops the king-elect. The effigy of Nyikang, which is kept in the principal of his provincial shrines, at Akurwa in the most northerly district of Shillukland, is brought out by his priests, to whom the king-elect has to make considerable gifts for their service in this matter, and together with the effigy of his son Dak is taken to beat the northern bounds of the kingdom and then southwards, supported by an army of the north, to fight the king-elect for possession of the capital. As the effigies pass through each district the people gather to pay their respects to Nyikang and to escort him to the next district, for it appears that during the interregnum the effigy is believed to contain the spirit of Nyikang, to be Nyikang in fact. Nyikang's army of the north meets in mock combat an army of the south, supporting the king-elect, at the Arepejur watercourse just outside the royal capital. In the words of Mr. Howell and Mr Thomson, this meeting in battle of the two armies on the Arepejur, the boundary between north and south, 'symbolizes the ceremonial division of the country into two moieties. The balance between them is strongly emphasized at all points.'[1] The army of the king-elect is defeated and he is captured by Nyikang and taken by him to the capital. The kingship captures the king. There Nyikang is placed on the royal stool. After a while he is taken off it and the king-elect sits on it in his stead and the spirit of Nyikang enters into him, causing him to tremble, and he becomes king, that is he becomes possessed by Nyikang. The concluding ritual acts follow. The new king has married a girl, traditionally provided by a certain clan, and this girl has an important rôle in the ceremonies of investiture. After the king's enthronement Nyikang seizes the girl and refuses to surrender her to the king on the ground that she was married with cattle from the royal herd, which is Nyikang's herd, and is therefore Nyikang's wife. On this issue Nyikang and the king

[1] *Op. cit.*, p. 48.

summon their supporters to a second mock battle, in which the king captures the girl. Nyikang thereupon pays the king a visit to make his peace with him. On the following morning the king receives the homage and exhortations of the chiefs and undertakes to be a good king. Nyikang does not again contest the king's authority and some weeks later the effigies are sent back to the shrine at Akurwa.

Even so brief a sketch as I have given enables us to perceive the basic symbolism of the events of investiture. Nyikang is always king of the Shilluk and when a king dies his spirit is conceived of as departing in some manner from the king's body to take up its abode in the new effigy specially made for its accommodation at the shrine of Akurwa. By entering anew into the body of a prince Nyikang once again rules in his capital. The most adequate interpretation of the succession of rites of investiture would therefore seem to be that when the effigy and the king fight for possession of the capital the army of the effigy is victorious because Nyikang is in the effigy, but when they fight again over the king's bride the army of the king is victorious because Nyikang is now in the king. Power has passed from the Nyikang of the shrine of Akurwa to the Nyikang of the king in Fashoda. The king is now reverenced and the effigy is sent back to Akurwa.

It is Nyikang, mark you, the symbol of the whole Shilluk people, who is the king-maker. The kingship belongs to all the people and not to the royal clan. Indeed, I think it significant that when Nyikang captures the king-elect the latter is ostentatiously surrounded by a block of his own clan. In this connection it is to be hoped that more will be learnt about the distribution now and in the past of the royal clan. The traditional home of Nyikang was Fanyikang, a settlement in the south, and the ritual equivalent to the southern half of the kingdom is Gol Nyikang. It seems likely on these, and on other, grounds that the royal clan was at one time found chiefly, perhaps only, in the south and spread from there to those northern settlements in which it is found today, as has happened among the closely related Anuak people. Hence in the ceremonies of investiture it seems as though the Shilluk people, represented by Nyikang and the army of the north, capture the king and take him away from his clan, represented by the army of the south, to be the head of the whole nation. The ritual of investiture appears to be an enactment of this central dogma, that it is not an individual who belongs to a particular clan or to a particular part of the country who is king, but Nyikang in whom are the continuity and welfare of the whole Shilluk people.

Royal Succession and Regicide

We may now examine, in the light of what we have learnt about the position of the kingship in Shilluk society and particularly about the polarity so clearly expressed in the ceremonies I have reviewed, the mode of succession to royal office and the tradition of regicide which is so closely connected with it. Although Professor and Mrs. Seligman say, 'We found no basis for the belief, common among Europeans in the Shilluk country, that there were two, or even three or four, branches of the royal house from which the kings were elected in turn',[1] the early *Sudan Intelligence Reports* make it clear that this was the case in recent decades and also that rivalry between claimants to the kingship in the second half of the nineteenth century was connected with the balanced opposition between north and south, for the halves of the kingdom fairly consistently supported rival candidates. Moreover, it is difficult to believe that the practice of the present day, by which it is more or less understood that the surviving lines of kings take it in turn to provide the king,[2] is new. A collateral royal line does not today contest an election on the understanding that they have next turn. The custom is for the reigning king to take under his wing a scion of a rival line and by so doing to indicate him as his successor, though he cannot nominate him and his choice may not be followed by the people. When this prince becomes king he takes under his wing a son of his protector. The reigning king insures by this convention against both rebellion by a rival line and his own line being excluded from the kingship in the future.

There can be no doubt that in recent times there has been an alternation on the throne of branches of the royal house, nor that the alternation is related to the structural dichotomy of Shillukland. We are told that if the ceremonial chiefs of the north and south fail to reach agreement in the election of a new king the chiefs of the northern settlements follow their representative and the chiefs of

[1] *Pagan Tribes of the Nilotic Sudan*, pp. 44–5.

[2] Westermann, *op. cit.*, p. xlvi; Hofmayr, *op. cit.*, p. 145; Howell and Thomson, *op. cit.*, p. 27.

the southern settlements follow their representative and the issue is fought out. It would seem probable that when there is disagreement it is an expression not of divergence of opinion about the merits of the candidates but of local loyalties in which different members of the royal house are associated with different parts of Shillukland. Whether disputed succession in the past was a product of local rivalries cannot perhaps now be determined, but it seems likely in view of the fact that in earlier times the king ruled from the settlement in which he was brought up or moved from one settlement to another and did not have a fixed residence at the central and neutral point of Fashoda.[1] I would also suggest that the association of princes with settlements and districts is clearly related to the custom by which they are brought up away from the capital. It is probable that the backing given by north and south to candidates for the kingship in past times arose from the fact that some princes were brought up in the north and some in the south. That this is the case is clear from Father Hofmayr's detailed notes on each of the Shilluk kings.[2] It is easy to determine because the shrines of dead kings are still maintained today where they were born and brought up. I would further suggest that the maternal descent of princes may be of great significance in that it may be the association of maternal lineages with settlements which attaches local loyalties to a particular prince or to a particular branch of the royal house. It is therefore important that the maternal clans of the Shilluk kings should be recorded by some future observer.

The Shilluk statement that kings should be put to death if they grow old or become sick and their further statement that any prince may at any time challenge the king to mortal combat, in which the king may not call for help, cannot, I think, like the mode of succession, be understood except in relation to the political structure as a whole. There is only traditional evidence that any king has ever been killed in either way, but as Mr. Howell and Mr. Thomson point out,[3] the belief that kings have been, or might be, so killed has political implications. The assertion that a sick or old king should be killed probably means that when some disaster

[1] Seligman, *Report of the Wellcome Tropical Research Laboratories*, p. 229, citing information given by Father Banholzer and Dr. Lambie; Westermann, *op. cit.*, p. 138; Hofmayr, *op. cit.*, p. 76.

[2] *Op. cit.*, pp. 59–136.

[3] *Op. cit.*, p. 11.

falls upon the Shilluk nation the tensions inherent in its political structure become manifest in the attribution of the disaster to his failing powers. The unpopularity which national misfortune brings on a king enables a prince to raise rebellion. The belief that a king may legitimately be assassinated by a personal rival is not substantiated by recent Shilluk history any more than the belief that he may be put to death, but it draws some support from tradition and from anxiety on this score shown by the king and his attendants and from the precautions he takes to protect himself against assassination, especially between his election and investiture and during the ceremonies of investiture. However, the evidence suggests that the anxiety may not be expressed, nor the precautions taken, solely on account of the king's feelings of insecurity but partly, if not chiefly, because he is compelled by tradition to act furtively. Moreover, it is difficult to reconcile the tradition that kings were killed in this fashion with the account we have of royal election and investiture. On the other hand there seems little doubt that Shilluk kings generally met a violent death. My own opinion is that we must interpret Shilluk statements about the matter as indicating not that any prince may slay the king on his own initiative, as has been suggested,[1] but that any prince may lead a rebellion as the candidate of discontent, particularly of the part of the kingdom to which the prince belongs. If the king has lost support in the part to which he belongs he will probably lose also both the resulting contest and his life in it. This is the conclusion I have drawn from Father Hofmayr's involved chronicle of the Shilluk kings.[2] It must here be remarked that Shilluk rebellions have not been made against the kingship. On the contrary, they were made to preserve the values embodied in the kingship which were being weakened, or it was believed so, by the individual who held office. They were not revolutions but rebellions against the king in the name of the kingship.

Conclusion

The divine kingship, to one, perhaps the best known, of the examples of which I have devoted this lecture, has been extensively

[1] Hofmayr, *op. cit.*, p. 64; Prof. and Mrs. Seligman, *Pagan Tribes of the Nilotic Sudan*, pp. 90–1. Howell and Thomson (*op. cit.*, p. 11 *et passim*) are more reserved.

[2] *Op. cit.*, pp. 59–136.

written about by ethnologists, particularly in reference to its occurrence in Africa.[1] I cannot discuss their conclusions here though I feel that I must say about them that they are not, for me at any rate, well founded. In this lecture I thought that I could make a more valuable contribution by a detailed discussion of a particular instance than by what would necessarily have been a very general and superficial review of the whole field, especially as the case selected for discussion has been investigated by a number of gifted observers over half a century and still permits further and more systematic research.

In discussing the Shilluk kingship I have not, as you will have noted, followed Sir James Frazer's method of interpretation. In my view kingship everywhere and at all times has been in some degree a sacred office. *Rex est mixta persona cum sacerdote*. This is because a king symbolizes a whole society and must not be identified with any part of it. He must be in the society and yet stand outside it and this is only possible if his office is raised to a mystical plane. It is the kingship and not the king who is divine.

But though I would insist that a sufficient explanation of the sacral kingship can only be derived from a detailed and painstaking comparative study of a wide range of monarchical institutions, which implies a yet wider comparative study of types of political structure, I do not wish to maintain that because all kingship has some of the features of the divine kingship the divine kingship is not in respect of other features a distinct type of institution. It is to the credit of Sir James Frazer to have shown that it is; and I would suggest that it is an institution typical of, though doubtless not restricted to, societies with pronounced lineage systems in which the political segments are parts of a loosely organized structure without governmental functions. In societies of this kind the political organization takes a ritual or symbolic form which in polities with a higher degree of organization gives way, though never entirely, to centralized administration.

I would further suggest that the acceptance of regicide in one form or another as customary can be explained in the same structural terms. The moral density is great enough for the segments to

[1] Leo Frobenius, *Atlas Africanus*, Heft 2, Blatt 7, 'Der König ein Gott'; C. G. Seligman, *Egypt and Negro Africa* (the Frazer Lecture for 1933), 1934; Tor Irstam, *The King of Ganda. Studies in the Institutions of Sacral Kingship in Africa* (1944).

be represented by a common symbol in the kingship but not great enough to eliminate the powerful tendencies towards fission in the structure they compose. These tendencies are expressed in relation to the symbol, and either the kingship itself, or the king himself, circulates through the competitive segments, as among the Anuak and in past times also in Shillukland, or the segments struggle for royal representation in the capital. In either case their particularist sentiments operate through dynastic rivalries. The kingship, that is Nyikang, is changeless and acknowledged as a supreme value by all the Shilluk. In that permanence and in that acknowledgement the unity of the nation is manifested. In the rebellions against the kings and in the regicides the segmentary structure with its opposed local loyalties is equally present to the view of the observer. The kingship tends in such societies to become identified, by the attachment of the king's person to one locality, with sectional interests and when this happens other sections assert their rights, and by their action the common interest of all the Shilluk, in the kingship at the expense of the king's person. The kingship embodies a contradiction between dogma and social facts, in a sense between office and person, which is produced by a combination of centripetal and centrifugal tendencies in the national structure and this contradiction is solved by customary regicide.

BIBLIOGRAPHY

BANHOLZER, P. L. and GIFFEN, J. K. *The Anglo-Egyptian Sudan* (ed. Count Gleichen), ch. VIII. 1905.

CANN, CAPT. G. P. 'A Day in the Life of an idle Shilluk'. *S.N. and R.* 1929.

CRAZZOLARA, P. J. P. 'Beiträge zur Kenntnis der Religion und Zauberei bei den Schilluk'. *Anthropos.* 1932.

D.I. 'Conspiracy against the Mek of the Shilluks in 1917'. *S.N. and R.* 1922.

HOFMAYR, P. WILHELM. 'Zur Geschichte und sozialen und politischen Gliederung des Stammes der Schillukneger'. *Anthropos.* 1910.

HOFMAYR, P. WILHELM. 'Religion der Schilluk'. *Anthropos.* 1911.

HOFMAYR, P. WILHELM. *Die Schilluk. Geschichte, Religion und Leben eines Niloten-Stammes.* 1925.

HOWELL, P. P. 'The Shilluk Settlement'. *S.N. and R.* 1941.

HOWELL, P. P. and THOMSON, W. P. G. 'The Death of a Reth of the Shilluk and the Installation of his Successor'. *S.N. and R.* 1946.

MUNRO, P. 'Installation of the Ret of the Chol (King of the Shilluks)'. *S.N. and R.* 1918.

OYLER, REV. D. S. 'Nikawng and the Shilluk Migration'. *S.N. and R.* 1918.

OYLER, REV. D. S. 'Nikawng's Place in the Shilluk Religion'. *S.N. and R.* 1918.

OYLER, REV. D. S. 'The Shilluk's Belief in the Evil Eye. The Evil Medicine Man.' *S.N. and R.* 1919.

OYLER, REV. D. S. 'The Shilluk's Belief in the Good Medicine Men'. *S.N. and R.* 1920.

OYLER, REV. D. S. 'The Shilluk Peace Ceremony'. *S.N. and R.* 1920.

OYLER, REV. D. S. 'Shilluk Notes'. *S.N. and R.* 1926.

OYLER, MRS. D. S. 'Examples of Shilluk Folk-Lore'. *S.N. and R.* 1919.

PUMPHREY, M. E. C. 'Shilluk "royal" Language Conventions'. *S.N. and R.* 1937.

PUMPHREY, M. E. C. 'The Shilluk Tribe'. *S.N. and R.* 1941.

SELIGMAN, PROFESSOR C. G. 'The Cult of Nyakang and the Divine Kings of the Shilluk'. *Report of the Wellcome Tropical Research Laboratories.* 1911.

SELIGMAN, PROFESSOR C. G. and MRS. B. Z. *Pagan Tribes of the Nilotic Sudan*, chs. II and III. 1932.

TAPPI, P. C. 'Notes Ethnologiques sur les Chillouks'. *Bull. Soc. Khediv. de Géog.* 1903.

TAPPI, P. C. 'Le Pays des Chillouks'. *Bull. Soc. Khediv. de Géog.* 1904.

THOMSON, W. P. G. 'Further Notes on the Death of a Reth of the Shilluk, 1945'. (Manuscript.)

WESTERMANN, PROFESSOR DIEDRICH. *The Shilluk People. Their Language and Folklore.* 1912.

5

ZANDE KINGS AND PRINCES

1957

All who have been in contact with the Azande people of Central Africa have remarked on the bearing of their rulers, the Avongara clan, and they have often given us a sketch of their appearance and an estimate of their character and intelligence. I have myself met many members of this ruling house and I have been most impressed by—in general, for not all are alike—their proud bearing, their politeness, fastidiousness, reticence, even shyness; their intelligence, sharpened by suspicion of Europeans to cunning; their conservative clinging to tradition, a demeanour and manners unsurpassed by any aristocracy in the world, even among those who have no political position, and a superiority which requires for its acceptance neither display of force nor ornament; the ability to take in a situation and assess a man quickly and decisively, combined with, among those with power, the capacity to act decisively and with great severity—some would say cruelty—when that is required; and in some cases a nervous aloofness, a self-consciousness, a loneliness, which are sometimes almost pathological; and a tendency in middle age to corpulency, the result of a life of ease, absence of exercise, venery, and beer. These characteristics are, of course, a product of their social status. Even under European rule their prestige was quite considerable and their power, though curbed by alien governments, was strongly exercised behind the scenes; their subjects, in spite of European efforts to undermine their dominion, continuing to submit to them to the point of subservience. I never heard a commoner question their authority.

I was not, of course, able to meet an independent Zande king. All had lost their independence over twenty years before I first

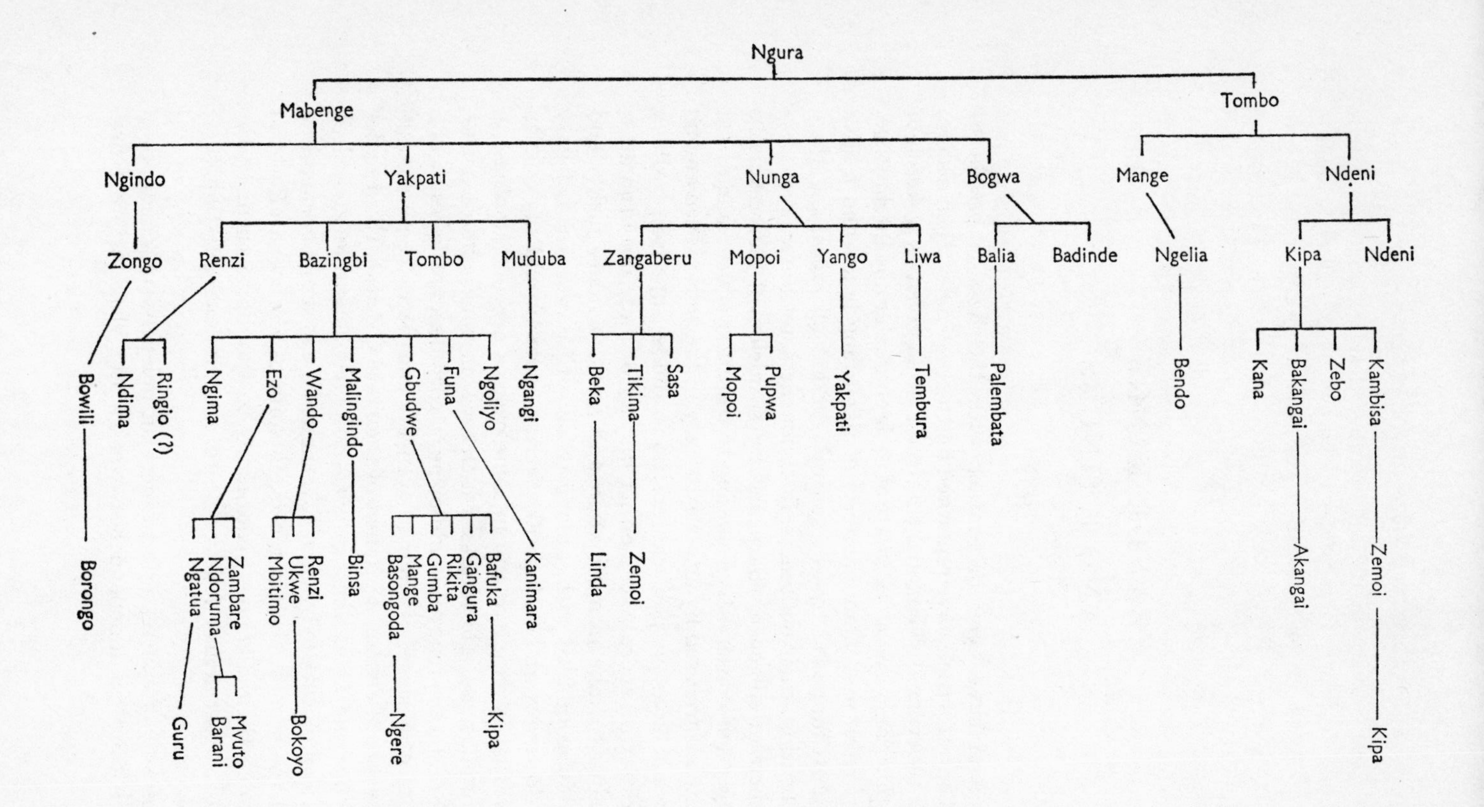

Most of the kings and princes mentioned by name in the text (the spelling of the names is not always that of the author).

visited their country in 1927. I obtained detailed accounts of one such king, Gbudwe, from many of his erstwhile subjects, among whom I lived for many months in the Sudan (what was the Anglo-Egyptian Sudan). I have recently published a description of his appearance and character,[1] and I repeat it here, adding a further assessment of his character based on a number of Zande appreciations. The period to which the description refers is round about 1900, when Gbudwe was a man of some sixty-five years, and the speaker is Kuagbiaru, who must then have been about eighteen years of age.

'Gbudwe was a short man, though not excessively short. He was short with the shortness of (his son) Gangura, though he was stout also, not, however, unpleasantly stout. He was stout with the stoutness of a man whose flesh is loose with it. His breasts protruded like those of a woman, but not altogether like a woman's for they were a man's breasts. His wrists were wrinkled with fat, and his forearm was like a man's shank. His eyes were little protruding eyes, and they sparkled like stars. When he looked at a man in anger they were terrible; then they went grey like ashes.

'His straw hat was woven with great skill and it had a wide brim all round it; and cowries were woven around the base of the crown, completely encircling it. He took two hat-pins, beaten out of white metal, and he stuck in one on each side. His hat was marvellously fine, and when he wore it, it suited him splendidly, and he looked a great king indeed. When he approached people from afar you could not mistake Gbudwe. He was a marvellous king.

'Gbudwe never wore black-stained barkcloth, only red barkcloth, and white barkcloth, which is that barkcloth which is soft. Gbudwe, on account of his wearing his barkcloth short, wore it wide at the sides. He tied it to the top of his thigh so that it did not reach to his knees. He wore it short but it covered both flanks, and (when seating himself) he hitched it up so that the extremities of it spilled over on to his thighs. He took his red cloth which he had brought back with him from (captivity among) the Arabs and tied it round his middle so that the end of it spilled over his barkcloth.

'He was on the whole light-coloured, but not excessively so. When he went into court his dogs took position on either side of

[1] 'A History of the Kingdom of Gbudwe', Zaire, 1956.

him. He carried two spears in his hand, and the third thing he held was his curved ceremonial knife. Those who wanted to see him climbed up trees to see him, because other people shut out their view. A man who had not seen Gbudwe climbed a tree to have a look at him. Gbudwe was a fine-looking man. He would never file his teeth, they formed an unbroken line in his mouth, and they were white.'

Other Azande have described him to me in much the same terms. They have said that the colour of his skin was dull copper, or as Azande put it, the colour of the leaf of the *nonga* plant, and the skin was smooth and soft. His plump hands ended in long nails, which he is said to have dug into the necks of erring wives. He swung his arms in a swagger cultivated by all of noble birth. His facial features were more like those of Gangura (in 1928) than those of any other of his sons, especially in the little black moustache and short bristling beard turning to grey. His hair was grey-black like Gangura's, and he resembled Gangura also in stature—though he was a little taller and also bulkier and stouter— and in loudness of voice and vehemence of speech. In his stoutness he resembled rather his son Rikita, though he was not so pot-bellied. His teeth were as white as those of his eldest son Basongoda in his young days. His legs were also like those of Basongoda, short and stumpy; or perhaps even more like those of his nephew Kanimara. I was told that when he was younger his hair was invariably dressed but that in his later years it was sometimes dressed but usually just cut short, the fashion adopted by his two eldest sons, Basongoda and Mange. When dressed, in the manner described in the text above, the skin of a monkey (*ngarangara*) was attached to the hoop of his hat so that it fell over the nape of his neck and his shoulders. In wearing his barkcloth short, so that his knees and part of his thighs were exposed, and as a close fit, he did not follow the fashion of many princes of his day of wearing their barkcloth loose and falling to the calf, or in the case of some princes, such as his sons Basongoda and Gumba, to the ankle. When threatening war he would pull the barkcloth right up his thighs.

Gbudwe generally carried a carved ceremonial knife in his hand and would lay it across his knees as he sat in court, and he used to assist himself in rising from his stool by pressing it on the ground. Princes, so I was told, seldom carried a spear, but Gbudwe used to walk about his homestead with one. He never smoked but would offer a pipe to others, and he let them smoke in his presence. Though fond of beer, he drank in moderation and was never seen intoxicated by his subjects.

Gbudwe was the Zande ideal of what a king should be and his name epitomizes to his subjects all that they are proud of in their past and all that they have lost by European conquest: their independence and the stability of their political and domestic institutions—all that they look back to with pride, longing, and regret. I have never met a Zande who had experienced Gbudwe's rule who did not speak of it with nostalgia and as better than the foreign administration which took its place. Before and after Gbudwe's death is not to them just a difference in time before and after an event. It is a deep moral cleavage of which they speak. It is well to remember that what these older men treasure most is associated with Gbudwe's name when we are trying to assess the manner of man he was, for all who can tell about him were grown up before his death and had been educated in the old traditions, and this early training of my informants may have led them to paint the past in too rosy a hue.

In the estimate of his character which follows I have relied on the general impression I received from hearing many accounts of him by Azande but also, and more, on stories of incidents in which he figured in which his actions speak for themselves and have not been recounted to me either to express a judgement or to evoke one.

Gbudwe was stern and sometimes morose, on account, Azande say, of misfortunes he suffered in his youth and the humiliations he endured when a prisoner of the Egyptian Government. But he was harsh only with wrong-doers—disloyal people, sorcerers, witches, adulterers, and those who flouted custom or good manners—and though he inspired fear among his subjects, he could unbend, and his bluff, open, sometimes even boisterous talk appealed to the men at court. He did not consider it—such was the custom of princes—beneath his dignity to banter and jest with a few of his old and trusted courtiers: Barafuya of the Angbapiyo clan, Baipuru of the Avokida clan, Kaleka of the Abakundo clan, and, above all, Zengendi of the Angumbe clan, mostly men of good Mbomu (true Zande) stock; though I was told that only Zengendi dared to play physically with him, clasping his master in mimic fighting and pulling him by the hand. Apart from these old courtiers, he joked with no one, though he relaxed towards his younger brothers Bagboro, Ngbutuma, Bagisa, Mukisa, Ngbima, and Gongosi, and treated them with kindness and condescension when they came to visit him. He was courteous to all and held aloof from none, and of his sons and the governors of provinces in my day, Azande say that in this respect Gangura and Ngere are most like him, and his great-grandson Ngindo perhaps the least like him, for Ngindo is conceited and makes no effort to converse with the faithful old men of his court who had served his grandfather Basongoda.

Some of his actions may strike us as being ruthless or savage, but Azande point out that it requires a strong hand to rule them. They admired also the frankness of his severity, for he attained his ends openly and not with the secrecy and slyness which, his subjects say, Wando and his son Renzi employed, nor did he practice, or allow others to practice, the insane cruelties carried out on the orders of some princes, notably Mvuto son of Ndoruma. Nor have I ever heard subjects accuse him of injustice, though they accused other princes of it. They say that, on the contrary though he ordered many executions (in fact, I have never been able to obtain details of more than a few, and I think Azande exaggerate the number) he often allowed a man whom he might have slain to pay a fine instead; and he saved from death men whom his courtiers wanted to kill. It is evident also that in the case of some brutal executions they were carried out in his name but without his authorization, for absolute monarch though he was, if his followers killed a man for some offence in his name he was compelled to accept the situation. His best friend, the commoner governor Zengendi, was killed without his knowledge. Moreover, powerful though he was, he had only limited means of controlling what happened outside his court, and there can be no doubt that influential men sometimes bullied those whom they administered in his name, especially such persons, mostly members of subjugated tribes, who never came to court and had no one there to represent their interests. It seems that Gbudwe took the view that it served them right if they stayed away from court and the polished society which frequented it and were ignorant and stupid enough to hide like wild beasts in the bush. Some discipline was required to civilize these barbarians and it was to impose it that he entrusted his sons and elders with administration under his authority. What went on in the provinces ruled by his sons was none of his affair, unless his own immediate subjects were involved. If we are to have sympathy for any of Gbudwe's followers it should, I think, be for some of his old commoner governors, whom, so far as I could understand, he sometimes ousted from their positions somewhat arbitrarily, and occasionally executed, and then replaced them by his own sons; but all kings did the same; Azande regarded the appointment of a commoner to a governorship as a political hazard.

Gbudwe always gave clear and decisive judgements when cases were brought before him, which is what Azande like, and they contrast him in this respect with his eldest son Basongoda, who vacillated in his judgements. Basongoda was of a quiet and gentle disposition and was anxious to prevent bloodshed, and executions at his court were almost unknown; but in his desire to spare or to placate people he wavered in his judgements and gave what became known as *ngbanga* Basongoda, Basongoda-decisions, attempts to show that neither disputant was entirely in the right or that both were in the right. Azande do not like this. Another trait which greatly gratified Gbudwe's subjects was that, whilst he destroyed without mercy any one who attempted to seduce one of his wives, he did not try to obtain the wives of his subjects by force or through a trumped-up charge or, relying on his immunity, to seduce them. Here again, they contrast his behaviour with that of other princes, such as his grandson Ngere, whom otherwise they like. His generosity was far-famed and none left his court because they were hungry or did not receive the gifts they came to solicit or because they were gratuitously ill-used by the men at court, as they are said to have fled from the courts of his sons Gumba and Bafuka. Gbudwe exemplified, Azande say, these three virtues which they demand in their rulers if they are not to change their allegiance: vigorous and decisive judgement of cases, no seduction of the wives of their subjects, and openhandedness. If a prince has these virtues, Azande will put up with a good deal of severity. But Gbudwe had other virtues as well. He had a reputation as a young man for remarkable boldness and personal courage. It was by boldness that he wrested his father's kingdom from the hands of his eldest brother Ngima, and we have Schweinfurth's testimony in support of Zande statements that he was a courageous fighter and did not, like most princes, keep well to the rear of a battle.[1] His subjects have often told me how excellent a father he was to his sons. He

[1] Georg Schweinfurth, *The Heart of Africa*, 1873, vol. 2, pp. 219–20.

was severe with them, as they think a father should be, and he never allowed them to take any liberties with him; and if they ill-treated commoners at his court or he thought they were trying to seduce his wives, he drove them away from it. But they always came back again, for he was deeply fond of them and he never put any of them to death or mutilated them as, it is said, Renzi and others did. From the beginning of his reign to the end of it, a period of almost forty years, there was no rebellion in his kingdom; neither did he have to take steps to anticipate a rebellion by murdering his kinsmen; nor was there civil war between his sons. I do not think that any other Zande kingdom enjoyed such internal tranquility, and it is without doubt at least in part due to Gbudwe's personality and the high regard in which his subjects held him that this was the case.

The Azande also liked him because he was not too self-conscious, was unpretentious in his demeanour, and did not humiliate them. They say that he did not laugh often partly because he was of a morose temperament but also partly because of a habit cultivated by princes of hiding their teeth and the interior of their mouths from the gaze of the public; so when Gbudwe was amused he would give a little cough, half cough and half laugh, and smile, putting at the same time his hand or his fly-whisk up to his mouth to cover it, a customary modesty on the part of royalty. But they add that Gbudwe, who showed none of the aloofness of his son Mange and his brother-in-law Tembura and of other princes in the presence of their subjects, would on occasions shout and laugh so that everyone could see his mouth and teeth, whereas Mange and Basongoda kept their hands incessantly before their mouths, partly because their teeth were not so good, but mainly to shield themselves from their subjects. It was the custom of some kings, of whom Tembura was one, to have a trumpeter standing at their side to trumpet whenever they laughed, the sound of the trumpet being called 'the king's laughter'. Likewise, Gbudwe would never be carried on the shoulders of his subjects as were his son Gumba and his grandson Kipa, who seldom walked in public. I was told that his elder brother Wando and some other of the princes in what is now the Belgian Congo never walked in their kingdoms but were always carried on the shoulders of servants. Gbudwe considered this practice foolish. Nor did he exact the crawling obeisance which some princes received from their subjects, though probably only those on the periphery of Zandeland where the vast majority of the population were conquered peoples or their descendants, and not in the heart of Zandeland where the Ambomu, or true Azande, element was more considerable. Gbudwe was treated with far less formal subservience by his followers than were his sons Mange and Rikita, his cousin Tembura son of Liwa, and, according to some accounts, of Kipa son of Ndeni, by theirs. The subjects of these kings were mostly conquered foreigners. Court custom in their kingdoms prescribed that a man who wished to speak with the king or make a case before him should crawl from a long distance to approach him. Gbudwe's erstwhile subjects have told me that it might be all right for barbarians (*auro*) to humiliate themselves in this way but that Gbudwe would never have permitted the true Azande of his court to act in so undignified a manner—they bent only slightly when approaching him—and had he done so they would have left him to follow princes with more respect for the traditional relationship between noble and commoner. Relations between king and subject at court are said to have been less formal still at the courts of Gbudwe's elder brothers Wando and Malingindo.

Gbudwe was a stickler for tradition, and in this he was naturally supported by the older men and the chief commoner families. He refused to imitate those princes who dressed like Arabs. Indeed he was hostile to anything the Arabs did, and he always spoke contemptuously of them. Any form of magic was intolerable to him unless it had been known to his father. He approved of witch-doctors (*abinza*) and other diviners (*aboro atoro*) and summoned them to divine for him, and he sent for the female leech Nambili to treat the ailments of his wives. Many forms of magic employed by Azande today, were not known to Gbudwe's subjects during his lifetime, and of those that were known one can count on the fingers of one's hands those of which he is said to have approved: war-magic, vengeance-magic, thunder-magic against wrongdoers, secrecy-magic (*gbau*) to aid the pursuit of vengeance, hunting-magic (*bingiya*), medicines for closing gardens against theft, magic for the protection of the person (*zuna*), medicines for increasing crops, medicines to increase sexual potency, and medicines to attract followers. He used some of these forms of magic himself, getting old commoners to bring the medicines and perform the rites, except in the case of the war-medicines, which he administered himself, from the large bongo horn in which they were kept, to his elders and his company commanders. He was suspicious of all kinds of magic other than those I have mentioned, and his hostility to some of those used by people in the kingdoms to the south of his own was probably the main reason for their not having entered his kingdom—such bad medicines as *togoligaka* and *ngwa gberesa kpolo* —by his subjects until after his death. The medicine he disliked most was *menzere*, a medicine used in sorcery, and I was told that if anyone were known to possess it his death was certain. He refused to condone the practices of the magical secret societies which were entering Zandeland during the last few years of his life. He is said to have destroyed the lodges and the members of the only one which gained a footing in his own country. I was told that he even frowned on such reputable medicines as the *zelengbongo* whistle, which a man blows to kill anyone who may be injuring him. Gbudwe is said to have asked why a man should have recourse to a magical whistle for protection when he gave all the protection against injury that a man could desire, and to have expressed the opinion that all this blowing of whistles only led to trouble. Nevertheless, he wore one or two whistles of an old type on his person.

Gbudwe was also violently opposed to circumcision, which the Azande took over from neighbouring peoples towards the end of last century, and he forbade the practice in his territories. His objection to it was that since neither he nor any of the married men were circumcised they might be subjected to secret ridicule among their womenfolk if circumcision became fashionable and all the younger men had undergone the operation. Circumcision was only practised in his kingdom, as far as we know, after his death, when his sons lost much of their authority and were no longer able to prevent this, the secret societies, and other innovations from spreading among their subjects.

Much more could be written about Gbudwe, but what has been said is perhaps enough to give some indication of the man's character. In summary, I do not think I am stating other than the general opinion of those Azande who experienced Gbudwe's rule when I say that he was regarded with fear, it is true, but also with something wholly different, respect. He was respected as a just man, a man without vanity, a brave man, and a man who hated deceit, shameful conduct, slander, jealousy and envy, and who loved honesty and honour. He must also have been a man of great physical stamina, of intellectual vigour, and, it may be added, of unusual virility, for he was begetting children up to the time of his death in about his seventieth year.

So much is part of what I learnt from Azande about Gbudwe the man. It seemed to me that it might be worthwhile to compare these secondhand impressions with such descriptions as we have of other Zande kings and princes by Europeans: kings and princes they met before their power was broken. They may be in part superficial impressions which, perhaps, sometimes tell us as much about the writer as about his subject, but taken together they give us a fairly vivid picture of an old-time Zande ruler.

We start with the Italian hunter and trader Carlo Piaggia, who visited the Azande from 1863 to 1865, living for most of the time as the guest of King Tombo. His account of his adventures was put together by the Marchese O. Antinori. He says of King Tombo: 'Tombo era un uomo nella sua piena virilità, di alta e svelta persona, di aspetto altero, ma non spirante alcuna ferocia. Aveva la sua lussureggiante chioma inanellata, adorna di penne variopinte e bizzarramente disposte. Le sue membra eran robuste; la tinta della pelle olivastro-ramacea, e si copriva d'una corteccia d'albero conciata di colore rossastro e che teneva legata ai fianchi mediante cintura. Si presentò al Piaggia colla destra armata da tre lunghe lancie, tenendo colla sinistra quella specie di arpa che essi chiamano *kondi*.'[1]

Later on he reports:

'Il capo di coteste tribù, che il mercante ed il cacciatore arabo chiamano Sultano, si distingue dai suoi subordinati per essere seguito da un numeroso stuolo dei suoi addetti, per il suo incesso grave ed autorevole, e per la sua foggia di vestire. Egli infatti porta legata un' ampia scorza d'albero che conciata somiglia perfettamente ad una stoffa, e che dal ginocchio si piega tra le coscie in su per le reni annodandosi ad apposita cintura: in sulla testa si adatta, bizzarramente disposte, un gran numero di penne dai fulgidi colori, e spesso le blù e rosse ali del verde cuculo a bianco ciuffo (*Corythayx leucolophus*), sono da lui molto disiderate. Alcuni fra loro aggiungono alle braccia ed agli stinchi armille di ferro e di rame, ed anche infilano al collo corone di duri noccioli di frutta, o di denti di animali carnivori, o di grossi serpenti e di pesci.'[2]

[1] O. Antinori, 'Viaggi di O. Antinori e C. Piaggia nell' Africa Centrale', Boll. della Soc. Geog. Ital. 1868, p. 112.
[2] *Ibid.*, p. 122.

He further remarks:

'Ad incutere timore ai suoi sudditi i Capi fingono talvolta di essere presi da un' agitazione e da una specie di frenesia di sangue. Essi figgono in tale stato i loro sguardi feroci in quelli che li circondano, ovvero si pongono errabondi quasi alla ricerca di qualche vittima, ed al più piccolo sinistro evento, sfogano gli impeti della loro ira simulata col dare a qualcuno perfino la morte. È credibile che un tale contegno sia adoperato onde essere temuti e rispettati dai loro sudditi. Il Piaggia ci narra come il capo Tombo desse piò volte lo spettacolo d'una simile scena.'[1]

Such scenes of cold-blooded murder, if we can accept the relation of them, are out of keeping with the character of a Zande king. Some kings may indeed have ordered executions and cruel punishments of commoners for trivial offences or for their personal advantage, but I have never heard of such behaviour as Piaggia describes. It is true that a passage in Schweinfurth's account suggests that kings occasionally behaved in such a manner: 'The defiant imperious bearing of the chiefs alone constitutes their outward dignity, and there are some who in majestic deportment and gesture might vie with any potentate of the earth. The dread with which they inspire their subjects is incredible: it is said that for the purpose of exhibiting their power over life and death they will occasionally feign fits of passion, and that, singling out a victim from the crowd, they will throw a rope about his neck, and with their own hands cut his throat with one stroke of their jagged scimitar.'[2] But Schweinfurth makes it clear that he did not witness this, and it seems probable that he was recounting what his Arab friends had told him or possibly that he here, as I think everywhere, made use of Piaggia's account. The only other early writer who describes a Zande king executing people with his own hands is Captain Burrows, a British officer who served in the Belgian Administration of the Congo from 1894 to 1898. He writes: 'The Azandé generally kill condemned criminals with the lance. I remember once an Azandé chief caught one of his wives attempting to run away with another man. They were both taken and brought back, and next morning, before an assembly of the people summoned to witness the ceremony they were tied to trees. The chief himself, after haranging the assembled multitude, at a distance of fifty yards from the prisoners, began to dance, stopping every now and then to throw a lance at either the

[1] *Ibid.*, p. 123. [2] Georg Schweinfurth, *op. cit.*, vol. 2, pp. 21–2.

woman or the man. This he continued to do, approaching nearer and nearer, until both culprits had been transfixed by two or three lances. A chief would not hesitate to mutilate his own son for such an outrage, inflicting the usual penalty by cutting off both hands at the wrists.'[1] This passage suggests that Burrows witnessed the event, but it is not clear why, if such was the case, he did not prevent it.

The famous German traveller and botanist Georg Schweinfurth, who visited the most easterly part of Zandeland in 1870, met two Zande kings, Ngangi son of Muduba and Wando son of Bazingbi, the first being the friend of Schweinfurth's Nubian protector Muhammad 'abd al-Sammad and the second being at that time hostile to Muhammad. Of the first he tells us: 'I found him perfectly naked except for a little apron that he wore. He was sitting on a Monbutto stool, quite unarmed, and with no insignia whatever of his rank. There were, indeed, some twenty or thirty natives who were armed and kept guard in the outer court, but apart from this any pretension to state was entirely wanting.'[2] He gives no description of Wando beyond observing that he wore a shirt, but only to please the Arabs. As soon as they withdrew, he took it off. He says that this was the common practice with all the nobility. They wore only barkcloth and would not dress in Arab clothes even when they had the opportunity to acquire them.[3] Schweinfurth also tells us that the leopard-skin was the insignium of royalty among the Azande, that only those of royal blood had the privilege of covering the head with a skin, usually the skin of the serval, and that the sons of kings wore their barkcloth looped up on one side so that one leg was left entirely bare.[4]

Romolo Gessi Pasha, the heroic governor of the Bahr al-Ghazal in the years 1878 to 1880, has left us a description of Ndoruma, whom he calls Mdarama, son of Ezo. Writing in 1879, he says: 'About a month ago news came to Dem Suleiman that a great Sandeh chief was on his way with a numerous suite. I gave orders that he should be received with due honour, and festive preparations were made. Mdarama soon arrived. He is a man about thirty-five years of age, more than six feet high, well proportioned, with broad shoulders, intelligent expression and a perpetual smile. He

[1] Guy Burrows, *The Land of the Pigmies*, 1898, pp. 66–7.
[2] *Op. cit.*, vol. I, pp. 441–2.
[3] *Ibid.*, vol. I, p. 502.
[4] *Ibid.*, vol. II, pp. 256 and 6.

examined our Remington rifles, the cannon, and the dêpots of ammunition and cloths with the greatest curiosity. He then presented me with forty large [elephant] tusks. I gave orders that he should choose some clothing from our stores. He was shown the best Arab clothes, but said that he wished to be dressed like a Frank [European], for he was no Jelabba [Arab trader]. Then he wished to see a cannon fired, and I hastened to gratify him, but when the piece went off he fell to the ground from fear.'[1]

Ndoruma's determination not to wear Arab clothes must have weakened, for when Wilhelm Junker, the eminent Russo-German explorer who travelled in Central Africa, chiefly in Zandeland, from 1875 to 1886, met him in 1880 he was dressed in a bizarre assortment of clothing, including the Egyptian galabiyeh (a sort of smock) and tarbush, put on in Junker's honour. 'On his first appearance,' Junker wrote, 'Ndoruma presented a somewhat comical sight, arrayed in an eccentric costume, which he had apparently put on expressly for this occasion. He had squeezed his long muscular legs into a pair of crimson trousers which were far too short and narrow for his brawny limbs, and which seemed to have at one time formed part of a huzzar's uniform. Over this he wore an Arab gelabiyeh, which was also far too tight a fit, compressing shoulders and arms into the smallest compass, and leaving chest and paunch fully exposed. Yet so calm and dignified was his bearing, so imposing his colossal figure, that I soon forgot his laughable appearance and at once became deeply interested in this striking personality.

'He involuntarily reminded me of the Mangbattu king, Munsa, as described by Schweinfurth in his *Heart of Africa.* On the countenance was stamped the unmistakable Niam-Niam [Zande] type—sharp, vigorous traits, animated eyes bespeaking a resolute spirit, combined with prominent cheek-bones and broad nostrils, which imparted a strange wildness to his Negro features. The lips, however, were but moderately everted, and were moreover relieved by thin mustachios, and a shaggy beard merging upwards in a sparse growth of whiskers. The hair, arranged Zandeh-fashion, though somewhat carelessly, in tresses, projected under a tarbush round the occiput. Like all the Niam-Niam [Zande] chiefs of the early period, Ndoruma scorned all personal ornament, his ordinary dress being the customary "rokko" which is prepared from the bark of a

[1] Romolo Gessi Pasha, *Seven Years in the Soudan,* 1892, pp. 348–9.

species of fig (*Urostigma*), and which is generally worn by many peoples of Central Africa. The Zandehs wear a comparatively small garment of this type, which is brought forward between the legs and fastened behind by a girdle, so as to spread out on both sides, and fold round the hips like a loose loin-cloth. In this national rocco Ndoruma's tall handsome figure showed to the best advantage. When seated he affected a somewhat careless attitude, though by no means awkward, but on the contrary displaying a certain natural dignity in every movement.

'In recent years Ndoruma had been brought into frequent contact with the Arabs and Khartum traders, and had already acquired some familiarity with their language. Some eighteen months before our interview his independence had been broken in war by Rafai Agha, the Mohammedan governor of Zibêr's former zeribas in the west Zandeh lands, a person who had played a leading part in the history of [the] Egyptian Sudan. But though compelled to recognize the suzerainty of the Nubians, Ndoruma, like the vanquished chiefs, had gladly welcomed the new relations growing up under Gessi's administration.'[1]

Elsewhere Junker says of Ndoruma: 'Ndoruma's dwellings, which lay scarcely five minutes from my station of Lacrima, were in no way distinguished from the ordinary native huts. Ndoruma himself, in accordance with the good old Zandeh custom, displayed the greatest simplicity in all things. His favourite dress was the "rokko", which had certainly seen better days, and which was fastened by a stout twisted bast cord. On his visits he was followed about by two or three boys carrying an old musket, the revolver I had given him, and a large Mangbattu *trumbush* [throwing-knife].'[2]

Junker met a number of other Zande kings and princes. One of these was Ngatua, Ndoruma's elder brother (Junker says that he was his uncle), who went about accompanied by an old red-brown Zande hound and a red-haired ape which rode on the back of the dog.[3] Another, belonging to the Nunga branch of the Zande royal house, was Zemio [Zemoi], a man who spoke Arabic and had adopted certain Arab habits. Junker wrote of him: 'This vassal of the Egyptian Government is a son of Tikima, and although not more than about thirty years old, is already somewhat corpulent, as many Zandeh princes are later in life. His small uniformly

[1] Wilhelm Junker, *Travels in Africa during the Years* 1875–1878, 1891, p. 101.
[2] *Ibid.*, p. 163. [3] *Ibid.*, p. 151.

rounded body supports a typical round head with an expression almost of kindliness and benevolence, at least so far as it is possible to draw a conclusion from a Negro's physiognomy as to his inner sentiments. His chubby oval countenance is lit up with the intelligent glance of large piercing eyes. A scanty growth of hair covers chin and upper lip, while the broad nostrils and prominent cheekbones recall the Niam-Niam [Zande] type, though his Arab garb with red shoes, tarbush, and cropped hair almost suggested a half-caste Negro. Even at this first interview he gained my sympathy, a sympathy which I was able to retain during long years of friendly intercourse.'[1]

This same Zemio or Semio or Zemoi became later a strong supporter of the Belgians. One of their officers, Jules Milz, described him in 1891: 'C'est un homme d'une quarantaine d'années, de taille moyenne et assez corpulent, doué d'une physionomie très intelligente. Il rappelle l'aspect des fonctionnaires du gouvernement égyptien. Il a une grande distinction dans son attitude.'[2] Another officer of the Belgian forces in the Congo, Gustave Gustin, wrote: 'En 1891, Semio semblait avoir cinquante ans. Il ne savait ni lire ni écrire, mais avait un scribe arabe ou katip [*kātib*]. Semio n'était pas quémandeur; il était au contraire d'une générosité vraiment désintéressée. Il saluait à la manière arabe le Blanc qu'il ne connaissait pas suffisamment; il prenait entre les mains celle qu'on lui tendait, la portait ensuite aux lèvres, puis au front et enfin à la poitrine, en prononçant avec recueillement le salut arabe. Quant à ceux qu'il connaissait mieux, il leur serrait chaleureusement la main entre les siennes, pendant que sa figure s'épanouissait sous un bon sourire.'[3]

[Zemoi was met twenty years later and in the year before his death (1911) by the German traveller Captain von Wiese. Von Wiese, who calls him Semio Ikpiro, describes him thus: 'The Sultan is a well-built man, about five feet nine inches in height. He is sixty-five years of age, and has a kindly expression. At first he reminded me of a self-conscious, obstinate, crafty old peasant, who evidently regarded me with profound distrust. . . . Semio's personal appearance was a striking contrast to that of the Sultan of Rafai [mentioned later]. He wore a long Arab dress, and his only Euro-

[1] *Ibid.*, p. 197. Also p. 203.
[2] R. P. L. Lotar, *La Grande Chronique de L'Uele*, 1946, p. 61.
[3] *Ibid.*, p. 61.

pean article of clothing was a large grey, broad-brimmed, felt hat. He carried a long spear, leaning on it as he walked. He stepped quietly along, with slow, measured tread, and deliberate movements, reminding me of one of the ancient patriarchs. When he paid me a visit, a low bench covered with carpet was brought in for his use, for he never sat on European chairs. The dignitaries who accompanied him either squatted on the ground outside the house or sat on mats which they brought with them. Although Semio is not a genuine Moslem, he inclines rather to Arab than to European customs. He has an Arab fakir living in the palace, but he does not conform to all the prescribed daily prayers. But he has retained much that he learned during the years when he was a vassal first of the Arab slave-hunters, and later of the Egyptian Government. . . . Our conversation was not very rapid, for the old gentleman took some time to consider each remark of mine before replying. Every day from morning till night, with an interval of two hours in the middle of the day, he sat patiently listening to my questions. But when I asked him about his family life, his religion, or the manners and customs of his subjects, he evidently distrusted my motives, and gave evasive replies. . . . I had, moreover, the feeling that both the Sultan and his subjects were impatiently awaiting my departure.'[1] Can we blame them?]

Junker also met Zemio's uncle, Sasa, one of the first kings in the Uele region to make submission to the Belgians. 'Zassa, brother of Zemio's father, Tikima, had for years maintained active relations with the Nubians, was familiar with Arabic, and, like Zemio, had adopted the Arabo-Nubian dress, so that his features alone recalled his Zandeh nationality. He was considerably older than Zemio, had a dignified carriage, and inspired confidence by his outward appearance and courteous manners.'[2]

Perhaps the king best described in the literature whom Junker met was Bazingbi's son Wando, whom Schweinfurth had met ten years earlier. His son Fero or Renzi presented himself to Junker on November 10th 1880 and told him that his father was too fat to walk any great distance but hoped to see Junker on his route to Ndoruma's.[3] This is how Junker describes their meeting: 'At one of these groups of huts were several hundred Zandehs, among whom

[1] Mecklenburg-Schwerin, Adolf Friedrich A. H., Herzog v., *From the Congo to the Niger and the Nile*, 1913, pp. 217–18.

[2] Junker, 1891, p. 309.

[3] *Ibid.*, p. 274.

I was at once able to single out the aged Wando by his corpulent figure. Like all members of the old Zandeh dynasty, he despised princely adornments, and even his rokko [barkcloth] was no better than those of his surrounding followers. His hand also grasped, not a warlike assegai, but a peaceful fly-fan! Our friendship was soon sealed, though he remained for some time absorbed in thought, which perhaps was natural enough, seeing that facing him sat his rebellious son, Hokwa.'[1] Wando's brother Ngoliyo resembled Wando but was younger and less corpulent.[2] There is lack of agreement between this portrait of Wando and that drawn by that remarkable man Eduard Schnitzer, a doctor from Silesia who took the Muslim name of Emin and was at the time he met Wando governor of the Equatorial Province of the Egyptian Sudan. He wrote in 1882, 'Wando, well known to readers of Dr. Schweinfurth's book, is a well-built, athletic fellow; he has a dark skin and a completely shorn head, which distinguishes him from the other Nyam-Nyam, who think so much of their frisures. The *rokko* trousers of the Monbuttu constitute his only dress. He was accompanied by three of his fourteen sons, all wearing the handsome hide-dress of the Zandē, and tall straw hats decorated with parrots' feathers. The indispensable trumpeters accompanied them, carrying gigantic horns and trumpets made out of elephant's tusks and decorated by leopard-skins.'[3] Emin does not seem to have had a high opinion of Wando, for in speaking about his son Mbitimo he says that it was in the young man's favour that he was totally unlike his father. Emin also speaks of a prince called Mbrú, whom I have not been able to identify, as 'a very aged, jovial fellow, with long white hair and a beard dyed red'.[4]

If Wando was corpulent in 1880 he was a monstrosity in April 1892 when the Belgian Commander Guillaume Van Kerckhoven met him on the lower Kibali. Milz described the spectacle: 'Une troupe déboucha en face de notre poste, puis la foule s'écarta afin de livrer passage à une masse animée s'appuyant sur un immense bâton et s'affalant lourdement sur une chaise qu'on s'empressa de placer derrière elle.'[5] Van Kerckhoven sent Gustin forwards to greet him. Van Kerckhoven himself describes Wando thus: 'Il ne

[1] *Ibid.*, p. 276.
[2] *Ibid.*, p. 281.
[3] *Emin Pasha in Central Africa, being a Collection of his Letters and Journals*, edited and annotated by Professor G. Schweinfurth, Professor F. Ratzel, Dr. R. W. Felkin and Dr. G. Hartlaub, 1888, p. 374.
[4] *Ibid.*, p. 445.
[5] Lotar, *op. cit.*, p. 121.

restait du grand et fort guerrier qu'un volumineux paquet de vieilles chairs, cachées par une chemise loqueteuse en kaniki, surmontées d'une tête grisonnante qu'entourait une bande d'étoffe d'une blancheur plus que douteuse. Bien que les yeux fussent noyés dans la tête et semblassent sans expression, on surprenait par moments son regard s'illuminant d'une flamme vive et intelligente. Chose curieuse, les dents étaient toutes à leur place, blanches et en parfait état de conservation. Les mains étaient très grasses, les doigts assez effilés, terminés par des ongles en deuil de deux à trois centimètres de longueur. Signe de race, disent les Avongara.'[1] Gustin wrote in his journal on this occasion: 'Par déférence pour le vieux chef vongara, Semio ne voulut pas s'asseoir sur une chaise semblable à celle dont Wando faisait usage; il se contenta d'un simple pliant, tandis que les fils de Wando s'asseyaient sur des peaux de léopard. Pendant que l'Inspecteur élaborait le traité à conclure avec Wando, celui-ci, très animé, retroussait sa grande blouse bleue, pour se gratter le genou. Semio était fort ennuyé de l'inconvenance du vieux Sultan et rabaissait discrètement la blouse dès que la main coupable de Wando l'avait relevée.' Wando presented to Van Kerckhoven his son Mbitimo and then his son Ukwe, 'onctueux autant que Mbittima était brutal et emporté'.[2]

Other kings Junker met were Badinde son of Bogwa, who, he says, was aged and a man of calm sound judgement, and his nephew Palembata, a young and arrogant fop. 'At a subsequent interview,' writes Junker, 'Badinde put me many other questions in civil and criminal jurisprudence, some of which I found it very difficult to answer; but in many things he himself displayed sound judgement, as well as a sincere desire to act in accordance with right and justice. Some of his difficulties had reference to the victims of the universal belief in witchcraft, and he evidently seemed to fear that perhaps many suffered innocently.'[3] Junker has left us also descriptions of two of the sons of the famous King Kipa, Kana and Bakangai. 'Kanna was of robust appearance, and less corpulent than many of his brothers. The expression of his sharply-chiselled, manly features bespoke firmness, combined with a degree of restraint or reserve. Not a movement betrayed either surprise or pleasure at my appearance, although I was the first European he had ever set eyes on. A full beard, already somewhat gray, enframed his cheeks and chin. an indication of advanced years, for the Negro turns grey later in

[1] *Ibid.*, p. 122. [2] *Ibid.*, p. 123. [3] Junker, *op. cit.*, 1891, p. 200.

life than cultured peoples. Discarding all ornaments, the prince wore nothing but an apron of fig-tree bark, and a leopard-skin head-covering like Bakangai's, which, however, was rather spoilt by a fastening of white European shirt-buttons drawn round the forehead.'[1] Prince Bakangai 'was of low stature, with thick-set figure, very stout, with plenty of flesh about the neck, and in his fortieth year. His features had a kindly expression, despite the quick, piercing glance that betrayed the consciousness of power. The oval face was adorned by a short, bushy black beard, and he wore his hair, Mangbattu fashion, raised high above the crown and gathered behind, while his royal blood was indicated by a leopard-skin cap in form not unlike a bishop's mitre. But the effect was somewhat spoilt by a rag of blue cloth fastened round his forehead. Dispensing with all ornaments, he limited his costume to the rokko of fig-bark girdled round the waist.'[2] Junker also says of him: 'Bakangai lacked the enterprising spirit of his father, Kipa. For him the world was limited to his mbanga [court] and the hundred huts of his women-folk. The short plundering expeditions against the A-Babua and other southern tribes he allowed his sons to carry out. Only once in earlier years he had personally conducted a warlike expedition to the south....'[3]

The Italian officer and cartographer Gaetano Casati, who spent ten years (1879–1889) in Central Africa, very largely among the Azande, and who was in Zandeland at the same time as Junker, has also left us a portrait of these two kings. Of Kana, he says: 'His ways and manners were harsh and rude, but he was sometimes frank. He was careless of his person and clothes. Though clever and brave, public opinion asserted that he was extremely avaricious.' Casati says that he was of an obstinate temper.[4] Of Bakangai, or Bakangoi as he spells the name, he says that he was the second son of Kipa and one of the most powerful of the Zande princes; and that: 'He was astute and clever, and the sturdiness of the barbarians was in him accompanied by an imitation of the courteous and kind manners which he had observed in the ivory merchants. He was little liked, and much feared by his subjects.'[5] Elsewhere, after remarking that in the despotic Zande states the welfare of the people much depended on the disposition of the ruler, he compares these

[1] Junker, *op. cit.*, 1892, p. 23. [2] *Ibid.*, pp. 1–2. [3] *Ibid.*, p. 9.
[4] Gaetano Casati, *Ten Years in Equatoria and the Return with Emin Pasha*, 1891, vol. I, p. 215. [5] *Ibid.*, p. 198.

two sons of Kipa: 'Bakangoi makes his power heavily felt by his subjects, and is hated by them, but revered as a matter of habit;' whereas 'Kanna, firm in his intentions, but intelligent and prudent, conciliates the affection of his subjects.'[1] Bakangai had adopted, at any rate superficially, some features of Arab culture: he 'almost always wore dresses, bought of the merchants. He had an Arab bed, with rich covers, elegant pillows, lamps, and all sorts of vessels and beads.' Casati adds that 'It is the general opinion among potentates of his rank that the greater number a king kills the stronger and more powerful he is; also that fear, not love, makes subjects obedient and faithful. In accordance with these ideas, he was severe and even cruel, and death was the punishment he inflicted for the least fault.[2] His son, Akangai or Akangoi was described by Casati as 'an intelligent man, with a sad and serene look and kind manners'.[3]

Another of Junker's acquaintances was Yakpati son of Yango and grandson of Nunga, whose family and estates had greatly suffered at the hands of the Arabs. Nevertheless, he 'still bore the unmistakable stamp of a Zande prince, his tall, manly figure reminding me of Ndoruma.' With it he had also 'a calm, dignified bearing, a sound judgement, and a pride which was far more justified than the senseless arrogance of the Mangbattu princes. But these qualities are largely shared by the Zandeh nation itself, and were doubly agreeable to me after my long intercourse with the cringing, importunate, and forward Mangbattu peoples.'[4] Later, when Junker was among the Bantu in Uganda, he recollected with nostalgia 'the calm reflective temperament of the A-Zandeh princes'.[5] And he more than once remarks how their bearing is found even among the children of a prince. Barani, a son of the Ndoruma mentioned earlier, 'a mere stripling, who three years before was an inmate of his father's household, received me with a princely condescension, while two of his retainers kept fanning him, which excited in me a feeling more of amusement than anger. He had often been sent by Ndoruma to the Mudiriyeh [capital of a provincial governorate], where he had acquired a good knowledge of Arabic.'[6] Then Junker relates: 'On the third day a short march led to the residence of Ngettua's son Guru, or Mange, a lad scarcely ten years old, who nevertheless gave me a stately reception, and

[1] *Ibid.*, p. 281. [2] *Ibid.*, vol. I, p. 199. [3] *Ibid.*, vol. I, p. 211.
[4] Junker, *op. cit.*, 1892, pp. 142–3.
[5] Junker, *op. cit.*, 1892, p. 482. [6] Junker, *Ibid.*, p. 313.

gallantly discharged all his princely duties. The same evening the new carriers were all ready, and he also sent us dishes of porridge with accompaniments.'[1] It is only rarely that Junker notes a lack of dignity among the Zande princes, as in the case of Gbudwe's eldest son Basongoda, of whom he says: 'He was a genuine Zandeh, already advanced in years, and betraying little princely dignity.'[2] Since he did not die, of sickness, till thirty-two years later and was not remarkably aged then, and his father did not die till twenty-two year later, and then by violence, he could not have been very advanced in years when Junker met him in 1883, but Junker showed good judgement in his assessment of his character, for the Azande of his father's kingdom regarded him as a weak character and a poor ruler.

Junker was attached to the manners and customs of the Zande princes of old times and deplored the changes he saw taking place in them, largely as a result of contact with Nubians and Arabs, especially in the west, where the contact was earliest and deepest. He laments that the western Avongara rulers had not only learnt to speak Arabic, but had also partly changed their way of life, for example, their dwellings were built on the Arab model.[3] We have earlier noted that several of the western kings had in Junker's time already adopted Arab modes of dress. Of another, Pupwa (Junker's Pupo), son of Mopoi (Junker's Mopa) he reports that 'He was a young man, who had acquired much of the Arab culture, and spoke Arabic fluently.'[4]

It was with pleasure, therefore, that Junker moved eastwards, where the people were still uncontaminated by the Arab way of life. 'At Linda's mbanga [court] I again met genuine, old-fashioned Zandehs, retaining their ancient usages, wearing coarse rokko garments, and adorning themselves with the skins of animals. At Zemio's the hankering after a show of Arab culture, which after all could lead only to partial results, had already effaced much of this primitive social system. But here the chiefs still presented themselves in their original elaborate head-dress, armed with shield and spear, as of old; and at the national gatherings they sang their melodious chants, in which, on this occasion, they glorified my

[1] *Ibid.*, pp. 317–18. [2] *Ibid.*, p. 322. [3] *Ibid.*, p. 177.

[4] *Ibid.*, p. 311. All the principal princes in the Western part of Zandeland probably spoke Arabic at the time Europeans entered the country. (*Anglo-Egyptian Sudan Handbook Series: Bahr El Ghazal Province*, 1911, p. 23.)

arrival, and strove to give me proof of their friendly feeling. At the mbanga I was even present at a veritable musical concert, in which the huge and extremely simple instruments were certainly all alike, but nevertheless formed the counterparts to the already-described *marimba.*'[1]

Junker also greatly admired the simplicity of dress and manners of the older kings and was inclined to be critical of the younger generation. We have noted that he called Prince Palembata a 'fop'. Another princeling he met was Binsa, son of King Malingindo, a youth who, he says, lacked the dignity of the older Zande rulers and was a typical dandy of the rising generation. These young lordlings gave considerable attention to the adornment of their persons. 'The hair especially is treated with amazing care, and, at an expenditure of much time, built up in a great variety of head-dresses. The triumphs of our European dames in this respect are far surpassed by the rich diversity of these elaborate coiffures. The towering toupees, or the arrangement of narrow tresses clinging close to the head and falling in wreathes down to the shoulders, are often decked with cowrie shells, glass beads, little copper plates, and other trinkets. A favourite adornment of the forehead is a string of dogs' teeth or of a small wild animals', while the neck is encircled by diverse fine copper, iron, or bead rings, and the like. But the most costly and highly-prized is an ivory ornament falling low down on the breast, and consisting of thirty or forty cylinders from one and a half to two and a half inches long, strung together according to their size, and terminating in a point downwards. The cylinders are supposed to represent the teeth of predatory animals, especially lions, which are very difficult to procure. Throughout the Zandeh lands the lion compared to the leopard is very rare, whereas in those regions where lions are numerous, leopards are seldom seen. These ivory ornaments, whose preparation with their primitive tools involves an amazing display of skill and patience, belong properly to an earlier, one might almost say a classical, period of native art, and are now possessed only by a privileged few.

'The toilet of the Zandeh fop is not complete without the little straw hat, which, as far as the form of the chignon allows, is set jauntily on the crown, and decked with a tuft of cock's feathers slit up through the quills to let them waive more lightly on the breeze. The whole effect is also heightened by smearing the body

[1] *Ibid.*, pp. 307–8.

with powdered red dyewood, or painting it with the juice of gardenia.'[1]

We have one other person to consider in Junker's account, Ringio or Ringa. He was at one time a servant of the Welsh trader John Petherick, the first European to reach the confines of Zandeland, in 1858. He later represented first Arab traders and then the Egyptian Government in the country of the Adio and Bombe (Makaraka) Azande, the most easterly extension of this people, whose ruler he became. Petherick says that he was the son of Gorea or Goria (?Ngoliyo), Shaikh of Beringi and grandson of Harquati, and that his brothers were Bashima and Basia.[2] Schweinfurth says that he was a brother of Indimma and a son of Renzi son of Yakpati.[3] Junker also says that he was Ndimma's brother but gives his father's name as Ngerria (Pethericks' Gorea or Goria); and he tells us that he had been captured in his boyhood and taken as a slave to Khartoum. Junker found him 'an intelligent-looking, robust negro forty years old, courteous in his demeanour, and evidently anxious to pass for a "cultivated" Nubian'.[4] Casati also met him and says of him: 'Endowed with an iron hand and a great amount of good sense, he had succeeded in disciplining his people, who were not only naturally inclined to freedom, but also to disorder'; and that 'He was a genial man, and his manners were courteous and respectful. Wando, the great chief of the Sandeh of the West, had paid him a visit a short time previously, and he told me, evidently with great pleasure, of the reluctance of the chief to change his old customs and habits.'[5] This Ringio served the Egyptian Government well, supplying them with troops and labourers. It was four thousand of his men who, at great cost to themselves, carried the sections of Gordon's steamers, *Khedive* and *Nyanza*, from Muggi to Dufile on the Nile when Gordon was Governor of the Equatorial Province. He was eventually murdered by agents of that same Government, and it is not surprising therefore that later his people showed some sympathy with the Dervishes. However, I include Ringio in this portrait gallery of the royal house with some misgivings, partly because there is divergence of opinion among our European authorities about whose son

[1] *Idem.*, 1891, pp. 287–8.
[2] Mr. and Mrs. Petherick, *Travels in Central Africa*, 1869, p. 63.
[3] *Op. cit.*, vol. II, p. 36.
[4] *Op. cit.*, 1890, pp. 481 and 304.
[5] *Op. cit.*, vol. I, pp. 252–3.

he was and also because I was told by a good Zande authority that he was a commoner of the Aboro clan. He might well have tried to persuade Arabs and Europeans that he was of noble birth. I can make no firm decision on this question, since I did not probe into it when I had the opportunity to do so.

In concluding Junker's testimony to the ability and character of the Zande ruling house of the Avongara clan I cite the reason, or one reason, he gives for their superior intellectual qualities: 'The higher circles, princes and nobles, are the most highly endowed with intellectual qualities. This is doubtless due to the fact that, despite his limited sphere of action, the Negro ruler is still compelled to think and act in his capacity as judge, law-giver, and captain, whereby his cerebral activity has more play than that of the common folk. To this must be added the fluency acquired by the long parliamentary speeches at the *mbanga*, a sort of witenagemote, where the winged word, often embellished with simile and metaphor, stimulates thought and promotes readiness of expression. The lower classes are doubtless also present at these assemblies, but in their slavish dependence assist only as dumb spectators, except when called upon to speak as plaintiff or defendant. Special gatherings and meetings of the commonalty to deliberate on any topic of general interest are unknown to these peoples. Every question is discussed at the place of assembly in the immediate vicinity of the royal residence, or at the *mbanga* [court] of the vassal chiefs.'[1]

I have earlier mentioned some of the kings and princes whom Casati met, as it seemed appropriate to place his impressions next to others when they were those of the same man. In Casati's case we have to remember that he had to rely on his memory as he lost all his notes when he was imprisoned by Kabarega, the king of the Banyoro, in Uganda. A letter he wrote to the Editor of the *Esploratore*, in September 1880, however, sets forth at the time of his meeting him his impressions of Zambare, brother of the aforementioned Ndoruma: he says that Ndoruma's brother arrived with a large following of dignitaries and about a hundred porters bearing ivory to visit Gessi. His name was Zambaré, and he was about twenty-five years of age. His features were perfectly regular, and only his complexion, which was dark olive, made him look different from Europeans. His hair was long and wooly, and was

[1] *Op. cit.*, 1891, p. 157.

entwined and ornamented with large beads. He had thin whiskers and a black beard some twelve inches long. He had round his neck a chain made of the seeds of *bogó*, the kernels of a wild fruit. His head-dress was formed of a monkey's skin with a thick plume of cock's feathers, resembling that of our Bersagliere, on the hinder part. Round his waist he wore a cord an inch thick, to which was attached a piece of barkcloth, the only stuff used by the Azande.[1] In his book he gives another description of the same man: 'During my sojourn in Wau, the brother of the Sultan Mdarama, chief of an extensive territory inhabited by the Sandeh or Niam-Niam, came to pay his respects to Gessi, with a numerous following of dignitaries and a hundred loads of ivory, and announced that his brother would shortly come in person, being desirous to continue friendly relations. Zambara, who might be a man of twenty-five years of age, was of regular features and dark olive complexion, middle height, well-proportioned limbs, with a small mouth and not thick lips; boasting of plaited hair, adorned with large beads. He wore a necklace of seeds of wild fruit; his head was covered with a monkey-skin cap, from which hung a thick bunch of cock's feathers, that made him known as a chief of warriors at a glance. He was girt about the waist with a thick cord, to which was fastened a linen skirt, made from the broken bark of a fallen tree (sic!); it covered his body to the knees, and one corner of it was tucked up.'[2]

Casati's opinion of two of the sons of Kipa, Kana and Bakangai, has already been given. He also met a third son, Prince Zebo, of whom he wrote: 'He was tall, with well-proportioned limbs. His countenance had a resolute expression of something more than boldness; it was ferocity. His face was blackened with charcoal dust, and he was wearing a torn garment made of bark fibres, which covered him from his waist downwards. He had no ornament either on his wrists or round his waist.'[3] He also met Kipa's brother, the aged Ndeni: 'A tall, upright man, with grey hair, and very cordial manners, with a smile always on his face.'[4] Kipa had died before Casati visited his country, but his appearance must have been described to him by Azande, for he wrote of him: 'Nti-kima [Kipa] was tall and well-built, with a keen and penetrating

[1] Gessi, *op. cit.*, p. 448.

[2] Casati, *op. cit.*, vol. I, pp. 57–8. 'Broken bark of a fallen tree' must be a mistranslation from the original Italian, which I have not seen. What must, I think, be meant is: made from the bark of a fig-tree.

[3] *Ibid.*, vol. I, p. 191.

[4] *Ibid.*, vol. I, p. 197.

eye. He used to dress plainly, and was in the habit of blackening his face and neck with fine charcoal dust.'[1]

I conclude these descriptions of Zande kings and princes by travellers with a few more quotations from the writings of Belgian officers, who had, when they were taking over the country, excellent opportunities for meeting some of the more notable Avongara rulers and assessing their temperaments, characters, and abilities, and some remarks by an Austrian and a German traveller.

Louis-Napoléon Chaltin in his notes describes the arrival of Mopoi, son of Mopoi, at the Belgian post of Amadis in 1896:' C'est une entrée triomphale; les tambours battent, les oliphants rugissent, les grelots s'agitent, d'autres instruments font entendre des sons de bois secs heurtés les uns contre les autres, les soldats tirent des coups de fusil. La masse s'ébranle, Mopoie marchant devant, entouré de sa cour, une cour qui obéit et marche au doigt et à l'oeil. Mais, précédant le tout, de malheureux Akaris (les anciens possesseurs du sol occupé par les Azande), portant des pointes d'ivoire et encadrés de fusiliers, d'archers et de lanciers . . . Mopoie s'avance donc, suivi de tout son monde. Il est radieux, fier, sa démarche est assurée. Il salue profondément Devenyns (chef de poste), qui est allé à sa rencontre. Le sauvage orchestre donne tout ce qu'il peut à l'entrée de la station; le tapage est assourdissant, affolant. Mopoie tire six coups de revolver: c'est son salut. Il se dirige vers nous, s'incline respectueusement, et c'est presque agenouillé qu'il presse ma main droite entre les siennes. Je suis obligé de lui demander de suspendre l'exécution "des morceaux choisis" qu'à tour de bras et à coups de gosier son orchestre nous inflige. . . .'[2]

He sketches a portrait of Mopoi: 'Mopoie est un homme de haute taille, bien découplé, bien musclé, aux proportions bien gardées. Son visage, d'un noir d'ébène, est rond plutôt qu'ovale; il est très agréable et éclairé d'une paire d'yeux vifs et très mobiles; son regard est franc; Mopoie regarde son interlocuteur bien en face; il ne détourne jamais les yeux. Comme tous les noirs, il a des dents superbes. Il porte le costume arabe et dans des sacoches suspendues à sa ceinture se trouvent des extraits du Coran. Il égrène parfois un énorme chapelet. Il m'a produit une excellente impression et a répondu avec franchise et sincérité, me semble-t-il, à toutes mes questions. Il m'a promis de servir d'intermédiaire avec Ndoruma et Mbima. Je l'autorise à faire la guerre à Badindé, qui l'inquiète et lui tue les hommes qu'il

[1] *Ibid.*, vol. I, p. 209.

[2] Lotar, *op. cit.*, p. 250.

envoie vers le Nord. Mopoie m'offre un sabre de derviche. Trait de moeurs: le fils de Sasa, Torombet, neveu de Mopoie, a refusé de s'asseoir à côté de son oncle, l'étiquette le lui défendant.

'Un soldat du poste, Zande de Djabir, est venu saluer Mopoie et a déposé quatre mitakos à ses pieds. Le Sultan n'a pas même daigné remercier. L'autre s'est néanmoins retiré satisfait.'[1]

I have earlier recorded descriptions of the aged and obese Wando. His sons Mbitimo, Ukwe, and Renzi quarrelled continuously among themselves during his lifetime and brought in Egyptian Government forces, the Dervishes, and the Belgians to serve their several and opposed ends. When Ukwe died in February 1896 Chaltin, who knew him well, wrote of him: 'La mort d'Ukwa débarrasse les Européens de Dungu d'un puissant voisin dont l'ambition toujours en éveil était sans limites. Il ne visait qu'à agrandir ses États et avait à ce sujet des démêlés continuels avec les autre chefs. D'après les indigènes, il avait empoisonné son père Wando et son frère Mbittima pour entrer plus vite en possession de leurs biens. Son fils Bokoyo est un jeune homme d'une vingtaine d'années, grand, bien découplé, a la physionomie ouverte et intelligente. Il aime le Blanc et l'accompagne volontiers en voyage.'[2]

Chaltin has also given us (1896) a portrait of Renzi, whom he also knew well: 'Cet Avungura, dépeint si différemment par ceux qui ont eu des rapports avec lui, a la figure intelligente, l'oeil interrogateur. Il étudie son interlocuteur, l'examine attentivement. Au physique, il ne ressemble pas aux fils de son frère Ukwe. Il a moins de robustesse, il est nerveux; les autres sont tout en chair. C'est un homme décidé et aventureux qui a été au service de tous les conquérants dont son pays a reçu la visite. Les mahdistes, il est vrai, ont usé de contrainte envers lui. Il s'engage à me conduire à Redjaf et à Lado, mais a condition que Bokoyo, dont il craint un mauvais coup, n'accompagne pas.'[3]

I add three other Belgian portraits of lesser princes. Clément Vande Vliet says of Borongo son of Bowili and a descendant of Mabenge: 'Borongo a à peu près la même taille que Suronga [a Barambo chief], mais il est plus corpulent et mieux conformé. Son regard inspire la confiance.'[4] Gustin's portrait of Kipa son of Zemoi and grandson of Kambisa, who was wearing a costume the Belgians had given him, is: 'Grand, svelte, bien proportionné, pas lippu, le

[1] *Ibid.*, p. 251.
[2] *Ibid.*, p. 237.
[3] *Ibid.*, p. 255.
[4] *Ibid.*, p. 102.

nez non épaté; moustache frisée; pas de barbe.'[1] Gustin says of Bendo son of Ngelia: 'Gendo [Bendo] est vêtu à la mode arabe; il porte une cartouchière soudanaise. Un boy de sa suite est porteur de son fusil, cadeau de Ponthier. Il est le fils préféré de Galia, dont il est l'héritier présomptif.'[2]

[The Austrian, Franz Xaver Geyer, Apostolic Vicar for Central Africa, in 1906 journeyed southwards from Wau to the kingdom of Tembura and what had been that of Ndoruma, of whom Gessi and Junker gave us so vivid a sketch. At the time of his meeting with Tembura, the king was about fifty-five years of age and was tall and strongly built. He had a deep black skin and thick lips, unlike the colour and lips of the average Zande. 'The scanty beard which surrounded his face heightened the expression of benevolence. The eyes showed cleverness and security enhanced by experience. But in his eyes there was also the fire of animal sensuousness and the mouth showed signs of brute force and cruelty. This masculine and commanding appearance was matched by simplicity and artless dignity of behaviour. He represented a sultan who excels the ordinary people in body and spirit, and one gained the impression that one was dealing with a rough-grained, able and cunning man, who might also be cruel and forceful and who could adapt himself to any situation and was capable of anything. He had heart but also unpredictable passion.' He was 'passionate, moody and cruel'; and he was 'an opportunist'.[3] Geyer described Tembura's half-brother Bekka as 'a tall man with lively eyes' who had come to the north while young and had there met Arab traders from whom he learnt Arabic: 'In contrast to the true native Niam Niam he is a cunning fox whose partly cringing and partly hypocritical and impertinent manner inspires little confidence and credibility.' Bekka's second son, Mashena, a youth of about twenty-three years, was 'tall and slim like a date palm', light copper in colour, and with a 'fiery and forceful expression'.[4] Of a son of Bati, a brother of Tembura, who had charge of a district at the early age of fourteen, Geyer says that he was 'of friendly and pleasing appearance'.[5]

Ndoruma's eldest son Mvuto was a man of barely forty, of little more than medium height, well-built and well-fed, and of copper-coloured skin. 'The clothes that he wore could not destroy altogether

[1] *Ibid.*, p. 57.
[2] *Ibid.*, p. 57.
[3] *Durch Sand, Sumpf und Wald*, 1914, pp. 281–2.
[4] *Ibid.*, pp. 291–3.
[5] *Ibid.*, p. 277.

the impression of savagery that surrounded him. He may have been benevolent, but he was certainly a savage (*wilder*) prince. To this was added a shadow of deep dissatisfaction which was reflected in his face.'[1] He was at the time having difficulties with his family. It is curious that Geyer should speak of him as benevolent, for he had among Azande a shocking reputation for cruelty. Geyer also met Mvuto's son Bujo, a copper-coloured boy of about fourteen years of age and of slender build and pleasing features.[2]

My last quotation is from von Wiese, whose account of his interviews with Zemoi has been cited earlier. It is about Hetman, a prince of the Bandiya family, who rule a section of the Azande to the extreme west, whereas the rest of the Azande are ruled by the Vongara family who have formed the subject of this paper. Political institutions are much the same in Bandiya and Vongara Country. Von Wiese met Hetman in 1911, and he says this of him: 'Sultan Hetman, the son of Rafai, has acquired European ideas and tastes. He speaks fluent French, wears a European uniform, and proudly displays upon his breast the order of the Black Star of Benin. He has been to the coast and has inspected the large European liners, with all their up-to-date appliances. He lives in a house built in the European style, with European furniture, a European kitchen and cellar, and he invites Europeans to dinner.'][3]

I have greater confidence in my own assessment, with which I opened this paper, of the character and ability of Zande kings and princes in that those who had the opportunity of judging them before they came under European administration are in general in agreement both with it and among themselves. It is only rarely that an individual has made a bad impression on these earliest visitors to Zandeland: one is unctuous, another brutal and hotheaded, another cruel, another arrogant and a fop, another harsh and rude, and another avaricious. On the whole, however, they speak highly of them. They stress their natural dignity of bearing, unostentatious pride, distinguished air, courteous manners, cordiality, self-assurance, composure, reserve, reflectiveness, and generosity, and their intelligence and calm, sound judgement, firmness, astuteness, and prudence.

[1] *Ibid.*, p. 298. [2] *Ibid.*, p. 194. [3] *Op. cit.*, pp. 210–11.

6

HEREDITY AND GESTATION AS THE AZANDE SEE THEM

1932

In this paper I am going to describe Zande ideas and behaviour with regard to conception and gestation. I shall break off my description before it reaches the final phase of birth and shall give main attention to Zande ideas about embryonic growth and to conventional behaviour of parents during pregnancy. It is possible to describe events in this way without making a great cleavage in their transition because they tend to fall into three distinct periods of activity: gestation, birth and seclusion of mother and child, and their ceremonial exit from seclusion. I shall restrict my description in this essay to the first of these periods.

Azande have no doubt about the cause of conception, they know that it results from congress of man and woman. They do not understand the full physiological processes through which conception takes place but they are aware that it is due to the semen of a man entering into a woman. Semen is called *nzira* or *mbisimo gude* the latter term meaning 'soul of a child', while the womb is called *ba agude* or *bambu agude* meaning literally the 'place or hut of children'. Azande believe however that the mucus (*nzira*) which a woman emits during intercourse also contains a soul or souls of the unborn, and that conception is a result of the union of male semen and female mucus. Thus two souls, one of the man and one of the woman, are necessary for birth of a child and if either partner lacks these souls marriage will be unfruitful. It is thought also that if the *mbisimo* (soul) of a man is stronger than the *mbisimo* of a woman a boy will be born whereas if the *mbisimo* of a woman is the stronger a girl will be conceived.

This dual causation of conception is asserted unequivocably by the Azande. They say: '*nzira kumba nagwali ka koda ti ru na ga de ka meka ti ru na kule ka sa ti ru ni gude*' ('semen of man goes to unite itself with that of a woman to build itself up with the blood and change itself into a child').

And again they say of a woman: '*nzira kumbani ki ta gwali na gani nzira nga ga de,si ki nigbia ti ru ka sa rogo ru dunduko na kina ha ki niza ti e ka du ni bakere kule ti e*' ('semen of her husband goes with her mucus, they meet together and thoroughly mix with one another and then begin to be in the midst of copious blood'). They think that a woman must also have souls of children in her mucus because they observe that children sometimes resemble their mothers and sometimes their fathers. They notice also that a child will often take after both parents. Thus its facial features may be those of its mother while its gait reminds people of its father. '*Si Azande naya ti ni mbisimo de na ga kumba si du nasa ti ru sale ka fu vungu, mbiko boro nabatika gu gude u ki wili nani, ki batika guru a u ki wili bani a.*' ('Thus Azande say about it that the soul of the woman and that of the man develop into a child, because they beget one child which resembles its mother and then beget another which resembles its father.')

Three points in these statements need further elucidation, the meaning which the Azande attach to the term *nzira* which they use alike for the semen ejaculated by the male during orgasm and for the mucus secreted by the female during intercourse; the meaning which they attach to the term *mbisimo* which is found in both semen and mucus and which I have translated 'soul', and the relation of their beliefs about the parts played by man and woman in conception to other opinions about the human body and its soul.

Before I comment on these points I may draw attention to another factor in conception. In Zande opinion Mboli, the Supreme Being, is responsible for birth. A woman cannot conceive unless it is the will of Mboli. '*Mboli nifu mbisimo fu boro ni batika, ka Mboli funga mbisimo fu boro ya ni abatikangate*' ('Mboli gives a soul to a man to beget a child, if Mboli does not give a man a soul he will not beget children'); and in speaking of the growth of a foetus in the womb I have heard a Zande stop in the middle of his description to point out that these things do not happen of themselves but that it is Mboli who arranges their disposition. As in all else Mboli is far-off, little-intruding, and seldom-thought-of, but is nevertheless, according to Zande notions, the final cause of conception, gestation and birth. Man, woman and Mboli, are the three factors which cause conception. I will not describe in this paper the various influences which can prevent conception, such as witchcraft, hostility of wife's mother to her son-in-law, curses of relatives, and various magical rites, nor will I discuss the methods of abortion which women are said to employ.

Men and women cannot beget children until they reach maturity. Azande say that in the early stages of male puberty the seminal fluid (*nzira*) does not contain souls of children (*mbisimo gude*) and it is only when a boy blossoms into manhood that his semen becomes fertile. That the souls of children are connected by a simple inference with the presence of spermatozoa in the seminal fluid is shown by the statement that the fluid becomes fertile when it ceases to have the appearance of water and becomes thick and slimy like the yolk of an egg (*wa kina parakondo, ni zelezele he rororo rororo*). Semen is thought to cause a boy's first ejaculation by collecting at the root of the organ and forcing its way out. This first ejaculation of semen is somewhat painful since the semen 'burns like fire' but afterwards the boy ejaculates without difficulty though for a long time his seminal fluid is like water. A boy of about twelve to fourteen years of age is said to have orgasms without emissions; from about fourteen to sixteen his emissions are 'merely like urine' and contain no *mbisimo gude*; at about seventeen years of age they contain *mbisimo gude*.[1] A man considers himself capable of procreating children so long as he is able to ejaculate sperm. Azande speak of urine and semen coming along the same path from the *bambu agude*[2] into the bladder and thence into the penis. Their paths separate somewhere between the kidneys and the spine. Doubt in my own mind about the exact organs to which Azande refer when they speak of physiological processes renders it difficult to ascertain the extent of their knowledge and to translate their opinions. Certainly they do not understand the function of the testicles which 'are just nothing at all but exist in order to support a man's organ and to carry it'. One informant said that a little of the water which one drank passed into the testicles.

[1] The Zande does not speak of people as of so many years of age. The ages given above are my estimates for actual persons designated as examples by my informants.

[2] The womb in a woman and a corresponding part in a man (the prostate?).

Women also become fertile only when they reach maturity. 'However much intercourse a small girl has her mucus is not capable of giving her a child. It is only after her breasts begin to grow and her hips broaden and strengthen that her mucus begins to contain souls of children. The mucus which a girl secretes shortly after her first intercourse is like water. Thus Azande say that a girl must grow up before she can have a child. If she conceives before she is properly grown up she will die in child-birth. This is why a man will not think his wife barren because she does not bear him children when she is small, but he waits till she is grown up, and it is only when her breasts have begun to fall without her having given birth to a child that her husband begins to think that she is barren.' Some women are thought to be more fertile by nature than others just as one soil is more fertile than another. Thus they will sometimes say of a woman who has born many children that her abdomen is *mbudu*, a rich, black, sandy soil, near the edge of a stream, which gives an abundant crop of ground-nuts. If a grown-up woman does not conceive, her husband will consult oracles to find out the cause, but the oracles may tell him that she is barren, in which case he can do nothing, for barrenness is due to Mboli and cannot be overcome. Azande consider that the birthrate has fallen considerably since European occupation of their country and they attribute this partly to widespread adultery which has followed on the destruction of their old institutions. Adulterous intercourse with a large number of men renders a woman less fruitful because 'the womb (*ba agude*) suffers from so many organs'.

A short paragraph must suffice to explain the concept of *mbisimo*, the soul. A foetus is a soul with an undeveloped body, and even when the child is born the soul has not become completely and permanently attached to its abode. Hence it is feared that the soul may flit away, and this is one of the reasons for confining infant and mother to a hut for several days after birth, lest '*mbisimo gude ka ndu ka inga*', 'the child's soul might get lost'. This idea of a new-born babe as not yet constituting a full human being is further displayed in linguistic usage for one commonly hears the foetus spoken of as *si* (the pronoun used for things) though often it is referred to as *u* (the pronoun used for animals and birds) and they continue to speak of a baby as *u* until it grows strong and they have no doubt that it will live when they will begin to talk about it as *ko* (the masculine pronoun) or as *li* (the feminine pronoun) according to its sex. In the early stages of infancy Azande are always anxious lest the soul shall fly away for it is still considered to be loosely fettered to its body. The *mbisimo* grows in strength as a child grows and it wanes as a man wanes in old age. It is the vital part which wanders in dreams, which is attacked by witches, and which weakens in sickness. In old age a man becomes again like a little child and as bodily power declines he returns nearer and nearer to the pure *mbisimo* stage and this *mbisimo* may at any time flit away. Hence sometimes one hears people say of a very old relative 'he is our *atoro*' for when *ambisimo* (souls) leave bodies at death they become *atoro* (ghosts of the dead).[1]

This brings me to the third point selected for comment, the idea that both man and woman contribute to produce a child through the union of their souls. Though the Zande appears generally to think of a person having a single *mbisimo* which at death goes to the land of ghosts, at the heads of streams, he often puts it forward in discussion that there is a second soul which changes at death into a totem animal of a clan. This second soul seems to be a spiritual emanation from the body itself whereas the first soul is independent of the body but Zande eschatology is never clear on this point. I regard it as legitimate nevertheless to speak of the first soul, which goes to live at the heads of streams, as the spirit-soul and of the second soul, which becomes a totemic animal, as the body-soul. The spirit-soul, which is what Azande mean when they talk about *mbisimo*, is derived from the father, in spite of what is said about the mother's co-operation in its creation, and this is what makes all children, irrespective of sex, members of their father's clan. But it is thought by many people, though opinion is not unanimous, that change into a totemic animal varies according to sex, the body-souls of boys becoming totems of their father's clan and the body-souls of girls becoming the totems of their mother's clan. I want to make it clear that no Zande has ever suggested to me a connection between their beliefs about conception and their beliefs about changing into totemic creatures after death. These beliefs are, however, to some extent complementary.

Of great importance in this respect are Zande doctrines about the inheritance of *mangu* or witchcraft which is a physical trait inherited unilaterally from either father to son or from mother to

[1] Like the Latin equivalent, *manes*, *atoro* has no singular form.

daughter but never from father to daughter or from mother to son. Inheritance of witchcraft goes together with inheritance of sexual characters. A female child is born with the sexual characters of its mother and if the mother is a witch the child will be a witch also. Nevertheless a child of either sex belongs to the clan of its father and not to the clan of its mother.

These ideas about the dual process of conception spring from the dual nature of the family itself. A man is related to his kin on his father's side and to his kin on his mother's side and he has obligations to carry out towards both. Knowledge that father and mother both play a part in the physiology of parenthood is surely bound up with this social balance. There is a tendency to emphasize the father's part in procreation beyond that of the mother just as the father's side of the family is stressed socially to a greater extent than the mother's side of the family. There is always a balance and a bias in such matters in every community in the world.

The woman contributes to the formation of the child's soul and it is she who provides the infant with blood and food for its growth while it is in her womb and afterwards suckles it at her breasts. When a Zande speaks of the functions of motherhood he points to the way in which a mother bears her child in her body, to the way in which she suckles it, and to the way in which she carries it in her arms or on her hips. Thus a maternal aunt will reproach a boy by reminding him of his mother's pains during parturition and her cares during infancy, while a maternal uncle will curse his nephew by blowing on his breast, which he takes between thumb and fingers, in reference to the part which their clan has played in his nurture. But when people speak of the functions of fatherhood they point to the original act of procreation rather than to any subsequent service which a father may perform. Everybody knows that a woman cannot conceive until a man has had intercourse with her and has sent his sperm into her body. This is the main contribution of a father towards his child's existence for he plays a very small part in providing for its nurture and in attending to its infant wants. Hence a father or a paternal uncle when cursing his son or nephew will slap his thighs saying that it is these thighs which he pressed against the bed when he begat the youth and he will take his organ in his hand and blow on it and utter a curse over it. There is no absolute regularity in modes of speech but as a rule when people of a man's father's clan wish to remind him of his duties towards them they ask him to remember that 'it is we who begat you', whereas people of a man's mother's clan recall their services by using the phrase 'it is we who carried you'.

Conception is the threshold of pregnancy. Pregnancy is marked by physical changes in the mother and child and is recognized also by certain conventions to which the father and mother are expected to conform. A man suspects that his wife is pregnant when menstruation ceases and he becomes aware of this change by observing that she continues to sleep with him during the whole month instead of spending a few days apart as is usual in menstruation, during which it is expressly forbidden for a man to have congress with his wife. In spite of this evidence the husband is doubtful for the first month whether his wife has conceived, since it sometimes happens that a woman misses her monthly period. He feels more confident during the second month of unbroken intercourse and when the third moon begins to grow without his wife sleeping apart from him he is certain that she is going to bear him a child. By this time other signs of pregnancy have become manifest. Azande say that the mother's skin takes on a new lustre and glistens with an unwonted reddish brightness; her body appears to fill out and its round contours become more pronounced; her breasts become firmer and their nipples stand erect and take on a darker shade of colouring; and her navel sticks out prominently. The surest sign of conception is the swelling of the abdomen and people judge from its size how far gestation is advanced.

The physical changes which take place in a foetus (*nganda*) cannot, of course, be observed directly, but the Zande has derived a certain amount of indirect information about them from opening up bodies of female animals and birds and no doubt also from examining premature human births. His knowledge of embryology is confused and he understands little about the physiology of the human body, but by putting two and two together he has formed a rough idea about what happens during gestation. Azande have seen ova in hens when preparing them for cooking and they think that the womb (*ba agude*) contains something of the same nature. They say that the womb is located between the navel and a corresponding point in the back; it lies behind the bladder near where the excreta pass from the intestines into the rectum. Their information may be more precise, but my own knowledge of the human body was often insufficient to follow the exact meaning of Zande descriptions in this sphere.[1] They connect the cessation of menstruation with the utilization of the economized blood to form a child in the womb and they are aware that when a woman has ceased to menstruate she has passed the age of child-bearing. 'When a woman is with child a great amount of blood collects in her body and the child is in the midst of this blood, a little thing like a young rat [or mouse]. It is just a tiny thing surrounded by a pool of blood and it begins to change its form and to grow in this blood. When it has reached the stage of a human being the blood, in the fullness of which the child has taken its shape, now forms a small net (*rukumbu*), in the centre of which the child lives. It continues to grow in this net. Copious blood collects together and forms the child and its residue makes a net around it. It is this which they call *likikpwo*[2] and of which one will hear it said that such and such a woman has given birth to a child but that the *likikpwo* has not fallen. The child remains in this little net and nibbles at it with its lips and rubs it with its nose until the mother groans in pain.' The child is thought of as slowly boring its way out of this web with its hands and face. A few days before birth the child begins feeling out with its legs and to twist and turn in the womb. In these final days a few drops of water tinged with blood, called *ndika sule*, make their appearance. Then the child causes its mother severe pain and they prepare for delivery.

Another informant spoke of the early foetus as huddled up in a pool of blood like a lizard. This same informant said that the child lacks only teeth for completeness when it has finished its growth in the womb. 'A child starts in the middle, then its head is formed, then its mouth, then its arms diverge while its limbs still form part of its back and then it begins to separate fingers and toes. Meanwhile its eyes and mouth are still closed, the mouth opening after about three months. The anus remains closed until the mid-wife

[1] For instance, it is possible that Azande distinguish between the womb and the ovarium.

[2] The same word is used for the part of a man which is removed and eaten by witches and also for the piece of barkcloth taken from a corpse, and its little finger or toe nail, which are used for making magic to avenge death. Here *likikpwo* refers to the *placenta* and I am indebted to Major R. G. Gayer-Anderson for the suggestion that *rukumbu* should be translated 'sack' or 'membrane' since it clearly refers to the sack attached to the *placenta*. He points out that since this membrane is often torn in many places during delivery it is understandable that the Zande speaks of it as a net.

opens it after birth.[1] If it is a boy the penis appears in the second month. If it is a girl a small vaginal channel appears in the second month.' The man who spoke these words was speaking loosely and intended to give a rough idea of the growth of a foetus, mentioning each point as it occurred to him without presenting a thought-out sequence of embryological changes.

The second element which builds up a child in the womb is the father's semen. There is no taboo on intercourse during pregnancy and a man continues to have relations with his wife during at any rate the first five or six months of gestation and even during the sixth and seventh months, though he is careful to lie at her side and not on top of her. Intercourse during pregnancy is considered most beneficial to the child for the semen assists in building up its body in its mother's womb. The function of the father's semen at this stage is to make the child grow. A rigid prohibition on cohabitation commences after the child is born. Nevertheless some people say that a man should cease intercourse with his wife when she is in an advanced state of pregnancy lest he should injure his child's mouth with his organ, for towards the end of gestation the child is thought to come down towards the entrance to the vagina. Hence people will say of a child born with a disproportionally large mouth that it has been spoilt by its father. Others say that a man may have relations with his wife up to the last month of pregnancy. One man asked 'how will the child be born if the path down which it must come is not kept open?'

The third factor which builds up a foetus is the food which a mother consumes. The child is thought to absorb a liquid extract of these foods (*ime liae*) since it cannot eat them in the solid owing to the smallness and ineffectiveness of its mouth. It drinks a little of the beer swallowed by its mother and is also believed to wash itself in beer so that they say of a baby born with a very clean body that its mother must have drunk much beer during pregnancy.

Lagae says[2] that the Zande woman is well aware that the period of gestation lasts nine months but I cannot agree with him in this statement. In the first place they do not know with any degree of accuracy when a woman has conceived and in the second place they do not reckon up future events by counting the number of moons which will elapse before they ensue, even though they have

[1] The midwife puts her little finger up the child's anus shortly after birth.

[2] Lagae: *Les Azande*, p. 166.

names for each moon. They know that the growth of a foetus is slow and that it will take many moons for it to develop. They can also tell you in which part of the year a woman is likely to be delivered. Thus a woman who is observed to be pregnant when the edible *akedo* termites are swarming (cir. end of March and beginning of April) will be delivered at the time of sowing millet (cir. August-September); a woman observed to be pregnant during the sowing of millet is expected to give birth when they are harvesting the remnants of the crop (cir. January-February), while a woman who manifests signs of pregnancy at the commencement of the millet harvest (cir. December) will have a child when the *abio* termites are swarming (cir. May-June) or later when people are starting to hoe their millet gardens (cir. July-August). If you ask a Zande how many months a child remains in the womb he cannot tell you because he does not count the months. We can make a rough reckoning from his time estimates which will show us that by long experience he knows during which period of economic activity a woman will be delivered by correlating the first sure signs of pregnancy, in about the third month, with the economic labour which is going on at this time. On his estimates this means a period of five to seven months, but the Zande reckons by seasonal undertakings. One woman told me that there are two kinds of pregnancy, the *nguru* and the *anabeleyulu*.[1] In the *nguru* there is little swelling of the abdomen and the period of gestation is shorter than in the *anabeleyulu* type of pregnancy in which also the stomach swells to a much greater size. To sum up we may say that old people, women especially, can tell roughly the time when an expectant woman will be delivered and that they can reckon more precisely the nearer the time for delivery approaches but that their opinions are subject to much variation and inaccuracy.

Besides undergoing physical changes an expectant mother is also being socially transformed. Society gives little recognition of the state of pregnancy by imposing prescriptions and prohibitions of behaviour on the parents. However both parents are expected to perform certain actions and they generally conform to what is expected of them. The father on his part observes no special taboos during this period but occupies himself in an orgy of oracle consulta-

[1] These are terms used for swarmings of edible termites which take place shortly after sunset and about ten o'clock p.m. respectively. Hence in their extension to denote pregnancies they mean 'early' and 'late'.

tions. Today, though to lesser extent than in earlier times, a husband, as soon as he feels sure that his wife is pregnant, hastens to consult the *benge* oracle whether the child was conceived in wedlock or is the fruit of adultery, and he has no peace till he is reassured on this point. It is obvious from what we have seen of Zande notions on the subject of conception that a woman can conceive equally well from relations with another man as with her husband, and no Zande puts any trust in the virtue of his wife. Moreover, even if the husband has in the first place impregnated his wife another man may add his semen afterwards and so contribute to building up the child. Thus they speak of *koda gude na kura kumba*, to produce a child with another man, *i.e.* two men produce the child. The greatest emphasis is laid upon legitimacy and a man will not hesitate to flog a pregnant wife to extract from her the name of her lover if the oracle tells him that she has conceived in adultery. It is said that in the past a man would sometimes kill a male child if it were illegitimate though he would spare a female child in order to obtain her marriage-spears when she grew up. It is necessary to say that I have recorded no instances of infanticide of this kind, but also to add that I neglected to inquire for them. The husband goes into the bush and there asks *benge* whether the child in the body of his wife is really his fruit, his *mbisimo*. When he is assured of the legitimacy of the child he commences a series of oracle consultations about its welfare and the welfare of its mother. He asks at intervals during pregnancy whether the child will be born without injury, whether the mother will survive its birth, whether witches are seeking to injure either of them, where is a propitious spot for the birth to take place, who shall act as midwife, and so on. Not only the husband but his wife's relatives and the wife herself may consult various oracles about similar questions. But the onus is on the husband. It is his duty to make these inquiries and if he does not do so there may be difficulty later with his parents-in-law because he has taken no steps to protect their daughter from the perils of child-birth.

Lagae says that Azande always make offering to the ghosts of their dead relatives at this time and that the future mother sits near their shrine while her father prays to the spirits to protect her. He says that the husband remains at a distance while his wife's father addresses the ghosts, sprinkles her with a sprig of the *bombili* tree dipped in water, and places an offering of food on the shrine. Lagae also says that they offer prayers to the Supreme Being, Mboli, asking his protection for mother and child.[1] I was told that a man might make occasional requests to Mboli at this time but that he would not make a ritual address to the ghosts, nor get his father-in-law to do so, unless something goes wrong with the pregnancy, which generally means that the *benge* oracle prophesies some misfortune; in which case the above-mentioned ceremony will be performed, especially if *benge* recommends it.

The ghosts are not likely to interfere with anyone to molest him if he is leading a reasonably respectable life for they bear him no ill-will since they are the departed souls of his nearest kin. Mboli is not thought to shape men's destinies by taking an active interest in human affairs. Witchcraft is the real danger and a husband is constantly alert to protect his pregnant wife from witches. He consults oracles at every opportunity to make sure that no witch has started to attack his wife since the last occasion on which he consulted them. From the Zande's point of view child-bearing is safe so long as witches can be kept at a distance. He must never relax his watch since pregnancy furnishes one of those situations in which Azande expect witches to be unusually active.

The mother on her part may have to observe a simple food taboo since it seems to be customary for the wives of some clans to abstain from certain flesh during pregnancy, though they cease abstinence as soon as the child is born. Thus the wives of the Akalingo clan will not eat wild pig or guineafowl, the wives of the Abauro clan will not eat hens or any other bird, and most women are said to avoid oil made from the *bangumbe* plant (a species of gourd), during pregnancy, though it is possible that this last prohibition depends upon which clans women have married into. Guineafowl seems to be the meat most commonly avoided but I think the majority of clans do not impose food taboos of any kind on their wives and daughters during pregnancy. My clearest information with regard to one particular clan consists in the statement that women of the Abadara clan use a special pot for their food when they are with child in order to avoid contamination with beer, guineafowl, and bushbuck. Wives of members of this clan observe the same taboos. Thus the wife of a man called Turugba told me that she has avoided these foods during the gestation of her children because her husband's mother's brother

[1] Lagae, *op. cit.*, pp. 166–7.

was a Badara. Turugba himself however drank beer and ate guineafowl and bushbuck when his wife was pregnant. Doubtless a father would not eat those things which are taboo to his wife's clan while she carried his child in her womb but it must be remembered that with one or two exceptions (*e.g.* the Abadara are not supposed to eat bushbuck) none of the Zande totems are considered edible. On the whole there seems to be a rule that a woman should not eat those foods which her mother-in-law abstained from eating before her husband's birth. These may be clan taboos or they may be individual taboos. I have been told by most women whom I have questioned on the matter that they observe no taboos special to pregnancy. Certainly we may draw a conclusion from the scanty information which it was possible to obtain on the subject, as well as from the bored lack of knowledge and interest with which men and women greeted my questions, that pregnancy taboos are not considered important among the Azande.

Other special behaviour of women at this time also lacks ritual significance. They remove their tight-fitting waist cord of beads lest it should do the children in their wombs an injury and they substitute for it a plain loose cord. I think that at the same time they generally remove other ornaments. A pregnant woman tries to avoid the more strenuous and heavier forms of labour, but she continues to perform her household tasks to within a few days of delivery and it is a common sight to see women in the last stages of pregnancy bruising and grinding corn, cooking, and carrying water. It is not until the child is born that society imposes rest on a mother by confining her to her hut. One informant told me that some women are weak and lazy shortly after conception though they soon pick up again and perform the daily routine as usual. Nevertheless they demand the best food during this period and their husbands make strenuous efforts to satisfy their desires. They are especially partial to all kinds of meat and fish and beer. They are also said to display a keen desire for certain acidulous foods, such as *anzike*, a species of tree-ants, and the fruits *ndavu* and *nonga*. They make a point of eating vegetables which are soft and liquid, probably because they are thought to produce milk. There are special medicines known to old women which are supposed to increase a woman's milk when she eats them or rubs them on her breasts. Lagae mentions the names of several medicines which a woman eats to encourage the growth of an unborn child[1].

A husband may treat his wife with greater consideration during her pregnancy than at other times; her relatives and friends may show a lively interest in her condition; and the news spreads that so-and-so is with child. In these ways the mother may gain a certain degree of prestige from her condition. But it cannot be said that there is any express recognition by society of her new rôle. There is no rite which marks a change in social status and we have to record, not the presence of taboos, but their absence or their lack of universality and rigour. We may contrast the position of a mother before and after the birth of her child. As soon as the child is delivered its mother becomes the object of social control. She and her baby are confined to a hut, where she is protected by seclusion and by medicines, which are planted in its threshold, and out of which she and her child are ritually removed in a public ceremony. After delivery she is prohibited from sexual relations with her husband. I think that this contrast is related to the fact that a foetus is devoid of social personality and that a new-born child is invested with it to a very limited degree. The baby is still more or less a soul which may return easily whence it came. When it is ritually brought out of the hut to which it and its mother have been confined it gains social personality, which is further increased by giving it a name, though Azande refrain from doing this until some weeks after birth when they are confident that the soul really intends to remain in its bodily abode. As a child becomes invested with fuller social status so the corresponding status of its mother changes, especially if it is her first child or her first male child.

[1] Lagae, *op. cit.*, p. 168.

7

ZANDE BLOOD-BROTHERHOOD

1933

I

Blood-brotherhood is a pact or alliance formed between two persons by a ritual act in which each swallows the blood of the other. The pact is one of mutual assistance and is backed by powerful sanctions. It may bind only the two participants to certain obligations, or it may also involve the social groups of which they are members. Alliances based on exchange of blood have been recorded from many parts of the world, especially from Africa where they are exceedingly common. Among some peoples the participants drink one another's blood directly from incisions made on their bodies, while among others the blood is swallowed on a piece of meat or ground-nut or coffee-berry. But though the actual method of consumption varies in different cultures the purpose of the rite is always the same, and there is often much similarity between the ways in which it is carried out. Blood-brotherhood is not only widespread throughout Africa but it is also a ceremony which a European may inquire into easily and may even take part in without involving himself in social difficulties. It is the more surprising therefore that descriptive records of the ceremony by which the pact is formed and of the obligations which it entails are so scanty.

The present essay is an account of blood-brotherhood among a Central African people, the Azande of the Nile-Uelle Divide. No attempt is made to compare their customs with those of other African peoples. The data recorded here was collected during three expeditions to Central Africa. In its raw state it comprises descriptions by informants, including verbatim transcriptions in

Zande texts, and observations of one exchange of blood between two Azande and of one exchange of blood between a Zande prince and myself.

A European living among the Azande will soon come across blood-brotherhood and he will meet it again and again in following many lines of inquiry into different social activities. He will probably first encounter the custom when he is still struggling with the initial stages of the language, for he will often hear the word *bakurëmi,* my blood-brother, used as a term of address.[1] In its primary sense this term of address refers to the person who has drunk the speaker's blood, but it is extended in a secondary sense to embrace all members of this man's clan. Thus if you exchange blood with a member of the Akowe clan all other members of this clan rank as your blood-brothers and you may properly address them as *bakurëmi,* though whether you will actually address them by this term depends on a variety of individual factors such as the conditions under which you are speaking and the degree of intimacy which exists between you and the man whom you are addressing. It follows that a man stands in the position of blood-brother to clans with individual members of which his kin have exchanged blood. The word is commonly extended in a tertiary sense as a term of address to persons with whom neither the speaker nor any of his kin have exchanged blood, a courtesy usage which implies friendly familiarity. These extensions are made in the same way as kinship terms are extended to embrace whole clans and even quite unrelated persons and, in my opinion, the sociological and psychological significance of these extensions is the same in both cases. The extension of the obligations of blood-brotherhood from a blood-brother to members of his clan and the use of blood as the material link between the two partners have given rise to theories which stress the collective nature of the pact as an alliance between two blood-groups. These theories will be treated at the end of this essay.

In pre-European days, when blood-brotherhood and its obliga-

[1] The word for blood-brother is *bakure.* The possessive suffix of the first person singular is *mi* when speaking of a blood-brother instead of the more usual *re* suffix.

Lagae and Plas give *gbakule* as the purer form (*Dictionnaire Zande-Français,* 1925), being derived from *gba,* to cut, and *kule,* blood. In the Sudan *bakure* is the more usual form and is the one which I shall employ in this essay. Gore's dictionary, compiled in the Sudan, gives *bakure* (*Zande and English Dictionary,* 1931). The term *nakurëmi,* my blood-sister, is occasionally used for the wife of a blood-brother.

tions were held in greater esteem than they are held today, a man could not enter into a pact solely on his own initiative, since its clauses bound also his kin, who became subject to its sanctions. He would therefore first consult his father and uncles and would only carry out the rite of blood-brotherhood after he had obtained their consent. It appears that in the past they frequently objected to the proposed alliance, generally on the grounds of some long-standing enmity between the two clans concerned. Today people care less for the opinions of their kin and will often enter light-heartedly upon an alliance of blood-brotherhood without even informing their senior relatives about the matter beforehand. However, young men usually conform to traditions, and by consulting their family before making an exchange of blood they pay respect to their elders and show that they are taking the obligations and sanctions of the pact seriously. The extent to which custom has crumbled may be gathered from the case of a Zande whom I knew well. One day he told me that when scarcely more than a boy he had exchanged blood with another youth, and when I asked him to which clan his blood-brother belonged he was genuinely ignorant about the matter. I doubt whether it would be easy to discover a duplicate case, but even a single case would be inconceivable in the normal working of Zande society.

A man is also careful to consult the *benge* oracle before committing himself to an exchange of blood in order to ascertain if the proposed pact will be successful or will lead him into difficulties.

Men may enter into a pact for many reasons. In my experience the motive has generally been to cement already existing bonds of comradeship by giving them a concrete organized form which is backed by sanctions. Friends will assist each other out of sentiment, but little social compulsion attaches to it. There is a pattern of behaviour between friends which is supported by social precept, but this pattern is faint. We may contrast its indistinctness with the clear prominent lines of the behaviour patterns which regulate behaviour between kin. Blood-brotherhood gives to the vague sentiment of friendship, with its indefinite obligations, a status comparable to that of close kin relationship. But, though I have observed that it is often friends of long standing who exchange blood with one another, I do not think that they are ever motivated by purely sentimental reasons. Each knows that the other can assist him in a number of ways. Some advantages which will accrue from the pact are quite specific: thus one partner possesses powerful medicines with which he can supply the other, who may be an efficient smith or hunter, so that he can make return in iron or meat.

Blood is often exchanged solely for commercial purposes. A man who is travelling in foreign countries will make blood-brotherhood with a native, who thereby becomes responsible for his safety since this is explicitly stated in the clauses of the pact. When a man is travelling through a strange district of his own country he will establish a contact which will ensure his safety by finding someone of his clan, or of his mother's clan, to whom he can introduce himself as a kinsman. In a foreign country this is impossible, and here blood-brotherhood takes the place of blood relationship as the traveller's passport. In old days the most frequent use of this kind of passport was to give protection to parties of Azande which sought to gather a magic wood, called *benge*, which is used for oracle consultations. This wood grows only in hostile regions occupied by such peoples as the Mangbetu and Abarambo, and before European occupation of the country its collection was a hazardous undertaking, though risks were considerably lessened by an exchange of blood with one of the natives of the country who, in return for various presents, conducted the travellers to the end of their journey. Exchange of blood in such situations sacralizes and endows with sanctions a politico-economic transaction. As the union of blood-brotherhood is considered sacred by a number of adjacent tribes, it provides machinery through which trade can be carried on with a minimum assurance of protection for strangers. It is also common for men to make a blood-pact for purposes of trade in which there is no high degree of personal danger. A man living in the heart of Zande country finds difficulty in acquiring various luxuries which are plentiful in distant districts. Thus Azande sometimes make blood-brotherhood with semi-Zandeized Mbegumba and Mberidi of the extreme north with the purpose of obtaining dried meats and vegetable oils. At the time of the year when these articles of food are abundant the Zande pays his blood-brother a visit and asks him for presents of oil and dried meats. He may bring some articles with him as return gifts or he may just demand them *gine kure*, 'in the path of blood'. In any case his blood-brother will have anticipated the visit and will have reserved part of his surplus oil and flesh to meet the occasion. When he feels inclined the northerner will pay a visit to the centre of Zande country where he will enjoy the hospitality of his blood-brother from whose home he will return laden with one or two spears, or some bark-cloth, or other such articles which are difficult to obtain in his far-off district. In travelling in a foreign country blood-brotherhood gives protection. In seeking an alliance with a man living in a distant part of Zandeland it is an assured base and favoured treatment in economic exchange which is aimed at.

Such exchanges of blood are, however, exceptional. Blood-brotherhood is generally made between neighbours, and while desire for protection and for favoured economic conditions are both factors in any pact, they are only two among other factors which form a complicated mesh of motives, varying with each individual case, as will be evident when I enumerate the clauses of a pact and describe how it works.

I have never come across an instance of a man making blood-brotherhood with a woman, though I have been told that rare alliances have been made between a man and a much loved and trusted wife. This is the only situation in which a pact between members of opposite sexes could occur since all other situations would involve an alliance either with someone else's wife, which would be an adulterous union, or with a female relative, which would be absurd, since they are already united by ties of kinship. It is necessary to say also that it is very seldom that nobles exchange blood with commoners, and hence it is seldom that they enter into an alliance of blood-brotherhood at all, since Zande society is divided into only two classes, commoners and nobles, and the nobles all belong to one clan and hence are of the same kin. A man cannot exchange blood with his own kin. I do not doubt that alliances between sons of nobles and commoners occur, though I have not observed them. On the other hand, I have been told of several nobles of two and three generations ago who made blood covenants with commoner subjects. It is, however, said that the powerful King Gbudwe, who ruled over a vast area in the Sudan, avoided all such entanglements, and I do not know of any important princes among his sons who departed from this tradition. The reason for their abstinence is obvious and clearly expressed by Azande themselves. Princes have to settle cases and dispense justice and direct administration. An alliance of blood would militate against the fairness of their judgements and paralyse their execution. Put concisely, the position is this: the behaviour pattern between blood-brothers (social familiarity and mutual assistance) is incompatible with the behaviour pattern between commoners and nobles (respect and obligations on the one hand and authority and privilege on the other). Moreover, many clauses of a blood-pact are especially framed with the purpose of circumventing justice, as will be seen in the spells which follow. It is well known to Azande that blood-brotherhood counts little with princes when it clashes with their personal and political aims, and there are illustrative cases which tell how they have killed persons to whom they stood as blood-brothers, i.e. people belonging to clans with members of which a prince or some of his relatives have made a covenant of blood. The evidence suggests that in past times when the rule of princes was less autocratic and centralized than during the last two generations they made blood pacts with their subjects more frequently than when their political powers developed into untempered despotism.

II

I will now describe the manner in which blood is exchanged today as I have been told about the ceremony, have witnessed it, and have participated in it. Two men decide informally that they will meet on a certain day in the homestead of one of them and will there perform the ceremony. Azande intensely dislike people knowing about their affairs, however innocent they may be, and the participants will inform only their closest relatives and friends about the proposed pact and they will try to avoid publicity in its ritual enactment. Slight preparation is needed, and when you enter the homestead you will see its daily work going on in uninterrupted routine, cooking, carrying of water, sweeping, and the dozen other tasks which women have to perform in order to maintain a homestead in working order. You will certainly find the men under the shelter of a granary if the sun is well up, or round a fire in the centre of the homestead if it is early morning or towards evening. Natives soon forget the presence of an often seen ethnologist and gossip freely among themselves upon every sort of subject. Sometimes the conversation will turn to blood-brotherhood, but you will not receive the impression that their minds are riveted on the ceremony which is about to take place, and you will observe this matter-of-fact attitude running cheek-by-jowl with ritual throughout the ceremony. It is relevant to mention that most Zande magical and religious ceremonies which I have witnessed are remarkable for the absence of that 'spiritual' frame of mind which we Europeans consider appropriate to ritual events. On such occasions the Zande's behaviour, outside the stereotyped ritual acts of the ceremony, can in no way be thought of as 'sacred'.

However the men have come together for a special purpose and soon one of them will remark, 'Well, we had better get our business done', and his partner will assent and ask if everything is ready. In all probability nothing is ready. The owner of the homestead sends someone to cut some pieces of *banga* wood or tells his little son to run and ask his mother for a few ground-nuts, and he shouts to his wife to bring some salt. The men continue to sit and talk about local and court news whilst the boy returns with ground-nuts and the wife brings salt and whilst a slight incision is made on the arms or chests of the two partners to the pact so that a few drops of blood ooze out. If the two men have brought relatives with them, these make the incisions and conduct the whole ceremony, but if they prefer to do so the partners make the incisions and conduct the rites themselves. One partner takes a small rectangular piece of *banga* wood, or several ground-nuts, and soaks them in the blood which oozes from the body of the other. Often the two men consume each other's blood at the same time, each taking some ground-nuts, rubbing them in blood, and dipping them in salt. They eat the nuts with exaggerated relish. When ground-nuts are used they consume nut and blood together, but when *banga* wood is used they chew the wood into pulp which they spit out after swallowing blood, salt, and wood juices.

One of the men, or his second, commences to address his blood in the body of the other and as he does so the hum of conversation ceases and all pay attention to what is being said. There are two recognized modes of action which may be employed by the speaker when addressing the blood. He may take some twisted *bingba* grass (or a piece of cord made from the bast of the *dakpwa* tree) and, standing behind his blood-brother, hold it with one hand in his hair while with the other hand he twists the other end of the cord round and round on top of his head, uttering a spell meanwhile. This dramatized action not only accompanies the spell, but is appropriate to its words. The address consists of a number of clauses, some of which refer to actions on the part of a blood-brother which will bring upon him vengeance of the blood, and others to actions which will absolve him from vengeance. When a man wrongs his blood-brother the blood is thought of as getting a grip on his vitals, so the former set of clauses are accompanied by a twisting of the cord in his hair. When a man assists his blood-brother the blood is thought of as loosening its grip, so as the latter set of clauses are spoken the knot, into which the cord has been wound, is untwisted. Instead of using a cord, the speaker sometimes takes the two knives with which incisions have been made and, standing in front of his seated blood-brother, beats them together over his head. Apparently the object of this action is to draw and keep the attention of the blood to what is being said. Whether the speaker uses the cord method or the knives method he keeps up his action with these objects the entire time during which he addresses the blood, a period of from five to ten minutes.

In the following paragraphs I give a verbatim account of what is said to the blood when it is addressed by each partner or by their seconds. It must be understood in this paper that when I speak of one of the partners acting in the rites his place may be taken by a second who must be a relative of his. The addresses which I give here are texts which I took down from informants. The spell uttered by the first partner is a single text, whereas in the second spell I have combined in one address several textual fragments. As I have heard four such addresses pronounced, I can guarantee that my texts give an adequate summary of what is said at these ceremonies. I have slightly simplified the original texts in respect to personal pronouns, since an English translation tends to become unintelligible when there is constant change from sentence to sentence in the object addressed, sometimes the blood-brother being addressed directly as 'you', while at other times the blood is addressed as 'you' and the blood-brother is referred to as 'he'.

'You are blood,' he says, 'which we exchange with the clan of the Akowe. If you see someone struggling with your blood-brother and you run and attack him also and strike him violently, may you not recover from the vengeance of the blood. If a child of mine is in danger of the law and he flies and hides in your hut and you give him away so that he gets into trouble, may you die from the blood. If I come to your house, my blood-brother, and I say to you that I have come to ask you for the gift of a spear and you go into your hut and see a spear there but do not give it to me, you will die from the blood. But if your spears are of unbeaten iron, the property of others, marriage spears,[1] and you send me away without them, may you not die from vengeance of the blood. May the blood untwist itself from you with respect to unbeaten iron.

'If I pay you a visit and you have beer in your hut and you do not draw it for me, but let me sit near it and then return home with this insult, may vengeance of the blood overtake you. If you see one of our wives on a path and you hear that it is the wife of those men with whom you have exchanged blood and you say to her "Friend, we will drink a gourdful", and then you make advances to the wife of your blood-brother, may you not escape vengeance of the blood.[2] If I pay you a visit and you possess some feast spears,[3] you must not refuse me a gift. If you refuse me those spears which are yours to exchange, may you not escape vengeance of the blood. If you kill an animal and we come and cut *bingba* grass and bind it round the beast's head and then you come and take it from us, may you die from the blood, for the head of an animal belongs to the blood.[4] When you have been on an expedition to collect *benge* and I come and say to you "My blood-brother, I have come to ask you to break off a little *benge* for me" and instead of giving me your good *benge* which you have gathered yourself you just give me the remains of some old *benge*, whilst all the time I am saying to myself "My blood-brother has given me good new *benge*", may you not escape the blood's vengeance.[5] When I am pursued by avengers and I fly to my blood-brother and say to him, "I have come to ask you to give me spears since vengeance is hard on my heels"[6] and you look at your spears and send me away empty-handed, may you die

[1] i.e. Spears which have not been beaten into weapons, but are being stored by a man as bride-wealth for his son's marriage.

[2] i.e. If you meet the wife of your blood-brother carrying beer, it is correct to ask her to draw you a gourdful; but if you use this as a pretext to making advances to her, you will die from the vengeance of the blood.

[3] i.e. Spears which you have received in ceremonial exchange at mortuary feasts. These are not generally of unbeaten iron and you cannot refuse to give one of them to your blood-brother.

[4] A man has the right to claim the head of an animal killed by his blood-brother and he establishes this claim by tying some grass round its head as soon as it has been killed.

[5] He deceives his blood-brother by giving him the remains of old *benge* (strychnic poison used in oracle tests) instead of freshly gathered *benge*. It is not easy to tell the difference by looking at the *benge*.

[6] i.e. He asks his blood-brother to give him some spears to compensate for the offence which is bringing vengeance on him.

from the blood. I come to your homestead and I see a girl there, who is your daughter, and betrothed to none, and I ask you for her hand in marriage and you reply to me in an off-hand manner "Ai! You cannot marry her, she is betrothed", whereas as a matter of fact no one has espoused her and you are just deceiving me, then you will die from the blood.

'Blood, I address you; if his daughter is a man's wife, he need not give her to me in marriage; blood, do not kill my blood-brother on account of this, but entirely loosen yourself from him with respect to his daughter who is a man's wife. If we commit adultery with a woman of yours, do not kill us, but rather say, "Ai! We must not kill our blood-brother". Instead we will pay you compensation in spears and you must accept them to escape vengeance from the blood.[1] If you do me ill, may the blood pursue all your wives, may it leap in their abdomens; let them not give birth properly. If the prince sends out a patrol to seize me and I escape from it and fly away and hide in your hut and you rescue me by closing the door after me, you will recover from the blood. If you give me away to the prince's patrol, then you will die from the blood. May your wives not cut meat with a knife and may your relatives not eat at the mouth of iron. Rather let all your wives cut their meat with a firelog and let this be an antidote to the blood by which you may escape its vengeance.[2] May none of your wives cut grass with a knife. When they arrange their grinding-stones in position may they drag them in hernia, may vengeance of the stones seize them on their knees, elbows, backs of necks, and tops of heads.'[3]

When one of the two partners has finished his address he sits down and the other rises and commences a similar speech: 'You are blood which we exchange with you.[4] If you do me an injury, may you die from the blood. If you commit adultery with our wives or

[1] A man was sometimes killed or mutilated for adultery, but normally compensation in spears was accepted. Here the man tells his blood-brother that their clan must accept compensation in the event of such an offence being committed by one of his kin.

[2] i.e. If you do me wrong, the only antidote by which you can escape vengeance of the blood is by cutting your meat with a firelog. This is a picturesque way of saying that there can be no escape from the blood.

[3] Actually he says 'May vengeance seize them here and here and here and here' and taps various parts of his partner's body. The women will get keloids on these parts and will suffer from hernia. At the end of this address the speaker throws down a stone at his partner's feet, a dramatic act appropriate to his words.

[4] This second 'you' refers to his partner's clan.

make advances to them, may you all perish: your fathers, your mothers, your mother's elder sisters, your mother's brothers, and all your kin will die. If there is beer in your house and you let me go away without partaking of it, your relatives will all perish. If I ask you for a spear and though you possess one you send me away empty-handed, may you not recover from the blood and may all your clan die. If your daughter is espoused to no one and I come to ask for her hand in marriage and you refuse to give me her hand in marriage, may you die from the blood, may all of your kin perish. But may you not die in respect to your daughter who is espoused. If you speak ill of me to the princes, may you die.

'My blood-brother, we exchange blood with you, it is blood which we exchange. If you refuse me spears, iron, hens, beer, heads of animals, you will die from the blood. If you give me any fine gift that I ask of you when I come to your house and you cook porridge and give it to me in the path of blood, may you not die from the blood.'

If either of the two partners wants any special gift, he will mention it in his address to his blood. Thus when a Zande makes blood-brotherhood with a foreigner to facilitate his journey to collect *benge* he will state exactly what he wants from his blood-brother, namely that he is to act as a guide, protector, and surety for the party of travellers, while the foreigner, on his part, will mention in his spell various objects of wealth which he knows Azande bring with them on such journeys for purposes of exchange. When two Azande are exchanging blood they also may mention some gift of value which they require from their blood-brothers. The ceremony concludes with a preliminary exchange of gifts. Each party throws down a gift, generally a large knife, which is taken by the party opposite. This is the concluding act of the rites.

Before making an analysis of the ceremony which I have just described, I will point out that it is subject to considerable variation in the order and composition of its rites. This is the case with all Zande ceremonial which I have witnessed and is also doubtless the case with most African ceremonial, though we are seldom informed of the fact. It can hardly be expected that an ethnologist shall describe every variation which he has noticed in a ceremony performed on different occasions, but he may fairly be expected to explain that in the society which he is investigating ritual is rigid and formulated or lax and variable. I have only twice witnessed the ceremony of blood-brotherhood among the Azande and I was surprised, accustomed as I was to the plasticity of their rites, to note how different were the ways in which it was carried out on each occasion. In the following columns I list only the main variations. In the ceremony recorded in the left-hand column I was myself one of the participants, but I have no reason to suppose that the rites were in any way altered on this account.

	A.	*B.*
1.	X and Y sit facing one another on stools.	X and Y sit facing one another on stools.
2.	Each is accompanied by seconds.	Neither is accompanied by seconds.
3.	Seconds make incisions on arms.	Each makes an incision on the chest of the other.
4.	Blood smeared on piece of *banga* wood.	Blood smeared on ground-nuts.
5.	X's second hands wood to Y who dips it in salt and chews it.	Both together dip ground-nuts in salt and eat them.
6.	Meanwhile X's second addresses the blood and twists *bingba* grass in Y's hair.	X addresses his blood in Y's stomach while beating knives over his head. Also uses stone in ritual.
7.	X swallows the blood while Y's second addresses it. Uses grass.	Y addresses blood in X's stomach. Beats knives.
8.	Exchange of presents.	Exchange of presents.

Besides these variations in the order and composition of the rites as they occur in one area, there also appear to be regional differences. Thus Calonne-Beaufaict, speaking of the Azande of the Belgian Congo, says that one of the men spits on the forehead, the breast, the nape of the neck, the hands clasped in his own, and on the feet of his friend who returns this act of politeness.[1] Gayer-Anderson says that the Azande of the Meridi district of the Anglo-Egyptian Sudan incise each other's foreheads, drink the outflow of blood, and smear a lock of hair in its residue. Afterwards they cut

[1] De Calonne-Beaufaict, *Les Azande*, 1921, pp. 204–5.

off this lock and keep it in a small cylinder of wood or in a neatly-woven hair-bag as a charm.[1]

One informant told me that in the past Azande did not drink each other's blood, but made a pact by drinking water from a gourd which contained an iron arm-ring, though at the same time they addressed each other's blood. The statement of this man was unsupported by others present, but he himself belonged to the Amiangba people now absorbed by the Azande and I consider it probable that he was recording one of the customs of his ancestors of which there is still a faint tradition.[2]

III

We can now proceed to analyse the main characteristics of Zande blood-brotherhood. The ceremony which I have just described has the configuration of a typical magic rite. The blood (*kure*) is the concrete nucleus of the rite, a substance charged with dynamic magical forces. It corresponds to the medicinal herbs and woods which form the concrete nuclei of most magic rites in Africa. It is admonished to act in certain ways in certain contingencies. The fact that it is more often the blood-brother who is directly addressed than the blood must not be interpreted incorrectly. It is a common feature in Zande ritual for a man to address persons directly, in the midst of prayers to the ghosts of the dead and in the midst of spells to medicines. Throughout the spell it is the blood which is the real object of address and which is thought to absorb every clause of the speech. The more pronounced the social nature of a Zande rite, the greater the tendency to speak directly to the persons whom it concerns rather than to the sacred object to which it is directed. In praying to the ghosts a Zande will make a direct appeal to them in his opening sentence and will then proceed to harangue the bystanders in the same way as he here starts off with a direct invocation

[1] Gayer-Anderson, 'Some tribal customs in their relation to medicine and morals of the Nyam-nyam and Gour people inhabiting the Eastern Bahr-el-Ghazel', *Fourth Report of the Wellcome Tropical Research Laboratories*, vol. B, 1911, p. 253.

[2] Pacts of friendship are made in other ways among the Azande. Each of two people eat one of the ground-nuts contained in a single pod. This rite is sometimes performed between a man and his bride or love. Calonne-Beaufaict mentions other rites such as two people eating together a kind of yam or placing burning brands into the same water. Women also make pacts between one another by sharing a head of maize, but these are not discussed in this paper.

to the blood and then proceeds to talk to his blood-brother as though it was he and not the blood that he was addressing. In both of these cases the final object of the rites is to compel people to fulfil their obligations and it is understandable that the Zande soon begins to talk to them, when he is speaking about them, since they are present. The spell is typical of Zande spells. It is a long unformulated rambling speech, adorned with imagery, and delivered in much the same manner as those made to oracle magic (*benge*) or magic of revenge (*bagbuduma*) or hunting magic (*bingiya*). As in every magic ceremony, the spell accompanies various actions, which we speak of as the rite, drinking of blood on ground-nuts or *banga* wood, beating of knives or twisting of cord in hair, throwing stone on ground and tapping of partner's body, making opening gifts, and so on. The attitude of the speaker, his behaviour, his manner of speaking, the form of his address, are all typical of Zande magic.

As I wish at the end of this paper to bring the Zande data of blood-brotherhood into line with anthropological theories about the nature of blood-covenants among primitive peoples, I desire in this place to emphasize the fact that to me, saturated as I was with Zande magical practices, exchange of blood appeared as a typical magic rite, since the point at issue between scholars has really been whether the blood represents the unity of a clan and its exchange the means by which a stranger enters into a psycho-physical kinship with the clansmen of his blood-brother, or whether the blood creates merely a magical bond between them. Also, since among those who consider that the blood creates merely a magical bond there is a difference of opinion about the manner in which it forms such a bond, whether through the sacred nature of blood itself, or through a belief that what was once part of a man continues to remain part of him though materially separated from him, or whether the blood is no more than a vehicle for a conditional curse, I wish to draw particular attention to the fact that the blood is a magical substance when it figures in this rite and has quite a different sociological meaning from ordinary blood, in the same way as a stone placed in the fork of a tree to prevent the sun from sinking ceases to be an ordinary stone and becomes a ritual artifact.

In every magical ceremony sanctions derive their force from a proper carrying out of the whole rite. Each partner must drink the blood of the other and must do so in a traditional manner while suitable words are being spoken to it. If the rite is performed according to custom, it is valid, its obligations are binding, and its sanctions are operative; but if it is not properly conducted, it has no potency whatsoever. Owing to the facts that no taboos are observed preliminary to exchange of blood and that the extreme plasticity of Zande ceremonial allows wide variation in rite and spell, the only invalidating circumstance is likely to be the failure of one participant to drink the blood of the other. It might appear impossible for such a thing to happen and I do not suppose that it ever does happen between Azande themselves, but an omission of this kind might occur when a Zande is exchanging blood with a foreigner and has no intention of carrying out his obligations, but merely wishes to obtain some privilege from his partner or to lull him into a false sense of security. In such a situation the Zande does not make mental reservations which would profit him little if he had once drunk his partner's blood, but he omits to drink the blood itself and thus renders the spell worthless verbiage. For the spell has no virtue in itself. It can act only through the blood. I only know of one instance of a man cheating in this manner, but I was told that it was not unique. A Zande prince went through the ceremony of blood-brotherhood with a *mamur* (Egyptian or Sudanese official) to whom he was bitterly hostile. When the *banga* wood is the medium on which the blood is eaten it is usual, before putting it in one's mouth, to break it in two, placing the half which is smeared with blood in one's mouth, and letting the half which one has held between one's fingers, when scraping blood from one's partner's body, fall to the ground. On this occasion the prince let the blood-soaked half fall to the ground and chewed the bloodless half. As he had not consumed any of the *mamur's* blood, none of the obligations of blood-brotherhood were binding on him and he felt quite free to act against the interests of the *mamur* and made full use of this freedom. The one absolute essential is that each partner shall swallow the blood of the other if the contract is to be valid. Little matter the exact words which are uttered or the precise actions performed so long as the blood of each is in the stomach of the other. On one of the occasions on which I witnessed the ceremony one of the participants swallowed his own blood by mistake. He did this by picking up and eating some of the ground-nuts which had been soaked in his own blood and laid on the ground beside those soaked in his partner's blood. This was done quite inadvertently and those present laughed. Nobody minded the mistake, which was at once rectified by smearing new nuts in the blood.

But once you have performed the ceremony and your stomach contains your blood-brother's blood the sanctions of the pact work automatically without your partner having to set them in motion. The ceremony of alliance initiates what Westermarck calls a 'Conditional curse'. For example, if you have relations with your blood-brother's wife, the blood will act of itself to destroy you and your kin while your blood-brother is still ignorant of your misconduct. You and they will die *be kure*, from the blood. Azande say that the blood goes down into the stomach[1] of a man and from there sees all that he does, and when a man betrays his blood-brother it avenges itself on him. The blood knows exactly what is required of the blood-brother because it has heard the address made to it when it was swallowed. 'The blood hears like *benge*' people say, and this is the highest compliment which a Zande can pay to its attention and foresight. In the case of some misfortune it is not always possible, without consulting the oracles first, to know whether a man is suffering from vengeance of blood or from some other cause such as witchcraft or bad magic. It is very seldom that misfortunes are thought to be due to the action of blood and doubtless this is largely due to the fact that people are careful to fulfil their major obligations. Most Azande can, however, quote cases in which there has been no doubt that the blood has taken a terrible toll of a family for a breach of one of the obligations of the pact, for the action of the blood differs from the actions of witchcraft and bad magic in that it does not attack a single individual but also wreaks havoc among his family and kin. Hence, when several members of the same family suffer consecutive misfortunes, as when several deaths occur in the same family at about the same time, people say, 'surely it is blood which is pursuing them'. I will give a single instance of blood working in this manner. There is a man, called Gbitarangba, who used to be one of my closest neighbours, who, when still a boy, was mutilated for having made advances to another man's wife. He denies that he was guilty of the offence, but

[1] It is difficult to decide whether the blood is thought to remain in the stomach or to reside in some other part of the body. I think that the Zande does not feel sure about its residence. He only knows that it is somewhere inside his blood-brother.

whether his denial is true or not, there can be no doubt that mutilation was carried out with undue haste and brutality. As a result, according to Gbitarangba, a series of misfortunes overtook the husband and his family. His brothers and sons died one after the other, and he himself died an exile without leaving children to carry on his name. He suffered these misfortunes because Gbitarangba's clan was bound to his clan by ties of blood. I am not certain of the exact relationship of the two original blood-brothers to the two principals in the tragedy, but it was certainly a distant one. Nevertheless the blood took its toll because the two clans were united by blood-exchange. In such an instance as this, when relatives die one after the other, the survivors will suspect that it is blood which is at the root of the matter and they will cast their thoughts around to consider who among them can have done an injury to his blood-brother, and will then ask the oracles whether it is this offence which has brought vengeance upon them.

Although the blood is thought to act on its own initiative, its action is sometimes fortified by a special rite. A man injured by his blood-brother takes the piece of cord which was twisted in his partner's hair during the ceremony and which he has carefully preserved, and he winds it into a knot while uttering a spell to his blood in the body of his blood-brother. He calls upon the blood to avenge the injury and exterminate his blood-brother and his kith and kin. He tells it what offence has been committed and directs it to scatter the clan of his blood-brother, against whom he utters an anathema of curses which will bring upon him and his relatives leopards, lions, snakes, thunder, dysentery, leprosy, European justice, and a host of all possible evils. While addressing the blood in this manner he winds the cord into a little ball which he wraps in leaves and hides in the roof of his hut. Here again he performs a typical magic rite with the blood as its agent. It is believed that misfortune will soon overtake a blood-brother who is the object of such a rite and that the oracles will inform him of the cause of his loss or sickness. It is said that he will then go to his aggrieved blood-brother, who can be appeased by gifts and persuaded to give to the sick man *ziga kule*, an antidote to the action of the blood. This consists of a medicine which is cooked in oil while a spell is spoken over it and is afterwards eaten. He will also take down the ball of cord from the roof of his hut and unwind it while addressing his blood in order to release his blood-brother from its grip. Everyone is aware of this additional sanction of blood-brotherhood, though I do not know of any particular case in which it has been brought into operation. Once more we may notice how the blood is regarded as an ordinary magical agent, for, like many Zande medicines, it has its *ziga* or antidote.

A further sanction is that of public opinion. Open failure to fulfil the obligations of the pact brings upon a man not only magical retribution but also public censure. He becomes an object of contempt to his neighbours and a shame to his kinsmen. If, for instance, a man is travelling in a distant district and he appeals to one of the clansmen of his blood-brother for hospitality and is refused it, this refusal shames his blood-brother and his relatives, who feel themselves responsible for the conduct of their clansman. Another important sanction of a blood-pact springs from the reciprocal nature of its obligations. If you do not carry out your obligations towards your blood-brother, neither will he carry out his obligations towards you. One asks for a gift or a service in the name of the blood, but it is well understood that one's blood-brother in presenting the one or performing the other will demand an equivalent return in the future. It thus happens that each partner keeps a mental tally of the various ways in which he has assisted the other from time to time and he expects that the tally of the other shall be approximately as long as his own. If his partner is generous, he will be generous; if his partner is mean, he will be mean. The reciprocal nature of blood-brotherhood thus provides an integral system of sanctions by the very mode in which it functions. Social systems invariably generate their own sanctions by their mechanism of mutuality.

These reciprocal duties incumbent on a man who has made blood-brotherhood with another are clearly enunciated in the spells which I have cited. A man must act always as a generous friend towards his blood-brother; he must give him food and beer when he visits his homestead; he must refrain from making advances to his women; he must not refuse spears or other gifts, which he is free to part with, on the request of his blood-brother; he must grant the hand of his daughter in marriage, if she is not already espoused; he must not speak evil of his blood-brother to the princes; he must render him assistance in quarrels; he must do his best to protect him against vengeance and justice; he must give his blood-brother the heads of any animals which he has killed in hunting, if he asks for them.

Generally speaking, a man must always support his blood-brother when he is in difficulties, especially when he is in legal difficulties. In the old days when a man was caught in adultery or accused of murder by witchcraft it was essential for his relatives to collect a sufficient amount of wealth to compensate for his offence without delay or he might be mutilated or killed. As he lay bound at the prince's court his relatives and relatives-in-law and blood-brothers brought spears and placed them beside him until they were of sufficient number to protect him against immediate execution. This was perhaps the main function of a blood-brother in the old days. He was a supplementary ally who could be relied upon to assist a man in conjunction with his kin and relatives-in-law on those occasions when the solidarity and relationship by blood (as we would say) and by marriage were most in evidence. When speaking of blood-brotherhood a Zande never neglects to mention among its foremost duties that of giving warning to a man upon whom his prince's displeasure has fallen. One of the main incentives to forming a pact was to have a friend at court who was acquainted with the designs of his prince. Such a man would hear, as a member of the confidential circle of courtiers, the intention of his prince to kill his blood-brother or to deliver him into the hands of avengers. It was his imperative duty to inform his blood-brother of the plot against him, and he had to contrive to do so without involving himself at the same time in open breach of confidence. If he could send word to his blood-brother's residence, he would do so, but often enough he would only hear of the plot while his blood-brother was already on his way to court to answer the prince's summons. In this case he would contrive, by making signs with his face, or by scratching his partner's hand as he shook hands with him, to convey a warning which would allow his partner to escape from court before he was seized. Another duty incumbent on a blood-brother in past times was to cut open the corpses of his partner's kin, if called upon to do so, so that it might be ascertained whether they were witches or had been falsely accused of witchcraft during their lifetime. None of these last three duties has prominence today, since summary executions by rulers are not allowed, and ample time is given for a man to collect fines, in default of which he suffers only imprisonment and not mutilation or death; and since corpses are no longer slit open to discover witchcraft. There are two further obligations of the pact, which are in full force today. A man must assist in digging the graves of members of his blood-brother's family and kin. It is not so essential for blood-brothers to perform this task as for relatives-in-law, but it is nevertheless considered most reprehensible for a blood-brother to absent himself on such an occasion if he lives in the vicinity. He must also attend mortuary feasts prepared for his blood-brothers and bring spears to exchange with them for beer. Here, again, what is an essential duty for relatives-in-law is more in the nature of an act of courtesy and good faith for blood-brothers.

The obligations which I have enumerated come into force on occasions when special social conditions show up vividly the nature of blood-covenant duties. The pact functions in a less spectacular but more continuous manner from day to day in the ordinary routine of social life. A man constantly eats meals at his blood-brother's homestead and is invited there to beer parties. When a man kills a large beast his blood-brothers come to ask him for a share of the meat. They pay each other frequent visits, in which they are treated as favoured friends and given the best hospitality which the owner of the homestead can afford. Often one will find a man living adjacent to his blood-brother, to whose homestead he has free access since the danger of adultery is reduced to a minimum by the terms and sanctions of a blood-pact. Occasionally a man is largely dependent upon his blood-brothers for the necessities of life. Such a case is that of the mutilated man Gbitarangba, to whom reference has already been made. He was not on good terms with his relatives, but lived with one of his blood-brothers, whose food he ate and whose household he assisted by making nets and by snaring guinea-fowl. Besides this man, whose home he shared, Gbitarangba had exchanged blood with several other neighbours and was always a welcome guest at their meals. Being physically impaired, he had made a point of contracting alliances of blood with two or three influential men of the neighbourhood, who were able to assist him through their influence at court and by their authority in the locality.

One of the duties most strongly emphasized in the spells addressed to the blood is that of making any gift which may be asked by a blood-brother, but it must not be thought that this leads to unlimited sponging. I was surprised that my blood-brother did not take advantage of my being a European to make extravagant requests for gifts and exercise of political influence. On the contrary, I received on the whole rather more than I gave during our partnership. Blood-brothers do not make unreasonable requests to each other among the Azande. Reciprocity of services makes this impossible since it is expected that there shall be an even balance in exchange of property.

IV

The pattern of behaviour between blood-brothers is one of intimacy and equality. One way in which intimacy and equality are expressed between the partners is by each publicly insulting the other, a custom commonly described by ethnologists as a 'joking relationship'. This is not the place to discuss the peculiar sociological problem posed by this custom, but a short example of the kind of insults which are bandied about between blood-brothers is desirable. Thus one will shout to the other:

'Ai friend! May they cut into your witchcraft! You are witches, you of the Akalingo clan!' To which the blood-brother replies:

'He! May someone spear you! Who told you that we are witches, my friend? You've just had a good meal over there so you come on a full stomach to pick a quarrel with me without cause. That's a bad joke; you're a nasty sly fellow.'

Sometimes a man will play a practical joke on his blood-brother, sending him on a fool's errand. I have a good example of this type of joke in one of my Zande texts:

'A. "While you were coming here that elder brother of your father who lives over there has died of rupture, so they say."

'B. "Hm! I don't believe that, my friend; you have a poor sense of humour."

'A. "Very well, if you don't believe me, go and see for yourself."

'B. "All right, I'm just going."

'He picks up his spear and he goes away and walks on till he reaches the homestead of his father's elder brother, where he sees a child and says to him, "Child, my blood-brother says that father's dead, is that true?" The child replies, "Who is spreading that lie? If he spreads such baseless rumours perhaps he will peg out himself."

'He passes on to see this elder brother of his father and says to him: "Father, it is you I have come to see because that fellow over there, that blood-brother of mine, said yesterday that you were dead."

'To which the old man replies, rather offended: "Hm! So when you heard that you believed it, did you? The fellow is a fool to play such jokes. If he tells you something, just reply, 'Really, is that so?' Now, my son, what little thing is the matter with me that I should die from it, eh? So! If I were ill wouldn't your elder brother send someone to you to summon you to come and see the evil that was happening to your father? Jests of this kind are no good, my son; if you don't know all about these jokes beforehand, you put your foot into the fire."

'It is thus they say about jests of this kind: if someone with whom you are on joking terms comes with a long sad face to tell you some story about your relatives such as "Don't you know that your relative has died?" You should take care not to be caught. He is jesting about your relative saying that he is dead, and you must not be taken in. Blood-jests, they say, are awful lies.

'Then when he meets him again in the path he says to him, "Ah, friend! You did play me a rotten trick. I went ever such a far distance. Friend, may someone spear you!" The man who has played the joke bursts with laughter and says, "Ho ho ho, so friend, ha ho ha ho, isn't he dead after all? Ha! While you were with this other father of yours have you heard this latest bit of news of mine, that father of yours who lives quite near here has been bitten by a snake. I saw that child of his, the girl, wailing the wail of death, *buba zoga re ooo, ako buba te, ako buba te.*"

'The man who has been fooled replies, "Ah! My friend, my blood-brother so! Why can't you tell the truth?" He bursts out laughing again and goes on roaring with laughter.'

As the behaviour pattern between blood-brothers is extended to the members of their clans, an extension discussed in the following section, a 'joking relationship' may grow up between two clans who may insult one another with impunity. I do not think that this is common in Zandeland, but it appears to happen sometimes, as, for example, between the Abauro and the Abangombi, the Akalingo and the Agiti, and in one or two other instances, who jest in this manner without offence being taken by either party, a relationship which is said to have arisen from blood-brotherhood between members of the two clans.

V

The pattern of behaviour between blood-brothers is extended, like the term *bakurëmi*, which symbolizes the relationship, towards their clansmen. In theory a man owes the same duties to members of his blood-brother's clan as he owes to his blood-brother himself, but in practice the obligations are of different quality. The form of obligation is extended, but its content becomes progressively weaker the wider the extension. The Zande principle is that all clansmen of *bakurëmi*, my blood-brother, are *abakurëmi*, my blood-brothers, but it is well understood that the obligations recited in the spells have less force in their application to people the farther they are genealogically from one's actual partner. His brothers and sons are almost equivalent to the partner himself, but distant clansmen receive scanty recognition.

No Zande would explain the mode of extension in quite the way I have done, since it is a dogma that every member of your blood-brother's clan is equivalent to your blood-brother himself, and when I pointed out to them that, whatever they might say, people did not in fact treat the clansmen of a blood-brother as though he was a direct partner to a pact, they defended the dogma by asserting that since European occupation of their country people no longer carry out their obligations as conscientiously as they used to do. They say that in the past no one would dream of refusing the same help and hospitality to any member of his blood-brother's clan as to his actual blood-brother. The impression which I formed, however, was that this assertion is largely fictitious, and that whilst people would give occasional hospitality to the clansmen of their blood-brothers, they would hardly expect to be asked for any substantial gift or service unless the relationship was a very close one. It must be borne in mind that the Zande clans are not cohesive localized groups, but are spread loosely over the whole of Zandeland. The consequence is that those clansmen of a man's blood-brother with whom he comes into contact in normal circumstances are those who live in his blood-brother's neighbourhood and are closely related to him. A Zande has not the faintest notion of his full blood-brotherhood relationships, since he does not know either who are all the clansmen of the man whose blood he has drunk nor with what clans all his fellow clansmen have made blood-pacts. If one were able to make a complete survey of Zande society, one would probably find that everybody was a remote blood-brother of everybody else. But when Azande talk of their clans they really mean their close paternal kin or those clansmen who live in their immediate vicinity and with whom they come into frequent contact. Clans function as small segments. A man knows the clans of his own blood-brothers and clans with which his fathers and grandfathers and uncles and brothers have made exchange of blood and he acts towards the members of these clans as his blood-brothers in so far as they come into his social milieu, that is to say, he gives preferential treatment to the nearest relatives of the actual participants in the rites. Nevertheless there is always a difference between the bonds which unite the actual participants to a blood-pact and those which unite their respective kinsmen. The reciprocal obligations which compose the first operate only in an attenuated form in the second. Just as a pattern of behaviour towards a brother is extended with ever-decreasing vitality towards more and more distant members of his own clan and generation, so when the pattern of behaviour between blood-brothers is extended towards their clansmen it becomes less and less a functional relationship and more and more a formal one. In three or four generations all memory of a pact fades and it ceases to have any significance. Eventually it is entirely forgotten.

The obligations of blood-brotherhood also bind to some degree relatives of the mother's clan. In the spells one hears the blood admonished to destroy not only members of a false blood-brother's clan but also his 'mothers, mother's elder sisters, mother's brothers', and so on. These people are included in the circle in which the sanctions of the pact are operative. I was told that a man would not exchange blood with a member of his maternal uncle's clan nor with a member of his maternal grandfather's or grandmother's clan since the people are his kindred. I may add that on the occasion when I performed the rite myself the blood of the prince who was my partner was addressed by a member of his mother's kin.

It sometimes happens that one observes flagrant breaches of the obligations of blood-brotherhood. I came across one instance of a man who committed adultery with the wife of his blood-brother and an instance of another who tried to do so. But such cases are, I am convinced, rare, though less rare today than in past times. People are undoubtedly very frightened of the consequences of failure to carry out their duties and one constantly hears Azande remark that 'Blood is no joke, it is a very serious matter.' A man does not enter lightly into an alliance, and in my experience people have the best intentions to fulfil their obligations. It was not long, however, before I began to observe that the Zande often tries to avoid fulfilling his obligations towards his blood-brother if he finds them irksome in the same way as he tries to wriggle out of his obligations towards his relatives and to other persons to whom he is supposed to act in certain ways. At the same time he protests vigorously his good faith. He would not make a deliberate breach of the pact, but the idea of reciprocity on which it is based gives ample scope for grumbling and for withholding gifts on the grounds that one's partner has done the same. In this respect blood-brotherhood displays the same opposition of egoism to social duties which is characteristic of other relationships and associations in human societies.

There can be no doubt of the general truth of the Zande contention that blood-brotherhood is no longer respected today as it used to be before European occupation of their country. All Azande with whom I have spoken about blood-brotherhood were unanimous in deploring the decay of the institution. They said that exchange of blood in the old days created a pact which was held as sacred by the two participants and their kin, while today people no longer regard their obligations seriously. Of necessity they feel that blood does not inevitably destroy a faithless blood-brother as it used to do. As in other departments of their life, custom has crumbled and blood-brotherhood is slowly losing its moral force. We must not attribute this phenomenon of social disintegration, as is often done, solely to the negative and destructive influences of white men and their culture. We shall find it intelligible only if we view it as a process of social change. European intrusion has created new conditions to which Zande culture is adapting itself. Adaptation takes place just as much by the decay and disappearance of old social processes which no longer have a useful function as by the appearance and growth of new social processes. Many of the obligations of blood-brotherhood have ceased to apply under modern conditions. No longer do people need protection from violence from princes, avengers, and foreigners. Money and the beginnings of trade enable Azande to dispense with circuitous means of acquiring various kinds of wealth through channels of blood-brotherhood. Marriage no longer presents its old difficulties to those not backed by kin or some other form of social relationship, such as blood-brotherhood or political patronage. Blood-brotherhood atrophies as it ceases to carry out its more important social actions, and it becomes more and more a mere formal acknowledgement of friendship between two individuals.

VI

Blood-brotherhood has long been a subject of scholarly enthusiasm and debate. Vast armies of facts, recruited from pre-history, contemporary European folk-lore, Biblical and classical literature, and accounts of savage tribes, have been marshalled for engagement. These mercenary armies were ready to serve one scholar today and his opponent tomorrow. Much of the controversy concerned questions which do not directly touch the institution of blood-brotherhood and posed problems which cannot be investigated by research, but in so far as they can be tested within our restricted range of data we must decide as briefly as possible on the relevance and validity of the main theories propounded to account for exchange of blood in primitive communities.

The main subject of controversy has been the nature of the bond which unites blood-brothers, whether it is a bond of true kinship or whether it is based on homeopathic principles of magic or on the mechanism of the curse, and whether it is formed by change of status or by simple contract. A subsidiary question has been whether it is a collective alliance between groups or a personal pact between individuals.

Robertson Smith[1] argued as follows: (i) there is no kinship without community of blood. (ii) There are no obligations in primitive society except those of kinship. (iii) Therefore anyone who wishes to enter into a reciprocal social relationship with another man who is not of his natural kin can do so only by an artificial creation of kinship. (iv) Since kinship is based on community of blood, it can be created artificially in one way only, by each of the two men partaking of the blood of the other. As clans are undifferentiated units, the bond between the two partners is also a collective bond between their respective clans.

In Robertson Smith's theory the god or fetish is also made a partner to the pact, and the argument given above is related by him

[1] W. Robertson Smith, *Kinship and Marriage in Early Arabia*, edit. by S. A. Cook, 1903, *passim.*

to other social phenomena, namely, sacrifice and totemism, but these need not trouble us here, since we wish only to test his ideas about blood-exchange by reference to Zande practice. Davy[1] points a conclusion to Robertson Smith's line of argument. (v) Since alliances in primitive communities can only be made by a man entering into a kinship relationship with another we can say that contractual ties are assimilated to kinship ties, i.e. contract is only possible through change of status. The contractual relation between blood-brothers imitates the status of kinship.

Frazer[2] has discussed the facts of blood-brotherhood as part of a wide range of similar data. Blood-brotherhood is a bond created by men who wanted to institute a form of contract. It is a derivative from residual notions about the nature of substances. These elemental beliefs in homeopathic magic assert that in absorbing part of a man one absorbs his physical, moral, and intellectual qualities, and hence one's fate becomes identified with his. Davy accepts Frazer's views as complementary to those of Robertson Smith, since, according to Frazer, exchange of blood is only an application of homeopathic magic and kinship is based on a similar idea of physical and mystical unity. Davy will not admit, however, that blood-exchange is intelligible in terms of homeopathic magic alone because he considers that the bonds of blood-brotherhood are of the same nature as the more fundamental religious and social bonds which unite family and clan.

Westermarck[3] strongly opposes the theory of Robertson Smith and his colleagues. He maintains that their point of view supposes that members of the same clan consider themselves as being literally of one blood, as a physiological unity as well as a social unity, and criticizes them for seeing in blood-exchange a crude artificial transfusion of blood. In Westermarck's opinion the really important element in blood-brotherhood is the curse which is uttered over the partners, and he regards the blood as merely a suitable vehicle for the curse.[4]

[1] *La Foi Jurée*, 1922, especially Chapter I. Sidney Hartland, *The Legend of Perseus*, 1894–6, vol. ii, pp. 237–58, takes the same view as Robertson Smith.

[2] *The Golden Bough: Taboo and the Perils of the Soul*, 3rd ed., 1911, p. 130, and *Spirits of the Corn and of the Wild*, 1912, vol. ii, ch. xii.

[3] *The Origin and Development of Moral Ideas*, 1908, vol. ii, pp. 206–9.

[4] The 'kinship theory' of blood-brotherhood is weakened by a comparative study of rites by which artificial brotherhood is created, for many of these make no use of blood. For a wide survey of evidence see P. J. Hamilton-Grierson, Art. 'Brotherhood (Artificial)' in *Hastings' Encyclopedia of Religion and Ethics*, 1909.

The facts of Zande society undoubtedly support Westermarck's contentions rather than those of Robertson Smith and Davy. I do not consider that any of the arguments of Robertson Smith are true of Zande society. Manifold social obligations exist outside the boundaries of kinship. The Zande does not regard kinship as a community of blood, and hence there is no idea of artificially creating bonds of kinship by transfusion of blood. I cannot recall a single occasion during my residence in Zandeland on which I heard kinship spoken of in terms of blood. Azande speak of members of the same clan as having sprung from the same seed, but the filiation is not spoken of as one of blood. A Zande thinks of his clan rather in terms of social function than of biological affinity. It is perfectly true that a man will not exchange blood with a fellow clansman, but I was never given as a reason for this abstention that they were of the same blood, but that they were kinsmen, i.e. that they were already bound to one another by the social ties of kinship. If kinship and common blood were synonymous in Zande thought their mode of reckoning descent would be matrilineal, since a child, they say, is formed out of its mother's blood.

No Zande ever thinks of a blood-brother as a member of his clan in any sense whatsoever. Not only is the idea of a man entering into his blood-brother's clan by consuming his blood quite foreign to Zande thought, but also there is no notion of social identification between clan brothers and blood-brothers. It is true that many of the obligations of blood-brotherhood are the same as those of real brotherhood, but this appears to me to be due, not to an assimilation, through an idea of social identification, of new ties based on contract to old ones based on status of birth, but simply to what one may call the logic of social situations. There are only a limited number of ways in which people can assist one another, and as these modes of assistance are in Zande society largely functions of kinship it is obvious that any pact of mutual assistance is likely to duplicate many of these functions. But the obligations of blood-brotherhood include behaviour which is directly opposed to the patterns of behaviour between kin. Thus, as I have already mentioned, a blood-brother must assist relatives-in-law to bury dead members of the clan with which he has exchanged blood and into which they have married. The dead's kin take no part in digging the grave and refrain from carrying the corpse. In ritual exchange at mortuary feasts blood-brothers and relatives-in-law form one party and exchange wealth with the kin who form the other party. Kin cannot exchange wealth with each other on these occasions. It is a blood-brother who cuts open a corpse to see if witchcraft is present. No kinsman can perform this task.

Another striking difference between brotherhood and blood-brotherhood is the fact that brothers are graded while blood-brothers are on an absolute equality. A man is not simply 'brother' to another, but he is either 'elder brother' or 'younger brother', and the younger always owes respect to the elder. Intercourse between brothers is always coloured by notions of seniority. We have seen, on the other hand, how blood-brothers have an egalitarian status and treat each other with open familiarity across the usual barriers of etiquette which Zande custom erects between members of society. Hence the behaviour pattern between a man and his brother is incompatible with the behaviour pattern between a man and his blood-brother and a man cannot therefore be a kinsman and a blood-brother. We have, moreover, seen that the sanctions of a pact involve members of the mother's kin, which is in direct opposition to the clan theory. There is thus no identification of social function between blood-brothers and clansmen, any more than there is biological identification through communion of blood. A man takes over none of the titles of clanship by exchange of blood. He does not adopt the clan-name of his blood-brother nor his totem. If he became in any sense a member of his blood-brother's clan, he would be subject to their rules of exogamy, whereas, on the contrary, we have seen that it is considered highly commendable for a man to marry his blood-brother's sister or daughter. No one would deny that the obligations of blood-brotherhood are coloured by the obligations of kinship and family, since all human groups are deeply affected by the fact that a man is born and grows up in his family and that his main social attitudes towards family and kin are built up long before he joins adult associations or forms new patterns of behaviour towards unrelated persons, such as princes and parents-in-law, but this is a very different notion from the idea of a blood-brother changing his status so that he becomes reckoned as kin to his partner and his partner's clansmen.

It is quite common in fact for Azande to contrast blood-brotherhood with kinship, extolling the first in comparison with the second. They say that a blood-brother is a much better friend than a real brother. He will not commit adultery with your wife or refuse to help you in time of need, whereas your brothers are always trying to corrupt your wives and to escape from aiding you when you find yourself in difficulties. But talk of this kind does not really mean that the feeling towards blood-brothers is stronger than that towards family and kin. The apparent discrepancy between what Azande like to say and what they actually feel and do probably springs from the compulsive nature of family and kin sentiments, the universality but indefiniteness of their obligations, and the peculiar psychological character of their sanctions. Contrast this state of affairs with the relationship of blood-brotherhood, with its well-defined set of obligations detailed seriatim in the spell; with its direct magical sanctions destructive of the other party to the pact; with its bargain of balanced exchange of gifts and services; and with its basis a magical rite quite unsupported by the slow process of conditioning of sentiments in childhood which forms and explains the sentiments of kin. It is true that the rite may give social recognition to any already strong friendship between two men, but the Zande knows as well as we do that friendship and kin are worlds apart. Friends change as contacts lessen or different interests draw them apart or quarrels rend them asunder, but close kinship resists distance, occupation, and disputes, with a resilience all its own. The fundamental basis of kinship is sentiment expressing and vivifying itself in social obligations. The fundamental basis of blood-brotherhood is a contract. My obligations towards my blood-brother are more directly binding than my obligations towards my brother. I can elude my obligations to the latter more easily than to the former. Yet, though more directly binding, they are also more limited. Lastly, blood-brotherhood is a contract entered into by two men of their own accord. Real brotherhood is a circumstance into which men are born without any act of their own.

In my opinion to argue that kin are people with one blood and that therefore anyone who drinks their blood becomes in any sense one of them, would be, so far as Zande society is concerned, a white man's interpretation of the facts based on his mode of thinking about kinship primarily in terms of blood relationship. This point of view also entirely fails to take count of the essential difference between the social links which bind a man to his brother and those which bind a man to his blood-brother. You are bound to your blood-brother not because you have become one of his kin by drinking his blood, but because his blood is a concrete magical substance impregnated with a spell embodying a 'conditional curse'. You are compelled to assist him, not because you are motivated towards him by the obligations of kinship, but because if you fail to help him in his need his blood will kill you in virtue of its magical power. A man does not become your blood-brother by linguistic usage, by biological relationship, by social status, or by the nature of the social sanctions which back his obligations towards you. He becomes your blood-brother by ties of magic, ties involving him in a special set of duties, sometimes the same as, but often different, even opposed to, the duties of kinship, and backed by a typical magical sanction of the 'conditional curse'. If we seek for a reason to explain the extension of the pattern of behaviour between blood-brothers to members of their clans we must look for it in the sociological nature of these reciprocal obligations which of necessity involve their kin.

It is abundantly clear from my description of the rite by which blood-brotherhood is instituted that it is a typical magical mechanism. It is impossible, however, to accept Frazer's interpretation, since no Zande would hold that by absorbing a man's blood you absorbed his physical and moral qualities. As far as I know, blood has no magical associations in Zande culture and is never thought to embody magical power *per se* any more than the hundreds of herbs and trees which the Zande uses as medicines can be said to have any magical value in themselves when growing in the bush. They derive this value from the way in which men use them in ritual situations. On the whole, therefore, Westermarck's explanation appears to cover the Zande facts better than any other, though I do not entirely agree with the stress he lays on the verbal element in magic. The blood is not simply a vehicle for the spell or conditional curse. The blood itself is the 'medicine', the material element in the magical complex, and it becomes such through association with the spell and rite. The social action of magic is not always evident from accounts of primitive peoples, and one may stress that in many institutions the basic link between members is of a truly magical character. Zande blood-brotherhood is an example of such social action.

8

ZANDE THEOLOGY

1936

I

About no subject in social anthropology is there more conflict of opinion than about primitive theology. It would not be surprising to find disagreement among students of comparative religion about the meaning of facts recorded by fieldworkers but there is often complete lack of unanimity among fieldworkers themselves about primitive notions in the same ethnographic field. The Azande of the Nile-Congo Divide are a case in point. Early travellers such as Schweinfurth and Junker give us very little information about their religious ideas and, among those who have had later and more intimate contact with the people, Colonel Bertrand makes Mbori a culture hero of Zande mythology like Ture, about whom there is a cycle of amusing stories told to children around the evening fire.[1] Major Larken tells us that '*Mbali*, the Deity, the creator of all things good and evil, appears to be an all-pervading spirit whose dwelling-place is supposed to be at the heads of streams that rise in the dark overgrown ravines, or in the great trees that grow in such places. Good fortune and bad flow from him alone. No moral sense is attributed to him. He is not pleased by good, or angered by evil deeds. He is a blind Providence—a glorified god of luck.'[2] On the other hand, Mgr. Lagae[3] and Captain Philipps[4]

[1] Colonel A. F. Bertrand in *Azande*, by A. de Calonne-Beaufaict, 1921, p. 172.

[2] Major P. M. Larken, 'An Account of the Zande', *Sudan Notes and Records*, vol. ix, 1926, p. 42.

[3] Mgr. Lagae, *Les Azande,* 1926. Figures in brackets after quotations from Mgr. Lagae's writings refer to this book. His previous article, 'Notes sur les êtres suprasensibles chez les Azande', *Congo,* 1921, was incorporated in *Les Azande.*

[4] Captain J. E. T. Philipps, M.C., 'Observations on some Aspects of Religion among the Azande ("Niam-Niam") of Equatorial Africa'. *J.R.A.I.*, 1926. The numbers in brackets given after quotations from Captain Philipps refer to this paper.

portray a personal God, kindly creator and father, moral ruler and judge of the universe, to whom men pray in humility and in faith.

Hutereau does not mention a Supreme Being among the Azande. Perhaps we are to understand his opinions about Mbori by what he writes of bad ghosts called *Bali*: 'Certains défunts deviennent *Bali* ou *Engese Ingisi*, parcourent les plaines ou les forêts la nuit et s'attaquent aux personnes isolées. D'après les indigènes le *Bali* est visible pendant un instant pour la personne qu'il guette, il a l'aspect d'une être humain recouvert d'une peau de poisson.'[1]

This diversity of opinion cannot be wholly due to religious convictions, or the lack of them, but must also be attributed to the amorphous, indefinite, character of the facts themselves which allows emotional and intellectual selection on the part of observers. For were Zande notions about their Supreme Being expressed in an organized ritual so great a disparity of opinion could scarcely have arisen. Herein lies the main difficulty of giving a balanced account of Zande notions of their Supreme Being. There are no shrines or other material evidences of worship; there is but a single public ceremony associated with his name and this is performed on rare occasions; prayers are individual and private ejaculations of more or less stereotyped expressions; and there is an unique myth about him. The fieldworker therefore has to rely upon a judicious interpretation of these scanty evidences supported by native commentaries which, in the absence of clear-cut doctrines, are often un-illuminating and contradictory. All I can do in this paper is to describe the different situations in which Azande act towards Mbori and speak about him, and to show how their ideas about him are related to other notions contained in their culture. If my descriptions and those of my fellow fieldworkers sometimes seem sparse and our interpretations vague, this must, in part at any rate, be attributed to paucity of organized ritual and absence of formulated dogma.

When speaking of Mbori I have often rendered his name in English as 'Supreme Being', but I wish it to be understood at the outset that I do so without prejudice to a conclusion about the Zande representation of him. Indeed I had better say at once that I cannot altogether agree with Mgr. Lagae's description of Zande theology, but I hasten to add that this is the only major point in

[1] A. Hutereau, *Notes sur la Vie Familiale et Juridique de Quelques Populations du Congo Belge*, 1909, p. 23.

Mgr. Lagae's book on which I feel that it is necessary to join issue with him. I have the greatest respect for his accuracy on all matters of fact and pay homage to my distinguished predecessor in the study of Zande culture. It is with regret that I feel bound to challenge his interpretations, and those of my friend Captain Philipps, of Zande ritual. In the spelling of 'Mbori' I have followed Canon and Mrs. Gore's Zande Dictionary[1] which conforms to the decisions of the Rejaf Conference, which was advised on orthographic matters by Professor D. Westermann, but I have retained the spellings 'Mboli' and 'Mbali' in quotations from other writers.

Captain Philipps says that he has been at pains to record only references to the Supreme Being from Azande of the bush and has discarded remarks made by persons who have had contact with Christians or Mohammedans. He also says that he has not obtained his professions of belief by questioning Azande about the Supreme Being, but by listening to spontaneous avowals overheard rather than elicited by him. Mgr. Lagae, on the other hand, though he has tried to eliminate possible Catholic influence, seems to have relied upon Christian converts, or boys attending a Catholic school, for most of his information, and to have received it in texts written for him by his pupils. In my opinion the danger of using information supplied by informants who have been in contact with Europeans and Arabs is often grossly exaggerated, but undeniably the dangers are great when the subject is that of religious conceptions. In my own view Zande ideas about Mbori are vague on the conceptual side and are little attached to institutions. I have found that in these circumstances Azande are not ill-disposed to accept European opinion and incorporate without difficulty, though often grotesquely, into their loose beliefs about Mbori, the certain dogmas of Christianity and Islam, backed as they are by the cultural superiority of the bearers of these religions. I speak of Azande of the bush who learn here and there an odd piece of doctrine, often from boys who have left the mission or market with scanty notions of teachings of Christ or Mohammed, and I am not referring to Christian converts of long standing.

We may contrast this readiness to accept foreign theistic concepts which, being theological notions, do not contradict indigenous thought because there is really very little to contradict in this

[1] *A Zande and English Dictionary*, compiled by the Rev. Canon and Mrs. E. C. Gore, 1931.

sphere, with the determined intellectual resistance Azande oppose to ideas which contradict convictions which have to be expressed in social routines, e.g. their faith in oracles, their devotion to the ruling class, and their opinions about the position of women in society. I found that they were open to correction on theological questions but not on such matters as these. Considerable caution has therefore to be exercised when using information supplied by boys who have studied at mission schools or resided in Government centres, for they may unwittingly substitute Christian or Moslem ideas for the vague beliefs of their own culture, beliefs which are moreover the expression of age rather than of youth.

Major Larken has often been so careful to record genuinely native thought that he has marked passages derived by direct questioning. My own information was gathered partly by observing ceremonies and partly by systematic inquiry from regular informants some of whose answers I took down in the form of texts. I have tried to make it clear when I have elicited information, when it has come my way by chance observation, and when my informant has been a boy who has studied at a mission school, and I have noted what were the situations in which spontaneous reference to Mbori occurred, and what were the psychological reactions of informants to the questions I put to them.

II

Mgr. Lagae and Captain Philipps are quite decided in their view of Mbori. Mgr. Lagae writes, 'The idea of a Supreme Being is deeply anchored in Zande mentality . . . ' (66); 'for the Zande there is no doubt about the existence of Mboli. It is not a question for discussion . . . ' (66); 'the influence of Mboli is not able to be neutralized by anything. Intervention of Mboli is the ultimate explanation of sickness and death . . . ' (66); 'The Supreme Being, Mboli, appears as the great master of everything, disposing of everything as he pleases without one being able to counteract his activity.' (67). The Azande 'know at least that he is the great Chief, that he has made all and that no one can do anything against him. The universe is his property; the animals of the bush belong to him; even the stars are his work. Mboli sees things and hears what is said. He does not remain a stranger to his handiwork. He intervenes continually, not only causing illness and death, when it pleases him, or producing abnormal phenomena, but he intervenes in daily life, as he pleases, above all to chastise men when they commit evil. The Zande feels himself in respect to Mboli in a state of complete dependence . . . ' (67); 'The Zande is penetrated with the universal action of Mboli . . . ' (67); 'There is no doubt that the Zande attributes to Mboli supreme authority, a power which nothing can neutralize, the unquestioned right to interfere in everything, since the universe is his handiwork. The Zande accepts all that without discussion, without ever blaspheming. In fact he is afraid of the Supreme Being. Although he does not know what happens after his death, he knows that on this earth he can fall under the blows of Mboli. The Zande is far from regarding the Supreme Being with the indifference which some wish to attribute to primitive man. His individual life is altogether penetrated with a reverent and respectful worship of the Supreme Being. One may say that the Zande is deeply religious.' (69). Mgr. Lagae sums up by saying that Mbori applies sanctions to wrongdoers. For example he will send thunder to kill a bad man. Azande believe that through prayer bad actions are pardoned to them by Mbori.

Captain Philipps tells us much the same as Mgr. Lagae. 'Mboli makes himself felt to the Zande in every phase of his daily activities. He is not, as are so many African deities, so much a god-to-be-propitiated. He is rather to be prayed to in order to avert evil, inflictable or inflicted by spirits. He is a 'Fixed power divine which moves to good', though haltingly. His general tendency is felt to be benignant. But if he is slow to anger he is slow also to good. His response to prayer is sluggish. He needs to be constantly reminded of the good disposition or merit of the human individual in order that his benignant potentialities may be stimulated and put into action on the individual's behalf. But, woe betide the Zande who calls casually or overweeningly to the Supreme Being, or who represents himself to be practising virtues or merits which he does not in reality possess. Hence it is to their negative virtues that would-be suppliants most frequently draw attention in protestation or in prayer. *Mboli* appreciates the moral virtues as they are conceived by the community, who feel themselves consciously to be beneath his ubiquitous and absolute dominion. He intervenes frequently in daily life to chastise ὕβρις by the stroke of illness, or to loose the bolts of death upon those who have neglected or inadvertently laid shame upon the *manes* of their clan . . . ' (173). 'The usufruct of earth, air, fire, water and the animals of the chase are consciously held to be conceded to man by *Mboli*, whom the majority of Azande consider to have caused them to be brought into existence . . . ' (173). Captain Philipps concludes, '*Mboli* appears to be continually present in the Zande subconsciousness. Nay, the idea of the presence of *Mboli* seems to hover at the edge of the Zande consciousness more strongly than that of the occasional, though dreaded, spirits who, though more acutely active, appear to fill only a secondary rôle in Zande life.' (175). He adds that, 'The reverence and respect shown to *Mboli* appear to be universal, and to date from a period considerably anterior to European occupation' (175).

Mgr. Lagae and Captain Philipps have had long experience of the Azande and speak their language, so that their opinions are not lightly to be set aside. Yet it is remarkable that neither Major Larken nor I have found the concept of a God who takes an ever-present interest in the world, rewarding good and evil, the guardian of moral law, an omnipotent, omnipresent, benevolent, personal, monotheistic, being, and that we have not found such a belief distinct from other mystical notions nor always on the threshold of Zande consciousness so that it is frequently and readily evoked.

Colonel Bertrand and Major Larken naturally do not give detailed information in support of their view of Mbori, but the accounts of Mgr. Lagae and Captain Philipps are well documented. Indeed, the subject has evidently been of primary interest to both of them; Mgr. Lagae's description of the Supreme Being is his first paper on Zande customs and Captain Philipps' article is his sole contribution on the Azande. Captain Philipps follows Mgr. Lagae so closely that we may consider their opinions together. These are formed from interpretations of three types of evidence, (1) prayers offered to Mbori, (2) the meaning of personal names, and (3) a ceremony carried out during periods of drought and other national misfortunes. I have attached my own observations to their accounts under each of these headings and have added further material.

III

According to Mgr. Lagae and Captain Philipps the Zande prays daily to Mbori. He does so specially when anything goes wrong, for example when he has a sore on his hand or leg, exclaiming, 'Alas

Mboli you do not grant me fortune', or, 'Alas this affair which is troubling me, if *Mboli* wishes it, it is sufficient for it to cease' (67). Thus also a pregnant woman blows a mouthful of water on to the ground from time to time and tells Mbori that she has not stolen the goods of another and that she is in his hands for good or for ill (68). But even if nothing in particular is troubling him, a Zande offers up his daily prayer. Captain Philipps remarks, 'The audible use of prayer to the Supreme Being is more frequent among the Azande than among any African race of whom I have direct or indirect knowledge. I would hazard the opinion that the average untravelled Zande of the bush seldom passes a day of his life without a spoken prayer to *Mboli*' (176). When the Zande performs his daily ablutions his final act is to wash out his mouth with a handful of water and 'he expectorates it on the ground near by, using one of the many variable formulæ according to occasion. One may cite a typical prayer which one very frequently hears if one sits and smokes a pipe unobtrusively with them by a twilight fire. *Bangile aboro wene nga yo dunduko. Kina lo, Mboli, nikasapa ga aboro gbwanga ni lengo,* "in my eyes all men are just (to me). Verily it is thou, *Mboli*, who art a judge over us" (176). Mgr. Lagae gives another of these prayers to Mbori: 'If I have failed in anything, if I have spoken words of anger, all is finished. I blow out water as a sign of my good-will.' He adds, 'In entirely native surroundings, this type of prayer to *Mboli* is made so to speak each morning.' He further tells us that there is a solemn and occasional prayer which Azande utter when menaced with misfortune or on the eve of a serious happening; for example a pregnant woman will utter it. It runs: 'Father, as I am here, I have not stolen the goods of another, I have not taken the goods of another without recompense, I have not set my heart after the goods of another, all men are good in my eyes . . . *Mboli*, it is indeed you who settle the differences between us who are men' (70). Mgr. Lagae quotes a Zande as saying, 'A thing deteriorates among the Azande, maybe a pot, maybe a gourd, maybe a hut, maybe anything else, and the Zande says: "It is the doing of *Mboli*. It is *Mboli* who has said that the thing must perish." One invokes the name of *Mboli* about all things among the Azande. The Azande think about *Mboli* in reference to everything' (68).

Mbori also figures as an object of address in situations of sickness and death. Mgr. Lagae tells us that a visitor to a sick friend will blow out a mouthful of water in a spray to the ground as a sign of his good-will, saying that he is innocent of causing his friend's illness and asking Mbori to drive away the witch who is responsible for it, and that if a man dies and his relatives use magic in vain to avenge themselves on the witch who has murdered him and no one dies as evidence of guilt, they will say that it is not a witch after all but the Supreme Being who has killed him, for Mbori is sometimes made the direct cause of death (66–7). Captain Philipps says that the Supreme Being often causes or permits death to supervene—in the words of Azande, 'Mboli has let the heart-beats fade'—and according to both these observers death by thunder is particularly attributed to the Supreme Being. Mgr. Lagae tells us that when there is a violent storm threatening his safety the Zande, knowing that the Supreme Being sends the thunder-beast to punish wrong-doers, takes a mouthful of water and blows it on to the ground, saying, 'If I have fallen short in anything, there, it is finished, I blow water as a sign of my uprightness' (70). Captain Philipps writes that during violent thunderstorms one may frequently hear Azande pray to Mbori to protect them from the thunder-beast: 'The remarks actually reproduced are those most frequently overheard in the mouths of different Azande on some dozen occasions: *Mi adinga ga boro ahe te*—"I have not stolen things of any man." *Ga Mboli pai du!*—"Mboli's affair it is!" *Ka Mboli aidanga te, ka mi kpinga haleme ya!*—"If Mboli dost not desire it (then) let me not die today!" ' (174).

When travelling in the Congo with nine conscripts for the Moto gold mines Captain Philipps noticed that after crossing a river of any size they washed and filled their mouths with water and spat it out in a shower to the ground. As they did so 'each in turn said with a quiet and simple reverence: *Mboli, ka mi kpinga ku watsa yo ya!*—"*Mboli*, may I not perish in Watsaland!" (Watsa is the distributing centre for the Moto mines.)' (176–7).

Although I have never heard Azande pray for aid to Mbori, on a number of occasions I have heard them use such expressions as 'Oh, Mboli, you have not done well with me,' in situations of unhappiness as when a man had lost his hens, and, 'It is the affair of Mboli,' when referring to something beyond human knowledge. People will also sometimes say that 'If Mbori helps me I will do so and so'. I was told that this is a new expression and that in the past they only used the expression 'If Mbori is well with me', e.g. 'If Mbori is well with me I will marry.'

To supplement the data already quoted I transcribe from my collection of texts other prayers which informants have told me are sometimes uttered to the Supreme Being. Though the physical union between man and woman is the cause of procreation in the eyes of Azande, they nevertheless believe that it would not take place if Mbori were not a complementary cause. In one of my texts a man admonished his son, exclaiming, 'Oh, my son, I have already reasoned with you and you have not listened to my words. Man does not come out of wood. You see this vast extent of country, it is Mbori alone who made it, and he controls everything in it. It is he who put a soul into my father so that he begat me and it is Mbori alone who put a soul into me so that I begat you my son.' During pregnancy Mbori is said to be fashioning the child in the womb and I was told that one should never wake a sleeping woman who is with child lest one should disturb the Supreme Being at work and cause the child to be deformed.

Azande will say of anything that is mysterious to them, such as sleep, 'Mbori in truth does wonderful things.' They say of sleep, 'Sleep is the younger brother of death; what wonders does Mbori perform; a man thinks when he lies down to sleep, sleep like death, that he will wake again with life though he does not know why he wakes, because sleep is like death.'

When visiting the home of a sick man a Zande will take a draught of water and blow it in a spray to the ground and say, 'Oh, Mbori, this man who is sick, if it is I who am killing him with my witchcraft, let him recover.' He blows water and utters this prayer as a declaration of his innocence and in order that, if he is inadvertently responsible for the sickness, the man may recover and he may save himself from death at the hands of avengers. Thus Azande say: 'The blower of water does not die,' meaning that a witch by blowing water cools his witchcraft and hence avoids murder and retribution.

Another text reads: 'Old men when washing in the morning wash their faces and rinse out their mouths and then blow out the water "fushiya" and say, "Oh, Mbori, I do not steal the goods of men, I do not wantonly commit adultery with the wives of men, oh, Mbori, let there be a test between me and men (i.e. if I have committed an offence let me die but if I am innocent, let me live); may no man give me his stolen thing so that I eat of it and die, but may magic (i.e. the medicine made by the owner of the stolen object to kill the thief) settle the affair equitably between me and the thief since it is not I who stole the thing. If perchance there is witchcraft within me let me not injure anyone's gardens with it but let the mouth of my witchcraft cool, let it spend its force upon animals in the bush, animals which dance on the graves of my relatives. Oh, Mbori so! You have not granted me good fortune. Oh, ghosts of my fathers, in what depths of poverty am I plunged! Of a truth you do not watch over me, for if you watched over me you would see that I catch animals to eat since I look like dying after the death of my father." '

An appeal to Mbori is often coupled, as in the last quotation, with an appeal to the ghosts. In another text a man says, 'Oh, if Mbori is good to me today an animal will rush into my net and I among all these people will kill it. Oh, what about it! I wait for long gazing into my net. Oh, so! Indeed the ghost of my father has deserted me.'

When a prince gives a case against a man the loser may say to his opponent, 'Mbori between me and you,' or 'Mbori himself will settle the dispute between me and you before we die.' This is a *zunga*, a test or challenge, and if the man's opponent in the case dies or suffers some grave misfortune shortly afterwards, they say that Mbori has settled the case against him. Men also say, 'If I die first my ghost will go to rest in the earth to make a case against you before Mbori.' I heard of a man whose knife was stolen from another. When the owner of the knife died he appeared in a dream to a friend and told him that he was awaiting the thief to make a case with him before Mbori. Everyone got to know of this dream and when shortly afterwards the thief died, he was said to have been summoned by Mbori to answer the case brought against him.

Though I have never observed a Zande praying to Mbori during morning ablutions, Azande have told me that people will occasionally do so, especially old men, at the time of new moon. One informant told me that a man would say, 'Oh, Mbori, do not let me die this month. Oh, Mbori, let me live to see another moon.' Another informant said that a man might utter these words, 'Oh, Mbori, deal well with me this month. Oh, Mbori, let me obtain spears this month.' New moon is the time when a man will go to his prince's court and ask him for a gift of spears.

When Azande pray to Mbori they often bend their arms at the elbow with palms of the hands uppermost as they do when asking pardon or assistance from a prince.

It is mainly upon the evidence of these and similar prayers that Mgr. Lagae and Captain Philipps rely to sustain their representation of the Zande Supreme Being. Leaving general criticism to the conclusion of this paper I wish to make a few comments upon the use of prayers as evidence of Zande notions of Mbori. When pieced together and presented in bulk by an ethnographer they appear to furnish overwhelming evidence for systematized doctrine, but in real life they are never so presented, but are dissociated phrases evoked in various situations of grief, anxiety, and fear, and have in their context of utterance emotional rather than conceptual significance. They are an idiom of emotional expression in certain situations. In so far as there is a religious doctrine it is found in the prayers themselves. We who are brought up in the poetic imagery of sacred books, are conscious of doctrines which are not only expressed in prayer and worship, but which at the same time explain and justify prayer and worship. But we shall seek in vain for such doctrines among the Azande and there is a grave danger lest we try to construct from their prayers a picture of a God which we would visualize were we to utter them.

Furthermore, there has been a selection of situations in which the word 'Mbori' appears and this would seem to be inadmissible as it limits its range of meaning. For just as we in our culture hear the word 'God' pronounced with many different implications, as 'I believe in God the Father', 'God help us!', 'My God!' and so forth, varying in doctrinal significance from a standardized statement of belief through responses to grief and fear to expletives uttered in anger or exasperation, so also the Zande uses the word 'Mbori' in many different contexts. Besides the prayers cited above, one frequently hears the phrase, '*Mbori amangi e*', 'Mbori did (or made) it' when a Zande sees or hears something unusual, as when he sees some strange product of European manufacture. Once when I read out to a song-leader the text of a song he had composed he exclaimed 'Mbori!'. The phrase is equivalent to our 'By Jove!', or 'Good Heavens!', or 'Well I never!'. To take another example: I once heard an old man tell his son to go a message for him and when the youth started to argue his father uttered several expletives of mingled amazement and anger such as 'By the limb of Gbudwe', and concluded '*Mbori amangi e*', 'Mbori has done it'. The utterance of the man whose hens had disappeared, 'Oh, Mbori, you have not done well with me' ought, I consider, to be translated in our own idiom, 'Oh, I never have any luck', and we ought not to suppose that he was attributing to the Supreme Being guardianship of his fowls or believed that if there had been divine intervention he would not have lost them. I have heard a youth who was being chaffed because girls did not care to flirt with him on account of his looks reply in anger that if he was not good-looking Mbori had made him so. I have heard a man remark in envy of another's marriage 'Mbori gave her to him—it is his wife' which means 'Well some people have all the luck'. Azande also speak of a great king who has died as 'Our Mbori'.

A further point concerns the frequency with which Azande mention Mbori in prayer or otherwise. Mgr. Lagae and Captain Philipps claim that Azande pray daily to Mbori but I have never heard these prayers although I have been on the look-out for them and present when in the early morning during ablutions, around twilight fires, and in thunderstorms, they are said to be spoken. Furthermore, though my informants said that people sometimes pray to Mbori, especially old men and at the time of new moon, as far as I could gather they themselves did not call upon his name. Major Larken, who has been in intimate contact with the Azande for more than twenty years, tells me that he has only once heard a Zande pray, the occasion being when a man asked Mbori to protect him from the rainbow, which is believed to be a large snake. I do not question the authenticity of these prayers—many occur in my own texts quoted on preceding pages—but I doubt the frequency claimed for their expression. I doubt also the justification for such sentences as 'The idea of a Supreme Being is deeply anchored in Zande mentality'; 'The Zande is penetrated with the universal action of Mboli'; 'His individual life is altogether penetrated with a reverent and respectful worship of the Supreme Being'; 'Mboli makes himself felt to the Zande in every phase of his daily activities'; 'He (Mbori) intervenes frequently in daily life'; 'Mboli appears to be continually present in the Zande subconsciousness'; and so forth. I do not wish to set up myself as a better authority on the Azande than Mgr. Lagae and Captain Philipps, but as a fieldworker I must record that I have never heard a Zande pray and that I have seldom heard people utter his name, and then only as an ejaculation of emotional intensity and with only the vaguest suggestion of doctrinal significance. I must confess also that I have found the greatest difficulty in obtaining either information about Mbori or arousing any interest in him, as I explain further on.

A specific problem suggested by these Zande prayers to the

Supreme Being concerns the causation of death. To ask a Zande whether Mbori kills men is like asking a Christian the same question. He knows that sooner or later everybody dies and he supposes that Mbori is aware of their death and permits it. But in sickness and death he thinks of witchcraft as their cause, and not of Mbori, who does not interfere in such matters, and he seeks to cure disease and avenge death through magical and oracular processes against witches and not by prayers to Mbori. Nevertheless, it appears that death is sometimes vaguely attributed to Mbori when no other cause can be discovered. One man told me that Azande will occasionally consult the poison oracle about a sick man, asking it 'Poison oracle, this man who is ill, it is not witchcraft, it is not magic, it is Mbori, poison oracle kill the little fowl.' But they only do this if all efforts to attach responsibility to a witch or magician have failed, and even if the poison oracle kills the fowl to the name of Mbori and the man dies they avenge his death upon some witch, because witchcraft is always a factor in death, and since to omit vengeance would be a stain on family honour. Azande have also told me that on the death of a very old man people may say, 'Mbori killed him, all his days were finished,' or, 'Mbori has taken our relative.' Sometimes also people will say of a very old man, 'He has lived long, his days are ended by Mbori. His little stick is finished.' Mbori is here pictured as breaking off bit by bit the stick of life, just as a Zande breaks the stick when he is counting point by point his statement of a case or is reckoning spears. 'Our fathers said, "Child, Mbori himself breaks off your little stick of days. When he comes to break off the final pieces your days will be ended." '

Zande notions of causation are complicated and vague. I have dealt with them at length elsewhere[1] and will only remark here, in elucidation of the part with which Mbori is credited in the causation of death, that whilst Azande have a hazy idea that he is aware of all deaths, he is not explicitly considered a factor in causing them except in the case of very old men. If a man dies in his prime his death is attributed to an interplay of natural processes, such as diseases, dangerous beasts and reptiles, spear-wounds, falling granaries and so forth, with the action of witchcraft. Witchcraft, being the only cause allowing intervention, is selected as the socially relevant one and a lengthy process of vengeance is based upon it.

[1] *Witchcraft, Oracles and Magic among the Azande,* 1937.

But when a very old man dies, to these causes is added the notion of the Supreme Being as not only aware of the death but of permitting it, even encouraging it, as the ordained end of a natural existence. Nevertheless, vengeance upon a witch will be exacted, however old the man is, for even granted his great age as the natural cause of his decline and the permission of the Supreme Being as the explanation of man's allotted span, it still requires a witch to give him the final push into the company of ghosts. Both the natural cause, age, and the accessory factor of the Supreme Being's encouragement, are thrust into the background by the necessity of vengeance which requires a notion of witchcraft as the cause of all deaths, except those of people who, in the old days, were themselves put to death as witches. In reference to the death of a leper I have heard it said that leprosy is *ga mbori pai*, the business of Mbori, rather than due to witchcraft. Leprosy may come from eating a tabooed animal, or from incest, or even from contact with an insect that walked over dung which a man has excreted in a riverside wood. But whatever may be the participating cause witchcraft is always the agent which provokes retaliation.

IV

The second type of evidence quoted by Mgr. Lagae consists of an analysis of Zande names containing the word 'Mbori'. He considers that they demonstrate Zande notions about the Supreme Being. 'The Zande,' he writes, 'is so penetrated with ideas about the Supreme Being that sometimes he gives his children names which embody a complete doctrine' (68). He gives the following list: Daduwamboli (Who is as Mboli), Mbolinabilo (Mboli sees you), Mbolimangile (Mboli made me), Mboligihe (Mboli hears it), Udimboli (Appreciated Mboli), Humboli (Thing of Mboli), Ngbamboligbwe (Mboli is very good), Kumboliyo (At Mboli's place). To these names I may add Mbori (Mbori), Gamboripai (Mboli's affair), Mborizingbare (Mboli has closed my lips).

Whilst it is true that these names bear witness to belief in the existence of a being superior to man they do very little to define his attributes, though Mgr. Lagae makes them bear a doctrinal interpretation which in my opinion they do not express. He does not mention that princes sometimes bear the name of Mbori, and it is hardly consistent with the picture of an omnipotent All-Father that men should bear his sacred name. Also when a man gives his son such a name as Ngbamborigbwe (Mbori is very good), he means simply that he is pleased and there is little reason to suppose that on this or on many other occasions upon which the name Mbori is mentioned by Azande that they are conscious of paying homage to the deity any more than when an Arab bawls out, 'Ya 'Abdallah!' he is conscious of having uttered the name of God. But this is not the whole point, and I have purposely mentioned the name 'Abdallah to bring out the rest of my objection, for in the case of an Arab who calls his son 'Abdallah we know that there is a doctrine which explains historically how the name came to be used by Arabs, and that this doctrine defines the attributes of God, but we would not attempt to derive from an Arab's use of the name an elaborate doctrinal concept and say the Arab is so penetrated with ideas about the Supreme Being that he gives his children names which embody a complete doctrine. To anybody acquainted with, at any rate Bedouin, Arabs this would sound absurd as religion sits very lightly on their shoulders. Zande names which contain the word 'Mbori' when viewed in the light of their method of naming in general cannot be used as evidence for the existence of a formulated doctrine defining Mbori as a supreme and beneficent father or of conscious devotion of Azande towards him, for they are in origin little more than idiomatic expressions of satisfaction and in use no more than names are to us.

It is necessary, moreover, to know not merely that such names are occasionally given to children, but also the context of their endowment. The name Ngamboligbwe may have been given as a joke or out of a feeling of exuberance, and there is no reason why we should suppose that it was given out of a feeling of gratitude or respect. The attitude of Azande towards the Supreme Being as registered in their names can only be ascertained by noting how their endowment and expression are associated with psychological states and doctrinal comments, and not by merely writing them down on paper and afterwards making a lexicographic dissection of them. I have never observed that Azande show any more sense of awe when uttering names in which Mbori occurs than we have in uttering such names as Christopher. I was only able to trace the occurrence which suggested the endowment of a name in a single instance. One of my informants was named Mborizingbare or Zingbarembori (Mbori has closed my lips). I asked the youth's father why he had called his son by this name, and he said that when he was asked by what name he would call his son he made this reply, which meant 'I really cannot think what to say.'

V

The third type of data instanced by Mgr. Lagae and Captain Philipps is a description of public ceremonial in honour of the Supreme Being. In times of drought, when there is danger that the crops may die from lack of moisture, or in times of serious pestilence, a ceremony takes place at the suggestion of ghost-diviners (*aboro atoro*) who are instructed to initiate it on directions from Mbori or from the ghosts of the dead by dreams, in cultivations and at sources of streams. However it is necessary that the prince's poison oracle shall confirm their dreams before the ceremony takes place, and if the poison oracle gives confirmation the prince tells his deputies to instruct the ghost-diviners to organize locally in each district a ceremony which is usually called *maziga.* Ghost-diviners are people who are able to communicate with the ghosts of the dead, usually through dreams, and are generally women.

Mgr. Lagae does not describe the ceremony in detail as he did not have an opportunity to witness it, but Captain Philipps, who has watched it taking place, writes, 'The bearers of the offering of first-fruits had, in this instance, been called forth by the chief amid the approbation of the people in increasing procession from house to house. Thence they moved with simple cadenced song towards the open table rock which gives birth to the source of a river and looks out over the whole countryside. The songs appeared to consist of chorused invocations of a very limited variety. Considerable alarm and despondency were created during our stay at the neighbouring village by a bursting storm which, occurring during the night, washed off a large proportion of the offerings into the stream below. Passing next morning about dawn on my way to shoot, I was an attentive witness and hearer of the impromptu meeting held on the spot by the earliest passers-by' (177). He says that the ceremony is usually held about December in the Zande month of *bandulo,* the month of mists, but if this is so it can hardly be intended to counteract drought as the Azande do not plant their crops till the end of March, and as in December the millet is ripening in the cultivations the last thing they want is rain. Mgr.

Lagae says that it is held at the commencement of the dry season and only once a year but not necessarily each year (71). This is a time when drought may destroy the millet harvest since it is still growing and needs moisture. Similarly I was told that it was held either when the young shoots of millet needed moisture (it is planted in August) or in the springtime (about May, in the Zande month of *malekoko*) for the benefit of all crops.

Major Larken describes the ceremony as in honour of Baati and not of Mbori. His description is as follows[1]: 'In the case that came under the writer's notice, no altar was raised, but only a small space was swept at the rocky lip of a ravine, and in that space a heap consisting of leaves of pineapple, bananas, elusine, sweet potatoes, ground-beans, *kpagu* and *ngbazi*, had been placed by the people.

A song is sung while the gifts are brought:

E, E, Baati, O.
E, E, Baati ti ali yo (E, E, Baati has tumbled down from above),
Ndu ko kati (His leg is broken).

(Chorus): *E, E, Baati O.*'

I have only once had the opportunity of witnessing the *maziga* ceremony and could not make use of this to any great extent as I was in high fever at the time and it was only towards the end of the ceremony that I became an eye-witness. On this occasion, in the month of August, there was a severe outbreak of cerebro-spinal meningitis which caused many deaths. The prince, Gangura, had consulted his poison oracle to find out whether the epidemic would cease if the *maziga* ceremony were held, and learning that this would be the result he sent for a well-known ghost-diviner and instructed her to commence the ceremony, which she organized with the aid of several other women ghost-diviners. In the early morning the women of several settlements collected in the house of the leading ghost-diviner and from there commenced to visit neighbouring cultivations through which they charged, rushing in all directions, shouting and singing, and swinging sticks into the air to bring them down with strokes to the earth in time to their songs. Besides sticks they carried in their hands leaves of manioc, sweet potatoes, and other food plants which they gathered from home-

[1] 'Impressions of the Azande', *Sudan Notes and Records*, 1927, p. 121.

steads and cultivations as they passed through them. They were preceded in this romp through gardens and cultivations by a small boy beating on a leather-topped drum. Men kept out of their way partly because it was not their business to take part in a women's ceremony and partly because the women become excited and do not observe, indeed are not expected to observe, the usual rules of seemly conduct. The ghost diviners and others among the women who accompany them perform a kind of belly dance which in ordinary times would be considered indecent and would not be allowed. I was told also that these ghost-diviners may make obscene gestures with their hands and utter expressions which are only permitted on rare occasions of prescribed licence.

The women finally gathered together in a homestead at the edge of the settlement in which I lived and I hurried out to meet them as soon as I heard that they were there. Only women took part in the ceremony and the few men who, like myself, were onlookers, happened to live nearby and could hardly have avoided being spectators. On the whole they seemed to regard the antics of the women as a joke. These were dancing wildly in the centre of the homestead and one of them was now beating the drum. They waved leaves of food plants in their hands and beat the ground with sticks singing various songs, usually consisting of a single sentence, for example:

Maziga oo Baati oo
and
Uwa uwa uwa Mbori ooo maziga ooo
and
Mbori di wiru be re Mbori ooo
and
Buba akpi te Mbori ako ako kpiyo ani ga ga.

No translations can be offered for the first two lines other than the explanations suggested below of the words *maziga* and *Baati.* The third line might be translated 'Mbori has taken his son from me, Mbori ooo', and the fourth line as 'My father has died Mbori alas, alas, death, we have departed'. During the singing and dancing the leading ghost-diviner became possessed by ghosts and twitched and trembled and shook as though she had convulsions. Some of the other women beat her on the back and poked their fingers into her ears. They must have danced thus for half an hour when, preceded by the leading ghost-diviner, they rushed off at the double along a path to a stream singing.

> '*Maziga oo oo ee ee uu uu*
> *Baati ti ooo uu uu oo ooo*
> *Baati ti ali yo nduko kati.*
>
> *Maziga oo oo ee ee uu uu*'
> 'Baati fell ooo uu uu oo ooo
> Baati fell from on high and broke his leg.'

On arrival at the stream head they continued to sing for a while and to beat the drum. Finally they cleared an open space on the floor of a shallow chasm at the head of the stream and placed their leaves there. It seems that they may place them instead on a granitic outcrop near the head of the stream. At this point the leading ghost-diviner swooned in convulsions, and the ceremony came to a conclusion. The women oiled their bodies in the bush and made themselves presentable before returning to their homesteads. I was told that on the following morning the ghost-diviners ate special medicines—ghost medicines—known only to them. The country was laid under a kind of general interdict against eating manioc leaves and the oil-bearing plant *ndaka* (*Hyptis spicigera-Sch.*), because the senior ghost-diviner had been given an order to this effect by the Supreme Being in a dream and her dream had been confirmed by Gangura's poison oracle.

These descriptions may be supplemented by several native accounts. According to one informant (Kuagbiaru) 'In the past all Azande used to think about Mbori as dwelling mainly at the heads of streams rather than in other places. They also thought about Mbori as being under the earth because when a man dies they bury him in the earth where Mbori is.

'In a year in which food plants do not bear well for Azande they collect on a certain day, shortly after sunrise, and go about ululating with a great noise. It is the same with rain also. If rain does not fall to make their crops grow they perform this ceremony at a stream-head, because they all believe that Mbori is at the heads of streams and that if they go there to cry out for rain he will surely give it to them.

'But now a good number listen to the teaching of the missionaries and think that in fact Mbori is on high because the missionaries always tell them that this is so. But the people who do not live near the Government station still retain the ideas of their fathers, for their fathers used to honour Mbori at the heads of streams in the old days. Most people still say today that Mbori is in fact at the heads of streams because when they go to celebrate *Baati* at the heads of streams Mbori will grant them rain on that day on which they go to celebrate *Baati*.

'Azande speak thus about Mbori, "Alas Mbori has become bad"; they say this when a relative has died and they say that it is Mbori who has taken him. Also they say thus at a house of mourning, "Alas that Mbori is aloof, Mbori has wearied, Mbori has done an unworthy thing, Mbori is responsible for happenings, Mbori has been wanton." All such expressions are uttered by those who are sad, by blind persons and lepers, by those whose relatives have died and those who cannot rise from poverty. These people speak all these things to the name of Mbori.

'It seems to be their cry of anguish to Mbori; but they do not know what to say. If they see a bad man with many fine wives, they say, "People have all married women except me, Mbori is being unworthy."

'All these sayings Azande have in no wise given up; they still speak them about any small matters which trouble them; they say it is indeed Mbori who has done it thus.

'If you ask a Zande today he would tell you that Mbori is certainly at the heads of streams. It is thus that you will hear it on the lips of all Azande.'

A Zande Christian (Zuzu) gave the following account of the ceremony: 'That which Azande used to do is as follows: in the past people used to say that Mbori dwells at the heads of streams. People collected together to perform the ceremony of *Baati*. They said that Mbori is at the heads of streams and near limonite outcrops. They performed the ceremony of *maziga* and rain came down and poured greatly. People went and straightway gathered [in the ceremony] all fruits, ground-nuts and sesame and sweet potatoes and leaves of manioc and fowls' eggs and bananas and every kind of produce to perform the ceremony of *maziga* and *Baati* to bring down rain upon their crops and cultivations so that refreshed by rain they might spring up, for if rain does not fall the plants will not spring up. Mbori gives rain and the crops spring up and that is why people perform the ceremony of *maziga*.'

A third account was as follows: 'People rise early and go out to beat *maziga* on account of the seedlings of plants. They say, "Let plants flourish, let this world be fruitful to men here, because if there be no food all men will die. Mbori grant it to us who are ghost-diviners." They then commence to sing a song:

Maziga ooooo baati oowo.

When they arrive in the cultivations they begin to break off heads of millet and *kpagu* [a species of gourd] and ground-nuts and earth-beans and *mele* [a yam] and heads of *abakpa* [a bean] and *detiro* [an oil-bearing plant] and to collect fowls' eggs. They beat all the cultivations and then their leader says, "Let us go to the head of the stream to present these things to Mbori." Well, they begin to go and arrive there.

'She tells them to remain on the bank and she collects all these things and takes them and throws them down in the chasm. Then she begins to tremble and starts the song of the ghosts for her companions, and they respond, to Mbori. She says to them, "Let us go home, the ghosts are chasing me, let us go." They commence to depart.'

A fourth account was compiled from statements of three women, who were leaders in the ceremony I witnessed, a day or two after it had taken place. Their statements were taken down by my Zande clerk in my presence.

They said: '*Maziga* is held when the country is quite dried up and rain refuses to fall. Those women who are ghost-diviners have already notified all their women friends, and at dawn they all collect, each carrying food plants and none lacking these. They take a leather-topped drum and give it to a small boy and he walks ahead of them and beats it. People proceed singing many *maziga* songs. They go and arrive there and the ghost-diviners descend right into the chasm at the stream-head. While they are there the boy beats the drum up above on the bank. They wait there for a long time and then suddenly emerge and tell the people that the ghosts praise their offerings and that their rain will fall on their millet. The ghost-diviners say that when they are in the chasm the ghosts speak to them. When they go to wait in the chasm the ghosts speak words to them and praise the food plants which the people have brought with them.'

They also said: 'It is the ghosts who speak about *maziga* that people must go and beat it at a stream-head. When rain has not fallen for a long time it is the ghosts who say to a ghost-diviner that she shall tell the people to go to cry *maziga* at a stream-head so that rain may fall. The ghost-diviners tell everybody to gather together in the early morning to go and cry *maziga* because thus the ghosts order it. The people gather together, men, women, and little children, with a great noise, plucking heads of manioc in the gardens and leaves of many food plants. They go singing these songs.' (Here follow songs. Some are similar to those already recorded while others are not transcribed because they do not shed light on the meaning of the ceremony.)

The manner in which each of these women became ghost-diviners was also recorded. One was called Nabaru. 'Her father had gone to the wars in the army of Gbudwe and the ghosts made her dream. They said to her in a dream that she must not eat those things which her mother will prepare (because she was in mourning). In this, her dream, she saw the corpse of her father on a bier and men carrying it home. She woke up because it was a terrible dream. In the morning, at dawn, she looked up towards the path and people came bearing the corpse of her father. Messages from the ghosts came to her ever afterwards. *Ngbisi* began from that moment to take up its place in her throat. *Ngbisi* is the little voice in the throat of a person. Only not many ghost-diviners possess it. They ask *Ngbisi* about the future and it reveals everything. But not many witch-doctors possess *Ngbisi*, only a few of them.'

The second woman, Naakadumu, recounted that, 'She went to scoop out water to catch fish. She continued for some time to scoop out water and caught a crab by one foot and one claw and caught a frog. She returned home and when she arrived she put water on the fire to boil. She took the crab and threw it into the water and threw the frog in after it. When the water got too hot for the crab, it clambered out of the pot and made off in haste to the head of the stream. It ran and ran and entered into a hole. Naakadumu found the tracks of the crab and tracked it till she arrived at the stream-head. She saw the hole and put her hand into it and seized the crab. She had just seized it when it cried out aloud like a man. The horror of it came upon her and she jumped up in haste with a cry and fled. She continued to run shrieking and fell into a chasm. People took a leather-topped drum and came and stood at the mouth of the chasm and beat it and after a while she came out.

They took her and returned home with her. She refused all food, but she ate flies for food. The ghosts continued ever afterwards to trouble her.'

The third woman, Nambua, said that, 'She died and they dug a grave for her and everyone wailed. Her soul went forth and appeared at the place of ghosts. She was just looking about when all her relatives collected and made a circle around her. It was her mother who said to her, "What have you come here for? Get up and go whence you came. Go away quickly." She departed from amongst these people and her eyes at once opened. Everyone ceased wailing and she began immediately to wake from death and recovered completely.'

The songs sung during the ceremony are quite unintelligible without native commentary and even to Azande they are little more than rhythmic chants devoid of meaning. The ghost-diviners say that they refer to the Supreme Being having turned his back on the people and are above all on the theme of death. It is of particular interest to know what, or who, are *maziga* and *Baati*. According to Captain Philipps the word is *beleti* contracted from *ba*, father, and *eleti*, cultivations, and he concludes that the word therefore means 'father-(of)-cultivated fields", and he says "This may not unreasonably be taken as an attribute of *Mboli*, one of whose principal functions consists in acting as the spiritual land-lord of the *A-zande* (*sande*, *sende*) or people-of-the-soil' (178). According to Mgr. Lagae and Major Larken the word is compounded of *Ba*, big, and *eti*, cultivations, and they conclude that it should be translated 'big cultivations'.

Major Larken speaks of *Baati* as a distinct personality and in his account of the ceremony does not even mention Mbori, showing that his informants certainly did not emphasize the Supreme Being in association with it. He writes of *Baati* that he 'inhabits the sources of certain streams which rise in deep ravines, shaded by great trees,or rocky outcrops which have a spring at the foot, and it is by revelation in a dream that his dwelling-places are known, divination [oracles] not being resorted to for the purpose of discovering them.'[1] He comments, 'What the people imagine Baati to be is difficult to say. Were he accepted as a spirit, or as a personification of the deity Mbali, he would undoubtedly be accorded the neuter [animal] gender, and the penultimate line of the song would

[1] *Ibid.*, pp. 120–1.

be: *Ndu ru kati.* He must have either a multiple personality or the power of responding to calls made for him at his various haunting places; and yet the Azande interrogated replied, "*Ko wa boro,* he is like a person," again using the masculine *ko* and not the supernatural neuter, *u.*'[1]

In a text written by a Christian convert the word appears as *batita* which means 'great ancestor'. Though it is evident that this is an elision in writing *Baati ti,* Baati fell, it shows clearly that the boy did not understand the sense of what he was writing and how very little meaning the song conveys to Azande. We are disappointed if we anticipate that it may summarize a myth. The word *Baati* is known to Azande only in this song and it is noticeable that Zande songs in general soon lose whatever meaning they may once have had and that at any time are seldom more than partly understood by those who sing them. They retain only sufficient grammatical form and limited sense to serve mnemonic purposes as accompaniments to rhythm. To most Azande *Baati* is the ceremony itself but as in one of the songs his leg is said to have been broken they think that he may have been somebody who had something to do with Mbori. The senior prince of Yambio district, Rikita, told me that *Baati* and Mbori were the same person and that the song came to a ghost-diviner in a dream. Another old man told me that *Baati* is the son of Mbori and he is spoken of as such in one of the songs quoted. I discuss later on the possibility of Christian influence through some, perhaps early, channel which would account for Mbori having a son whom he took from men (the ghost-diviners say, however, that this line means that they are weeping for their dead children), and who fell down from on high and broke his leg.

Mgr. Lagae says that there are two ceremonies, the ordinary one being known as *baeti* and the other, carried out by an important person living near Dungu (a place in the Congo), being called *maziga.* This second ceremony is carried out on a path. It is possible that the first ceremony is one to bring rain and the second a ceremony to end pestilence, but in the Sudan Azande do not appear to distinguish between them. None of my informants knew what *maziga* meant beyond the action of the ceremony. Here again the word only occurs in the single context where it is a symbol for the whole ceremony. Thus one says *ta maziga,* to celebrate *maziga,* just as one says *ta baati,* to celebrate *baati.* The meaning of the word

[1] *Ibid.*, p. 121.

might be *ma ziga*, to place an antidote, *ziga* being the usual word for magical antidotes, but it would be hazardous to attach importance to this or any similar guesses. Mgr. Lagae does not suggest a meaning for the word and Captain Philipps and Major Larken do not mention it at all. Nevertheless the meaning of *ta maziga*, the usual expression in the Sudan, or *ta baati*, is at once suggested by the ceremony itself, the part which is stressed in the action of the women who perform it and which is emphasized by Azande when describing and commenting on the ceremony, being the beating of the earth with sticks by the women as they run through the cultivations and gardens. *Ta maziga* or *ta baati* is therefore 'to beat (*ta*) the *maziga*' or 'to beat the *baati*', and as in fact what they actually beat are the large cultivations in which are sown the principal crops (millet, sesame, oil-bearing plants, peas, beans, and manioc) the inference of Mgr. Lagae, Captain Philipps, and Major Larken, that *Baati* is compounded of *ba*, big, and *ati*, cultivations, is probably correct, though if this is so it is a puzzle how the expression came to be personified.

Neither Mgr. Lagae nor Captain Philipps have any doubt that the ceremony is held in honour of Mbori, the Supreme Being, and that Azande are expressing in it their theological doctrines. Mgr. Lagae writes, 'Great droughts and floods have on many occasions destroyed entire harvests. The Zande still recalls that in the past invasions of locusts have destroyed everything. Would not this be a punishment from Mboli? It is necessary to make a public offering of all kinds of food to Mboli, not only to obtain abundant harvests and freedom from all illness, but also to purchase in some way the right to use the goods of nature' (70–1). Captain Philipps, who speaks of Mbori as the 'spiritual landlord of the Azande', writes of this ceremony that it is 'one of the few manifestations of communal tribute to the Supreme Being', and he concludes that 'the offering is in the nature of an insurance against defective productivity, and also, perhaps, is a tangible recognition of the power of *Mboli* to concede or to withold the full usufruct of the earth' (177).

In watching the ceremony and in talking to Azande about it I have never received an impression of such a devout and poetic interpretation as is drawn by these two observers. In the ceremony itself there are no signs of deep reverence for a Supreme Being. Also I could not elicit from Azande theological notions which would explain the custom. What they had to express they expressed in action and they had little more to add by way of commentary. Always I found their ideas about the songs and about the purpose of the rite were very hazy, and from Major Larken's description it is evident that such were also his impressions. They seemed vaguely to associate drought and pestilence with Mbori and to believe that if he were honoured by performance of the ceremony he could end them, but their notions could hardly be said to define relations between God and men. Indeed at these times of national peril their speech and behaviour furnish no evidences that we are able to co-ordinate into a coherent conception of a deity. The ceremony does not express religious doctrines so much as it is in itself the doctrine, and there are no further theological beliefs that can be called upon to explain it. Its two main actions in the eyes of Azande are undoubtedly the beating of the earth and the placing of leaves of food plants at the heads of streams.

Moreover several Azande have told me in good faith that the ceremony was carried out to honour the *atoro*, the ghosts of the dead. When I asked one informant why other people told me that it was performed in honour of the Supreme Being he replied that he did not know but that he himself had always been told that it was carried out in honour of the ghosts. The three women ghost-diviners considered that the ceremony had reference only to the ghosts. Also the royal class takes no part in the ceremony other than consulting their oracles whether it is desirable to perform it, for they place offerings in their shrines and ask the ghosts of their fathers to stop the drought or pestilence. Rain is closely associated with the ghosts and when Azande wish to prevent rain from falling and spoiling their millet, spread out to dry in the centre of their homesteads in preparation for feasts, they appeal to the ghosts to prevent rain from falling. There can be no doubt that Azande do not clearly distinguish between the Supreme Being and the ghosts of the dead when performing the ceremony and that they think of them both together as the object of their ritual. On the other hand one informant, Kisanga, said that people ought to distinguish between Mbori and the ghosts.

Besides the Supreme Being and the ghosts it is thought that certain men have an influence over the rain and can stop it from falling and can therefore be persuaded in one way or another to withdraw their opposition and allow it to fall. In my own experience this belief plays very little part in Zande life and the people whom it concerns are unimportant and unfortunate. Indeed I have only come across them by hearsay and during my residence in Zandeland have seldom heard of action being taken against them. However, Major Larken attributes social importance to them.

He says: 'A general belief exists in rain-stoppers. The power of controlling rain runs in certain families, and descends from father to son, but the particular root or medicine used in the family must be made known to the latter, or he will not be able to exercise his gift.

'If a drought occurs, and there be living in the neighbourhood any person credited with such power, he may be tied up, or beaten or dipped in a stream or sluiced with water until rain comes. On one occasion, at Tambura, a rainmaker buried his rain charm with the body of his son, in revenge for the latter's death, which he suspected to have been caused by magic. A drought followed, and when the situation became serious the grave was violated and the charm thrown into the stream. Rain fell. In 1915, on July 23rd, a man came in to the District Commissioner to complain that he had been beaten by his neighbours for holding up the rain. On the 24th rain fell. On the 25th, his Chief came to make a formal complaint against him for his action in ruining the crops. In Chief Sasa's country crops were withering from a drought. Sasa sent for the man who was supposed to be responsible and had him dipped in a stream or beaten, and heavy rain fell at once. Similar conditions obtaining in Chief Gbefe's country, the Chief sent a message to one of his subjects, whose forefathers were known to have been rain-stoppers under the Vungara régime, to the effect that he would hold him responsible if the drought continued. It did not. . . .

'It seems to be the general opinion that rain-men only put forth their power when they suspect their Chiefs or neighbours of not sending them as many presents of food as they should. Chief Ninda [Ngindo?], a most enlightened and exceptionally intelligent Vungura, shares his first maize crop with one of his men, fearing that if he does not do so the rest of the crop will perish through drought.'[1]

It will have been noticed that in the texts I have quoted and in Major Larken's statement about Mbori that the Supreme Being is spoken of as living at the heads of streams. The text written by my Christian informant speaks of it as an old belief, while Kuagbiaru

[1] *Op. cit.*, 1926, pp. 44–5.

contrasts this belief still held by all Azande of the bush with the new belief that Mbori lives in the sky which he had heard from 'people of the post' who have either been to the mission school or are to some extent aware of Christian teachings. Both emphasize the fact that in Zande belief Mbori resides at the heads of streams because the modern challenge to it has focused their attention on the point. Mgr. Lagae and Captain Philipps expressly state that Mbori has no particular dwelling place and neither mention that he lives at the heads of streams, yet this is about the only clear and unanimous belief that I found associated with his name. It is to these dark ravines that the souls of men go, when they die, to lead there the shadowy life of ghosts. Doubtless the association of both the Supreme Being and the ghosts with rain is connected with their residence in these moist ravines where water everlastingly bubbles from the ground.

To the information about Mbori given under the headings of prayers, personal names, and the ceremony in times of drought and pestilence, must be added a Zande creation myth known to many persons but by no means to all, even among the aged. I have heard several versions of it which differ slightly from one another. All agree in telling how Bapaizegino, or Bapai, who is the same person as Mbori, put mankind with the rest of creation into a kind of round canoe which he completely closed except for a small hidden entrance by which it could be opened. This entrance he closed with wax. Bapaizegino, sent a messenger, in one version the Bongo (*Boöcircus euryceros isaaci*), to his sons, the Sun, the Moon, the Night, the Cold and the Stars, to say that he was dying and that they were to come immediately. All the sons of Bapaizegino received well their father's messenger at their homes and each showed him the path to the home of the next son, but it was the Sun alone who treated him with the consideration a messenger from their father deserved. Here we find Zande notions of princely obligations colouring the story. The sons of Bapaizegino should have behaved as a son of King Gbudwe would have done had a special messenger from his father arrived at his court. This is just the way a Zande king might have tested the character of his son. For the messenger, in one version, acting on his master's orders, chose the Sun on account of his munificence to be the greatest of the sons of Bapaizegino and explained to him the secret of opening the round canoe which contained mankind. He told him to look for a stain, made with fruit of the *mbiango* (*Gardenia jovis-tonantis Walw.*) tree, on its surface, and when he saw that he would know that there was the hidden opening.

When the sons of Bapaizegino arrived he told them that he had sent for them to open the round canoe of the universe and had it placed in the centre of them. Each in turn made an attempt to open it without success. When the Sun was called upon he saw this stain but pretended he had seen nothing and so appeared to meet with failure like the other sons. Their father upbraided them for their inability to open the canoe and the Sun then stepped forward a second time and scraped away with his nail the wax beneath the stain and with a great noise poured out men and beasts and trees and grasses and rivers and hills. The first clan of men to emerge were the Ambata, the First Ones, and the last clan to emerge were the Aboro, the Men, so-called because Bapaizegino had used up all the names he could think of on the other clans.

Hence it is that the Sun is king of all things and that none can hide from his face. The Azande say that the Sun is the greatest and that this is why men say, 'Take care not to do it at night.' Still, the Night is good because termites fly in it. The Moon is bad because if it shines brightly the termites rise towards it instead of flying downwards to the flame which is held to attract them. Still, the Moon is also good and second only to the Sun for men say, 'Wait for the Moon to rise before you do anything.' Also the Stars are good because when you see *Tungu*, the Morning Star, you know that dawn is at hand.

This is the only creation myth, if it can be so called, found among the Azande. Another aetiological myth, obviously a late tradition, is found in one form or another among several other tribes in the Sudan and is perhaps diffused throughout Africa generally. In this myth, told to me by Rikita, the eldest surviving son of King Gbudwe, Mbori placed on a tree a spear, a shield, and a rifle, and gave choice of weapons to the Azande who foolishly chose the spear and shield and left the rifle to the Europeans. European domination is accounted for by this myth.

In their myth, known to many Azande, accounting for the origin of death I have never heard the name of Mbori mentioned. It is a typical African myth attributing death to fortuitous circumstances and runs thus: 'Azande say that the cause of the moon not dying is that a human corpse and the corpse of the moon lay at the side of a grave. Then it was said, "Let the frog and the toad jump with them over the grave. That corpse—let them jump with it over the grave and he will never die again." The frog jumped over the grave with the corpse of the moon. The toad intended to jump over the grave with the human corpse but fell with it into the grave. Therefore they said about the moon that it would not die again but that man would die altogether. It is for this reason that the moon continues; always it comes to daylight and grows old and changes into a little moon and rises again in the west. When the toad fell with the human corpse it meant that man would continue to die always and for ever. But people only think this story may be true for no one actually saw the thing happen.'

There are certain natural objects which are explained by reference to Mbori. In Yambio and Maridi Districts there are numerous holes in rock outcrops, presumably made by earlier occupants of the soil, probably in grinding grain, which are generally known as *fua Mbori*, footprints of Mbori. I was told that they were made by Ture, the main character in Zande folklore, when he ground his corn and crushed his sesame. This was ever so long ago in the time when Ture used to walk about with Mbori. Other Azande say that they are the footmarks of Mbori but that they do not know when or how he made them. I have also been told that they are footmarks of the ghosts. One man even told me the Christian story of the Garden of Eden to account for these holes but in a form so stamped by Zande culture that it was a long time before I discovered its origin. Once upon a time there was, I was told, no bush, but only rich, open, country in the soft earth of which Mbori imprinted his footmarks. Later Mbori became angry with men and changed everything into bush and the ground hardened here and there into granitic rock in which the footprints of the Supreme Being are preserved. Major Larken tells us that fireballs are known as *hu Mbali*, God's property or thing,[1] and I have myself heard Azande speak of meteorites by this term.

In the Tembura District there is a natural object known as *kura Mbori*, Mbori's whistle, which is known to the Azande of Yambio District by hearsay. Major Larken thus describes it: 'Spirits of the deceased, if successful application be made to them and small offerings placed in the altar, will send rain. Certain places, and perhaps certain spirits, seem to be more effective than others. For

[1] 1926, p. 43.

instance, the rock Wanga, in the Pambia Hills where Liwa, father of Tambura, lies buried, is a good place. It may be because this rock is vaguely connected with *Mbali* that it has a special reputation. For it possesses a curiosity in the *kura Mbali*, God's charm. The grey rock face is bare and sheer, rising precipitously for perhaps two hundred feet. At half its height there is a small hole, through which protrudes what looks like the snapped-off root of a tree. This withdraws into the hole, or stretches out from it for a yard, according as to whether rain is coming or the reverse, and is the *kura Mbali*. Moreover, if a gun were discharged against this rock, at all events in Chief Tambura's time, the man who fired it would be drenched by a storm before reaching home. But in spite of this it is Liwa's spirit, and not *Mbali*, that is supposed to be the rain-giver here. It is said that only the application of Renzi, the heir of Tambura, or one of Tambura's surviving brothers, is certain of success, as Liwa probably would not trouble about the wants of any less important people.'[1]

Besides these particular objects the existence of Mbori furnishes a general vague explanation of all natural objects. When walking in the bush with Azande I have often asked them the names of plants and for what purposes they are used and they have replied that a plant has no uses but is just a plant. It is not for men, Mbori just made it. Similarly if you ask them about granitic outcrops they say simply that Mbori made them. Also if you press a Zande to say where his fathers gained knowledge of magic and oracles, he will reply as a last resort, 'Mbori gave them to us.' Pretty well everything can be explained in this way. Especially abnormal natural objects, such as the whistle of Mbori described above, and any human abnormality, such as an abnormal birth, are attributed to Mbori. Thus Major Larken writes: 'No superstitions appear to be connected with the hair, except that occasionally someone is seen with an abnormal growth which has never been cut. It is held that such hair is made to grow in profusion through an act of Mboli, and that the bearer of it would fall ill if it were tampered with. The late Chief Mainge of Maridi had a leonine head of hair, falling to his shoulders, matted and unkempt. He had never had it cut for this reason.'[2] [This is contrary to what I was told. He may have changed from one mode to another.]

Zande folklore is concerned almost entirely with a man called

[1] *Ibid.*, pp. 45–6. [2] *Ibid.*, p. 33.

Ture who is the hero of numerous tales, and as he is sometimes mentioned in association with Mbori attention must be paid to him here. In a note signed (B) in de Calonne's book on the Azande we find the following statement: 'It is generally accepted that Boli [Mbori] is the Zande God. I have not been able to find anything on this subject in the notes left by de Calonne. Boli [Mbori] seems to belong rather to the category of culture heroes like Tule [Ture]. The fact that the native sometimes compares himself, or compares his ancestors, to Allah or to Dzambi, makes it clear that he has in no wise assimilated Christian metaphysical ideas but rather that Christian entities have been integrated into ancient Zande beliefs. The God of the Christian Zande is no more than a demi-god. In the same way the sexual prohibitions of the exogamous clan are extended to all those who have had the same patron in baptism.'[1] (B) is doubtless Colonel Bertrand to whom we owe so great a debt for his arduous task of editing de Calonne's notes after his death.

Before mentioning Mgr. Lagae's reaction to this comment it will be as well to say that the Azande of the Sudan have been subject to shorter and less intensive foreign influence than those of the Congo and that the question of direct Christian teaching in their ideas does not arise except among those who are living around a Government post or who have been educated at mission schools.

Mgr. Lagae does not accept with equanimity this suggestion of M. (B). He replies: 'La question revient à se demander si les Azande assimilent Mboli à Tule. Tous ceux qui ont appris à connaître les Azande, doivent savoir qu'il y a, sur le compte de Tule, toute une série de légendes, qui constituent avec les fables et les contes animaux de folk-lore zande. Ces *sangbwa* Tule, contes ou dits de Tule, se racontent le soir autour du feu, au grand délassement des assistants. Voilà déjà un fait important. Car, qu'on ne s'y méprenne point, Tule n'est entouré d'aucun respect, pas plus que Uylenspieghel dans nos contes à nous. Tule apparaît dans les différentes légendes comme un personnage qui se pique d'être plus intelligent et plus rusé que ses semblables, mais qui bien souvent est roulé d'importance par un plus malin que lui.'[2] Mgr. Lagae refuses to identify the author of the universe with a liar, a thief, and in general a 'bad hat'. 'De

[1] *Op. cit.*, p. 172, Mgr. Lagae refers to an article on dynamism by de Calonne in which the same statement, slightly differently worded, and under the same initial (B), appears, in *Notre Colonie*, October 1920, p. 10.

[2] *Op. cit.*, p. 72.

fait, les mensonges et les vols de Tule, mentionnés dans les légendes, ne se comptent pas. Toutefois, aucun Zande ne prend au sérieux les exploits et les mécomptes de Tule. Cela se raconte, on en rit, et le temps passe agréablement. Des représailles ne sont pas à craindre. Tule n'est qu'un personnage légendaire.

'Quel contraste avec le respect qu'ils témoignent à Mboli, le véritable Être suprême qui régit leurs destinées. N'équivoquons donc pas, et n'imposons pas aux Azande des idées qui leur sont totalement étrangères. Eux-mêmes ne disent-ils pas de Tule: *ira sawiya nga kù*, ce qui peut se traduire en langage européen: c'est un monsieur qui fait de sa poire. Ils sont loins de lui témoigner un soupçon de culte ou de lui adresser la moindre prière.'[1]

Major Larken and Captain Philipps agree with Mgr. Lagae's opinion of Ture. Major Larken writes: 'The Zande equivalent of the fairy story is the string of tales, called *Sangba Ture*, relating the trials and experiences of a mythical personage named Ture, who was always getting into trouble and who was terribly hen-pecked by his wife Nanzagbe. There are scores of these tales, which are told to the children by their parents.'[2] Captain Philipps says, '*Tulé* could perhaps best be described as "a card". The collection of the *Asangbwa Tulé* or tales of the *Tulé* form the daily fairy-tale literature of the people.'[3]

On the whole my conclusions about Ture are like those of the authorities I have quoted. Certainly Ture belongs to folk-lore rather than to sacred mythology. He embodies all the charm and humour of the average Zande and for this reason the stories about him never fail to amuse listeners around an evening fire. But do Azande believe that he exists or that he has ever existed? It is very difficult to answer this question and perhaps the correct reply would be that they half-believe in Ture. If you ask them they reply, 'We Azande think that he must have lived because our fathers have told us so.' In a vague sort of way Azande think that he is still alive today for they say that the English captured him and took him to their country and that it is he who taught them how to make motor cars and the various other products of European manufacture they have seen. One can only say that Ture lives in the stories told about him. It is no use asking who he was or is because Azande only know him as the hero of a cycle of stories. Impossible things happen in these stories—animals talk and so forth—but this does not make

[1] *Op. cit.*, p. 73. [2] *Op. cit.*, 1926, p. 28. [3] *Op. cit.*, p. 174.

Ture incredible to Azande. To them he is a real figure in the situation of story-telling. But since he lives in the stories nothing much is known about him outside them. Nevertheless he is sometimes vaguely associated with Mbori and is said to have walked about with him.

Both Mbori and Ture belong to the hazy supra-sensible world. The representation of Mbori is no more developed than that of Ture, and the proof that Azande advance for the existence of the one is the proof they advance for the existence of the other, the word of their fathers. Belief in Mbori is a function of certain emotional situations and he is therefore by the circumstances of human relations with him endowed with supernatural powers and given a vague transcendental personality. Ture on the other hand is never regarded as divine. No one prays to him or makes any ceremony in his honour. His personality is untrammelled by the necessity of having to furnish an idiom of emotional reaction, and art has had free play in creating one of the most delightful characters in the unwritten literature of Africa.

It is also possible, of course, to ask Azande direct questions about Mbori—'This Mbori of whom you speak, who is he?' If there were any formulated doctrines about him this would give Azande opportunity to enumerate them, if not as a complete dogma at any rate in bits. I have never been able to elicit any interest in, and have found that Azande are frankly bored by, questions about the Supreme Being. They are seldom able to give more than a vague statement of belief and after asking several men such questions the inquirer feels very confused about the Zande notion of a Supreme Being. Mbori is a big king of ghosts ('All Azande say that the ghosts are subject to Mbori') but he can also assist people in this world, although his sphere of influence is more directly among the ghosts who join him at the heads of streams, and if a man prays to the ghosts of his fathers they will ask Mbori to grant his request. It is possible for the ghosts to make cases among themselves before Mbori if they have not been settled justly by a prince during life. The ghosts can see Mbori, who seems to be generally considered to lead the same shadowy kind of existence as themselves, although Azande do not pretend to know much about the life beyond the grave. Men occasionally visit the ghosts, and may even see Mbori, in dreams.

Most people say that Mbori is never seen in waking life and that no one knows what he looks like, but some Azande have told me that human beings have been known to see him, though this was not regarded as a privilege but as *hu kpele* or a thing of ill-omen. Some people say that he does not walk about the earth while others declare that he occasionally walks in mists. He is greater than ordinary ghosts. Some say that he has the features of a man but is a giant and carries a huge spear. Others say that ghost-diviners can see him at heads of streams or as he walks in the early morning on granitic outcrops. Yet others say he is a short man and wears tall feathers in his hat. I have even been told that Mbori was brought into the country by Europeans and that before the missionaries came Azande paid attention only to the ghosts, and these informants have maintained their testimony against conflicting native opinions.

My general objections to the representation of the Supreme Being as interpreted by Mgr. Lagae and Captain Philipps will have been already noted in the various criticisms of specific points which I have made. Mbori may justly be described as a god, as a spirit, and as a person, it is true, but the concept is very hazy; indeed the very conceptual vagueness of Zande belief allows us the more readily to read into it the notions of our own culture. The assumption is that because Azande invoke Mbori in a way that resembles our prayers to God they have a theistic doctrine similar to ours. From Zande behaviour we construct a concept in terms of our own thought. But I do not believe that Azande have any clear doctrinal opinions, for they actualize their beliefs, expressing them in rite and prayer, rather than intellectualize them and think of them in dogma and myth. In treating of Supreme Beings we are very likely to give to primitive speech a meaning which it does not contain, for we ourselves possess analagous modes of ritual behaviour and these are linked to patterns of thought through which we at once apprehend the behaviour of primitives by attributing to them as definite notions as our own. When dealing with magic and witchcraft there is so vast a gap between our notions and primitive notions that there is less danger of apprehending their ideas by assimilating them to our own, and consequently we treat them behaviouristically as ritual responses and do not attempt to create for them an ideology that will explain them by seeming to cause them. Indeed magic and witchcraft are difficult to describe for precisely the reason that we do not act as primitive peoples act in these respects and have no stereotyped patterns of thought relating to them. In treating of religion, however, we have only to translate primitive religious terms into our own language, and our interpretation of them is already made by the very process of translation. Once we have translated Zande words into such English expressions as 'Supreme Being' and 'soul', the notions and feelings these words evoke in us already intrude to colour our apprehension of the meaning they possess for Azande. Merely by translating 'Mbori' as 'Supreme Being' we ascribe to him supremacy which implies for us personality, omnipotence, benevolence, and other divine attributes. In my opinion Mgr. Lagae and Captain Philipps have inferred from Zande behaviour a doctrine by which they then proceed to explain the behaviour.

I have already made it abundantly clear that I have searched in vain for dogma and that I have found Azande bored by the subject of Mbori and unable to express more than the vaguest ideas about him, their most definite belief being in his presence at the heads of streams. Prayers and the ceremony in times of drought and pestilence are their beliefs and not merely the way in which they express a religious conception. Their story of creation alone gives them a mythological background, and I have no evidence that the creation myth is called upon to buttress belief. It is known to only some people and seems to have little functional relationship to prayer and ceremony, although this is suggested by their juxtaposition in an anthropological account.

This does not mean that we must refrain from all comment on Zande behaviour and from any effort to interpret it. It is true that any complete interpretation must take into account all cultural interrelations, a task which is impossible here and must await a final account of Zande society. But even in this place one may attempt in a preliminary way to analyse the situations in which Mbori is invoked and even to show certain logico-emotional dependencies between religious categories.

It is clear that in all cases where Europeans have actually heard Mbori called upon for aid and have not merely recorded Zande statements about prayer the situation was one of fear and anxiety and despair, e.g. in thunderstorms, when threatened by the rainbow, certain situations of pregnancy, in continual loss and misfortune, and in death. Mbori seems to be especially called upon as a last resort when all other channels of assistance are closed. So that whatever other meaning may be contained in invocations to Mbori they have at any rate an emotional significance. Since I have heard the ghosts and medicines called upon in situations identical with, or similar to, those in which Azande are said to call upon Mbori, these modes of seeking mystical intervention may be regarded as alternative and equivalent idioms of emotional expression.

Azande make no clear conceptual distinction between the Supreme Being and the ghosts and these notions overlap one another.

We have seen how in praying Azande intersperse their remarks to the Supreme Being with appeals to the ghosts, e.g. 'Oh, Mbori so! You have not granted me good fortune. Oh, ghosts of my fathers, in what depths of poverty am I plunged.' Lagae and I have recorded that Mbori is thought to be a creative factor in the birth of children but Major Larken quotes Zande authority both for the statement that 'a baby is a gift from the spirits' [ghosts][1] and also for the statement that a baby 'is given by *Mbali* (the Deity) to the mother',[2] showing here again the confusion amounting almost to functional identity between the Supreme Being and the ghosts. What are probably grinding places in rock outcrops are said to be both footprints of Mbori and footprints of the ghosts. Where the whistle of Mbori protrudes from the face of the rock it is the ghost of Liwa who sends rain. I have even heard Azande speak of the soul as Mbori. In saying that in dreams their soul goes ahead to see if the way is free from misfortune they will sometimes speak of *mbisimore*, my soul, and sometimes of *atorore*, my ghost, and sometimes of *gi mbori*, my Mbori.

We have also noted that Azande are apt to speak of the rain ceremony as though it concerned both Mbori and the ghosts, or rather that they do not really distinguish between them. Also the ghosts are appealed to in drought to send down rain without Mbori being approached. It is the ghost-diviners who organize the ceremony for rain; they sing ghost-songs and the ghosts speak to them in chasms at heads of streams. Indeed the ghosts are emphasized just as much, as if not more than, Mbori, in this connection. The three ghost-diviners who organized the ceremony I witnessed referred always to the ghosts and not at all to Mbori.

Indeed it is clear that the relationship between Mbori and rain and the ghosts and heads of streams is one to which Lévy-Bruhl has applied the term 'participation'. These heads of streams where

[1] *Op. cit.*, 1926, p. 25. [2] *Ibid.*, p. 26.

bubble eternal springs are the antithesis of drought and it is here that the ghosts and the Supreme Being reside and it is they who have mystical control over rain. The same participation may be observed in the notion of earth, for the dead are buried in the ground and are sometimes thought to reside under it, and Mbori also is associated with the earth and its fruitfulness, and perhaps the main rite in the *maziga* ceremony is the beating of the earth. This interrelation is also shown in prayers of potters who call alike on Mbori and the ghosts when they are digging for clay. They ask the Supreme Being to assist them, and beseech the ghosts to go away so that they may dig in peace.

It is also clear, from my experience, that Azande do not properly differentiate between Mbori and the ghosts in their notions of death and in their eschatological beliefs. Indeed, it is in this confusion of representations that I see the main intellectual action of belief in a Supreme Being. When a man dies he goes to the ghosts at the heads of streams. But what happens to him then? Azande say that a father's ghost will sometimes frequent his grave and will sometimes visit the homesteads of his children and take an interest in their affairs. But no one takes much interest in a grandfather's ghost and none at all in the ghosts of yet more distant ancestors. The notion of Mbori accounts in a vague and general manner for all the ghosts—'they go to where Mbori is', 'they are with Mbori', say the Azande. I have no doubt that Mbori may be considered, that is to say that he is felt by Azande to be, a vague generalized unity of the ghosts of the departed. Their ideas about the ghost of a father are comparatively sharp and definite but ghosts genealogically further removed tail off into the notion of Mbori. Their individuality is lost and only the notion of Mbori remains to account for them.

It is of some interest to observe that Mbori is not given a personal gender but like the ghosts has what is sometimes called an animal gender. I do not want to go deep into this question but I may say that in Zande persons are given the personal pronouns *ko* (masc.) and *li* (fem.), while animals, the ghosts, the Supreme Being, certain of the heavenly bodies, and a number of vegetables and tools which have an especially intimate relationship to human beings, have the animal pronoun *u*.

In their intellectualization of Zande feeling and action Mgr. Lagae and Captain Philipps have not only constructed such a doctrine as we would require were we to feel and act as they do but have separated and given distinct conceptual individuality to notions which are confused in Zande mentality. They make of the Supreme Being one thing and of the ghosts another thing, but to the Azande themselves they tend to form a colourless amalgam. Hence they appeal now to the one and now to the other as though they were the same and, as prayer is a function of situations of emotional stress and is expressed in the simplest of rites, the meaning of the one partakes of the meaning of the other since the meaning of both is almost entirely of an emotional and motor character and little controlled by ideological patterns. Not only is this the case but I would say that missionary influence rather than inculcating entirely new notions has rather the effect of breaking up a complex of ideas and giving to each an individuality of its own and distinct from the others.

Mbori is also associated with moral regulations and though he is not thought to be the direct retributive agent in breach of custom he is nevertheless felt to be a distant and final sanction. It seems that while leprosy assails a man on account of incest and ulcers waste him on account of retributive magic, Mbori is vaguely felt to permit these happenings or at least to do nothing to prevent them. The name of Mbori is sometimes associated in prayer with observations of laws and customs. However, when a sick man reminds Mbori in prayer that he is not a thief nor adulterer he means that he should escape magic made to avenge theft or adultery. I also found an opinion current that attributes to Mbori, though vaguely, responsibility for deaths by witchcraft or sorcery, for Azande say that he knows what is happening and does nothing to prevent it. Moreover it must be remembered that here again the association of Mbori with moral law does not ascribe to him sole authorship and responsibility, for I have heard Azande address medicines in a precisely similar manner saying that they have robbed no man, have committed adultery with no man's wife, and so on. On the other hand people do not seem to insist upon like virtues when addressing the ghosts. For the ghosts of a man's fathers are concerned only with intra-kin morality and are not a sanction of his conduct towards unrelated persons. Mbori being a sort of generalized ghost is associated with sanctions of conduct which concern the whole community. I have never heard Mboli's wishes quoted by a Zande as a reason for doing anything or refraining from any action.

Morals and the notion of a Supreme Being are not directly associated in Zande culture. It is not Mbori but magic that punishes evildoers and Mbori's part is to furnish an explantation for the magic and its actions. As a rule conduct rests upon quite other than religious foundations and even when Mbori participates in sanctions his participation is of a distant and secondary nature.

Finally, it emerges that the notion of Mbori furnishes a remote cause for anything and everything in the world. It is the horizon of Zande thought, an ambient haze into which every chain of causation ultimately fades. We have seen how Mbori is a kind of generalized ghost. The souls of men become ghosts and the ghosts go to live with Mbori and their personalities merge into his. We have seen also how he is a kind of generalized cause, being the single common participant in all causes. The immediate sanctions about which Azande trouble themselves are the princes, medicines, the ghosts of their fathers, private vengeance, and so on. But beyond all these and in the distance their single common factor is Mbori and this notion enables Azande to comprehend why the sanctions exist and how it is they work equitably. Magic, like *bagbuduma*, vengeance-magic, acts justly, that is to say it kills only witches and thieves and adulterers. But if you ask Azande from where they obtain such excellent medicine and why it works as it does they say that Mbori gave it to them and that perhaps he supervises its action, though they do not seem so sure of this. Azande do not think that Mbori directly avenges crime but he furnishes them with a justification and comprehension of vengeance.

As Mbori gave men magic and oracles so he is the final argument for the existence of anything at all. This is well shown in R.P.A.-M. De Graer's excellent paper on Zande leechcraft. He remarks that if one asks Azande about their drugs ' "Who has shown you these remedies?" They will invariably reply "Our ancestors". If you continue and say to them "And your ancestors, from whom did they obtain these remedies?" They reply: "From their ancestors in their turn". Until at last they declare to you: "It is God who has first taught us the plants which may cure us." '[1] If you take a Zande back step by step to the limits of his knowledge you will reach Mbori, whose name takes the place of understanding. He is the horizon that rounds off knowledge and tradition. He made the

[1] R.P.A.-M. De Graer, 'L'art de Guérir chez les Azande', *Congo*, 1929, Tome I, p. 223.

sun and the moon and the stars, the rivers and plains and mountains, men and beasts and birds and trees. When Azande do not understand something, it is vaguely explained by citing Mbori. Man and woman beget children but Azande perceive that they alone will not account for conception because some people do not beget children, or wait many years before conception takes place. Conception also depends on Mbori and if it were not for his participation children would not be born. What is the cause of a monstrosity? Azande do not know but say, 'It is the affair of Mbori'. Who made the curious phenomena of nature, smooth holes in rock outcrops, an expanding and contracting tree root in a rock face, long luxuriant hair of men? 'Mbori made it,' say the Azande. Death is the most obvious limit to experience and beyond lies Mbori who personifies and accounts for the ghosts.

A final word may be said about the possibility of foreign cultural influences in the Zande notion of a Supreme Being. No proof of this influence can be offered but there are certain indications which compel one to admit at any rate the possibility of it. These indications derive mainly from the presence of ideas which do not seem to fit in with Zande culture and bear a foreign stamp. We cannot help noticing that these same traits that we would suspect as foreign on account of their cultural inappropriateness correspond with Christian teachings, and it is therefore possible that they are derived from a Christian source and were, perhaps, very early and widely diffused. We have seen that the name of Baati presents difficulties for he is said to have fallen from on high and to have broken his leg, while he is also said to have been the son of Mbori who took him away from men. Moreover, he is given the pronoun used for humans and not for the pronoun used for ghosts and souls. The creation myth shows evidences of having been borrowed, for men and other creatures are said to have emerged out of a *kurungba*, a canoe or boat of some kind. Azande—at any rate those of the Sudan—have probably only seen canoes among foreigners living on the banks of big rivers like the Uelle River in the Congo. It is curious, therefore, to find the canoe or boat as the central theme in their creation myth. It may be remarked also that Zande culture is very poor in mythology and that the only traditions comparable to the creation story in detail and completeness are stories concerning a great witchdoctor of the past who cut a river in twain to allow the Azande to pass over to the other side and who eventually ascended into the heavens, reminding us in these two feats of Moses and Elijah. I have even heard Azande of the bush identify this person with the Christ of the missionaries. I have already recorded that some people say that Mbori was brought by the missionaries. It is remarkable also that Mbori is sometimes not even mentioned in connection with the rain-making ceremony and appears almost to have been incorporated into a performance directed towards the ghosts of the dead. It is impossible to determine whether these notions are due to old Christian teaching or not, and even direct Christian teaching of today is difficult to identify when it has been incorporated by Azande of the bush into their own traditions, as witness the story of the Garden of Eden related in this paper.

9

SANZA, A CHARACTERISTIC FEATURE OF ZANDE LANGUAGE AND THOUGHT

1956

In my book *Witchcraft, oracles and magic among the Azande* (1937) there emerged from the treatment of these three topics a picture of some features of the Zande mind, revealing itself often as a suspicious, distrustful, hostile mind. Another facet of this mentality is revealed in the Zande concept of *sanza* (pl. *asanza*).

Frs. C. R. Lagae and V. H. Vanden Plas in their excellent *La langue des Azande* (vol. II, 1922, p. 140) translate this word 'animosité; haine; jalousie. *Sanzale kpwotolo yo*: la haine de moi dans ton corps, tu me portes de la haine, (à noter que le possessif *le*, pronom suffixé, amène la traduction littérale suivante: ma haine dans ton corps; c'est-à-dire: la haine qu'il porte à mon égard). *Sanzale vulo yo ku ti le*: ma haine (la haine que tu as pour moi) dans ton ventre à mon égard. *Sanza bangilise*: haine de l'œil, signifie un clin d'œil. Celui qui constate que son interlocuteur cligne des yeux à une tierce personne, le prend généralement en mauvaise part. *Sanzako namanga le*: la haine de lui (c'est-à-dire: contre lui) me travaille.' It is strange that they do not give 'proverb' as one of the meanings of the word. The dictionary compiled by the English missionaries Canon and Mrs. E. C. Gore (*Zande and English dictionary*, 1931, p. 138) lists separately, as though they were two different words, *sanza* 'parable, proverb', and *sanza* '(with verbs *ba* or *gumba*), spite, hate, envy, jealousy. *Sanza bangirise*,[1] a meaning look, a wink, a scornful or disdainful look.' They are,

[1] The same sound in Zande is sometimes written *l* and sometimes *r*.

however, the same word and I hope to show, among other things, why proverbs are referred to by a word which also means spite, hate, envy, and jealousy.

I do not intend to give a long list of Zande proverbs, only a few as examples. A hundred specimens are given by Canon Gore (*A Zande grammar*, n.d. [1931], pp. 134–46) and a vastly greater number by Fr. S. Bervoets '"*Hinapai*": Enige spreekwoorden van bij de Zande', *Zaïre*, 1952, 1953, and 1954); but my slight knowledge of Flemish is insufficient for a full appreciation of Fr. S. Bervoets' study. What I intend to do rather is to see what light is shed on Zande ways of thought by a consideration of what Azande mean by *sanza*, in the course of which we may also learn how they use proverbs and think of their use.

Some examples of proverbs or aphorisms in more or less our sense of the words, with Zande comments on them, are as follows (I give free translation):

(1) *I ni kpisidi bakumba na gani kpata roko* 'they bury an elder with his old barkcloth'. Comment: 'In the past when an elder died he was buried with his old wife, the one who was always at hand to see to his wants. People said that she was his old barkcloth. It was the custom to bury princes with their old barkcloths, that is, with their wives.' (Before Europeans began to administer Zandeland wives of princes, and sometimes of important commoners also, were, at any rate sometimes, buried alive with their dead husbands.)

(2) *Wo na ora nga rimo ru te* 'a snake does not disown its name'. Comment: 'Azande ask one another what are their clans. If I meet a man on the path and I ask him what is his clan he speaks out the name of his true clan; he would not hide it, because a snake does not disown its name. The meaning of this is that you must never hide your clan. Even if it is not a good clan name, you must not hide it.' (Fr. S. Bervoets gives *wo naoranga ngbwatungalu te* 'de slang verloochent haar geslacht niet'.)

(3) *Aboro ni ta gunde be go, ya sumba we u i a gunde be ru* 'when people were afraid of the termite mound cricetus said that it was he they feared'. Comment: 'A man says he is going to kill another on account of adultery with his wife. His prince calms him and says to him that it is better for the offender to pay spears in compensation; and the husband consents to what the prince says. He says to the offender "I am afraid of the prince, while you think I am afraid of you. If it were not for the prince I would kill you. It is that when

people were afraid of the termite mound cricetus said it was he they feared." The cricetus is a tiny beast which flees at the sight of man into a deserted termite mound or into a hillock; the man just stands wondering at the firmness of the termite mound.' (Gore has *i ni ta ora go, sumba ki ya, u i a ora ru* 'as they swerved because of the anthill, the cricetus thought it was he they were running from'; and he comments that this is said 'of the man whose wrongdoing is overlooked or forgiven, and who thinks it is because they are afraid of him'. Fr. S. Bervoets has *i nitaora go, sumba ki ya: i naora lu* 'ze zijn voor de termietenheuvel gaan lopen (uit de weg gegaan) en de *sumba* (veldrat) zegt: "zij vrezen mij")'.

(4) *I ni ini bawo rago zo ru* 'they know a male snake at the time of roasting it'. Comment: 'If you have done a man some wrong, such as committing adultery with his wife, he being ignorant of it, other men will tell you that you had better stop acting as you are acting because the husband might get to know about it. It is about that that you speak this *sanza*; however, it is as though one said "you will know it on that day when it comes out, you will then know the truth of it". It is about that that one says they know a male snake at the time of roasting it; because when they begin to roast a python its male member rises to come right out with the heat, so that people see it, whereas before, when it was alive, it was hidden.' (Gore's comment: 'A man's character is known at the time of trial or testing.')

(5) *Ba gude uwe te* 'a child has not two fathers'. Comment: 'There is a man whose father has died. After his father's death he is truly miserable, for his kinsmen are not agreeable to him, nor also do they marry him a wife. He begins to prosper by his own endeavour and marries several wives and begets children by them. His kinsmen come to his home but they get nothing to eat there and they begin to speak ill of him, saying that he is a mean fellow. He brews beer and invites all his kinsmen to come and drink it. When they are all assembled he rises and speaks to them thus "Why have you spoken ill of me, seeing that I prospered by my own endeavour and no one married me a wife? A child has not two fathers; because these many children, I alone am their father. If my father were alive, it is he who would think of me."'

(6) *Sa gara a kati rogo mbaro yo* 'the lizard's tail broke off in play'. Comment: 'This means that there is a man who jokes with you all the time, but his joking is not straight, it has malice in it for you.

It is such that should you lose your temper with him he will lose his also and wish to have a quarrel with you. It is about this that people speak this *sanza*, because the man's joking is not well-intentioned.' (Gore's comment: 'Do not get angry when at play.' Fr. S. Bervoets gives: *Sa gala nakiti rogo mbaro* 'de staart van de hagedis breekt af onder 't spel', and some variants.)

(7) *Gude a ri ga bako kondo mbiko badia bako* 'a child has eaten his father's hen on account of his father's friend'. Comment: 'In the past an elder did not eat a hen with his son in any circumstances. It is that when his friend arrived and he cooked a hen for his friend, his friend called the son of this owner of the homestead to come and eat it with him. The child's father said "you eat first and then I will give what is left over to the child". His friend would not give way and the child came and sat down to eat the hen with his father's friend. It is about that that he spoke this *sanza*.'

(8) *I na yugo nga sanza fu awiri ira sanza te* 'they do not teach a *sanza* to the children of a person who knows it'. Comment: 'The meaning of this is that a man should not try and teach a prince *sanza*, because it was the princes who originated *sanza*. Princes tell Azande not to teach them *sanza*, who are princes, because it was they who started *sanza*.'

(9) *Anyogi na batika zi* 'a bee has begotten a fly'. Comment: 'A man begets many children and he watches them carefully all the time and he sees that one of them is stupid and he says "the bee gave birth to a fly". For the bee is a courageous insect and one not to be trifled with. It is that this outstanding man has begotten children who are not all alert as he is.' (Fr. Bervoets gives: *nioge vungi azi* 'de bie heeft vliegen gebaard'.)

(10) *I ni kpe miri bi ango kina ngba ru yo* 'they rub the black dog's dung in its own mouth'. Comment: 'This means that they do not kill a man on account of what another has done, only on account of what he himself has done. If a man has done ill they do not say on account of that man who always goes about with him that it is good to act as though that friend of his had done the ill.' (If the black dog steals things they kill it, and not the red dog.)

(11) *Bamongo yo na nye nga ko o gbua te* 'a man does not go on laughing for no reason'. Comment: 'If a man is smiling he has had a good meal and is satisfied; laughter appeals to you then. If you are hungry or sick, laughter altogether leaves your lips; if a man jokes

then, it does not at all please you. Therefore people speak this *sanza*, saying that there is no laughter without a cause.'

(12) *Gbate a siri kunduru ni sa ru* 'the francolin has rent its crop by itself' (in trying to escape from a trap). Comment: 'This means that a man gives you something, saying "do not mention it to anyone". You then go and meet a company of men and say to them "you, you are hungry; I have eaten something good". It is about this that they say that the francolin has rent its crop. You talk about that food which is in your stomach; if a witch hears it he bewitches you, thinking about your having eaten something good; it is as though you yourself had told him to rip open your stomach, of your own doing, since you said that you had eaten something, for it was on account of that that they bewitched you.' (Gore gives *gbate nga mo na siri kunduru*? 'are you a partridge that ripped open its (own) crop?' He comments: 'do not lie against yourself'.)

(13) *Boro ni kpamu ti ni ni wiri nzaga kurani* 'a man scratches himself with the nail of his companion'. A man gains a reputation for generosity by being free with the goods of others. Another version is *boro na kpama nga ti ni na wiri nzaga kura te* 'a man does not scratch himself with the nail of another'. Comment: 'This is as though one said, a man's possession, I cannot give it to you, he would take it from you.'

(14) *Ka renvo rundu bamo ti ngia u arundu ro a* 'if a cane rat bit your father, perhaps it will bite you also'. Those who have injured others may injure you too.

(15) *Mbara nga mo, mo na imi ira ati*? 'are you an elephant that killed the owner of the garden?' First an elephant spoils the garden and then it kills its owner. This is adding, as we say, insult to injury, as when a man commits adultery and then insults the husband. (Gore's comment: 'are you angry with a man for keeping what's his own?'.)

(16) *I na gumba nga rimo sumba na go te* 'they do not criticize the cricetus to the termite mound'. One does not speak ill of a man in the presence of his friend, his kinsman, his blood-brother, or his relative-in-law. The cricetus has its home in termite mounds. Fr. S. Bervoets has: *i na penga limo sumba na go te* 'men noemt de veldrat niet in het oor van de termietenheuvel'.

(17) *Fufurafu na ke pati miri mama* 'the butterfly circles near leopard's dung'. Comment: 'Should you be journeying with your child and trouble start between you and some man and should he,

while leaving you alone, turn on your child to beat him, you say to him in *sanza* "the butterfly circles near leopard's dung". This *sanza* began with regard to a prince's things. If you trifle with a prince's thing your companions say to you "you circle near leopard's dung". This means that a prince is dangerous like a leopard, which does not play with a man.' (Fr. S. Bervoets translates this: 'de vlinders staan rond de drek van de luipaard'.)

(18) *I a kuru vura ngbaya ku kpakasira yo* 'they begin the war on the maize on the pumpkin leaves'. Comment: 'This means that a man comes and, as he looks at you, suddenly begins to insult your child, or your wife, insulting him, or her, almost to the point of assault. You speak to him thus, "they begin the war on the maize on the pumpkin leaves", that is to say, he insults you through your child. For a man goes to pluck spinach, which is the leaf of the pumpkin, in the maize garden, and while he is plucking spinach he turns to strip off maize cobs. So Azande say about it in a *sanza* "they begin the war on the maize on the pumpkin leaves"; that is, "you direct your assault towards my child and you assault me in him to do me ill".' (Maize and pumpkins grow together. This proverb, as will be seen later, meaning that in doing or saying something to a man you are really aiming at another, epitomizes a common form of Zande *sanza* behaviour.) (Gore translates it 'they went out of the attack on the corn into the pumpkin leaves', and he comments 'said to one who leaves one job unfinished and goes to another'.)

(19) *Mi du wa munga* 'I am like a stone-flat'. After drought a heavy shower of rain on to a stone-flat brings thousands of small insects to it and they chirp there all day till nightfall. A man speaks this *sanza* to, or about, his sons who have left him to go and live in different parts of the country away from him. They will all come back to him one day.

(20) *Da na ya fo roni mbara du gi go yo*? 'who told you that an elephant is behind the termite mound?'. The meaning of this *sanza* is that only those who show themselves ready to help others are likely to receive help from them. If a man has no friends no one tells him when they see him approaching a termite mound that there is an elephant behind it. An example given to me of its use is of a man who comes to the home of another who is eating in his hut, being a mean man. The visitor is hungry and he asks the son of the owner of the homestead where is his father. The boy replies, having

been told what to say on these occasions, that his father has gone to court. The visitor guesses that this is a lie but does not wish to say so outright. Instead, he speaks this *sanza.* The boy tells his father later that the visitor spoke to him and that he did not understand everything he said. The father tells him to repeat what was said and if he is a man who understands *asanza* he will understand what was meant. (Gore gives *da na ya fo ro mbara du gi go*? 'who told you that an elephant is behind the anthill?'. He comments: 'when one warns another of something of which he was not aware'.)

(21) *Gine ime angba gbe, runge a kpi ngbwa a* 'the path to the water was excellent, but the pot was smashed on it'. However well-kept the path to where one draws water may be, one may still stumble and smash a pot on it. This proverb is probably used in many situations. One is when a wife says it *to* a friend or co-wife but *at* her husband to tell him that she and his other wives are displeased because he is always sleeping with a favourite young wife and neglecting them—'since you are always going along that path you had better be careful'. If the husband is a man who does not understand *asanza* well (but suspects some allusion to himself) he will ask his wife what she is talking about. She replies 'no sir, I was not speaking about you. I was just telling this girl to be careful with my pots as one can never be too careful even on the best paths.' She has chosen to say this *sanza* when a co-wife is about to fetch water, so that her pretence that she was talking about her pots appears reasonable.

(22) *Boro na kita nga gani mvuko ti ga bakurani biri te* 'a man does not break his billhook in the wood of his friend'. Comment: 'This means, a man does not send his wives, or his followers, to go and hoe another's gardens, only his own.'

These examples must suffice. Their general sense is plain, but it must be emphasized that not only may there be variation in the form of any given proverb but also that it can be used in a wide range of different situations, the meaning changing somewhat to meet the situation. But the meaning of *sanza* covers much more than what we call proverbs and aphorisms. It includes any remark or action which is intended to be oblique, opaque, ambiguous, any words or gestures which are intended to suggest a meaning other than they have in themselves, which have, that is, a double meaning, a manifest meaning and a hidden one. Moreover, Azande are very sensitive and self-centred and often attribute a hidden meaning, an innuendo, where possibly none may be intended. It is true that not all circumlocutory remarks they regard as *sanza* are malicious. They distinguish between *wene sanza* and *gbigbita sanza*, good *sanza* and bad *sanza*. But a *sanza* is generally in some degree spiteful, and even a good *sanza* can in a suitable situation be twisted to serve malicious ends.

Azande often prefer a circumlocutory way of speech to directness in their dealings with their fellows and it enters into all their social activities, though it is more evident in some forms of relationship than in others. It will be best, therefore, before entering into a more general discussion to give some examples of its use. These were given me by Azande, whose statements, as with their comments on their proverbs, I recorded sometimes in English and sometimes in the Zande tongue.

(1) A man says in the presence of his wife to his friend 'friend, those swallows, how they flit about here'. He is speaking about the flightiness of his wife and in case she should understand the allusion he covers himself by looking up at the swallows as he makes his seemingly innocent remark. His friend understands what he means and replies 'yes, sir, do not talk to me about those swallows, how they come here, sir!'. (What you say is only too true.) His wife, however, also understands what he means and says tartly 'yes, sir, you leave that she (wife) to take a good she (wife), sir, since you married a swallow, sir!' (Marry someone else if that is the way you feel about it.) The husband looks surprised and pained that his wife should take umbrage at a harmless remark about swallows. He says to her 'does one get touchy about what is above (swallows), madam?'. She replies 'ai, sir. Deceiving me is not agreeable to me. You speak about me. You will fall from my tree'. The sense of this reply is 'you are a fool to try and deceive me in my presence. It is me you speak about and you are always going on at me. I will run away and something will happen to you when you try and follow me'. *Sanza* language is very common between man and wife and in reference to the relationship of spouses. It is usually the husband who speaks it, often in reference to his sexual life with his wife.

(2) A man complains to his parents-in-law that his wife is refusing him his marital rights: 'she has made a new thing and kills me with too much porridge, for I did not marry her for big porridge alone; I married her for all my affairs'. (She gives him huge evening meals

to send him to sleep, but to eat is not the only purpose of marriage; congress is another one.)

(3) This is a typical conversation piece between two men. One wishes to tell the other that his wife will not have congress with him, but he does not want to say so in so many words, so he goes round and round, imparting his meaning by oblique hints. He says 'my condition is bad'. His friend replies 'how might one set about bettering it?'. He answers 'if I were to say that these wives of mine were against me in my home how would it be?' (Would not that about hit the mark?), and he adds 'ill fortune pursues me, my household are against me nowadays'. He also makes some obscure reference to witchcraft and explains his wife's attitude to him in the matter of congress in roundabout ways, such as 'I talk to my wife, but she does not listen'. If he were making a case about it before a prince he would be more explicit, though still keeping to *sanza* speech, in these circumstances for the sake of good form. He would say 'I go to her couch and she turns away from me like a little girl, prince'; or, even straighter to the point, 'she moves to the side of the couch for me' or 'she lies on the ground'. Or he might say 'she divides huts with me'; and a woman in like circumstances might say 'prince, he has left me with the hut'.

(4) Azande are secretive about their consultation of oracles, and this frequently leads them to employ a *sanza* mode of speech, of which I give three examples. A man wants to say to a boy 'let us get along and consult our poison oracle', but there are women present and he does not wish them to know of his intention, and there may be men present also whom he does not want to go with him and listen to his private affairs and also use his poison and chicken for their own affairs. So he might say 'get up, lad, let us be moving, go and operate your rubbing-board oracle for me' (he does not mention the poison oracle). One of his in-laws who is present asks him 'friend, really the rubbing-board, sir?' (and not, as he rightly suspects, the poison oracle). He replies 'yes, sir, my relative-in-law, master, since I am so poor, where do you think I am likely to know the journey of men?'. (The journey of men means where men go to, and only men, and hence here either to obtain poison for consultation or to consult the oracle.)

(5) A man, A, is hurrying off, with a basket containing some chickens in his hand, to consult the poison oracle, which has already been prepared in the bush by a boy sent on ahead. Just as he is

about to turn off into the bush to the place of consultation he meets another man, B. A does not want B to know where he is going or for what purpose and tries to greet him and pass on, but B is inquisitive and asks A where he is going. A replies 'no, sir (I am not going anywhere in particular); I have just been to that fellow over there to ask him to catch a little chicken for me to throw it (consult the oracle with it), because my condition has been really bad recently. If I were to obtain a little poison from those people who frequently consult the oracle I would choke the chicken with it (use the chicken to consult the oracle)'. He cannot pretend that the chickens he is carrying are not for consultations of the oracle—it is all too obvious that they are—but he pretends that he has only just been to beg some chickens from a neighbour to consult the oracle about his affairs on some other day. He now says goodbye to B and continues a few paces on the path but as he has then to turn off into the bush to reach the place of consultation he gives a sharp cry of pain and sits down, saying to himself, but so that B can hear, 'oh, where is a knife? what a thorn!' When B turns his head and asks 'what is the matter?', A replies 'nothing, just a big thorn, you go on your way'. He then watches B out of the corner of his eye till he is out of sight, when he rises and proceeds on his way to consult the oracle.

(6) A man is going, with perhaps another elder or two, to consult the poison oracle. A neighbour meets him on the way and guessing his purpose wishes to accompany him, hoping to satisfy his curiosity about the man's affairs and also that he will be asked to make use of his chicken and poison to put some affair of his own before the oracle. He says to the man 'friend, where are you going to, sir?'. The man replies 'master, my mother-in-law keeps on being sick and I am about to go to my blood-brother here to get him to send a boy to her home' (to inquire about her health). The neighbour sees through the man's deception and, realizing where he is really going, makes a further attempt to be invited to the oracle consultation: 'oh, sir, I will join you on your path and we can go there together'. The man replies 'no, my blood-brother (my friend), I am first going to that fellow over there, and I shall be there some time. There is something owing to me there and if I get it I shall be pleased because I can then send it with the boy. I shall afterwards go on ahead to my blood-brother's home to arrange to send a messenger to my mother-in-law'. (What he is saying is that since he has to see

the other man first and that is not the way his neighbour is going he need not bother to accompany him; and anyhow he will be wasting his time because all these arrangements are going to take most of the morning.) His neighbour replies slyly 'oh, friend, what a busy person you are!' The man says to this ironical sally 'we had not arranged to go anywhere together today, had we, sir? You carry on and go to where you are going'. There is a slight awkward pause, and he continues 'take my hand (say goodbye), friend, I must be getting along'. The neighbour says 'well if you are quite sure'. He is quite sure and says so: 'yes, sir' (I must really be getting along).

(7) Other occasions of use of *sanza* are in connexion with food and drink, especially beer. A man wants to invite a couple of friends from a company of men sitting in his home to drink beer with him but he does not wish to invite the rest of the company. He gets up as though to go away from them, and as he walks away he calls out to these two men 'now get up, please. That journey (business) of ours which we talked about yesterday, I am anxious to get it done'. The others think that he and his two friends have something to do and will be moving out of the homestead or be conducting private business in it, so they take the hint and leave. When they have left, the owner of the homestead and his two friends start their beer-drinking.

(8) A man hears that his blood-brother's beer is ready for drinking and comes to his home for a drink. He enters the homestead and says to members of the family 'oh, children, you draw water for me, sir, I am dying of thirst'. The owner of the homestead can hardly refuse to take this hint, especially as the visitor is his blood-brother, but he is determined to give him as little of the beer as possible. He says 'my blood-brother, the wife has made a little maize-beer (it is really millet-beer), just a wee drop, for it mostly got spoilt in the straining. However, I am not a bad blood-brother and you shall have a sip of it since you are thirsty'. The visitor started with a *sanza* by asking for water and his blood-brother excuses himself for not offering him more than a gourdful of beer by two other *asanza*, that the beer is not of the best quality and that it got spoilt in the straining. The visitor drinks the beer offered to him and, being pleased, says 'oh, sir, when I tell people what a good fellow you are, it is this sort of thing I am thinking of'; and he continues in the language of the joking relationship—what Azande

call *buga*—between blood-brothers: 'my witchcraft is so active inside me that I might have killed you (I was so longing for a drink of beer); now the rubbing-board oracle would not accuse me (of witchcraft)'. He says that he would not harm his blood-brother because he is so grateful for the drink. The reference to witchcraft is a joking *sanza*. He does not confess to being a witch, though Azande would say that one cannot tell when a man makes this sort of remark in fun whether his pretence to be a witch may not be a double pretence, a subtle indication that he really is one.

(9) A man passes through a homestead where its owner is eating. Being a hospitable man the owner invites him to join him at his meal. The invited man is shy or hesitant, perhaps being uncertain whether the owner of the homestead really wants him to be his guest or is merely being polite, and the owner of the homestead says to him 'perhaps you do not eat manioc leaves, sir'. At the suggestion that he would not care to partake of a humble meal (Azande only eat manioc leaves when there is nothing better) the visitor can hardly refuse to accept the proffered hospitality. In fact, what the man is eating (with his porridge) is flesh or fish or oil.

Should one eat at one's mother-in-law's home and be offered a meal of manioc leaves one should smack one's lips to show one's appreciation. This is a complimentary *sanza*. But it must not be overdone, or it may be taken to be ironical, a malicious *sanza*, at which the mother-in-law would take great offence.

(10) There is also much *sanza* in making love, and Azande particularly stress its significance in inviting adultery without actually suggesting it in so many words. A man meets on the path a married woman with whom he wants to have an affair. After greeting her he says 'were a man to go to your home would he see your little ways?'. She understands what he is after and replies 'is there any place without little ways?'. This is an intimation that she is not averse to his advances, so he approaches her, saying 'I draw near you just to take your hand, madam'. She replies 'ehe! Oh, my brother, sir, there is nothing against a hand, sir'. This reply, together with her expression and manner of speech, is tantamount to her saying that she would welcome illicit congress. Emboldened, he asks 'oh, my sister, is there any man there with you who might be angry with me on your account?'. She goes off at a tangent: 'oh, my brother, nowadays the ways of men are not good, sir! My brother, do not men's ways get worse nowadays? I am tired of making blood

brotherhood with men, sir, because you tire of a man who does not think of you, sir; have not the ways of men become bad nowadays, the days of the Europeans, sir?'. There is here a double *sanza*. Blood-brotherhood is a *sanza* for sexual intercourse and when she says that she is tired of making it (women do not in fact make blood-brotherhood) she is complaining that those who have made love to her before have not given her sufficient presents and that is why she has given them up, for one makes blood-brotherhood for the sake of the gifts one will receive from one's partner. He pleads 'oh, my sister, I am not like those people' and she answers 'ai! You talk just as they did, sir'. The conversation continues on these lines of circumlocution and innuendo.

(11) A man wants his blood-brother to allow him to have pleasure of his daughter. Though some blood-brothers might permit this if the girl were unmarried, many would refuse such a request and it is not an obligation of blood-brotherhood to grant it; so the man proceeds warily, making his suggestion in *sanza* saying 'does one not know what a man is longing for, my blood-brother, sir?'. His blood-brother replies 'what are you talking about?'. The man says 'eh sir! Those women in this home, sir, how shall I say it? What shall I put in the mouth of the dog, sir?'. His mention of women gives a hint of what he really wants, then he goes off at a tangent, asking how shall he say what he wants, and ends by remarking that as a dog eats everything how should one know what it wants. By his allusion to women he tells his blood-brother what he wants but then goes under cover, as it were. The father of the girl laughs 'aha ha ha, aha ha ha, my blood-brother, then those thoughts inside you, sir, with which you have come to my home here, why do you hide them from me, sir?'. He knows what his friend wants but is not going to say so directly, and his friend knows that he knows but is also not going to say so directly. He replies 'master, I was frightened of you; master, I was frightened of you, my lord'. Then they both laugh together, for this is *wene sanza*, good *sanza*, which, though it conceals a purpose, is good-humoured, as it should be between blood-brothers.

(12) *Sanza* is spoken by a man to his in-laws but he has to be very careful how he does it. An innuendo to a father-in-law or mother-in-law must be well covered by the innocence of its outward meaning. Thus a woman is always coming to call on her daughter and son-in-law and the son-in-law says to her, sarcastically but with

every appearance of sincerity, when she next visits his home 'alas, mother, we have not seen you today. What is the matter? Perhaps you do not like us any more?' The mother-in-law may not see that this solicitous inquiry is ironical, and even if she does see it in that light she cannot very well make a scene, because the man would deny that he meant other than what he said, and, since she could not prove that he did, she would be in a weak position if it came to a dispute.

(13) There is a well-known story about a mother and her daughter, involving an in-law situation, which Azande often tell as a warning of the danger of speaking in *sanza*. It is called *sanza diwi*, *sanza* of the moon. A mother came to visit her married daughter and her husband and stayed with them many days. One night, on entering her hut, the daughter lit a handful of grass to see by, and happening to glance into a pot she saw an adder in it. As her husband was in the habit of killing adders for food she thought it was a dead adder he had killed and hidden in the pot so that she and her husband could eat it together when her mother had gone. She was, anyhow, discontented with her mother's prolonged stay. Had she come to eat them out of house and home? The daughter came out of the hut and sat down by her mother in the courtyard of the homestead. After waiting a long time she looked up at the moon and, as she gazed at it, she said in an absent-minded way, as though the thought had just then occurred to her, 'what a fine moon there is tonight; were a person to travel to our home by its light he would arrive before daybreak'.

Now the mother was a woman who understood *sanza* and she was very angry when she heard her daughter's remark, and she said 'I will go now by the light of the moon'. The daughter called her husband, who tried to appease her, saying 'what affair is this, mistress?'. But she would not listen to him, saying 'no, I will return home tonight by the light of the moon'. They went a little way with her to see her on her way home, then they bade her good-bye. Quickly her daughter returned, thinking 'now I will cook the adder my husband killed and we will eat it together'. She entered her hut in the dark and placed her hand in the pot to take up the snake to prepare it. The snake, which had not been killed by her husband and was not dead, but had entered the pot to sleep there, bit her hand and she died. The husband sent a messenger after her mother to recall her, saying 'your daughter has been bitten by an adder and is sick unto death'. The mother refused to return because her daughter had spoken a *sanza* to her; for it was on account of this snake that she had hinted to her mother that she should go away by the light of the moon. Therefore, Azande say, it is not well to speak to a person in *sanza* because a woman died on account of having spoken a *sanza* to her mother. They say also that when your relatives-in-law come to visit you, you must be very careful not to mention the light of the moon, as they may consider this to be a hint that their departure is desired and take offence. If you have guests of any kind it is best not to remark on the brightness of the moon. If a man speaks to you in this wise it means that he wishes to push you out, he does not want you to stay in his home any longer.

(14) A commoner may speak or act a *sanza* towards a prince, but unless it is an entirely harmless joking kind of *sanza* or a highly complimentary one he runs a grave risk in doing so. A harmless *sanza*, what Azande call a *sanza mbaro*, a *sanza* in fun, is the habit of old commoner favourites of a prince of placing their hands before their mouths when speaking, especially when beginning to speak to him. This is a playful introduction to what a man is about to say. An insulting *sanza* to a prince in the old days might have been severely punished, even if the man who said it belonged to the aristocratic class and was therefore a kinsman of the prince. Gangura son of Gbudwe emasculated Mbitiyo son of Badiya, because he said 'the red duiker will eat ground-nuts'. This animal does not eat ground-nuts. I was never able to understand what precisely the allusion to the red duiker meant, but I was told that what was implied in the words was 'your country will become poor and you will lose your province'. Mbitiyo had been given a small part of the province to administer by Gangura, but he was dissatisfied with it.

(15) Another story told about Gangura is a literal application of the proverb *i na ni nga ku rogo kuru guga te* 'one does not excrete into an old water-hole'. The story is that 'there was a man called Ngawe who was a subject of Gangura. Ngawe said that Gangura was no good as a ruler. He arose and went home and when he had arrived there he excreted in his granary, in his huts, and into his water-hole also. He then departed to go to Basongoda's country. While he was in Basongoda's country the sons of Narepa of the Akpura clan showed themselves hostile to him, saying to him 'you killed our father Narepa with sorcery, and he died. Why have you

come back again among us? What happened to you in Gangura's country?". Ngawe fled back to Gangura's country. When he had arrived there Gangura told him to go and live in his deserted home and clean up his water-hole which he had excreted into; if he made another new home he, Gangura, would drive him away. Ngawe went and resided in his old homestead where he had polluted the place and drank from that same water-hole he had excreted into. Thus people say "do not in departing dirty your old water-hole" '. Ngawe had polluted his home as a *sanza,* to show his contempt for Gangura and that he was going for good. But one never knows what future circumstances may determine. That is the meaning of the proverb.

(16) One must be very careful not to speak at court the *sanza* Azande call *wawa.* This is to rise after a long wait saying *wawa,* a noise corresponding to such noises as we might make when stretching ourselves when tired and hungry. A Zande comment is: 'When a man has waited in vain at a man's home, and also at a prince's court, waiting vainly and eating nothing, then as he gets up he utters this *sanza,* since he has waited in vain and has eaten nothing. Azande often speak this *sanza,* they speak it much about their fellows; but at court they are afraid to speak it, for were they to do so the men at court would seize them on account of it. In the past at Gbudwe's court, had a man uttered a *sanza* like this, the men at court would have killed him, because he spoke a *sanza* about Gbudwe. It is the same as this: "you leave me alone, sir, at this time". No one would have said this at Gbudwe's court. But nowadays Azande say it to their fellows all the time. However, there are those among them who dislike those who utter this *sanza*; they say that they are envious men because they set their hearts on the possessions of their fellows'.

(17) The princes, on the other hand, can speak in *sanza* about each other or about commoners without fear of retribution. Azande relate how Nangbwagita of the Akalingo clan took a gift of some fish to King Wando, who was very fond of fish. He was told to wait a little on the path outside the king's enclosure. Then Renzi, Wando's son, came to see his father and, as they talked, Wando forgot all about Nangbwagita and that from where he waited he could hear what he and Renzi were talking about. What Nangbwagita heard was Wando saying to his son 'when I send a message to you to tell you to fight, do not take part in the fight yourself. When I say do

not fight, take part.' The message would indicate what the poison oracle had declared, but in a reverse sense. This was to deceive the Azande (commoners), who would go into the fight confidently thinking that few men would be killed as they had *sangbwa ga Wando benge*, the verdict of Wando's poison oracle, behind them; whereas Renzi would secretly leave the field, and many Azande would be killed.

(18) One of the proverbs princes use to threaten their subjects is *gbodi a ya fu ngungu gau kina o u a mangi ngungu na ni* 'bushbuck said to mosquito that he had something and would do ill to mosquito with it'. The prince is the bushbuck and the Zande the mosquito. Another proverb they speak to Azande is *mi ni du wa ranga ni sungu kina bare* 'I who just sit in my place am like the vulture'. A prince says this about a subject who has left him. He can afford to wait. (It can also be said by a husband about a wife who has left him or by a man about another who has done him an injury which he intends to avenge.)

(19) An action may express a secret meaning without any words being spoken or in addition to the spoken word. I give a few examples. Some have already been mentioned. A woman confesses adultery at court by, in addition to half-statements such as 'master, he said to me "let us go into the bush" and I went too', hanging her head down and picking at the ground with her fingers. Someone at court says to her 'woman, raise your head and speak out all you have to say'; but she keeps on picking at the earth, asking in a shy voice 'what more can I say?'. The prince knows by the hanging of her head and her picking at the ground that she has committed adultery but is ashamed to say so in so many words. Indeed, though it is not a subject I discuss here, *sanza* of word and gesture plays an important part in legal cases, so much so that it would often be impossible for a European to know the full grounds on which a prince has based his verdict without Zande comments to guide him, for it is as much on how evidence is phrased and presented as on the evidence itself that a prince decides whether witnesses are credible.

(20) So much is a wink a sign conveying some hidden meaning that, as has been noted, the Zande word for 'wink' is *sanza bangirise*, *sanza* of the eye. One purpose for which it is used is to commit adultery. A man winks at a woman on the path or at a dance, while at the same time slightly turning his head in the direction he wants her to go and wait for him. Other *asanza boli*, *asanza*

of adultery, are to pout the lips and turn the head or to put out the tongue and turn the head. Putting out the tongue may, however, easily be observed, and a man would not do this if there were people present. If he is quite sure that no one is looking he may beckon the woman with his hand. In past times a prince would indicate to his retainers at court that he wanted to slay someone by half closing his eyes. This had the double advantage that the man received no warning of his fate and that the prince could afterwards, since he had said nothing, disclaim responsibility for his death, should he wish to do so.

(21) In old days also a man's blood-brother would try to warn him as he entered court that there was trouble brewing for him there and that he had better get away quickly. He did this by greeting his blood-brother in the joking manner of greeting that obtains between blood-brothers, that is, by shaking his hand, and in doing so pressing a finger into the centre of the hand or scraping it with a finger. Since in the past Azande did not shake hands in greeting unless they were blood-brothers a man who did this would be suspect if his blood-brother escaped punishment or vengeance (*bape*). One way of escaping was to throw one's spear a little way as though in play and then again till one was out of sight. If a man did this after his blood-brother had shaken hands with him the blood-brother would be involved in complicity, so men adopted a new way of giving warning, the *sanza bangirise*, the *sanza* of the eyes. The man giving the warning quickly closed both eyes, screwed up his face, and turned his head round from the person whom he wished to warn, to urge him to get away at once.

(22) A man's barkcloth is out of place and his genitals are exposed. Another wants to make malicious fun of him, so he catches the eye of a friend and by moving his own head round he directs it to the exposure.

I have given a few examples to illustrate what Azande mean by *sanza* and how they think of it. As we have noted, a *sanza* is a circumlocutory form of speech or action in which words and gestures have hidden meanings different from their manifest meanings and generally malicious. All Azande employ *sanza* to some extent, though some more than others; and some are able to see a man's intentions beneath the cloak of words he throws over them more easily than others. People who habitually speak in *sanza* aim to be spiteful without exposing themselves to retaliation. They say something nasty about someone in the presence of others without his seeing the point of what is said while the others see it and go home and joke about it. A man says about his wife, whom he dislikes, in the presence of other women 'this stupid dog, I keep it only because of my cough'. A dog licks the phlegm its master spits out. The inner meaning of the words is 'this stupid woman [his wife], I keep her only because she hoes my gardens'. Were the wife to understand this she would make a row, but should she do so then or later, someone in the meanwhile having explained it to her, her husband would feign innocence, saying that he was speaking only of his dog and meant no more than he said. He is careful, when making the remark, to look towards his dog.

How far one goes in *sanza* and what words one uses depend on the situation in which one is speaking, and most importantly, to, or about, whom one speaks it. The great thing, however, is to keep under cover and to keep open a line of retreat should the sufferer from your malice take offence and try to make trouble.

This does not apply to the same extent to the proverb, though it does so to some extent. Many Azande do not know the meaning of many of their proverbs but they can see that a metaphor is being used and ask someone to explain its meaning. One uses a proverb because it is more effective than *kusa pai*, direct speech. A man might argue with you were you to say 'since a woman has said that she committed adultery with you, why do you deny it?'. But if you say *pi sende yo na gumba nga zire te* 'water on the ground does not lie' (it is conclusive evidence that it has rained), you make a statement that no one can confute and you thereby shake the other man's confidence and knock him off his balance, as it were; or again, you obviate any argument if, instead of saying 'you are bringing trouble on your own head', you say *ndiko agbe mai ku ri ru ni sa ru* 'the frog brings down rain on its own head'; or yet again, if instead of saying 'have you no compassion?' you say *ngangangangu atindi wiri nai mbiko inapai* 'the centipede carried its brother out of kindness'. (Fr. Bervoets gives: *ngangangangu naaka wilinaï kango hinapai* 'de ene duizendpoot draagt de andere uit dankbaarheid'.) By using metaphorical language you take the wind out of the other man's sails. He cannot start disputing with you whether water on the ground is a sign of rain or whether frogs bring down rain on themselves or centipedes carry their brothers out of kindness. You clinch the argument, you put a full stop to it; and you come out of it uppermost. But one also uses *sanza* rather than *kusa pai* because it stings more. The other man is not only placed in a disadvantageous position, but you hurt him at the same time. One says to a man, for example, *imi mbara na kpi mbata pa umbaga ru ne ka gbera* 'if the slayer of the elephant dies first it is bad for the second spearer'. If the man who first speared the beast survives he will admit the second spearer's part and claim to his share of the spoil, but if he dies his relatives may dispute the claim. This is a somewhat involved metaphor. I was told that it meant, or could mean, 'since you quarrel with me, sir, if I do not die first, I will see the end of it' or 'since you are so offensive to me, I will see the matter out'. Azande said that one would use this roundabout way of speech because it would hurt the other man more than direct speech, and also to express a *mokido*, a threat, and one which, because it was not made in plain language, could, if necessary, be withdrawn without loss of dignity.

The *wene sanza*, good *sanza*, said as a pleasantry, is spoken in various situations where a direct statement would be impolite or shameful or not hit the mark so effectively. For one reason or another it is best to be circumlocutory. The *gbigbita sanza*, the bad *sanza*, is more common. One uses it because subterfuge is advisable —it is not merely that one wants to score a point and to hurt, one also dares not say openly what one wants to say because of the relationship involved, the wife to husband relationship, that of commoner to prince, that between blood-brothers, that of a man to his in-laws. etc, And even what passes for good *sanza* may be malicious by a sort of double inversion. With certain persons, particularly with blood-brothers, it is permissible to use a joking language, called *buga*, in which things may be said which would not be proper if said to other persons. Azande work off a lot of *sanza* under this cover. An insult to one's blood-brother is presented as a joke. He is not supposed to take it seriously, but he may in fact take the words to be intended to bear their overt meaning in the guise of a joke, and they may indeed be intended to carry this meaning. Or two blood-brothers may sling insults at one another knowing that there is a third man within earshot, the insults being intended for him. Men who frequent court are there to serve their own interests and in competition to win the favour of their prince, and they are well-known for their skill in getting in sharp, sly little digs at one another in the form of apparently innocuous jokes and harmless small talk, and even in the form of compliments. A favourite way of doing this is to say the opposite of what is meant. The more the words are cloaked by expression of sincerity and friendship the more successful is this method of pricking the victim. Even if he does not see through them himself others may, so the effort is not wasted. Thus one says to a man who is, in one's opinion, talking nonsense 'oh sir, how well you know how to speak'. This sarcastic mode may also be employed discreetly with in-laws or in the home. For example, a wife says in *sanza* to another man's wife in the presence of her husband 'the renown of your home is greater than ours'. In fact, she means the opposite and is having a dig at the owner of the homestead who, she well knows, hears what she says. He understands the innuendo and asks 'what is the matter here, mistress?'. His wife replies in another *sanza* 'yes, sir, our home has a great reputation; she was saying nice things about it, sir, that people say that you would not eat anything and leave your wives without it' (which is precisely what he does do).

Indeed, any remark, even the most commonplace and trivial remark, can be made to express a double meaning by a slight emphasis of tone or manner. One says *rengo du* 'it is true', or *pai ti ni te* 'it does not matter', with just that intonation which suggests that it is not true or that it does matter. One can greet a man with one of the ordinary greetings in such a way as to ridicule him, show contempt for him, show hostility to him, make him a laughing-stock to others, or whatever it may be, by a slight inflexion or by a slight change in facial expression. I give one example. When a Zande greets a man he generally does so by saying *mo ye te*? 'you have come?', or *mo ye te ba*? 'you have come, sir?'. One replies *i* 'yes', or *i ba mi ye* 'yes, sir, I have come'. Said in a certain tone, this means more than appears on the surface. A man goes to see someone on whom he has a claim, perhaps his younger brother, and he replies to his greeting with the usual form of reply but with the intonation which makes it signify that he has come to eat something good or to hear, or say, something unpleasant. It may mean that last time he came on a visit he got nothing good to eat and that he expects something better this time.

Even such an action as washing one's face or arranging one's dress is *sanza* in that it has a purpose more than cleanliness or tidiness. It is aimed at drawing attention to oneself with the purpose of influencing other people's attitude and behaviour to oneself.

'Azande say thus, *sanza* is to pay attention to oneself, because a man looks after his appearance so that he will present a pleasant sight to others. Azande say that *sanza* are all these matters.' Again, 'the daily toilet is *sanza*. When a man comes out of his hut in the morning to wash his face he does that because he wants his face to be clean in the eyes of people. He does that in *sanza*. When a man washes himself well and wears his best barkcloth he does that in *sanza*, because he wants people to see himself as handsome, lest he should seem to them to be a dirty person.'

All this is very well known to Azande themselves. I have not recorded my own observations but theirs, both in the examples cited and in the interpretations put forward, though my own support theirs. Azande are under no illusions about human nature. They know very well how spiteful, resentful, jealous, envious, etc., men may be, and they are also well aware of what psychologists today call projection, that those a man thinks hate him are often those whom he hates. A Zande, asked to say what *sanza* was, summed up the matter in the following account.

'*Sanza* is cheating, because a man is very friendly with you and you, on your side, do not know that he is meditating ill to you, whereas under the surface he dislikes you. If a person sends you a present by such a man's hand he takes these things and eats them all up and does not give you, to whom they belong, any of them; and he says nothing to you about them. You know nothing about the gift; it does not get further than him.

'A *sanza* man goes and visits your relatives-in-law and tells them lies about you, saying that you said nasty things about them, and then that you want your bridewealth-spears back from them because you do not want their daughter. He speaks lies about you to your relatives-in-law so that when they hear them they make up their minds to return your spears. But what he says about you is all lies. That is one of the habits of a *sanza* man.

'Much *sanza* is spoken by people in relation to in-laws and to blood-brothers because people solicit gifts from them. Because if a man has a thing, he will give it to you gladly, that is a man who has thought of it himself to give it to you, out of kindness. But that which you pester him about, he gives it to you with resentment. He will not give it to you without saying *sanza* about it; he says "I give it to you to die of poverty, because I have only one of that thing, that which I give to you." If he speaks in this wise it is that he does not give it to you with goodwill. There is *sanza* in all these affairs.'

Those who have read my book on Zande witchcraft will know that the feelings Azande consider to be motives of bewitching, malice in its many forms, are also those they consider to be the motives of most *sanza* speaking. The idea of *sanza*, oblique speech and gesture by which a nuance, generally spiteful, is conveyed is, therefore, closely related to the idea of *mangu*, witchcraft. A man who uses *sanza* may very well be a witch. On the other hand, one may use *sanza*, go round the point, as it were, just because one regards the man with whom one is speaking as a witch. If one openly ridiculed him he might bewitch one in retaliation, so one does so in such a way that he is held up to derision without his knowing it.

A Zande expressed the similarity between *sanza* and witchcraft thus:

'Those people who speak *sanza*, they are all witches, because those people who speak *sanza* want misfortune to fall on a man. If a man often speaks *sanza* to others, it is that he is spiteful towards his fellows.

'Men get hold of women with *sanza* because all those things they say to a woman, they say them altogether in *sanza*.

'*Sanza* is resentment, because if a man is always resentful against another he speaks about everything in *sanza*. If a youth takes a girl as his sweetheart and then another begins to make love to her, the one who courted her first, if he knows of it, speaks *sanza* to the other all the time, because he hates him. If misfortune overcomes that other, it gives him the greatest pleasure.

'If you are going somewhere and arrive at a man's homestead on your way and see him sitting with many other men, and when they see you one of them says "it is just as you see", this is as though he were to say "that man whom we were speaking about has come"; because if a man is speaking ill of you, and when you appear someone says "it is just as you see", you know that they were talking about you before.' ('It is just as you see' is a rendering of *a ti mo a bi re*, a phrase difficult to translate. It corresponds to a too hasty change of subject in similar circumstances among ourselves.)

'That step which a man walks with haughtiness for another, he walks with a *sanza* step. It is like a man who, after quarrelling with another and giving him a good beating, does not fear him at all any more, and he goes about his affairs in *sanza*.'

In this essay on the Zande concept of *sanza* I have used only a fraction of the material I have at my disposal. The information I have cited is, however, perhaps sufficient for the reader to have an appreciation of its meaning. Before I draw a few conclusions, even of a preliminary kind, I must explain that what I have discussed is not a rare occurrence in Zande social life. That I have chosen to base my account very largely on texts might give this impression, but were it to be received it would be inaccurate and unfortunate. Azande speak in *sanza* so frequently that one may say it is a characteristic mode of speech, that is it an indication of their mentality.

It is, of course, true that other peoples speak in a veiled language and that there is something analogous in our own speech to the Zande *sanza*. But there is also something different in it from anything we are familiar with. The Zande attributes all his misfortunes to the ill-will of others. It is not merely that he thinks they are ill-disposed towards him, but that he believes that this ill-will, through the power to bewitch, causes all his woes and ills and pains. He feels himself, therefore, to be always on the defensive. He peers out of his shell, like a snail, and then withdraws, and he sees that all the other snails do the same. His world is a world of that sort, a world in which what happens is caused by man himself, a somewhat malicious and selfish man, and therefore a hostile world.

The *sanza* way of speech fits in, therefore, with the dominant feature of Zande philosophy, the witchcraft motif; and both go together with the idea of superordination which runs right through their social life. This is too big a theme to develop here, but a few words may be said about it. The princes were—more so in the past than now—very powerful, even despotic, and all members of their clan, the Avongara, were, and still very largely are, an aristocratic class of masters, responsible only to themselves. The commoners were subject to them and feared them. Those who frequented court were sycophantic towards their masters and jealous of each other in relation to them. Others kept away from court and tried to avoid the attentions of the princes and their agents and retainers, before whom they humbled themselves. Both alike kept their affairs as concealed as possible and were suspicious of others lest some word or act might be reported to those in authority and get them into trouble. Their anxious animosity was directed towards one another rather than to the princes, towards whom they refrain alike from making accusations of witchcraft and speaking *sanza* as they do to their fellows. These princes have always said, and Azande have always recognized the truth of what they said, that Azande (the commoners) are cheats and liars and practise every form of duplicity and deceit, and that it needs a firm hand to rule them; and I feel that, as is so often the case, those who accuse them of having an unpleasing character and justify their superior status and their severity accordingly, are those whose power, and the exercise of it, are, at least to some extent, responsible for that same character, that this sort of social system breeds this sort of personality. For the *gbia-vuru*, master-subject, relationship of Zande political life is a model for all their other social relationships. A father is *gbia*, master, to his sons, an elder brother to his younger brothers, a husband to his wives, and a father-in-law to his daughter's husband. Indeed, when Azande act together in any activity, however informal and temporary, their relations to one another in it conform to the same pattern. Someone always assumes, or is given, a superior rôle in it, the *gbia*, master, rôle. All their social relationships have this authoritarian pattern, and it seems to me that this, as well as their belief in witchcraft, tends to produce a tortuous mind which prefers concealment and, when it expresses itself, circumlocution.

Whether these are the causes or not, there is no doubt about the fact and Azande are the first to admit it; indeed, it is they who draw one's attention to it. It adds greatly to the difficulties of anthropological inquiry. Eventually the anthropologist's sense of security is also undermined, his confidence shaken. He learns the language, can say what he wants to say in it, and can understand what he hears; but then he begins to wonder whether he has really understood, when he sees how often Azande themselves take it for granted that what is said means something other than what is said, and when he cannot be sure, and even they cannot be sure, whether the words do have a nuance or someone imagines that they do, or wants to think that they do. One cannot know what is going on inside a man. That is the meaning of one of the most quoted proverbs: *i ni ngere ti boro wa i ni ngere ti baga*? 'can one look into a person as one looks into an open-wove basket?'.